D1244660

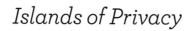

Islands of Privacy

ISLANDS
OF PRIVACY

Christena Nippert-Eng

THE UNIVERSITY OF CHICAGO PRESS · *Chicago and London*

CHRISTENA NIPPERT-ENG is associate professor of
sociology at Illinois Institute of Technology. She is the author
of *Home and Work: Negotiating Boundaries through Everyday
Life.*

The University of Chicago Press, Chicago 60637
The University of Chicago Press, Ltd., London
© 2010 by The University of Chicago
All rights reserved. Published 2010
Printed in the United States of America

20 19 18 17 16 15 14 13 12 11 10   1 2 3 4 5

ISBN-13: 978-0-226-58652-6 (cloth)
ISBN-13: 978-0-226-58653-3 (paper)
ISBN-10: 0-226-58652-9 (cloth)
ISBN-10: 0-226-58653-7 (paper)

Library of Congress Cataloging-in-Publication Data

Nippert-Eng, Christena E.
  Islands of privacy / Christena Nippert-Eng.
     p. cm.
  Includes bibliographical references and index.
   ISBN-13: 978-0-226-58652-6 (cloth : alk. paper)
   ISBN-13: 978-0-226-58653-3 (pbk. : alk. paper)
   ISBN-10: 0-226-58652-9 (cloth : alk. paper)
   ISBN-10: 0-226-58653-7 (pbk. : alk. paper) 1. Privacy—Social
aspects. 2. Social psychology.   I. Title.
  BF637 .P74N566 2010
  302.5—dc22
                                              2009051468

♾ The paper used in this publication meets the minimum re-
quirements of the American National Standard for Information
Sciences—Permanence of Paper for Printed Library Materials,
ANSI Z39.48-1992.

To Catherine, my delight

Out of the counterplay of these two interests, in concealing and revealing, spring nuances and fates of human interaction that permeate it in its entirety.

GEORG SIMMEL

Contents

Acknowledgments

In addition to the participants in this project who gave so freely of their time and experience, my heartfelt thanks also go to the remarkable interviewers who helped elicit their insights. It was participants' generosity in sharing their stories and insights that forced me—happily—to change my plan of action a couple months into this study. Everyone I spoke with was so forthcoming and so interesting that I wasn't making nearly the headway that I thought I would in terms of the sheer numbers of people I was talking to. I decided to hire some extraordinarily talented people to help do the interviews.

Gitte Waldman Jonsdatter, Linda Pulik, Margaret Alrutz, and Meghan Carlock Gonnissen are amazing researchers who brought so much to this study through their abilities to listen, to prompt, to think on their feet in respectful, enticing ways, and even to tap into their own social networks to produce some of the wonderful participants whose insights are included here. The semiformal nature of the interviews meant we each brought our own talents to bear on every conversation we had. I am all the richer for the conversational and analytical efforts of these women—not to mention their companionship along the way.

Gitte Jonsdatter also contributed inspired graphic design to the cause. She's a gifted sociological thinker and also a visual one. Along with Jay Melican and Eric Swanson, she helps me show and say what I mean here in ways I never could, especially through her careful reading of and feedback on the entire manuscript.

In addition to her interviewing, Meghan Carlock Gonnisson was an undergraduate, all-purpose research assistant who spent long hours doing whatever needed doing, part office manager, part colleague. We shared a number of happy planning breakfasts with Nick Nimchuk, who brought fabulous programming skills as well as general research assistance and smart thinking to this project for a couple of years, too, even after he'd graduated. Most recently, John Dominski, another undergraduate whose love of sociology has influenced these final pages, worked tirelessly to help assess and proof and index this manuscript. His curiosity and energy brought a fresh view to these pages that reinvigorated the whole process.

When Jay Melican came on board as a post-doc for a year in 2003, I had a perfect collaborator—just so excellent to think and work with. We shared many interesting and fun experiences in that short time, and it was exactly the intensely rewarding effort I needed to coalesce much of what had happened up until then. He is my coauthor on chapter 2.

Lydia Aletraris, another beloved undergraduate at the time, spent a couple weeks cleaning data and mining her store of first names on my behalf. Maud Schaafsma, Eric Swanson, Rachel Hinman, and Ryan Pikkel also worked hard with us for a couple of weeks and helped develop early thoughts on some basic behaviors that interested me. My thanks also to Candace Brooks, Lucas Daniel, Jeffrey Dunn, Ric Edinberg, Katie Luby, Lucas McCann, Dionne Smith, and Josh Stonehouse, who assisted with some coding and theme development during a semester-long workshop on qualitative data analysis, as well as Peer Fiss and Japonica Brown-Saracino, who also provided early assistance on this project. As always, Rotena DuBois Nippert, my mother and self-appointed, unremunerated research assistant, sent endless clippings through the post for me, inevitably useful and thoughtful.

The transcribers of these interviews were absolutely amazing: Gretta Wahlstrom Nippert, Vicki Aitchison, Carole McKaig, and Lisa Thorne. Hats off for a brutal and utterly impeccable, beautifully nuanced job, as well as all your encouragement! This book could not have happened without you.

My husband and daughters were of course critical to the endeavor. They let me know about things that they thought I'd find interesting and supported me along the way in more material, practical, and symbolic ways. This book is dedicated to the one and only Catherine, though. When she was seven, we were talking about a party I was going to throw for the summer students who'd worked on this project. "Do you have any decorations?" Catherine asked. "Well, no, I don't," I replied. "Talk to me," she said. "Tell me more about what you've learned." She then captured the essence of this book in the way that only a born designer can. "You need a sign, Mom, so your students will know where the party is. But it shouldn't be a sign that just anyone can see. You should only be able to see it if you're invited to the party."

Many astonishingly helpful conversations later, I still have that sign in my office, made with Sharpies and sparkles and glitter on transparency film. I'm thinking especially hard now about one of her many pieces of sound advice: "You should consider writing shorter books from now on, Mom—maybe for children."

This study would not have been possible were it not for a very generous grant from the Intel Research Council. As a result of Chris Riley's original invitation, I have met some fabulous colleagues, found new ways of working, and got to delve into something that would have remained shelved for a long time, in ways I could not have done otherwise. Thanks especially to Chris, Scott Mainwaring, Ken Anderson, and Genevieve Bell, and all the rest of the People and Practices folks.

Other colleagues who have been encouraging and helpful during the many years of this project include: Beth Angell, Mary Chayko, Lin-Lin Chen, Ira Cohen, Paul Dourish, Carlos Duarte, Mitch Duneier, Gary Fine, David Franks, Ken Friedman, Jeff Gilliom, Judith Gregory, Ben Gross, Sara Ilstedt Hjelm, Thor Hogan, Patrick Ireland, Mark Jacobs, Lori Kendall, Nalini Kotamraju, Martim Lapa, Cheryl Laz, Steven Margolis, Tim Marshall, Gary Marx, Simona Maschi, Noah McClain, Morten Engedal Nielsen, Kristina Orfali, Maritsa Poros, Eduardo Corte Real, Alberto Redolfi, Dan Ryan, David Smilde, Rebecca Trump, Vered Vinitzky-Seroussi, Nina Wakeford, and Judy Wittner. Some people, though, have actually read and critiqued an earlier draft of some or all of this book as well. A very special thanks to Kris Cohen, Kevin Delaney, Lara Hoegel, Bernie Hogan, Jay Melican, Harvey Molotch, Eviatar Zerubavel, and two extraordinary, anonymous reviewers for the Press.

To the brilliant, witty, and ever-so-generous Doug Mitchell: you have the patience of a saint. This book is proof of it. Doug, I'm so grateful we *both* held out long enough for this to happen. Thank you. Thanks also to the truly adventurous Tim McGovern, the very kindly Kate Frentzel, and the wonderfully talented Matt Avery, along with everyone else at the Press for using your remarkable expertise once again on my behalf.

Islands, Oceans, & Beaches

Would you say that privacy is a problem for you?

Are you kidding? Listen to what happened to me just a couple of days ago.

We were all at the pool, and—I had my period. And when I went to the bathroom I found out I'd lost the string to my tampon. It was up there somewhere, but I couldn't find it. So, okay. I decided to wait until I got home and I'd take care of it then.

So later on, we get home. I get all the kids and all their stuff out of the car. We get inside. I let out the dogs, took care of the towels and stuff, let the dogs back in, made sure they had water, checked for messages, made sure everyone had snacks and drinks and that they didn't need anything else. I took care of everything. Then I told them all I was going upstairs to take a shower and not to bother me for fifteen minutes.

I go upstairs to the bedroom. I close the door and lock it. Then I strip off my suit and go stand in front of the mirror. I mean, I've had five kids. You know? There are no mysteries here. I was just going to take care of the problem and that would be it. No sweat, right?

So I stand with my back in front of the mirror and I bend over, looking in the mirror, you know, so I could try to see what the heck I was doing. And there I am, poking around, trying to get that string out.

All of a sudden (Sarah) pops her head out from under the bed—with this big smile—and yells, "Hi, Mommy!"

Oh my God! I just about—"Sarah! What are you—out! You—get out of here, NOW!"

Well, she crawled out from under there and ran out of that room so fast. (*Laughing.*) She probably didn't have a clue about what she did and why I was so upset. But she knew she did something! (*Laughing.*)

I mean, can you imagine?

GINA, self-employed wife and mother of five

This is a book about trying to achieve privacy. It is about ordinary people's sometimes extraordinary efforts to draw the boundary between what they would like to be private, on the one hand, and what might turn out to be a little (maybe a *lot*) more public than they'd like, on the other. It is a book about the breadth and depth, the creativity and the mundanity of our everyday attempts to "do" privacy.

Like the best-laid plans of mice and men—not to mention moms—people in the United States often do not get our privacy wishes. Sometimes, though—as we shall see in the dozens of stories included here from mostly middle- and upper-middle-class people living and working in Chicago—we do. This is a book about successes *and* failures, then. It's a story about privacy gifted as well as denied, privacy violated and protected, along with the terms of negotiation underlying all these outcomes. And if this tale is told through anecdotes that are funny or familiar, there are stories in this book that are definitely a little sad and strange, too.

During the seventy-four formal interviews conducted for this study and an assortment of interactions I observed in public, it became clear that what I now think of as the process of "selective concealment and disclosure" plays an important role in how we try to achieve privacy. This is the daily activity of trying to deny or grant varying amounts of access to our private matters to specific people in specific ways. Whether focused on our space, time, activities, possessions, bodies, ideas, senses of self, or anything else we deem more private, this is the chief way in which we attempt to regulate our privacy, given the social, cultural, economic, and legal constraints at hand. The result is a collection of detailed, rich, and nuanced activities—like Gina's—that are as endless as the challenges that give rise to them.

Eventually, I selected certain private-public boundary behaviors for closer study so that I could look at this process of selective concealment and disclosure with an especially fine-toothed comb. In chapter 1, for instance, I look at the ways we try to keep, reveal, and find out secrets. What is the actual work involved in these processes, so critical to managing one's privacy? What can the work of secrets simultaneously teach us about the connection between managing privacy and managing relationships? In chapter 2 I look at what we carry in our wallets and purses and how we classify and use these nominally private things to protect our privacy and senses of self while nonetheless engaging in a very public realm. In chapter 3 I explore the ways we try to find privacy given the daily torrent of messages so many people in this study receive from cell phones, email, and other communication channels—at home, at work, and everywhere in between. And in chapter 4 I ask, if a person's home is her or his "castle"—guaranteeing a certain amount of privacy while inside it—how do we find privacy along its far more porous perimeter? What do we do to achieve privacy on the doorstep, in the yard, along the curb, and beyond, out in the neighborhood? Theoretically driven yet empirically rich, each of these chapters explores the microscopic practices through which we do privacy, every day, as well as the macroscopic concerns that underlie them all. As I argue in the conclusion, the heightened fear of one's privacy being violated is an especially important thread driving much of what we will see throughout these four case studies of the work of privacy.

In terms of the sheer level of challenge she faces trying to manage her privacy, for instance, Gina actually turns out to be rather typical of study participants. The culprits may differ—ranging from intrusive corporations and the U.S. government to hackers, noisy neighbors, and disrespectful coworkers. But for the people I interviewed, it can be quite difficult these days to claim any place, time, or activity as well and truly private. There is a general feeling now that the condition of privacy has become relegated to rather tiny islands of one's existence, few and far between, scattered across the vast ocean of accessibility that dominates so much of our lives.

It's as if a distinct cultural climate change is underway. The ocean has risen, shrinking our islands of privacy[1] and even submerging many of them altogether. Like Atlantis, perhaps, some private spaces and times and matters are fading into the realm of folklore—even legend—their very existence destined to rest one day on the unsubstantiated claims of prior generations. The result is an intriguing combination of rigorous island defense in some corners and fatalistic relinquishment in others.

What interests me, however, are not so much these islands or this ocean, or their relative proportions over time. Rather, what fascinates me is what happens on the beach—the place where islands and oceans most obviously meet. Specifically, I am drawn to two questions, both of a classificatory nature. First, when we consider a beach, where, exactly, do "the island" and "the ocean" begin and end? Second, how do people try to settle the matter when their answers to this first question differ?

On our planet, bodies of land and water are not discrete; they are connected in a continuous and inverse fashion. We perceive and emphasize more or less of one, and complement this with a decreased or increased perception of and emphasis on the other. The beach is so fascinating because here is where individuals' different expectations about the edges of the land and the water—where they are and where they should be—come together. At the beach, one might observe both conventionality and cleverness as individuals recognize, negotiate, and even leverage their classificatory differences—and then celebrate or cope with the consequences.

The shoreline on which this book is focused, for instance, reveals not only the endless potential for categorical conflict over what is "private" and what is "public," but the much more interesting and nuanced issue of just *how* private, just *how* public, we believe something is. "Private" and "public," "privacy" and "publicity" are concepts that are coupled and related to each other in the same way as islands and oceans, land and water. This is key to understanding how our culture conceptualizes privacy (Nippert-Eng 2007.)

Specifically, and in its purest form, privacy is one ideal-typical endpoint of a continuum; "publicity" is at the other end (Zerubavel 1979b). Given our culture's access-based understanding of these concepts (e.g., Allen 1988) purely "private" things are completely inaccessible to others. Purely "public" ones are completely accessible to others. Privacy and publicity, what is private and what is public, are each defined with and by each other along this conceptual sliding scale.

Privacy	Publicity
|	|
The condition of (pure) inaccessibility	The condition of (pure) accessibility

("Private"	"Public")
That which is completely inaccessible	That which is completely accessible

As with all ideal-types, this is only an analytical tool, useful to think with and help make sense of the world around us. Real-world experiences, real-world things, fall somewhere in between these two analytical endpoints. Something may be relatively more private or relatively more public, but it is never purely either.

When we think of privacy, then, what we really think of is a condition of *relative* inaccessibility. Any point on the scale has both a degree of privateness and a degree of publicness associated with it, that is, and an emphasis on one may far outweigh but never completely displace the simultaneous presence of the other. This means not only that an increase in one condition is associated with a decrease in the other but also that it is fairly easy to make mistakes about and/or intentionally challenge the amount of either that is actually present.

Consider the moment when Sarah's head popped out from under her mom's bed, for instance. This was when Gina discovered that the actual degree of privacy she possessed was quite different from what she originally thought. Right then, Gina instantly found herself transported from what might have been the dead center of her island of privacy to a metaphorical position much closer to the water—perhaps standing knee-deep in it. She was still *on* the island and certainly nowhere near over her head. It's not as if the entire family was watching her, nor even anyone old enough to really understand what was happening—much less everyone with access to the Internet. But, thanks to Sarah's playful challenge, Gina's actions were definitely not nearly as private as she'd previously thought.

The interrelated nature of these concepts is linked to everyday privacy behaviors in yet another important way. To be precise, acquiring privacy is only part of the problem facing the people in this book. The totality of the task is to achieve a balance between the need and desire for both privacy *and* publicity—for a certain degree of concealment *and* disclosure, for denying *and* granting access to others.

In Gina's short story, for instance, we see activities that center on disclosure as well as on concealment, on accessibility as well as inaccessibility. In order to get a driver's license so she can drive her kids to and from the pool, in order to get a mortgage for the house they leave and return to each day, Gina had to disclose who she was to various state and institutional representatives. She had to make ostensibly private information accessible to them and, in the process, meet some of the most rigorous, formal demands we have for proving identity and trustworthiness. The fact that she has a family and engages in the kinds of daily activities we hear about in her story signals a desire for disclosure of another sort: the desire to share much of her life and who she is with others, in some of the most meaningful ways exhibited by humans. The expectation for self-disclosure and the quest for intimacy are inextricably intertwined in our culture. Disclosure also occurs each time Gina gives an order to her children or tells them what she thinks, of course, as she makes her thoughts accessible to them.

At the same time, Gina clearly seeks privacy and the right to conceal certain things from others. She scoffed at the question about whether or not privacy might be problematic for her, immediately implying both its desirability and its absence. She promptly supported her reaction with an account of a remarkably thwarted attempt to make herself inaccessible— in spite of a problem that most people would see as intensely private. With this one story, she thus signaled at least an occasional desire for disconnection, for moments of freedom from her constant accessibility to others, for the opportunity to keep at least some things to and for and of herself.

In fact, creating pockets of accessibility is an important way in which we try to achieve a few pockets of inaccessibility, too. Making some parts of ourselves accessible to some people in some times and places actually helps us get away with denying them access to other parts or at other places and times. We might agree that "you can know this about me, you can use this thing of mine, and you can reach me here, at this time, and in this way" in part to better insist "but I won't let you know this about me, you can't touch this, and you need to leave me alone now."

This is the fuller context for understanding the process of defining and defending islands of privacy. This process is an utterly central aspect of life in the United States because, for us, "privacy" is where a rather large and important collection of concepts, ideological goals, and practical matters come together. Privacy is about nothing less than trying to live both as a member of a variety of social units—as a part of a number of larger wholes—and as an individual—a unique, individuated self. The tension this creates for every member of society is a central problem of sociology, my chosen discipline. It is also the driving force behind classical liberalism, the political, economic, legal, and cultural backbone of the United States.

This tension creates a problem that must be repeatedly solved by everyone, on a daily basis, then. It is embedded in every relationship—and potential relationship—that we have. And it is this need and desire and demand to connect as well as disconnect that is the very crux of the quest for privacy (Westin 1967, 7; Altman 1975, 10–12). Certainly, this need to be both *part of* and *apart from* is what makes individuals' attempts to achieve privacy so fascinating and complex.

This is particularly true since the power of the State, of corporations, indeed, of any of the social groups to which we belong (and want to belong) far outweighs that of the individual. These associations—sometimes armed with extensive computer technologies that allow for the unprecedented collection, analysis, and mass distribution of all kinds of information (Garfinkel 2000; Levine 2002)—set the terms of engagement for our daily lives. It is no wonder that legal scholars from the time of Warren and Brandeis (1890) to Rosen (2000) and Smith (2000) have noted the increasing importance of individual control over what is and is not disclosed to others for individuals' senses of privacy. This reflects the fact that while the acquisition of privacy is socially constrained (Etzioni 1999, 196; Schwartz 1968, 741), it is also interpersonally negotiated. In fact, in individuals' daily attempts to achieve privacy, we often see some extremely creative responses to whatever wiggle room there is.

Overall, then, Gina shares the problem of daily life experienced by so many people these days: achieving comfortable amounts of publicity *and* privacy, disclosure *and* concealment, given others' demands as well as our own preferences. It is not just a sum total, a given amount of disclosure and concealment that we want to achieve, though. The goal is to achieve *selectivity* in both—to carefully choose exactly what is disclosed and concealed, to whom, and how.

In fact, this is the very goal revealed by study participants when they discuss what it means to have "good' privacy. Early in their interviews, for instance, fifty-seven study participants answered the question "What does privacy mean to you?" Three common themes emerged from their answers that, not coincidentally, form the backbone of many Americans' views of privacy.[2]

What does privacy mean to you? (Total respondents = 57)
1) The ability/power to control access to some thing, place, or piece of information and its dissemination
   (*n* = 45)
2) The condition of being: alone/without others' demands, interruptions, intrusions/secure, safe, at peace
   (*n* = 17)
3) The freedom to do/live/make decisions, without regulation/restriction
   (*n* = 7)

The need to *manage* one's privacy runs throughout all these definitions of privacy. We see this managerial element especially in the most popular conception of privacy, which focuses on an individual's ability to control the accessibility of something. Yet participants also find it incumbent upon themselves to create their own pockets of uninterruptible time and space, or to make decisions without letting anyone else unduly pressure them into a particular choice. We must manage these dimensions of privacy, too.

An overtly managerial conception of privacy is built on the idea that there is nothing intrinsically, inherently private. In principle, study participants believe that anything may be shared or accessed. Whether or not it is (or should be) depends on the situation and one's relationship with the potential sharer. The key to this sense of privacy is the extent to which the individual has the ability to decide whether or not someone else needs to know or access something and to have her or his wishes followed.

For the people in this study, then, "good" privacy exists when the things they want to be private are as private as they want them to be. It's a wonderfully subjective, relativistic standard, yet this definition accounts for a full range of behaviors in the U.S. Some people choose to broadcast their entire lives over the Internet, for instance, placing pinhole cameras and microphones throughout their homes and workplaces, Tweeting their movements in between. Others move their families to a mountaintop and off the grid, avoiding all kinds of contact with others. With a definition as flexible as this, people at both of these extremes could feel as if they have good privacy, because *control* over the amount and type of disclosure and concealment is what really defines their assessment of the situation.

For the people in this study, though, the process is exponentially more complicated. They are not guided by blanket privacy policies in which they try to make themselves totally accessible or totally inaccessible to everyone around them. Rather, for the people I spoke with, a decision to make something accessible to one person in one way may or may not have anything to do with the decision to make it inaccessible to another person in a different way. And this is why the work of privacy is such a daily, dynamic task for them—as it probably is for most of us. Given whatever privacy is gifted to or withheld from us, it generally takes an extraordinary amount of knowledge, judgment, skill, and attention for these people to achieve whatever they think of as "good" privacy, selectively concealing and revealing as they wish.

Both types of these behaviors are critical to the process. Yet one of the reasons intentional, individual acts of concealment are such an interesting part of this process is because they are so much more difficult to achieve than are acts of disclosure. An individual's attempt to make something accessible to others rarely seems to be as much of a problem as an attempt to make it *inaccessible* to them.

The curiosity of our species seems to play a large role in this. Humans are constantly scanning, constantly receptive to and looking for whatever they can perceive about each other, for whatever is put out there. In such an environment, disclosure is a relatively easy endeavor. It is only when *selective* disclosure is the goal that one runs into problems. This is when the desire for concealment—and an assortment of much more complicated problems and behaviors—comes to the fore.[3]

Moreover, when a species operates the way we do—and when groups can have so much power over any given individual—privacy must be intentionally, socially gifted to anyone. Other peoples' eagerness to learn about us means everyone must engage in quite a concerted effort if we want to declare some things off limits, to reach at least tacit agreement that X is none of anyone else's—or at least most people's—business.[4] The only alternative is for individuals to intentionally, personally try to claim their privacy in spite of others' wishes. That is no easy task.

It can be especially difficult for someone like Gina to keep some things private, for instance, because the ability to conceal things requires collaboration from others, even if it's unintentional. For Gina to have privacy, her family has to have a sense of when she might want it, based on what she—not they—would like, and/or agree, at least tacitly, that some particular time, space, matter, activity, et cetera, can, in fact, be private for her. This may be simply because they don't care what she's doing or where she is at a given time. Then they have to actually grant that privacy to her.

The (possibly unwitting) collaboration necessary for her to have privacy is why the whole privacy thing could—and often does—fall apart for Gina. Someone might have never guessed that X or Y was something that she wanted to keep private. Sometimes Gina herself might not know that she would like to keep something private—until it is too late. Sometimes, either intentionally or accidentally, there may be just no way she is going to be permitted to have privacy or to keep something private—maybe especially when everyone knows she wants it that way. This may happen simply because the people around Gina might lack the understanding, emotional fortitude, and/or skills necessary to grant her the privacy she desires.

At some level, of course, Gina knows all this. Part of what makes her opening story so great (amusing, horrifying, typical—the list of appropriate adjectives could go on) is all the work she did to try to anticipate and head off any violation of her privacy, given her experience in the matter. She thought ahead and organized a tremendous number of variables so that she could conceal what she thought of as a very private thing from everyone around her.

In order to better assure her privacy, she started by deciding to wait until she was home to deal with the problem. She then took care of everyone else's needs first, even the dogs'. She asked if anybody wanted anything else, in case she hadn't thought of something. She clearly signaled to her kids that she was expecting privacy now, announcing that she was going to take a shower—a space and time commonly understood as relatively private. She then reinforced that signal and her intentions by explicitly ordering them to leave her alone for fifteen minutes. Finally, Gina left their space, went to another floor of the house, to her bedroom, and locked the door.

So much effort to stake out her desired place on such a little island of privacy. Such a carefully planned sequence of actions to prevent not only inadvertent disclosure but also intentional exposure, based on years of experience and guessing what was likely to come next. Gina really did do her best to meticulously design this pocket of time and space. At least this time, she might have thought, the private-public boundary would be drawn just as she wanted it to be.

This is precisely the kind of activity I include in the concept of "boundary work": the strategies, principles, and practices we use to create, maintain, and modify cultural categories (Nippert-Eng 1996, 7). In this case, Gina was focused on the category of what she wanted to be private, trying to keep her actions from becoming more public. Boundary work is rooted in such cognitive distinctions, but these are further enacted and enhanced through a striking collection of visible, practical activities. It is through these visible, felt behaviors that we make sense of classificatory distinctions and continue to challenge, defend, change, and solidify them over time. In fact, boundary work along the private-public divide is my focus throughout this book.

Categorical boundaries are not only locations for work, however; they may also be a great source of play. Sarah, for instance, threw quite a wrench in her mom's efforts when she decided to play with the very same boundary that was the focus of her mother's work. "I know!" she might have thought. "I'll go upstairs and crawl under Mommy's bed. I'll wait 'til she comes in and thinks she's alone. Then I'll jump out and surprise her! It'll be so funny!" Such "boundary play" (Nippert-Eng 2005a, 302) shows how the public-private boundary—or any semiotically linked, cultural-cognitive categories—can be used for amusement as well as underlie more serious endeavor.

Of course, once Sarah made her attempt to play with this particular boundary, Gina riposted with even more work, reasserting her vision of what that time and space was supposed to be, that is, very, very private. Gina ordered her daughter out of the room in no uncertain terms. The private-public boundary is actually a great place to see contests over the issue of whether play or work is going to prevail at any given moment. In this case, Gina was the more powerful person present (at least, once the playing field was fully revealed). Thus, her wishes (1) to draw the boundary in a certain way and (2) to not play with it trumped Sarah's attempt to draw it differently, as the focus of her proffered game.

Gina's story, like the rest of this book, is about a specific beach—the beach that bridges and blurs what is truly on an island of privacy and what is truly in the ocean of publicness. It is a place where we can see a tremendous amount of boundary work—and even a healthy dose of boundary play—as we negotiate how much land and water we think is present at any given time or place, how much of both we want to be present, and which one we think should be emphasized. It is certainly the place we see my main interest—people actually trying to do privacy on a daily, interpersonal, microsociological level.

This kind of personal privacy work depends heavily on myriad laws, institutional practices, services, objects, and features of the built environment, each of which actively constrains our options. I will talk about all of these. But my special interest in this study lies within the margins set by these broader constraints. Here is where these types of private-public negotiations are not only most highly visible but also most keenly felt.

The interactions at an actual, geophysical beach are useful for demonstrating my approach and the kinds of concerns and activities I am interested in throughout the remainder of this book. One of the public places I visited to do background fieldwork for this project, for instance, was North Beach in Chicago. It proved to be a great place to think with if one is interested not only in "beaches" but also in what constitutes boundary work or boundary play. I'll draw now on its familiar images to help illuminate my perspective.

Management of the private-public boundary, for example, is in striking evidence at this beach. One could write a separate treatise on how clothing alone is used in this regard, as people selectively conceal and reveal what they will. Such a treatise would note not only what kind of clothing is used at the beach to help manage one's private-public boundary, but also *how* it is used. What body parts are selectively concealed and revealed, which ones are classified as most private or most public? How are they emphasized and deemphasized for public consumption? How are clothes incorporated into other behaviors and carefully choreographed movements designed to bring attention to—or deflect it from—the wearer? Indeed, how does clothing alone show people recognizing, drawing, and leveraging the line between the private and the public?

There are plenty of examples at the beach of private-public boundary work—and play—that have nothing to do with clothing, of course. Figure I.1, "Zones of Boundary Work and Play, North Beach" is a diagram that represents some of the interesting behaviors I found on one of my visits as I explored the ways people engaged various boundaries at this beach.

As indicated in this diagram, for instance, people stake out their own territories at the beach, using umbrellas and strollers and blankets and

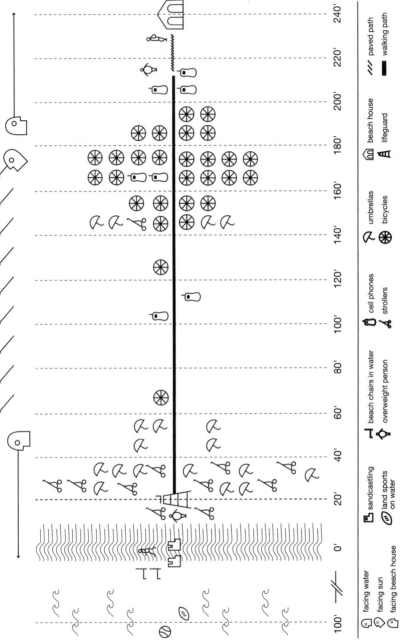

FIGURE I.1 Zones of boundary work and play, North Beach.

facing water
facing sun
facing beach house

sandcastling
land sports on water

beach chairs in water
overweight person

cell phones
strollers

umbrellas
bicycles

beach house
lifeguard

paved path
walking path

0'   20'   40'   60'   80'   100'   120'   140'   160'   180'   200'   220'   240'

100'

towels to claim little islands of temporarily private turf within this emi-nently public domain.[5] The amount of energy individuals put into claiming and defending "their" space is amazing, actually, from planning an early arrival to bringing an assortment of objects that help demarcate and fill the space, deterring encroachment. This kind of work includes the endless commands and directions given to children, too, as adults try to educate them about the family's territory versus other people's, including things like where and how the kids should walk and whose toys along the water-front are fair game.

Private-public boundary work may focus on auditory space, too. Indi-viduals set up their spaces away from the beach-house music loudspeak-ers, wear headphones, and/or complain when others' beach blanket boom box songs or inane cell phone calls bleed into their auditory space. The quest for auditory privacy can be highly selective, too. I heard one set of gorgeous twenty-something females decree that they didn't care where they set up their blanket as long as it was far away from the family section; they all agreed that they couldn't stand the sound of kids shrieking, laugh-ing, and whining at the beach.

In fact, I saw a fight over visual and olfactory privacy that took place in the middle of this same kid-friendly section of the beach. One woman left her family's blanket to check on her children at the water's edge. In the meantime, another fellow arrived and set up in front of her place, in a rather small spot that no one else had claimed. It was just big enough for the towel he laid out for himself and the contraption he parked next to it, which held his infant. This was a high-end stroller/buggy approximately four feet tall and three feet wide with its own solar deflector, which would now perfectly block this woman's line of sight to the water, where her chil-dren were playing.

When the mother returned to find this in front of her, she was not happy. A most important if neglected aspect of visual privacy was at stake—the right to see what she wanted to see, to have access to the view she wanted to access, not what others forced upon her—especially since what she wanted to see were her kids, playing safely. She didn't say anything. This was, after all, a public beach. This fellow didn't actually try to park it on the spot covered by her blanket, and she had sort of abdicated her right to protest by not being there when he set up in the first place. She positively reeked of annoyance, though, making a show of trying to see this way and that around the stroller and huffing and puffing loudly in frustration.

In what may have been a stroke of symbolic interaction genius, a few minutes later this mom lit a cigarette. She exhaled the smoke directly in front of her, right into the newcomer's and the baby's air space. That did it. Words were exchanged. His enormous stroller and her cancer-inducing particulates were intruding on each others' territories as well as the experiences to which each felt entitled. Eventually, the fellow grudgingly moved his stroller a few inches to the left and the woman exhaled her smoke to the right. Neither was happy with the outcome, though, and both took turns looking to me for validation of the injustice and stupidity they were forced to endure.

The privacy principles of the right to be left alone and not to have to experience (see, smell, hear, think about, et cetera) what one doesn't want to experience were the focus of repeated scowls and mutterings I heard from a group of young people later that day, too. Latecomers, they were forced to claim the only remaining largish beach space available, located far away from the water and—not coincidentally—within feet of an especially hirsute, grossly obese man wearing nothing but a fluorescent yellow thong. To them, he sprawled most unappealingly on his blanket. As the group looked on, he spent hours working on his tan, snoring loudly, first on his stomach and then his back, smiling happily at the world whenever he sat up to look around and change position.

Privacy violations occur not only when others intrude into our private territories; they also occur when others force us to enter what we think should be theirs. When our ideas about what others should keep private— and should therefore be concealed from us—do not match with what they insist on revealing to us, visible forms of boundary conflict may ensue. Given their complaints about having to endure this view and the accompanying soundtrack, I wondered if this group of beachgoers would try to arrive earlier next time. Perhaps they also would bring a CD player and their own soundtrack along with an umbrella in order to better control their auditory and visual privacy. Experience is one of the best teachers as we adjust our boundary knowledge, skills, and expectations over time.

One could see plenty of evidence of successful and unsuccessful private-public boundary work in other ways, too. Sometimes going to the beach isn't just about focusing on the private side of the boundary. It's often about working the public side of it, too.

The wheels on figure I.1 indicate the location of bicycles, for instance. At North Beach, people with bicycles strategically place themselves and their bikes near the blue rubberized mat that serves as a walkway between the beach house and the shoreline. Naturally, this makes it easy to walk a bike to an available spot on the sand, then flip the bike upside down, wheels up, where it can rest for the duration of a rider's stay.

But this strategy of sticking close to the mat serves other practical purposes, too. On the day I observed them, people with bicycles were uniformly meeting up with other people at the beach. The easiest way for them to see someone else, or to be seen by them, was to be on the edges of the crowd. The people I noticed using cell phones also were uniformly located along these edges—again, a good place to be for microlocating and trying to meet up with someone.[6] In fact, positioning oneself along the edges and keeping a cell phone on and handy are both ways of better disclosing one's presence, increasing one's accessibility at the beach.

A trip to the beach isn't just about work, though. It's also a grand place for a bit of play. Playing with the private-public boundary will be in evidence throughout the coming chapters, whether it's a game of truth or dare, a flirtatious tour of a potential mate's wallet, talking on one's phone while having sex, or waving from inside a stopped train to a stranger in a nearby apartment whenever she looks out her window.

For now, though, consider the left side of the beach diagram, where the water meets the sand. This represents the part of the beach where I found numerous examples of boundary play. With the exception of flirtatious behaviors[7], it was not so much the private-public boundary that was the focus of playful efforts here. Instead, play at this location focused on the geophysical nexus between the land and the water.[8]

An assortment of activities normally engaged in on land take on additional delight when they are executed in the water or on the water's edge, for instance. This is where people "wade," for example, rather than merely "walk"—pants rolled up, sneakers in hand, occasionally picking up treasures embedded in the sand or skipping stones as they go along. Adults sit in squat little chairs here, too, perhaps clenching a soda can on the armrest while feet, legs, and bottoms stay immersed in the water. Farther out, waist-high in the water, teenagers play land sports like football, baseball, and Frisbee, but with the added twist of being in the water and, sometimes, new rules to go with it.

Note that when the object being thrown hits those who are *not* players in the game—especially repeatedly—a variety of boundary work often ensues. This focuses on the private-public *and* the land-water boundaries. Comments like "Keep your stupid ball to yourself!" or "Do it again and I'll get the lifeguard" are common as nonplayers assert their rights to be in the water and to be left alone. Other disgruntled but more conflict-averse swimmers, perhaps, simply leave the water when this happens, making themselves less accessible to the players in a more expeditious way.

In terms of boundary play, though, most interesting of all to me were the children I saw building sandcastles, also depicted on the diagram. I witnessed two distinct types of sandcastlers. The first did her or his work in the damp beach sand that was farther inland. If the sand needed to be wetter or if the moat was ready to be filled, this kind of engineer grabbed a plastic bucket, went to the water, filled the bucket, and returned to the building site, adding however much water was deemed necessary.

The second type of sandcastler, though, was a little more daring. This person built her or his castle right on the edge of the lapping water. When she or he was ready, a temporary barrier would be removed and the moat would be filled by the natural action of the waves. Of course, these architects ran the risk of losing the entire structure due to a renegade wave or the rising tide. But they seemed quite happy to run that risk in exchange for the satisfaction whenever their clever, kinetic design actually worked. Each time their structure was accidentally demolished, they'd simply adjust the position a bit and start building all over again. It was a lovely demonstration that, whether one considers flirts on the beach or sandcastle builders, there are degrees of boundary playfulness, where one's skill level and desire to take risks play a visible role in whatever level of game one seeks.

The work, play, and overall wealth of effort that can be seen at the metaphorical beach I explore in the rest of this book include similarly familiar yet strikingly revealing behaviors. Taken altogether, they help tease out the ways "normal" people think about and do privacy. Much has been written about privacy by scholars, and privacy is certainly a regular topic of conversation in the media today. Yet I have found relatively little that actually asks everyday citizens what they think about it. And if little has been written about how middle- and upper-middle-class people in the U.S. *think* about privacy, even less has been written about how they actually *do* it, each day. These behaviors constitute such a fundamental aspect of what it means to be human, though, that the process begs for attention. It seems to me absolutely central to daily life. I hope readers will find that this book offers a contemporary picture of all of these elements for at least some people living today in the United States.

THE STUDY AND ITS PARTICIPANTS

This book is the result of a larger project on which I worked from 2000 through 2009. It was funded from 2000 to 2002 by a generous grant from the Intel Research Council. The project included archival research using both scholarly and popular media sources, a content analysis of over 52,500 newspaper articles on privacy between 1985 and 2006, ethnographic work in various homes, workplaces, and public spaces, and seventy-four formal interviews conducted between June 2001 and December 2002.

I want to be clear that this is a study based entirely on insights that probably are quite specific to the United States. This is a preliminary study, at best, one that only sets the stage for comparative domestic and international work. Indeed, my limited experience suggests that privacy and what is considered private or public are such culturally specific ideas and practices that I would be extremely reluctant to try to export what I've found here to any other society—or even to certain subcultures within the United States. I took a number of trips to England, Italy, Portugal, Sweden, and Denmark during the years I've been working on this subject, for instance. In addition to conversations with individuals from many more countries, what I saw and heard in these other places made me realize how different the conceptualization and practices—and importance—of privacy might be in other parts of the world. However, these travels and conversations also made me realize just how central whatever happens in the U.S. can be for shaping conversations and practices and policies throughout the world.

The political world that surrounded this study throughout its duration had an undeniable effect on it. Privacy is part and parcel of our daily lives, an important tenet of U.S. citizens' worldview and their everyday behaviors. Yet it is not always easy to get people—including politicians, critics, reporters, and the participants in this study—to talk about what they assume and what they do and why they think it is so important. A post-9/11 United States, however, with George W. Bush and Dick Cheney at the helm, seemed to have highlighted and challenged Americans' thoughts on privacy in rather remarkable ways.

This study is certainly all the richer for the enormous amount of media coverage on privacy—and especially secrecy—that resulted from this administration's choices. The number of column inches and televised minutes dedicated to my interests were invaluable for thinking about privacy. They were especially helpful regarding the selectivity of what is concealed and disclosed, the work that secrets and secrecy require, the tradeoffs that may or may not exist between privacy and "security," and the importance of the distribution of power for individuals' abilities to achieve privacy.

All this coverage was extremely helpful in getting study participants to talk about their views on privacy, too. Like my international acquaintances, participants used what was reported in the news during this time to reflect on and express their own views, and they had much to say about what happened to them, their clients, friends, and families, and their visions of the future, in light of all this.[9] The timing of this study offered a tremendous opportunity for anyone who wants to understand this subject, then, even if it was often for the most troubling of reasons.

Table I.1 presents a summary of some key socioeconomic statistics for these study participants.

Most of these individuals were contacted because of my personal knowledge about them and my desire to speak with them. Some of them were contacted because an interviewer who joined the project later believed they would be a good person to interview. If I agreed with the interviewer's

TABLE I.1 Summary Characteristics of study participants

RESIDENCE		HOUSEHOLD		EDUCATION	
Live in Chicago	74	INCOME		High school	3
US citizens	74	(45/74 data points)		Some college	6
Born in US	70	Range <$20K–$250K+		College graduate	20
Raised outside Chicago	57	Average $90K–$100K		Some graduate school	7
				Master's degree	27
SEX		LIVING		JD	2
Men	38	ARRANGEMENTS		MD	1
Women	36	2–7 person household	61	PhD	8
		Live alone	10		
AGE		College dormitory	3		
Range	20–80			OCCUPATION	
Median	41			Professional/technical	50
				Executive/management	3
RACE				Sales	2
Caucasian	63			Administrative support/	
African-American	6			clerical	5
Other	5			Military	1
				Service occupations	3
				Private household	4
				Students	6

rationale, the individual was approached. Seventy-five individuals were invited to participate; only one person declined to be interviewed.

The result was not only a remarkably articulate, insightful group of people to whom I am extraordinarily grateful, but also an undeniably privileged population. All of them lived in the Chicago area, too. Their socioeconomic and urban status as well as their current residency in Chicago are all reasons that that the insights I report here may or may not hold for other populations in the U.S.

However, the vast majority of these conversants had lived in multiple locations all over the United States as well as in other parts of the world. Most had traveled extensively as well, including a great deal of international travel. Most came from far simpler backgrounds than their current profiles would suggest, too. Some individuals, so accomplished now, were raised on public assistance in urban public housing or poor rural family homes. There were a number of solid working-class childhoods here, too, spent among both nuclear and extended immigrant families. In other words, the totality of participants' privacy experiences is far more diverse than one might expect from their current paychecks and living conditions.

Without additional work, it is impossible to know whether what I've learned from these individuals represents anyone other than themselves. They certainly have resources to achieve privacy now that many, many other people lack. That alone suggests the need for additional work with additional populations if we are to truly understand what privacy means and how it is achieved in the U.S.

In fact, the people who participated in this research project may be characterized as a "judgment sample" (Honigman 1973); they were not randomly selected. Rather, individuals were asked to participate based on some foreknowledge of their living arrangements, biographical histories, and/or professions. I believed that each individual would likely possess (1) an interest in privacy and what is private, (2) specific insights into the nature of these concepts and the practices that surround them, and (3) a willingness to talk about these things with me.

I asked participants for one and a half to two hours of their time. Early on, I approached some individuals as experts in certain fields to help me think about a particular aspect of privacy. I used my questionnaire (see appendix A) only loosely for them. For most people who agreed to be interviewed, though, I identified a specific section of the questionnaire for that individual, given what I knew of her or his interests and experiences. This became the focus of that person's interview, which was conducted in her or his home, private workspace, or a public meeting place such as a coffee shop.

Upon finishing the designated part of the questionnaire and/or at the end of the agreed-upon time, the interview would begin to wrap up. At this time, however, participants almost always offered to continue—if not then, then at another time. I was delighted to accept these offers. Thus, nearly every participant's interview was conducted across multiple sessions of two to three hours' duration per session. Each session was recorded to audiotape and transcribed for analysis. In total, the interviews were between one and a half and seventeen hours long, with most of them between eight and nine hours in length.

Individuals' identities have been protected by changing their names and any uniquely identifiable biographical information whenever necessary (e.g., age, dates, numbers of children, sex of children, place, firm, school names, occupation, etc.). A single person's insights are often attributed to multiple fictional names, too, whenever a particular combination of stories might make it a little too easy to identify someone. I do this not so much to protect participants' identities from strangers, but rather to protect them from people who know them well enough to figure out who they are. As we shall see, it's often the people who know us well who are the biggest threats to our privacy.

CHAPTER ONE

Secrets
& Secrecy

When I was a kid and I had just started masturbating, I had an accident, and I actually had to go to the hospital. I lost a testicle, and-- 'cause it twisted and the blood circulation got cut off. It was bad news. And I was mortified.

And I was so mortified of course that I didn't tell my parents what I was doing, because I was like twelve or thirteen. So I lied to them about what I was doing at the time.

And, I remember like, at some point during the whole thing, my mother gave me this little talk about how, you know, this was private and I didn't have to tell anybody. And, you know-- "And you don't even have to tell your wife when you have one."

And I thought, "Okay." I think I kinda, sort of took that to heart.

So anyway when I was telling you before about, has there ever been anybody who didn't respect, you know, privacy that you thought you had--My ex-boyfriend once-- when we were in a situation that was a party or with some friends or something—told or wanted to tell people at the party about this. And I was so angry at him because I just felt like--

And it's funny that I should feel that this was so private. But, I feel, I guess-- It's tied up in sex, but it's also tied up in that early shame about masturbation and stuff like that.

So anyway, that was-- What was the question?

Lessons about privacy that stem from your childhood.

Yeah, so this is one of the lessons, was that-- That there are-- That you have a right to keep things private, if you want to, certain things. And that other people should respect that. That's all what my mother taught me.

MIKE, twenty-eight-year-old single, gay administrative assistant

The privacy lessons that stem from our secrets are as rich as they are undeniable. Nothing better illustrates the principle, goals, and art of selective concealment and disclosure than how we manage our secrets—whether we are successful at it or not. In fact, secrecy and the work of keeping, revealing, and finding out secrets are important parts of the work we do to achieve privacy. Secrets are therefore a great place to begin looking closely at the work of privacy.

At its core, managing privacy is about managing relationships between the self and others. Altman (1975, 10), for instance, refers to privacy as a "boundary regulatory process by which a person (or group) makes himself more or less accessible and open to others." When we regulate our accessibility to others, though—including the accessibility of information, objects, space, time, or anything else that we deem private—we simultaneously regulate our relationships with them. In general, the better we are at making good decisions about what to conceal and reveal—and at carrying out these decisions—the better we will be at managing our relationships.

Relationships are built on pieced-together perceptions of each others' identities—our characters, priorities, and abilities, all manifested in and demonstrated by our visible behavior across time. As Simmel (in Levine 1971, 10) pointed out, "We cannot know completely the individuality of another. . . . It is impossible . . . to see anything but juxtaposed fragments."[1] The fullness of who we are—and what we do—is simply not accessible to anyone else.

Nor would we want it to be. There are plenty of aspects of who we are, have been, and will be that we would not want accessible to just anyone. Whether a painful childhood event, a favorite daydream that makes it easier to get through the day, a dubious workplace practice, our financial state of affairs, or our cell phone numbers—whatever—there are reasons we may want to keep some things about ourselves to ourselves. We share them with only the most trusted of souls, and/or the institutions, agencies, and people who are liable if they fail to protect us as they are supposed to.

We do this because we eventually learn that what others do and do not know about us has consequences for us and for our desired relationships with them. Others will allocate to and withhold from us all kinds of support, opportunities, and resources based on whatever fragmentary knowledge they have of us. It is precisely this desire to shape our relationships with others in particular ways that makes controlling what they know of us so important to us.

This is the very context for Bok's (1982) and Rosen's (2000) arguments, in fact, which assert that the most central claim to privacy in the U.S. is the desire to control identity, that is, "the sense of what we identify ourselves as, through, and with" (Bok 1982, 20). This, they argue, is the foundation of what we see as our "right" to privacy.

With some people, for instance, we may want only a very public, limited kind of relationship—if any at all. Identity thieves, child molesters, telemarketers, and Jehovah's Witnesses were regularly mentioned by study participants, for instance, as people with whom they want no relationship. Participants are very careful to hide all kinds of information from such people and to avoid any encounters with them in either the virtual or physical worlds. With others, though—say, a neighborhood, work, church, or softball friend—we may want personable, yet hardly "tell-all" kinds of relationships. We share much more information with them, accordingly, granting access to the very things we deny to others, but still holding much back. And with still other people, we may desire extremely intimate relationships. Accordingly, we choose to share the most private of our thoughts, feelings, belongings, and actions with them. Anthony, for instance—a thirty-six-year-old accountant—explained the situation like this:[2]

To, to expose the private part of your self is to make yourself vulnerable and that's not something that people generally do lightly. . . . There's definitely a huge differentiation between who you expose your, your more private self to and, and sort of the rest of the world that gets one facet or another of this sort of public persona-- or this public part of yourself that you allow others to see.

Erving Goffman's work (especially 1959, 1966, 1982, and 1986), for instance, focuses on a number of identity-related concealment and disclosure activities. He especially draws our attention to face-to-face encounters and the ways we offer up certain things about ourselves while omitting or actively suppressing others. Through our "presentations of self," we engage in "impression management," sometimes using space (e.g., "frontstages" and "backstages") to organize what we do and do not let others know about us. Goffman beautifully sensitizes us to the fact that all the while we're busy doing this, everyone else is, too. In the meantime, we're all trying to decide whether to accept, reject, and possibly protect the information we give to each other—and whether we want to find out more.[3]

It is the desired nature of our relationships with others that helps drive much of our efforts to manage our privacy, then, including what others know of us, as well as what we know of them. The management of information—specifically, private information—is therefore our starting point as we look closely at how, exactly, we try to achieve privacy. In the rest of this chapter, I first discuss the relationship between secrecy and privacy and between secrets and other private things. Next, I look closely at the nature of secrets and their connection to social relationships. Finally, I delve into the actual work of secrets, that is, the effort necessary to make, keep, reveal, and find them out.

SECRECY AND PRIVACY

The work of secrets and secrecy needs to be placed into the broader context of what we do to try to achieve privacy. Sometimes we need do very little to obtain privacy; we are given the discretion to set the private-public boundary pretty much as we like it. Our physical location, others' lack of interest, their good manners, and/or an assortment of personal agents and institutions may ensure our privacy along numerous dimensions without having to attend to it personally.[4] At other times, however, privacy may be highly problematic. It may be quite scarce or we may have little confidence in its persistence even when we have it.

Secrecy is a way of achieving privacy whenever individuals wish to ensure that the most private and important of their matters are kept that way. If privacy is the condition in which private things are as private as we wish them to be, secrecy is the condition in (and through) which we try to *insist* that our private things are as private as we wish them to be.[5] Secrecy is a means to an end,[6] a process in which we actively work to manage our private matters.[7] Here, we leave little about our privacy to chance, others' agendas, and/or their well-known (or even suspected) privacy-gifting/withholding tendencies.

Secrets are thus distinguished from the broader category of "private things" by their intentionally, personally protected status as well as the rich variety of work that people do to keep, share, and find them out. Sometimes we engage in secrecy work happily, as in the case of surprise parties and the carefully wrapped and hidden gifts we present at them. Sometimes we engage in secrets work under duress, as when we expect extremely negative consequences should significant others, coworkers, the IRS, the police, or an international ring of identity thieves find out something about us. Individuals in this study describe secrecy experiences that are a distinct mixture of both of these emotions—and more.

No matter how oblivious, delightful, or dire our frame of mind, though, at an interpersonal level, there appears to be a continuum between the most personally active and passive ways in which we obtain privacy. At one end, the concealing, perhaps dissimulating behaviors associated with secrecy are the most active of techniques through which we achieve privacy. At the other end, the noninterest of others associated with social ambivalence and/or proper etiquette are among the more passive ways we get to keep our private things private. And while we may leave less important or as-yet unchallenged matters to these more passive techniques, we actively, deliberately work to protect everything else—more or less—especially our most cherished secrets.

Secrets also are a subset of what might generically be called "unshared information." "Unshared information" includes subject matter that is both intentionally and unintentionally kept to oneself. It may have never occurred to us to share something that we know, do, or possess with a certain person, for instance. This is not a secret. Rather, the birth of a secret requires an intentional decision to make it so, at least an intuitive realization that someone else might want to know something and that we would not want that to happen. Likewise, once a secret is no longer intentionally withheld from others, it may well revert back to the category of merely unshared information, simply irrelevant to the matters at hand.[8]

THE NATURE OF SECRETS

Anything can be a secret. The form is analytically distinct from its content. As Bok (1982, 5) puts it in her seminal work on the subject, "A path, a riddle, a jewel, an oath—anything can be secret so long as it is kept intentionally hidden, set apart in the mind of its keepers as requiring concealment."

Secrets, moreover, are good and bad; harmless and dangerous; big and little; happy and sad. Participants in this study, for instance, are just as likely to classify their most intimate, treasured goals and future aspirations as "secrets" as they are past actions and thoughts that evoke especially negative feelings. Of course, the adjectives one might pick to describe a particular secret may well vary between those who share the secret and those who don't. This is particularly true if the excluded believe they have a vested interest in the secret and/or the relationship it establishes between those who share it.

Secrets may be short lived and long lived. They may be of planned and unplanned duration. And, like even the best of plans, the temporal boundaries of both ends of a secret are subject to the most unexpected events.

Secrets may be consensual and/or coerced. It is not uncommon for secrets to feel like they have elements of both. Guilt and/or anxiety in possessing knowledge of a secret—much less in participating in a secret behavior or experience—may be rooted in this hybridity.

Secrets may be autonomous one-offs that stand on their own in their implications and the work needed to maintain or reveal them. Secrets also may be deeply and widely interconnected with other secrets. In smaller or larger clusters, like an island that is part of an archipelago, the underlying connectedness of secrets may be discovered only by those most motivated to explore it, using talents that others lack.

Secrets may be singly owned or collectively shared—perhaps by millions. A single person may be the only one who knows a secret. Dyads, triads, and other small groups may share secrets, too, as might entire neighborhoods, departments, or corporate divisions. Yet as my all-time favorite example of widespread collusion in the making and keeping of a secret shows, literally hundreds of millions of adults can share and keep and be bound together by a secret: the secret of Santa Claus.

Like the secret of Santa Claus, or the wrapped gift sitting in plain sight, there are secrets whose existence is known. It is the precise content of the secret that is concealed from others. There are secret secrets, too, though. Others do not even know these kinds of secrets exist and may never even suspect their reality.

There are formal (legal-institutional) secrets and informal (personal-interpersonal) ones. Nondisclosure agreements, state secrets acts, insider-trading laws, attorney-client privilege, judge-enforced gag orders, and constitutional amendments are but some of the formal ways in which people try to ensure secrets. Informally, various social and physical consequences—both desirable and undesirable—tend to provide the tools through which secrets are kept—or not.

In terms of content, secrets are predictable and unpredictable, stable and dynamic. This is because things that become secrets are so context dependent: socially (especially culturally, geopolitically, and historically) and personally (particularly across simultaneously held life-worlds and reference groups as well as over the life course). One person's secret may be another person's calling card. The secret of one's childhood may become the focus of an adult's fondly and frequently retold story. The outed secret that leads one person to quietly commit suicide after a life lived in fear may give another a much-relieved new lease on life.

Secrets are the territory of professionals and amateurs. Some people literally get paid to keep them, reveal them, find them out, and/or encourage others to do so. Others acquire, give up, and uncover secrets for the simple reason that they are normal human beings living normal lives. And still others find the fascination with and opportunity to be involved in secrets their most compelling reason for getting up in the morning.

In other words, secrets can be more central or more peripheral to self-identity. This is true for those whose ability to keep, strategically reveal, *or* find out a secret is an important part of who they are. It is also true for those who have made a conscious commitment to living without secrets, often a key to identity reform for those who have lived previously stigmatized—or potentially stigmatized—lives. Indeed, the centrality of secrets work for self-identity may well change over the life course.

SECRETS AND RELATIONSHIP WORK

No matter what the secret, no matter how it is manipulated or what its fate, to consider a secret is to simultaneously consider the relationships (perhaps entire social networks) that it throws into relief. Indeed, from a sociological perspective, perhaps the most significant aspect of secrets is their selectively shared nature. They are secrets *with* and secrets *from*, intentionally disclosed to and concealed from specific individuals at specific times and in specific ways. Simultaneously inclusive and exclusive, secrets are quite effective at achieving social boundary work,[9] an excellent measure of the social distance between individuals.[10]

Simmel (1950b, 317–29) argues that every type of social relationship is defined by the expected degree of secrecy and secret sharing—what he terms "knowledge reciprocity"—associated with it. Yet this is an incredibly dynamic phenomenon. As the currency of relationships, secrets are exchanged and withheld in remarkable quantities and ways not only across different kinds of relationships, but across any given relationship, over time. They are a fine measure of the ebb and flow of intimacy. Consider this story.

Occasionally somebody we know might tell us something that they seriously want to keep private from others but we don't think it would be so awful if other people found out. Have you ever had that experience?

Be so awful? Yeah, probably. Um, I'm trying to think of some-- Probably the, the worst-case example is when my twin sister got pregnant and--

And she told you and she considered this a secret?

Um, actually, she got an abortion and didn't tell me until afterwards. 'Cause she was afraid to tell me. So that was a very, very interesting moment in our relationship, you know.

. . . She said that nobody else knew except for one of her roommates, who actually took her to the place, and then her boyfriend at the time. So, but-- She was like, nobody else in the family is going to know, that kind of thing. She wasn't going to even tell me for the longest time, so.

Was it really hard not to just tell anyone?

When it came to her, no. That wasn't an issue. I was more upset that she didn't come to me right away. It was-- You know-- That was kind of the most challenging thing. I'm like, she didn't want me to-- She thought I would judge her, and I was like, no way would I judge you on that.

Neither the content nor the existence of her twin's secret was upsetting to this participant. Rather, it was the fact that the sister withheld this information from *her* and, in fact, did not tell her about it for quite a while. The secret and its sharing signaled an unwanted, growing distance between these sisters that deeply affected this participant. A secret reinforces and heightens intimacy among those who share it. It simultaneously increases the sense of being distinct—if not cut off—from those who do not share it, even if preservation of the relationship is the very reason for the secret.[11]

The structurally binding effect of secrets undoubtedly rests in tension with the effect of the actual knowledge imparted when a secret is shared. There may be something about the content of the shared secret that makes us want to keep it as far away from a given individual as possible, even though to share it would be an undoubted request for and perhaps even result in intimacy. This participant believes this is exactly what worried her twin and led her sister not to tell what she was going to do—or, later, what she had already done.

In this next, more humorous story, we can also see the selective decisions made about what we will and won't share with each other, based on the desire to have others think of us in certain ways.

Yesterday, my friend (Stephanie) told me an excellent story, which I think should be on this tape. She said, "You know, it's interesting"—she's not married, never been married—and she said, "I just find it fascinating what people tell their spouses and what they keep secret."

Stephanie had a friend who called her the day before, saying, "Oh, I have to tell you what I did to my husband." She—this woman—went to the bathroom. And she knew that she had a hundred dollars of bills in her back pocket. And she went to the bathroom, flushed the toilet, got up and went to do something, and reached for the bills and they weren't there. And she said, "Oh, my God, I flushed my $100 down the toilet."

And she looked in the toilet and she scooped the water and she couldn't find it. And she got her husband and they bailed out the rest of the water. This man unscrewed the toilet and they're looking in the drain for the $100 and they can't find it and just like, "Oh, damn." And so he puts the toilet back and, "Oh, that's $100 gone."

Down the toilet.

Down the toilet.

That night, she looks in the front pocket of her pants and there's the $100.

And she says, "Can you imagine, Stephanie? I made my husband—rather than looking in another pocket of my pants—I made my husband, who I complain about constantly, unbolt the toilet and look for the money. Instead of just looking in the other pocket of my pants. Because I'm so sure I'm right."

And Stephanie said, "Oh, my God. So what did (Dennis) say?" And she said, "Oh, are you kidding? I didn't tell him."

And I thought, man, I would never tell my husband that I lost $100. And I would have no trouble not telling him that. But that wasn't the thing that *she* couldn't tell.

Notice all the relationship and presentation-of-self work in this story. In her panic, the wife decided it was okay for her husband to think of her as someone who had been careless enough to drop $100 in the toilet—but also as someone who would immediately confess to such a mistake and, in her contrite condition, try to make good on it. At the same time, she did not want her husband to think of her as someone who was careless enough to put him through so much trouble without bothering to check all her pockets first. *That* was something he could not be told for fear that it really would diminish her in his eyes. Our storyteller, on the other hand, would eliminate all the fuss by never confessing to the lost money in the first place. Her "what he doesn't know can't hurt him—or me" approach would completely sidestep the potential damage to her character and their relationship—as long as her husband never found out about any of this in the first place.

A secret withheld from others operates as a brick in the wall between its holder(s) and all potential sharers. This may or may not be a good thing. If walls can be detrimental to relationships, they can also allow happy and peaceful cohabitation. The same is true of secrets. What matters is the extent to which the decision to share or not share the secret takes specific relationships in the directions that the secret owner wishes—for the short *and* the long term.

The following story, for instance, is one in which the storyteller had little initial control over what she thought had to be kept secret from her mother precisely because of her mother's reactions.[12] She learned to engage in secrecy very quickly, as a result. One gets the distinct sense that the direction this took her relationship with her mother—indeed, her childhood, in general—was not one she would have freely chosen.

My mother couldn't really talk about certain things. I mean, like, she could never talk to me especially about things like, like getting my period. We learned certain things in school. But I remember when I got mine, and I asked her to help me, show me, something, how to use a tampon. She just wouldn't. Couldn't, I guess. And I had to figure it out myself.

Oh, my God, I just remembered! I used to have this bra, too. You know? I needed a bra. I wanted one, too, but I needed it. But I couldn't talk to her about it. So I bought one and just didn't tell her. And for—years, I think—like, two years, I slept with it under my pillow. It was like this old, brown, stinky bra that I kept under my pillow. When I took it off at night, I'd put it under my pillow. I don't think I ever washed it. It was, I don't know, this, this thing that I thought I had to hide from her or something.

Yeah. Body things. And other things. Emotional things, too. She just couldn't handle it, I guess. I grew up keeping a lot of things to myself.

A secret is, then, a source of acute self-differentiation, separating those who know it from those who do not. Sharing the secret, however—even with one person—almost tangibly differentiates the sharers from those around them. As a consequence of the previous money-down-the-toilet story, for instance, two middle-aged girlfriends are now delightfully bound to the owner of that $100 in a way that her own husband is not. Similarly, when a mother cannot bring herself to discuss so many important matters with her daughter, a sense of distance may permeate the entire relationship.

The next story also shows how the offer to selectively share a secret can be a compelling, overt invitation to friendship. Here, women quickly strike up a bond with each other as they offer to share their separate secrets.

I had a c-section and it was an emergency so it was something else. And I've met a couple women like that and we will actually show each other our scars in public places. (*Laughing.*) But that just cracked me up. I was actually at a party and talking to a woman and she shows me-- She just dropped her pants and shows me her vertical scar and we're, like, peeking, showing her mine. (*Laughing.*)

The female protagonist in the next story illustrates the same bonding effect of secrets, but also shows the ways they can be used more insidiously to draw and redraw social boundaries.

Have you or has someone you know ever made a mistake and told or showed someone something that, in retrospect, seemed too private to have shared with that person?

Yeah. I'm sitting there with this one girl, who-- She was a single mother. We were close friends and, you know, the guy [the father] was gone. And we were friends, but I had no really romantic intentions or anything like that, but we wound up having sex, right? A few times.

And finally she's, like, getting ready to come to term. . . . She's over at my house, like, "I want to fool around tonight." I don't want to fool around. I'm like, it's just too weird, you know? I'm just thinking like banging the kid's head in or something like that. And she's like, "Well, the doctor said one of the best ways to induce labor is to have sex." I'm like, oop, I can't argue with that.

And we did and she broke her water that morning on my bed getting up. You know, it was like splash. . . . And so, you know, I leapt out of the bed, pulled on my pants, and stuff like that. And, like, why don't you get your things? I'm going to get you in the car and I'll take you straight over to the hospital. 'Cause she's, like, panicking, you know, not sure what to do.

. . . Years later, she's dating this [other] guy seriously, but she has reservations. But she's not admitting them, yet.

. . . She brings this up. She's like-- She brings up that she broke her water on my bed, in front of her [new] boyfriend.

I was just like-- Oh, no! You don't talk about--! She's like, "What?" I'm like, never mind. So I tried. But she kept going on about it and getting people into the conversation. They're like, "Really? You broke her water?" Yeah.

What was her boyfriend doing?

Looking like it wasn't bothering him. But, later on, we talked and I said, "Look, dude. I'm sorry. I totally respect your relationship, you know?" He's like, "(Sam), I really appreciate that you say that because I feel like shit right now." I'm like, "She just doesn't know. She cares about you." Or something.

I didn't know if she cared about him. It turned out she was having reservations, and that was her nice little way of sabotaging it, I guess. Thanks for bringing me into that.

In her work on "uncoupling," Vaughan (1990) argues convincingly that secrets play a key role in defining and redefining specific relationships over a period of time. In this last story, we see that by revealing the secret from their shared past in the way she did, the mother not only aligned herself more closely with the participant, but also distanced herself from her current boyfriend. It is a subtle, yet quite effective move that nudged both relationships onto slightly new trajectories.

Interestingly, the bonding effect of a shared secret seems to hold true whether the secret and/or the relationship are wanted or unwanted. An example of the latter is seen in this next story, from a twenty-nine-year-old woman. She was inappropriately kissed and touched by the director of a summer camp that she attended as a teenager. Her shame was exacerbated by her choice to keep the secret, later, even after she'd found the courage to confront the perpetrator.[13]

There was a director of a camp who definitely I would consider invaded my privacy in terms of crossing the boundary.

. . . And this is when you were a child?

Yeah, when I was fourteen and fifteen.

. . . I had wanted to speak with [the director] and he suggested a meeting over here. It's in an outdoor woods place. So-- In a barn, which is where everybody meets, and it's across the street from the main house.

He definitely-- We talked and he definitely crossed the boundary, you know. Not violent or anything, just definitely crossed that.

And then when I confronted him the next year, I definitely watched my world on one level. And I felt guilty and all that. Probably his wife hated me. And the next year I brought it up, and he said maybe we should just keep that between you and I.

Oh. And what did you say to that?

I said okay. Which was bad.

Or so she decided years later, when she sought counseling for relationship difficulties that turned out to be related to this. In the circumstances, it would take an unusually empowered teenage girl to do anything except agree to keep such a secret. Unfortunately, doing so also meant allowing the relationship it signified to persist. Only by sharing and exploring her feelings around this secret with her therapist was she eventually able to alter both her understanding of that relationship and begin to better shape the ones she wanted to have with others.

Of course, a potential secret sharer may well choose to deny a proffered relationship by refusing to keep a secret quiet. Disclosing another's secret for spite is a relationship tactic I have seen perfected by extremely young children. It is used with relish against others as an effective way for the secret teller to claim status and/or deny status to others. This is also a critical tool used in organizations by individuals who wish to dissociate themselves from other members, particularly when they disapprove of what those members stand for. This is the case for whistleblowers (Zerubavel 2006; Vaughan 1996), for example, and those who are hired to "clean house" and refuse to hide the incompetence of incumbents (Hermanowicz 2008).

Someone who is intentionally excluded from a relationship may also try to extract a secret from those who currently have it, precisely because of the social bond it signifies. Young children are equally good at trying to overhear or persuade others to share secrets with them, for example, even silly, meaningless secrets. It is an attempt to insert themselves more fully into the social unit of those in the know.[14] Sometimes the whole point of a secret is the sharing or not sharing of it. What matters most is the relationship it confirms, offers, or denies—not the secret's actual content.

The effects of secrets on relationships are noticeable even in situations in which a secret originator chooses not to share the secret with anyone else. There are positive rewards for these secrets, such as feeling satisfied, special, or powerful because of the preciousness of this knowledge, feeling, or thought and/or what it allows one to do or know about the world.

Keeping these secrets also may help avert any anticipated negative social consequences associated with their disclosure. This operates as a different but equally compelling reward for keeping secrets to oneself.

However, these kinds of secrets do not allow for the same kind of interpersonal, relationship-confirming rewards associated with secrets that are shared. Instead, especially where the secret is kept out of fear, the effects of solely known secrets include at least one undesirable outcome: the possibility of an unwanted and saddening sense of social isolation.[15] With these secrets, Simmel's (1950b, 334) observation is especially clear: "the secret is a first-rate element of individualization." Moreover, the more important the solely known, fearful secret is for an individual's sense of self, the more it may produce this isolating, individuating effect.

The ages-old institutional act of confession recognizes this propensity. Here, individuals are encouraged to share even the worst of secrets with one safe person, knowing the power of such sharing to prevent giving way to despair. Today, the act (and importance) of confession may persist partly for this reason—whether with a clergy member, physician, therapist,[16] twelve-step group, or under the anonymity afforded by helpline volunteers, chatroom facilitators, or a community artist and a project such as PostSecret.[17, 18] The fact that one is no longer separated from others by a solely kept secret offers comfort to many.

Perhaps this is at least partly because unlike solely known secrets, shared secrets help confirm an individual's place in a group—whether a group of two or one as large as all of humanity.[19] In fact, the rewards associated with sharing secrets are significant and tempting in a way that the rewards of solely known secrets are not. This is true whether we intend to keep such secrets, betray them, or do the careful work of giving up and reconciling them.[20, 21]

To sum up, the making, keeping, revealing, and finding out of secrets is a critical dimension of making, keeping, revealing, and discovering social relationships. Individuals are judged in the success of their relationships—by themselves and by others—at least in part according to three factors: (1) the secrets they feel free to keep, share, avoid or seek out; (2) the secrets for which they feel obligated to do the same; and (3) by how, precisely, they do all of this. The more one's sense of self is defined by the relationships one has—or denies—with others, the more important will be an individual's success in managing this aspect of one's privacy.

HOW WE DO IT: THE WORK OF SECRETS

Success in the work of secrets means being able to keep the secrets one wants to keep, to reveal the secrets one wishes to share—with the people with whom one wishes to do so—to find out the secrets one wishes to know (or thinks one does), and to make good decisions about all of this in light of the kinds of relationships one wishes to have with others. This means that secrets work requires deep cultural, personal, and interpersonal knowledge at every level if one is to do it well.[22]

This is especially true because success in the work of secrets isn't just about managing content. The precise *ways* in which we keep, reveal, and find out secrets are just as important as the content of the secrets themselves, if not more so. This is because how and when we choose to keep, reveal, or find out another's secret tells us much about the ways each party perceives their relationship to the other.

For example, consider something as simple as timing in the sharing of secrets and how this, alone, matters to the person on the receiving end. Timing in the disclosure process is an important facet of how one manages a secret. It may well overshadow the importance of the secret itself, if it is mishandled, becoming its own source of contention, above and beyond the secret's content.[23]

Sharing secrets in a timely way is only one aspect of managing them, of course, even though this alone requires a fair amount of judgment and skill to do it right. If one gets it wrong, the skills needed to make amends because of the untimeliness of a revelation are quite substantial, too. They include the need for excellent judgment regarding whether or not one can actually expect forgiveness if one confesses later than one should have along with good ideas of how one might convey sufficient remorse and integrity in order to be forgiven. The highly skilled may even strengthen, certainly rescue, the relationship in this way.

In his excellent essay on the social norms of notification, in fact, Ryan (2006, 28) explicitly argues that the "how" of a revelation directly affects the "what." In his words, "even when the timing, sequence, and manner of notification are instrumentally inconsequential, how one conveys information affects the meaning of the telling." In the case of secrets, this is because the way we do secrets work directly demonstrates what we think of others and what we think of ourselves.[24] In fact, form may well trump content when it comes to what our secrets work reveals about us.

The work of secrets falls into two interrelated clusters. First, there is the decision-making work of secrets. This is the effort of determining not only if something should be a secret, but also whether or not—and how—to selectively disclose, conceal, or try to find out a secret in order to achieve a desirable outcome. Several factors are especially important here. First, there is the simple structural logic of a secret's life with all the decisive moments it entails. In addition, there are considerations such as customary practices regarding who "owns" a secret, one's personal knowledge of secrets work and how well one can do it, and the anticipated consequences of the disclosure and/or concealment of a secret for one's relationships with others.

Second, there are the skills, techniques, knowledge, and mindset necessary to manage secrets, for which individuals have widely varied competencies. These run the gamut from efforts to manage the tangible and intangible aspects of secrets to the work needed to manage both individual and collective secrets. I turn to both of these aspects of secrets work now to learn more about how we do privacy, every day.

THE WORK OF SECRETS, PART I: DECISION-MAKING

THE LIFE OF A SECRET

In order to more fully understand the decision-making process involved in personal secrets, I have selected a story about a small, utterly mundane secret that was quickly outed. I have mapped the plot of the story, including all the moments in which something might have happened differently from what was told to me. Table 1.1, "Mapping the life of a (very simple, short-lived) secret," is the result.

This chart presents what seems to be the structural logic of the concealment and disclosure of a secret—the logical possibilities that face any secret maker and the individuals around her or him. I trace what might have happened from the birth of this secret to its death, looking at the moments in which it was kept, disclosed, or exposed and how that might have happened. I do this by sticking very closely to the story as it was told to me, adding only what I know happened to this story after the events recounted in it took place. Here, then, is an analysis of Forrest lying to his mother one morning about brushing his teeth. The complete story is as follows.

Has there been a time recently when somebody didn't want you to know something but their face or their body language gave them away?

Sure. For example, my son, (twelve)-year-old son. "(Forrest), did you brush your teeth today?" "Yes!" And I didn't even have to look at his face, but it was just the intonation in his voice and the response. I knew he had not brushed his teeth. And so I went over and I looked at him in the eye, and he marched off and went to brush his teeth. Because he was lying through them. (*Laughing.*)

A few insights emerge from the mapping of this secret. First, note that the work within each wave of disclosure/exposure is highly iterative, as is the number of waves that may follow the first one. The possibilities can require an extraordinary amount of attention. Decisions are consciously and unconsciously made to keep, reveal, or try to find out secrets—or not—multiple times in the course of any single secret's life (much less any single individual's day). New or extremely important secrets—or relationships—may intensify the process, for instance, making many moments feel pregnant with the potential for disclosure/exposure and the need to make decisions. Those that have become less important or taken for granted may result in only certain moments grabbing one's attention, posing fewer noticeably acute threats/opportunities.

Second, competency in the skills and knowledge necessary to do secrets work plays an important role in what happens to a secret, affecting one's ability to carry out whatever decisions one has made. Individual competency in the work of secrets is not the only important factor, either. One's competency relative to another person's (agency's, institution's, government's) may be the more definitive measure of what is and is not likely to happen next. In this respect, we especially can see the advantage of detailed personal and interpersonal knowledge in secrets work, which leads to knowing when to press one's advantage or not, as well as how to do it best. Attentive mothers of young children, for instance, can be very good at knowing when to be suspicious and how to best act on that suspicion in order to achieve their desired outcome.

Third, we see the ever-present reality not only of intentional acts designed to keep, reveal, or find out a secret, but also of accidental or unintentional disclosures/exposures throughout the life of a secret. Individuals who feel they have a vested interest in a secret are most likely to act in ways that are designed to alter the path of a secret and create decision-demanding moments. However, the possibility always looms that things may go very differently than one might expect even though no one intended for it to happen. This is a theme that runs through all participants' stories about privacy violations.

Fourth and finally, whether the secret is intentionally or unintentionally disclosed/exposed—or whether it simply falls off the protective radar screen and reverts to the land of merely unshared information—this mapping reveals the logic underlying both the birth and the death of a secret. A secret begins with a decision to keep or hide something from other people. It ends when it is no longer consciously guarded—for whatever reason.

Note that the possibilities for what happens next in the life of any secret mean that there are inevitably certain paths that remain untaken. For instance, in the center of this chart, there are three columns of possibilities that are absent from the events of this story as it was told to me. One is "Another person unintentionally behaves in such a way that she/he does

TABLE 1.1 Mapping the life of a (very simple, short-lived) secret

The making of the secret	I possess unshared information.				
	1. Son: I didn't brush my teeth.				
	I decide to have (make) a secret.				
	2. Mom: "Did you brush your teeth?" Son: I'm not going to tell her that I didn't.				
First wave of exposure/ disclosure: From only secret originator(s) know(s) to somebody else knows, too.		I intentionally do not share it with (an)other person(s).	I unintentionally share it with (an)other person(s).	I intentionally share it with (an)other person(s).	Another person unintentionally behaves in such a way that she/he does not find out the secret.	Another person intentionally behaves in such a way that she/he does not find out the secret, even if its existence is suspected.
		3. Son consciously tries to bluff, adds lie: "Yes."	*4. Son's "Yes" sounds suspicious to mom.*			
			5. Son fails to present or sustain nonverbal portrayal of innocence to mom.			
				7. Busted: Son "confesses" by going off to brush teeth.		
Second (third, fourth, fifth) wave of exposure/ disclosure: Highly iterative, continuing for the life of the secret,						
when it is no longer intentionally protected.						

Has there been a time recently when somebody didn't want you to know something but their face or their body language gave them away?

Sure. For example, my son, (twelve)-year-old son. "(Forrest), did you brush your teeth today?" "Yes!" And I didn't even have to look at his face, but it was just the intonation in his voice and the response. I knew he had not brushed his teeth. And so I went over and I looked at him in the eye, and he marched off and went to brush his teeth. Because he was lying through them. (*Laughing*.)

Another person unintentionally behaves in such a way that she/he finds out the secret.	Another person intentionally tries to find out the secret.					
	6. *Mom goes over to "look him in the eye."*	Another person intentionally finds out the secret.				
		8. *Mom now knows son's secret.*				
	9. *Interviewer asks mom to tell about a time when someone's face or body gave them away.*		Another person unintentionally shares secret further.	Another person intentionally shares secret further.	Another person unintentionally keeps the secret.	Another person intentionally keeps the secret.
				10. *Mom tells story to interviewer.*		
				11. *Interviewer shares story with transcriber.*		
				12. *Transcriber shares story with me.*		
				13. *I share story with readers.*		14. *But I hide the identity of the mother and the son to hide the fact that it used to be his secret.*

not find out the secret." Forrest has a sister, for instance, a couple years older than him. She might have been going about her own business getting ready for school and remained oblivious to what was going on with her brother's toothbrushing. At some point in her story, Forrest's mother might have said that she asked her daughter to verify whether Forrest brushed his teeth, but the daughter might have said she had no idea. Had Forrest's mother mentioned something like this in her story, it would have been recorded in this column.

A second possibility omitted from this tale is represented by the column "Another person intentionally behaves in such a way that she/he does not find out the secret, even if its existence is suspected." Rushing to get herself ready, for instance, Forrest's sister could have noticed that her little brother failed to follow his usual routine of barging in on her in the bathroom while she was brushing her own teeth. Half suspecting that he was probably trying to get away with skipping it that morning, she might nonetheless choose not to confront him, not to seek independent evidence, and not to raise the issue with her mother. She might be thankful for having the bathroom to herself for a change, or for being exempted from yet another ridiculous confrontation between her brother and her mom. In fact, even Forrest's mom could have decided to give herself a break this one morning and simply not ask if he'd brushed. Forrest's mother didn't mention anything like any of these scenarios, though, so this column, too, remains blank for this story.

There is another possibility still, found in the column immediately to the right of that one: "Another person unintentionally behaves in such a way that she/he finds out the secret." Here, perhaps the sister might have overheard her mother and Forrest talking, just as she accidentally brushed her hand against Forrest's toothbrush while claiming her own. This might have led her to discover that her brother's toothbrush was perfectly dry and that he was, in fact, lying to his mom at that very moment. Or perhaps she might have walked by the bathroom and caught sight of Forrest trying to camouflage his shirking, making faces in the mirror while running the water and hoping to fake out his mother. In scenarios like this, the secret discoverer may well find out the protected information but without meaning to do so. Again, Forrest's mom made no mention of this, so it is not part of the mapping of this telling, even though it is a theoretical possibility.

As I was working my way through this chart, perhaps the most stunning insight for me was just how extensive, exhausting, and relentless the work of keeping a bigger, more consequential secret might be, over a much longer duration of time. Imagine the length of such a chart, for instance, if one tried to map the secret of either one of the main characters' sexuality in Ang Lee's film *Brokeback Mountain*. Even if one limited oneself to analyzing only the exact events and decision moments depicted in the film, it would be a daunting task.

Clearly, secrets can mean a tremendous amount of work. It is no wonder that the more study participants understand about the nature of keeping secrets, the less willing many of them are to do it. Some participants make this their life's work, of course; finding secrecy provides a highly necessary and even desirable backbone to their day and their identity. Yet for most people, the big lesson seems to be that avoiding secrets is much easier than embracing them. Knowledge of secrets work can at least result in much greater selectivity in deciding when secrets are and are not worth a given kind of effort.

DECISIVE FACTORS: OWNERSHIP, COMPETENCY, AND THE POTENTIAL CONSEQUENCES FOR RELATIONSHIPS

Three factors seem to be key in making a decision regarding what to do about a secret: (1) who "owns" the secret and what the distribution of power is across the stakeholders associated with it; (2) how good an individual's knowledge of secrets work is and how competent she or he is at it; and (3) given the former—and content-specific knowledge about the nature of the secret—what the anticipated consequences are of the secret's disclosure and concealment for the future, particularly in regard to one's relationships with others.

It is important to note that much of the asking and answering of these questions may be done with an individual having little awareness of the process or specificity of details. According to study participants, decisions about secrets are often instantaneous, intuitive, and based on a great deal of ambiguity.[25] This does not mean these decisions are not based on real experience and what may be acute insight or wisdom. It does mean, however, that it would be misleading to think the decisional work of secrets always resembles a careful, rational, unhurried, and analytical exercise. It might, but it often does not.

Nonetheless, I turn now to the part of secrets work focused on the times when we do exert whatever control we have, making quite conscious decisions about how to handle a secret. In deciding what and how to selectively conceal, reveal, and seek out, the first influence on participants' decisions is the distribution of power around a given secret. Whatever another's ability to act, it is her or his right to do so that seems paramount when deciding what to do next about a secret.

Who Owns the Secret?

As shown previously, there are numerous moments in which an individual other than the secret originator might intervene in the life of a secret. In addition, the outsider might intervene either on their own initiative or at the invitation of the originator. The questions of whether or not—and how—to intervene are greatly wrapped up in the issue of who "owns" the secret. That is to say, one of the first factors that is taken into account in deciding what to do about a secret is whether or not one believes one has a right to independently decide what should be done about it. Thus, the work of secrets includes the work of discerning who owns a secret, which then allows secret sharers to do more work in the form of making a decision about what to do next.

Among the participants in this study, secrets are viewed as property. The "owner" of a secret possesses the moral right to decide what should happen to the secret and, by extension, to any of the stakeholders associated with it. This includes all co-owners, in cases where secrets originate with more than one individual. If you do not wholly own a secret—that is, if you were not the only person who "gave birth" to it and, therefore, it is not only "yours"—then you do not have the right to make an independent decision about what to do with it.[26] It is a violation of a secret owner's privacy—her or his right to selectively reveal or conceal this information—for a non-owner to do something with that secret without all owners' permission. Thus, if you accidentally find out someone else's secret, are merely a sounding board for it, or are even the co-originator of a secret, the default moral position is that you may not independently act on the secret.

It may be that you cannot acknowledge that you even know this secret, as seems to be the case in the following rather heartbreaking story. Here, the storyteller still wonders if her intended revelation of a particular secret was done in not nearly a selective enough fashion.

My father.... Well, he was a very complicated man. He was a very loving man and also a very easily angered man and so on and so forth.

... When I was about eleven, maybe twelve, one day I was reading my diary to a cousin who lived across the fields. And we were on one side of a hedgerow. I got to the point that it said that I hate my father. And we heard something on the other side of the hedgerow. It was my father out for a walk, and I felt, you know, that I don't know if he heard or not. He was already somewhat hard of hearing at that point but that felt as if my, well, with my privacy, I'd been invaded, and as if I was, you know-- It was a shameful thing for me to have written down and, um, and he knew it.

And it's also very strange because it was that evening—must have been in October—that my father asked me if I would like to go board at the school because that year I was the only day student. It was kind of lonely.

. . . I said yes, I would like to. And I thought, but, you know, is this because he knows I hate him and he wants to get rid of me? So it was very complicated. But I didn't dare say anything about that. And he never said anything.

She never did find out if he never said anything because he didn't hear anything, or because he did, but, in essence, could not acknowledge what he heard because it was clearly supposed to be a secret from him, one that he did not own.

If one does not solely own a secret—and with only a few exceptions—rather than acting on it, one has the moral obligation (1) to confer with the owner/co-owners about any actions you might be tempted to take regarding the keeping, revealing, or finding out of that secret; and (2) to respect their wishes at least as much as your own. If you do wholly own the secret, however, you may proceed with it as you wish. As we shall see, this assumes that your ownership remains uncontested.

The owner of a secret must be distinguished from someone who simply knows the secret. As previously noted, a hallmark of secrets is that their value frequently rests in what their sharing does for relationships with others. For this reason alone, a secret originator—or usurper—may share a secret with one or more others who also now know the secret. Knowing a secret is not the same as owning a secret, however, and the person who shared it with us would be the first to point that out,[27] as Mike did at the start of this chapter.

Clarity of thought about who owns a secret is extremely important when individuals make decisions about whether or not they should keep, reveal, or seek them out. The following stories, for instance, demonstrate the ways in which a clear sense of ownership is directly tied to the decisions made by participants about the future of a specific secret—and the subsequent work they do and do not engage in regarding that secret.

In this first example, we see a situation in which a participant with a history of bulimia has a clear sense of whether or not she owns another person's secret.

I have had the experience where I was in the bathroom and I thought someone was throwing up, and I remember saying over the wall, "You know I go to Over Eaters Anonymous 'cause I used to be bulimic and, you know, if you're bulimic, you should check it out." (*Laughing.*) You know, that sort of thing, but--

Yeah. But that's funny so you'd say it over the wall rather than wait for them to come out?

Yeah, because it's very private. It's very embarrassing and I can't imagine being more humiliated than to be caught throwing up, really.

. . . So, I would never want to confront somebody. I mean I, my, my purpose would be to give them the information and let someone know that they have a choice, but I would never want to browbeat somebody into getting help or changing because it's-- It really is serving a function. You know, compulsive behavior protects you from something that you don't want to deal with, you know.

Yeah.

And I'm going to say what you should be dealing with or not? I don't think so.

Thus, even if she guesses another woman's secret, this participant does not believe she owns it. It is the other person's secret to keep, explore, or reveal in her own way, in her own time.

The next example shows clarity in the issue of ownership, too, although in this case, it's regarding a secret that is explicitly, collectively owned. That fact greatly influences this mother's work to both keep and reveal the secret that her daughter has leukemia. In the process, she must juggle the competing preferences and practical needs of several individuals, negotiating especially with the daughter to find terms of disclosure and concealment that everyone can accept.

How do you feel now about (Ashley's) desire to not have people know about her condition?

It was insanely difficult for me, insanely difficult, because I'm just the opposite kind of person. I work things out by talking to other people about them. So, you know, we weren't even allowed to say the *L* word in the house. We weren't allowed to tell her brother. We, you know-- This is months into the diagnosis. It took six months before we could tell (Luke). So she was insanely private.

And then we kind of came to this agreement where, number one, we had to tell people who were going to take care of her, like her teachers and the school. And we had a break-- For me, a huge breakthrough was going to the school and having a meeting with the counselor and the school nurse and her teacher and Luke's teacher, in which for the first time I, like, got to tell other people about it. And they were so supportive and so professional, it was really great.

But now, Ashley is at the point where she doesn't mind if other people know, but she wants them to know that she doesn't want to talk about it. So it's been a real process with her. She is a person who plays her cards pretty close to her chest.

Note that at no time did this mother deny her daughter's right to privacy, that is, to decide who would be privy to this secret. Instead, she waited for her child to change her mind about what to do with it, helping her to understand and weigh the desire for secrecy against other individuals' need to know.

This is not to suggest that clarity of ownership always results in respecting an original secret owner's wishes. In fact, it is not unusual for the holders of what are unquestionably others' secrets to nonetheless stake a claim of at least joint ownership, and then use it to trump and override the original owner's wishes. This inevitably shifts the nature of one's relationship with the original owner, of course, and may even bring it to a swift conclusion.

At what point might someone who simply knows a secret establish actual ownership of it? For many shared secrets, the answer is "never." For others, though, the most obvious moment when this happens is the one in which the secret owner tells the recipient that she or he is now the owner. "Here's my secret," the owner might say, "now it's yours, too. You decide what to do with it."

Far less obvious, and far more fascinating, are the moments in which a secret holder assumes ownership without the owner's permission and perhaps even without the owner's knowledge. This may happen because the secret holder believes that there could be even greater personal rewards if she/he were to usurp ownership of the secret and do something with it rather than if she/he were to stick to whatever the original secret owner has in mind. This includes scenarios in which the secret holder wishes to prove to others her/his importance and/or power by revealing what she/he knows (possibly also demonstrating to others the existence of a treasured degree of intimacy with the secret originator). It also includes occasions in which the secret holder dislikes the owner and thinks the secret matters to her or him—or a third party—a great deal. Here, revealing or threatening to reveal the secret is an overtly and intentionally hostile act against the original owner. A secret holder also may usurp ownership if she or he believes that the secret owner's decisions regarding this secret could eventually lead to highly undesirable outcomes for the holder, perhaps simply because she or he is now thoroughly implicated in the secret by virtue of their knowledge of it.

However, a final, common reason for claiming the ownership of a secret is that the secret holder becomes convinced that by continuing to keep the secret, the original owner is putting her/himself—and/or others whom the usurper cares about—in harm's way. The holder assumes ownership in order to look out for someone else, often the original owner, perhaps in spite of an explicit request to keep it quiet. The moral imperative of a secret holder to respect ownership thus comes into direct conflict with a competing moral imperative to challenge and perhaps disrespect the owner's idea of the same, for her or his own good.

The fact that secrets and their fates are direct indicators of the strength of social relationships is clearly seen in these circumstances. Without doubt, a secret holder's capacity for and allotment of discretion play an extraordinary role in shaping the outcome of these events. As Bok (1982, 43) puts it, such discretion includes

> an ability to evaluate what was asked of them, to judge when claims to group or family loyalty are legitimate or on the contrary manipulative or excessive, and to decide when promises of secrecy or revelation should be accepted or refused, kept or broken.

Consider the following stories, all relayed by one individual as he reflected on the decisions he has made regarding certain secrets. Here, the participant does not contest the secret sharer's ownership in either case—not until he believes their decisions regarding their secrets are not only wrong, but dangerous. He is keenly aware that denying a friend's decision-making rights over her secret may result in the loss of that friendship, too. However, that loss is a price this person is defiantly, if not happily, prepared to pay.

There's this woman. She has shared secrets with me that I kept. But there was one-- See, she fractured her skull. This is not like skinning your knee. A skull fracture, you can have blackouts, seizures. I mean there's just a lot-- You just can't ignore it, that kind of injury. But she is so fucking private. I mean, she told me. She said you cannot ever tell anybody. I said okay. But I did tell one person because I thought, you know what? Her parents should know about this, even if she hates her guts—which her mom, she hates her guts. Her dad, she's sort of okay with. Fuck, man. They gotta have some sort of access to this. But if I say that to (Mary) she would go ballistic.

That's not her real name. Plus she lives in an unlisted country, so it's--. (*Smiles.*)

So, you know? I don't know. Sometimes I make judgments about other people's privacy. I really don't have any right to, but as I said earlier, if it's about their own health, then I might say something. Which I did in that case. I mean she's told me some other secrets that I have kept and nobody knows and that I won't say here. So if she's pissed off at me for that one, this other thing I'll never say anything about.

I have had conversations with people-- I have not been a good steward sometimes when people have had very private conversations with me, where I haven't been-- where people have asked me to keep things in confidence. Which I have, a lot of things. But when things are hurting them, when people ask me to keep a secret that is hurting them, I don't do that. Even if they get pissed off at me, which I've lost a couple friends over that. But I don't care.

. . . My ex-sister-in-law was in an abusive relationship. This guy was crazy. I mean, he broke her kneecap when she was pregnant. I just finally went and got him, basically. Me and her brother and her dad. We said, you get the f-- You know, Dick, you will be—that's not his real name—you will be so severely harmed if you ever come near (Courtney) again. And she finally got divorced and married a beautiful guy, a fantastic person. And this other guy committed suicide about eight or nine years ago. I mean I feel sorry for him; he was crazy. But Courtney way didn't deserve that.

Anyway, I digress. But, I mean, I'm very flawed and-- extremely flawed. People share secrets with me that are about personal-- where they've been harmed and they want me to keep it secret-- You don't tell me that. I mean, that's where my codependency as a recovered alkie [alcoholic] gets-- I will take action.

Here, the moral obligation to reveal a secret that is causing (or is highly likely to cause) harm to someone for whom he cares is just as clear to the participant as is the obligation not to reveal other kinds of secrets. In fact, he uses his duty to protect his friends as a counterclaim that trumps and usurps his friends' claims of ownership. He may normally think of himself as only the holder of another's secret, not an owner of it. Once this fellow believes the secret is going to result in harm, though, he becomes an owner, too, and claims the corresponding right to decide what to do with the secret. Moreover, because his decision involves telling others about the secret—and the other owners' decisions involve remaining silent—his actions automatically negate theirs.[28] This is very similar to the logic used by parents to justify violations of children's privacy in situations that range from finding out their toothbrushing secrets to potentially much more harmful behaviors they might be hiding.

In the decision-making process about what to do with a secret, the important role played by knowledge of who owns a secret is clear in the following story, too. Here, we also see the principle of assuming ownership of a secret if one believes harm will otherwise occur. However, in this case, the participant couldn't really tell what was going on. The indecisive behavior that resulted—and that has lingered in his mind for years—stems from never really knowing if this is a secret that he should have outed or simply never seen. Should he have called the cops? Or was this an accidental violation of someone's privacy? Did it merely require that he follow standard etiquette and pretend he never saw it?[29]

I went to see my friend (Joe) and his girlfriend, his wife. I went to their apartment and they lived in a typical Chicago six-unit, you know, three-story brownstone, where there are six units. And I went up to the, you know, door. We were going out to dinner and I went up to buzz them. And they lived on the second floor, right? And on the first-floor space—it was eye level with the door, and you're buzzed in—and on the left-hand side, there's the window [for the first-floor apartment]. And the blinds were open.

And I'm, you know, standing there, I'm looking in, and there's a man tied up to a chair, naked. . . . He may have been wearing underwear. He may have been naked. But I couldn't tell. He looked pretty naked, and he was, like, in, you know, "bondage."

And I asked "What's this?!" And I was, you know, first-grade tourist, and staring. He saw me and he was trying to say something, you know, to communicate somehow. And I'm like, "Oh, my God." And I'm like-- I can't remember what I was trying to mouth to him but he was kind of, like, moving his chair. And I was like, this is freaking me out, this is freaking me out.

And so I'm buzzing to get in and I get up to their apartment and I tell them what has happened and they come downstairs and the guy is gone. And we were sort of, like, are, like, you know, trying to figure out-- Okay, was this something bad or was this, or was it some, you know, some weird sexual scenario. You know, as in, "Oh, I wasn't supposed to see this."

And he was moving around, like-- Was he trying to, like, shuffle out of the way?

We never found out.

To this day, ambiguity prevails in how to define this situation, including a distinct lack of clarity regarding whether or not he should have claimed ownership over this particular secret. A sort of paralysis lingers because of this, in which the event and the participant's actions remain in a kind of liminal classificatory state.

Clarity of ownership does not equal peace of mind, however. Conflict and disdain (if not more concrete forms of retribution) abound in situations where people do not agree on who owns a secret and who has a right to reveal it. Here, an attorney describes the actions of one of the lesbian professors at his college. Because of his early penchant for protecting the privacy of the people around him and his interest in doing the work of secrets, he had become involved in organizing meetings for a covert support group of gay and lesbian students, teachers, and administrators.

Some of [the professors] would come. And I knew who they all were. Because one of them was a blabbermouth. She was a big blabbermouth.

Did she [the professor] say something inappropriate?

She outed people. She outed my roommates.

What happened?

They [my roommates] were real pissed. They were good friends with her, too. I don't know what happened. She and I always kind of butted heads because I didn't-- I was not her-- I wasn't her choice [to organize this group]. . . . There was another guy who was also one of my roommates for a little while that she liked a lot more, mostly because I was more interested in people's wishes [than the professor was]. If they wanted their issues to remain private, then they could be assured that I wasn't going to tell anybody, no matter what happened. And I think that always pissed her off.

She couldn't relate to that?

Yeah. I don't know. She was older, too, and so she would bang the gong a lot about how, you know, you should all come out and blah, blah, blah. And it's like, you know what?

You should come out and I'm going to help you.

Yeah. When she outed (Scott) and (Matt), they were-- I mean, his family eventually came around, but it was years.

And who did she out them to?

One of her classes.

Oh! My goodness!

Yeah. A full outing. She outed all the other professors, too, at some function.

It sounds like it's hostile.

She was hostile, now that you mention it. I just ran into her a couple weeks ago, too, so it's somewhat fresh in my mind. Yeah.

You don't think she was trying to help them?

No. Not at all. I don't know what her deal was.

Clearly, this participant does not believe the teacher owned these secrets; accordingly, she had no right to share them, and he has no respect for her actions.[30]

One could imagine various reasons why the instructor might defend her actions, thinking she had a proper claim to expose the students and the teachers. This participant shares none of those with us, of course, and in his telling makes a persuasive case for the teacher being quite out of line. Yet in other situations, participants describe much more ambiguity regarding the issue of ownership.

Joan's story, for instance, shows just how difficult it can be to tease this out and how different answers to the ownership question may lead to profound conflict between people. She is an incest victim who was abused by her father for several years when she was a young girl. Her story has become for me a hallmark in thinking about the question of who owns a secret and who has the right to disclose or conceal it as they wish.

Years of postcollege therapy had helped Joan claim a pretty normal life for herself. She was now in her late thirties and continued to maintain rather strained relations with all of her family except her father. She did her best to completely cut him out of her life. Joan's mother remains especially problematic for her, however. The mother claims she never knew about the abuse and, like some other mothers of daughters abused in this fashion, talks and behaves as if she doesn't really believe it happened. Joan had never discussed the matter with her brothers, so she didn't know if they knew anything about it.

Joan was recently subjected to intense pressure from her family to attend her father's sixtieth birthday party.[31] He is ill, and they are all worried that this might be the last opportunity to throw him a big party. Joan's mother has been especially insistent about Joan attending—what would the rest of the family and all their friends think if she didn't come? Joan refused requests from her mother and her brothers repeatedly, dodging the queries of a few extended family members, too. They would not take no for an answer.

As a result, and after many years of living with her secret and the misery she continues to endure, Joan changed her mind about keeping quiet about what her father did to her. She told her mother that she was going to tell her brothers what happened. She also threatened to tell anyone else who continued to call, wanting to know why she wasn't going to the party.

The ensuing fight focused squarely on the issues of ownership, power, and whose privacy matters most.[32] Joan's mother was furious. This wasn't Joan's secret to tell. Didn't her mother have a right to privacy? Didn't Joan's brothers? What about the rest of the family? Who did she think she was? Too astonished to even begin feeling the outrage that would come later, Joan's mother added a final pound of salt into Joan's now fully gaping wound: her father should have a choice in this, too, shouldn't he? Why should he have to live what little time he had left suffering the consequences of Joan's selfishness?

The idea that her daughter had been a repeated, helpless victim of incest at her husband's hands never evoked anything like this woman's vehement reaction to the idea of her daughter telling people about it decades later.[33] Every argument came back to the issue of who owned the secret, who had more power—to either give it up or make sure it was kept—and the consequences for everyone's privacy. Every argument came back to the consequences of this secret for each family member's relationship to the other. No story better illustrates Bok's (1982, 19) arguments that "conflicts over secrecy . . . are conflicts over power: the power that comes through controlling the flow of information."

We also see Zerubavel's (2006, 41) observation, of course, that "Secrecy . . . tacitly stabliz[es] existing power structures." It does so by protecting the behaviors of those who are powerful enough to demand and maintain the secrecy surrounding their acts. The fact that this secret has been kept for so long is a clear indication that the mother and the father continue to have the upper hand in their relationships with their daughter. Joan's threat to finally tell is a threat to finally upend those relationships, to redistribute power throughout the family in a way that would be anathema to those who currently possess the lion's share of it. Challenge a secret, challenge the secrecy, and one challenges the very distribution of power and nature of the relationships that enabled it.

Competency in the Work of Secrets

If decisions about secrets depend on individuals' assessments of ownership, they also rest on how well one does the work of secrets. Again, Bok (1982, 19) is insightful on the matter:

> To be able to hold back some information about oneself or to channel it and thus influence how one is seen by others gives power; so does the capacity to penetrate similar defenses and strategies when used by others. To have no capacity for secrecy is to be out of control over how others see one. . . . To have no insight into what others conceal is to lack power as well.

Competency at secrets work rests heavily on two factors. First, there is the range of techniques and skills one has mastered. Second, there is the extent to which one has mastery over the ways in which one uses them. This is particularly true when it comes to using these skills in a specific sociophysical setting.

I begin by noting the general principle in which individuals learn from their own secrets work to anticipate others'. The following participant demonstrates this nicely. He shows how his efforts to protect his secrets are influenced by his own behavior when it comes to finding out others' secrets. Here he is, on snooping in other people's medicine cabinets.

I'm interested in your habit of looking in medicine cabinets.

Medicine cabinets?

Yeah.

Something that I have always done. And I-- The last twenty years, I've always done. And I'm not-- I don't hide it, I mean if someone, you know, "Oh, I opened your medicine cabinet."

(Laughing.)

But I don't feel embarrassed, you know, saying that I did. I-- I don't-- And I only do this if I'm using the bathroom. I don't run in, you know, and that's someone's house and I don't walk into their bedroom and open the medicine cabinet. But I sort of feel that if you have a, you know, a powder room or whatever bathroom you're using as your public bathroom, you know, it's a public bathroom. I mean, you're going to have people going in and out. So--

What kind of things do you look for?

I just open it and look. I look to see how it's arranged.

Right.

Is it neat? Is it messy? You know, I don't only-- I'm not looking for anything, you know, specific, um--

Would you ever read bottles? Like medicine?

Oh yeah, like cold bottles, prescriptions, oh yeah. I'm fascinated by those, yeah. That goes back to massive drug taking in college. What is someone on, um--

(Laughing.)

Can we get this legally? Now, I'm excited.

(Laughing.)

Um-- But yeah, I don't, um-- That's probably one of my, you know, one of my secrets. One of the worst things that I do in life.

Would you be mad if somebody looked into your medicine cabinets?

No, there's nothing in there. No.

No kidding. How foolish would he be if there was, given his own response to the siren call of this bathroom fixture? However, the decisions we make about secrets work are not simply about the kinds of things we think others might do, given the kinds of things we ourselves have done. They are also influenced by how well we think we do this work relative to specific others. The following participant, for instance, now a system administrator, describes his competence with an insightful range of secrets knowledge and skill. Throughout his interview, it was clear that this was a person who reveled in the challenge and responsibility of secrecy. This undoubtedly influenced decisions he made regarding the sheer number of secrets—and relationships—he could manage both in the past and the present.

When I was in college, I used to be one of the officers of the university's (Skull and Bones) organization, and so I was one of the people who did the secret meetings. You arrange them, organize them, contact people. You know, I was the security guy, the confidence man, the, you know. That's probably where I learned the whole camouflage thing is by arranging conversations with people such that I could pass on the information about the meetings and no one would know that it was anything out of the ordinary that I was passing on information.

... Okay. What kinds of things would you do to camouflage when you were passing messages?

The easiest way is to be around a lot and just randomly show up and just intimidate people from asking questions.

... They knew who I was and didn't associate me with anything but just some campus weirdo. And I was a TA [teaching assistant] too, a lot, so I had a lot of reasons to be different places. I worked for the university computing department. I also worked at the theater, so I had reasons to be a lot of places. A lot of people knew who I was.

... So, yeah. And people wouldn't ask me questions. I mean if I showed up at some frat house and asked to see somebody, nobody was asking any questions.

Because you intimidated them out of it?

Yeah.

... Are there specific things you do to make people know that you're not personable or—?

Oh, sure.

Like what kinds of things?

Body language, physical language.

What kinds of things?

Body language is easy. You just maintain rigidity and aggressive defense of personal space.

How do you do that?

The easiest way is you just back up a lot. The more difficult way is you basically enter their personal space and make them back away. That's the more aggressive method.... I am an extremely aggressive person.... So you just use that.

So, just, like, getting too close to somebody.

Or just being aggressive.

Like how else? With your tone of voice?

Voice tone is easy. Eye contact, especially unwavering eye contact, generally is a sign of aggression. And, yeah, just-- The arms crossed thing. Being curt. Tone of voice.

Staving off questions in the first place is certainly one way to avoid inadvertently giving out information that one wants to protect. In general, though, such a competent and confident secret keeper will be able to engage in secrecy in ways that others simply cannot, and this will inform his decision to get involved in all kinds of secrets work.

It can take someone equally determined and gifted in doing the work of secrets to counteract the intelligence and resources of someone who is especially good at it. Here, for instance, the head of a large nonprofit organization had to fire the center's director, "Alice." He had to do so while keeping his reasons from most of the center's staff and the public, who were simultaneously trying to force him to explain himself. Some resourceful, selective concealment and disclosure saved the day.

Her father was in the Pentagon, had been in the Pentagon. (Alice) had grown up at the feet of this very powerful (man), and she was no wimp, I mean to say. At the very least, she was no wimp. But she had begun out of fear to become more and more dogmatic and dug in, and she actually built an office in the center with no windows, sort of in the middle, like a fortress. And she began doing things that I thought were really unethical. And I couldn't tell people what she had done, because once you start doing that, you know, it's just-- (*shaking head side to side*).

Well, I was going to ask you. I mean in part you can't really defend-- If you're sort of an ethical person, you can't really defend your decision because it's inappropriate for people to hear this.

Precisely. And I never would do that and that made people furious. They wanted me to tell them the dirt and I wouldn't tell them. And it just made them—eeuhhh. They became-- They got into a rage about it. . . . So then finally I had to [fire Alice]-- And fortunately I had the total backing of the board of directors.

Good. Because eventually this just turns into an issue of authority. Do you or don't you have the authority to fire this woman?

Well, that's precisely right. And, of course, everyone knew I had it, but they were determined to do whatever they could to make me so miserable that I would give in, which I just couldn't do. So what I finally did was I called a meeting of the board with the CEO present and we made three decisions. One was to put her on administrative leave that day. The second was to hire an interim head that day, and I had someone ready. And the third was to appoint a search committee for a new head so it was clear that I wasn't totally—

In unchecked charge.

In charge, right. I was going to give them a say. I was going to involve them. So I went to the telephone and I called Alice. And-- the hardest thing I think I've ever done, just about. I called her and I said, as of this day, you are on administrative leave and you are not to enter this building again. And she said, may I come and get my things? And I said, if you come this afternoon, you may.

So she came with her sons and her husband, big sons, and I had to go into her office and I took two other men with me and to tell her that she was not to take anything from the building that did not belong to her. And she said, "Do you think I'm a common thief?" and I didn't answer the question. And she stole all the center's records. We had to send the police to retrieve (critical files) for the coming year, et cetera. So. Then I felt totally justified in my-- But I never even told people that.

Reverting to a strategy of selectively telling a small circle of powerful individuals who would not tell anyone else the details around this firing was a fine solution to the problems described here. Later, turning to the legal system to handle the retrieval of their stolen records also kept the matter quiet, further demonstrating the participant's competence in the work of secrets. These actions reinforced his power in the situation and still maintained his reputation as someone who would not break the professional code of silence expected among his rank.

In this next story, however, we see what happens when a participant who is particularly inept at the work of secrets tries to keep something from her husband.

I cannot keep a secret. It's physically-- It makes me sick. I can't breathe, I can't talk about anything else. I feel like a robot moving around.

What kind of a secret? I mean, a secret that matters?

Or, well, let's hear what I did last night to my husband. (Barry) [her youngest son] came home with head lice on Thursday. It was our first time. The big kids never had it. . . . Because we hadn't had it, I called all these mothers and said, "What do I do?" And everyone gave me different advice and I sort of made an amalgam and I attacked the problem and eventually it subsided. And I kept washing things and I looked it up on the Internet and so-- Then it was fine.

Then yesterday my head was itching, and I had to have been itching the whole time because it's so psychologically disturbing. But I had also gotten hit in the head with a snowball. I got caught in the crossfire and I had big bruises back there and so, as it heals, it itches anyway. So I just thought, you know what, I can't stand it any more. I'm just going to put this Nix [anti-lice shampoo] on me and do me, which I did. And then I did all of our sheets and I just did . . . I mean, it was this flurry. And when I said, okay, I'm just going to assume I have head lice. I'm going to say it, I have head lice. And I called one friend and I said, "(Gloria), I'm just going to tell you, I have head lice now. And I'm telling you so I don't tell (Curt) because if I tell Curt, I'll make him miserable." And she said, "Okay, I know. You have head lice."

So I get through the whole day, I do all this stuff. I just wash every comb. I wash all of Curt's . . . every coat. I take everything away and I try to make everything look normal by the time he gets home. And then I get into bed and the bed is all fluffy because everything is clean. And I say, oh. And I looked at Curt and I thought, don't tell him. And I said, "You know what? I thought I had head lice today, so I just washed everything." And he said, "WHAT?" And I said, "But I don't think I did." But I just, you know, I just took all these precautions.

Oh, because he had said to me, "Where's my comb?" And I said, "I just put all new combs in our house." And he said, "Oh." So then we got to bed and I just, I said it. And this is about 11:30.

At 1:30 he just bolts out of bed. And I just hear him scurrying about, running down the hall, and I said "What are you doing?" And he said, "Where's that Nix?" And I said--

I am so bad. I told him. I said I wasn't going to tell him. I told him at *bedtime*. And Curt has eczema and so he's just a very itchy man and he always has been his whole life. And it was so cruel. But I had to share. I had to.

. . . So we were up all night. I said, "Okay, now you can't use that Nix" because he's also-- He's allergic to so many things. I said, "We're going to cause a much bigger problem if we put insecticide on your head."

If you could write these things down, you could have a great sitcom.

I could, yes. Yeah. Well, Jesus said it: "The truth will set you free." I mean, it's not *knowing* the truth, it's *telling* the truth. (*Laughing.*)

One can't help but note that this participant is keenly aware that while telling the truth sets her free, it may well entrap the person to whom she tells it. Without question, though, her acknowledged incompetence at keeping secrets continues to influence the decisions she makes—and remakes—about what to do with any sensitive piece of information that comes her way.

In the next case another participant similarly has trouble with keeping secrets, but describes quite a clever compensatory skill. The result is yet another type of secrecy tool. Of course, it turns out to be a bit of a hindrance if her friends actually want to talk about their secrets after they've shared them with her.

When someone tells me a secret and they say you really can't tell anyone, what I do is forget it. Because I can't be trusted—knowing something and not talking about it. So I forget that I know it.

You can make yourself forget something?

Yes. I have very little room in there, so I have to choose. And I'm not sure that I'm conscious-- I wasn't really conscious of this, but I have a friend, a dear friend, who I walk with three days a week, and the point of our being together is really not the walk, but it's the talking. And over the course of twelve or fifteen years, however long it's been, we have both accumulated vast stores of secrets and sometime-- You know, a lot of them I think don't go beyond either of us. I mean, we hear them from other people and my friend will tell me and she'll say, you really can't tell anyone. So I effectively forget it and then she'll bring it up five years later and I say, "What? That happened?"

"You never told me."

"I can't believe you don't remember." And I say, "Well, I don't remember." And then later I realize, because she told me I couldn't tell anyone, I had to forget it. Because I don't have the brain power to remember it and remember also that I can't talk about it to anyone. And I'm very aware of my limitations.

I think actually you surpass the vast limitations of most people.

Well, you see, I really couldn't be a doctor or a lawyer. Well, I probably could because it's a different-- I keep people's confidence. I could. I could.

As long as you wrote it down so you could look it up. (*Chuckles*.)

Exactly. I think I could do that. But being kind of a freelance good citizen, I-- There are certain things I'm just not capable of doing. Just keeping a rumor that I hear secondhand, thirdhand, no can do. I mean I'm not going to go out and call everyone I know, but if I'm in a conversation and the topic comes up and someone says this, I'm going to blurt it out.

Unless you've told yourself to forget it.

Yeah, and then I don't know it.

Like competency with keeping (or forgetting) secrets—especially relative to another specific stakeholder—competency at revealing them is also important. As seen in these next two stories, the ability to effectively share secrets may rest on personal innovation, too.

When I was in college one year, I had one of my roommates, or a roommate that I was living with, which you know is one of the good things about college is the time where you probably learn more outside of your classes than what you learn in class. You know, where you have that mind set. And we used to read each other's journals.

Right.

And then write in each other's journals.

Oh, okay.

But it was like this thing where we didn't really talk about-- You would talk about it in writing but not verbally. And it was for this weird, um, you know, carrying on, let's say public life, private life, sort of thing. That's part of the game.

Right.

But it was like-- And it was definitely very much sort of an experiment in, you know, what you can get away with. And I'm sure that I wrote things that I wouldn't necessarily say to him, but I wrote them down and he didn't verbally respond, he just resolved that part of the problem. But it was written so there are two different dialogues going on. I really don't remember how it started.

So did it affect your relationship at all?

Um, I think that, I think it made us better friends at the time. You know, it intensified your relationship.

Right.

It's easier to say, you know, say something in writing than it is to, sometimes, say it verbally.

The next participant also describes what amounts to a clever technique for revealing secrets even though it's superficially couched as an accidental and unwanted one. Indeed, what one might classify as incompetence in keeping secrets turns out to be extraordinary competence in revealing them.

Well, we watch the finances 'cause I'm not working right now and we're just trying to raise two kids on a single income and Matt just has this running joke with me that anytime I buy (*laughs*), like, clothes shopping. He doesn't put the screws to me, you know, and go buy the clothes or anything. But I always feel the urge to, like, make sure I let him know that I got a bargain. And sometimes if the bargains aren't good enough, I'll drop the price that I paid by about $10 or $5 just to make it feel like a better deal and then he'll just give me this look.

(*Laughing.*)

I'm really, like, relieved. And inevitably he gets out of me that, okay, it wasn't as great a deal as what I was saying it was, so—yeah, I mean, that's a minor one but, yes, my face can usually can give away if I'm fabricating something.

Here, the inability to lie is actually an astonishingly effective mode of revelation. By lying badly, this woman ultimately manages to (1) preserve her identity as an honest person, (2) reinforce the integrity of her relationship with her husband, (3) maintain the power relations underlying her and her husband's roles, and (4) still keep it all at the level of a relatively harmless and amusing event. The effectiveness and success of the relationship/secrets work going on here is just remarkable.

When people do not actively participate in revealing their secrets to us, we might turn to other techniques in order to find them out. A great deal of post-9/11 news stories in the United States are about the work of finding out secrets, both because of worries about terrorist activities and because of a presidential administration that chose to operate under a historically extraordinary umbrella of secrecy. As a result, competency in the secrets work of those in law enforcement and intelligence work was a daily talking point during this study.

The following lengthy description of how an undercover detective does his job, for instance, gives excellent insight into the many techniques and skills that a competent detective must develop in order to find out the bad guys' secrets. Note that his reflections consciously include an awareness of how good he is at doing all these things.

If we have enough for a search warrant, we do a search warrant. If not, then we'll have to get enough for a search warrant.

And what's enough? So you have-- a what? A representative at the district attorney's office that you go to?

Right, we have an ADA, assistant district attorney.

Okay.

And tell him what we've got and if it's enough, then he gives us one or she gives us one. If not, then we've got to keep working. You know if you have enough or not.

Well, give me an example.

You have to have a crime occurring within that particular structure and you have to KNOW it; you can't just say, "Well, I think." Then you have to explain and show what you know. You have to have facts.

Well, how can you know there's a crime? I guess if somebody was a known felon—

You have to have-- There's two ways. One, you don't have to have a crime that you're looking for. Say they're stealing cable at the house, so, well, that's a crime. We need a search warrant to go in to get that cable box.

And you know this because you can see cables connected and somebody figures to go ahead and see if they're—

And you know somebody at Cablevision and they can pull the records and say, yeah, these guys are definitely stealing the cable. They haven't paid a bill for two years.

Oh, wow!

Well, let's go in now and get that cable box and while you're in there, oh, my God! What is that!? Trickery and deceit are the best friends of the police department.

I'm sorry, say that again.

You can write that one down, 'cause that'll be a quote. Trickery and deceit are the best friends of the police department, or law enforcement.

Holy cow! Well, give me another example like the cable box. Is there anything else that routinely gives you an excuse to come in?

Let's see. That's an easy one. A lot of times, though, you know what the crime is ahead of time and you can actually get enough material to get the search warrants. Or you send undercovers in to go into the house.

Ahhh. And they get admitted, you know—?

Well, you can go on your observations.

Okay, okay.

I'm a Jehovah's Witness. Can I talk to you a little bit?

Oh, really?

Trickery and deceit.

Now, how do you—?

But that person now is out of the game for the rest of the whole case.

Because they're recognizable.

Yeah.

. . . Have you ever blown it? Have you ever done something where you dropped character and something went wrong and either you were found out or the whole situation fell apart?

No. We're not dealing with a lot of brain surgeons here, for the most part. And it's a quick thing. Once you're in, that's it and you're out. It's not like you're sitting down and having lunch with this guy or anything like that.

You don't have to sustain it.

No.

So what kinds of personas have you had to adopt?

I had a good one. Actually—I have it on videotape, actually.

Your audition tape.

Right. I had a house, a guy, a city sergeant lent me his house and what I did is, I pretended I was the homeowner and I had a guy that I was looking at to install illegal cable in my house. So I got wired up and the guy comes to the house, have a little conversation with the guy, and he goes, yeah, yeah, it'll be 150 bucks. I said okay, no problem. I gave him 150 bucks. He goes up to the, you know, climbs up. He's got the [cable company] truck, everything, hooks up the cable to the house, brings it in, hooks it all up, and that was it.

And it was illegal.

Yeah. And then we did a search warrant at his house in another precinct because we wanted to recover all the equipment that he used to commit that crime. And what he was was a former [cable] employee who stole, like, $10,000 worth of equipment and then just went into business for himself by doing illegal cable hook-ups.

Are you having an internal dialogue almost while you're in the middle of doing this with this guy? Are you like thinking to yourself—?

I'm not that smart. I just shoot from the hip.

It's interesting. What other roles have you had to adopt?

Girl comes up and hires me for, like, $100 to steal her car. It was an insurance fraud. That was a two-minute conversation.

How did she find you?

From a guy who's looking to do nine years upstate in prison gave her up.

So he's up for auto theft or whatever—

On numerous insurance jobs.

And he turns her over as being somebody who has this great scam that she's running.

Yeah, that she needs somebody to steal her car for her.

And so how did she know where to find you? What? He told her—?

Yeah, beep me. . . . The department gives us beepers and cell phones.

. . . We do a lot with the State Liquor Authority, which is in charge of the liquor licensing in bars and package stores and stuff like that. And you go into the bars and you have to blend in with the crowd for a couple of hours. Of course, you have to drink, but that's part of the job.

Somebody's got to do it.

And they pay for it, so-- . . . And then we've had a lot of drug busts that way because the bars and drugs go together. You just keep your eyes open while you're there. You'd be able to see who's doing drugs and where they're getting it from.

So these are bars whose liquor licenses have expired or something?

No. They're all legitimate places, but once a year, actually any time you can if you have a problem with it, but once a year you're supposed to inspect these places. Called a state liquor authorities' inspection. That's part of it. And then, you know, in a couple of hours you'll just take yourself on out and call in. And then the troops will be in in about ten minutes and they just raid the place and everybody's up against the wall.

This same police officer describes himself as having no trouble at all with his secretive, sometimes traitorous undercover work. It's all for a good cause—getting the bad guys—and he has no doubt about who the bad guys are. He serves as a good reminder that the ability to live with secrets—your own or somebody else's—is an important part of one's competency in doing the work of secrets. It can be critical in deciding whether or not you want to do it, too.

This same participant described a number of his colleagues who struggle to keep workplace secrets from loved ones at home, though. In their efforts to put the day behind them and protect spouses and children from the horrible behaviors they witness (and the less than civilized ones that they sometimes display themselves), quite a few of his coworkers cope by drinking heavily at the end of the day. Our participant says he chooses instead to go to church regularly, stay very involved with his extended family as well as his own nuclear family, and work out each day. Of course, in a way, these coping mechanisms can be placed in the realm of secrets work, too—right alongside his coworkers' drinking.

A number of people in this study profess an ability to do a great deal of the work of secrets. However, they claim to stop short at being able to live with the consequences of it. Whether it's the consequences of keeping secrets, revealing them, or finding them out, they find it too difficult to sustain lives that are focused on such work.

The following participants illustrate this well. In the first case, both a daughter and her mom have learned it's hard to keep secrets—so hard that it's just easier to avoid it altogether.

We just had an experience with our daughter, (Amy), who is going through-- She seemed very tense and kept asking me questions about something, and I guess Amy did something that she felt bad about, she didn't feel-- She didn't want to disappoint us, she didn't want to tell us, and finally, um-- You know, I tried to tell her that no matter what, we love her. Um, and that she was safe to tell us anything. But I was interested that at this early age she was able to keep something inside of her and it was actually physically causing her problems, her eyes were twitching and, um--

Did she wind up finally telling you?

She did. You know, you don't-- Since it was such a big thing to her I didn't want her to feel it was minor, but, really, I had to point it out that at this early age she needs to know that-- It was her inner issues about ever being wrong. She was having trouble.

So she said something that she knew was wrong?

She did something that she knew was wrong and that she felt bad about, and she'd been holding it inside of her for months.

It was like totally inconsequential?

Yeah, and it was, you know, probably every kid does it all the time, but to her, it was a lower standard or something, I don't know. And so we've been talking about mistakes more, so she sees that we all make mistakes. And that we move on. We don't like it, but we just move on.

Has that happened to you recently, where you didn't want to reveal what you were thinking, but you felt like, like your body language gave it away?

If it's in my head, I've got to let it out. And [Carl] can see, like, if I wake up with something on my mind, he can sort of tell right away, so I don't even try anymore. We share it.

... I guess, my husband now, when we first started seeing each other, we had to (*laughs*) keep our relationship a secret. So, so I did. And I wasn't very good at it. Sort of, out there. So, I couldn't keep a secret. (*Laughs.*)

What kinds of things would you do to keep it secret, inasmuch as you were successful?

Well, at the time-- I'll just tell you. I was married at the time, and I started seeing (Carl). And so, obviously, when you got home you just didn't talk about that (*laughs*) part of your life, or you lie about where you were, and things like that.

Is it really hard to do? I mean, I guess it was.

It's—exhausting. Somebody once told me if you don't lie, you have nothing to remember. So you're constantly trying to keep everything straight in your head. And then when you realize that you-- When you decide you're not going to lie anymore, it's like this big weight is off your shoulders.

The decision to reveal secrets may be made in at least partial desperation because keeping them causes such distress.[34] This next story, like several others, suggests that ultimately the inability and/or the refusal to keep secrets may be an important and valued facet of one's personal identity. Here, a former New York state congressman is grateful he was outed in the *New York Times*. It appears to have saved him quite a range of secrets work. In fact, in his words, "it was very freeing" from the extraordinarily difficult work in which he previously engaged in order to keep his sexuality a secret. It also saved him a great deal of subsequent work since he never had to reveal his sexuality to anyone who lived near him in the future.

But what I'll tell you is, I mean this whole issue of my sexuality and private and public is-- I mean, I have a rich history around this. I was outed on the front page of the *New York Times*.

Were you really?

Yeah. I had a very powerful position. And my office was enormous. And I-- It actually was done-- It happened because people in the House who were "power people" wanted to hurt me. They thought that I would be embarrassed and resign.

I also think I forced them to look at something that they were able not to look at. They had even said, they being people who were in the leadership of the House, had even said things like, to me, "We don't mind having gay representatives at all, but we don't want them to make us deal with it." And I didn't even-- I mean, I never made a public announcement or anything because I didn't think that was the best way to go about it. I mean even strategically I just would have thought that was a dumb way to go about it. But I did tell the leadership that (Alex) and I were a couple and that I expected him to be honored in the same way that they had previously honored my wife, whom they didn't like, actually.

. . . [Their sense of] betrayal, I think, was less my being gay than it was my not maintaining the "Don't ask, don't tell." That was, I think, the real betrayal.

And so, these people, thinking they were going to humiliate me and force me to resign-- I mean, I'm a fighter. They didn't know what a fighter I was.

... It was okay. And, in fact, I think the people would have been very surprised at my reaction. It was very freeing. I mean, when you talk about private/public stuff, I mean everyone in New York knew my business--

And you didn't even have to tell them.

Exactly. I've never had to come out to another person as long as I was in New York. And I was the hero of all kinds of people.

The decision to widely reveal an extremely important and protected secret was taken away from this participant. Once the right to make that decision was taken away from him, though, he found himself forced to decide how he would live with the public's newfound knowledge of his orientation. A positive, life-affirming outcome was the result—as well as the rejection of any further work he might have done to try to contain the secret, such as changing his name, moving, and/or dissociating from his partner.

Stories like this one focus primarily on individuals and their secrets. However, like this last case, many of them remind us that decisions and outcomes regarding the willingness to live with secrets are by no means limited to individuals. Families, organizations, institutions, and nation-states make these kinds of decisions, too. And what they decide about how willing they are to have secrets and to maintain a culture of secrecy may well affect the kinds of individuals who are attracted to them.

In the following story, for instance, a businessman reflects on both the range of competency individuals can be expected to have as well as what he believes to be his own skill level. Clearly, his company could not exist without embracing this level of secrets work. He could not have the job he currently possesses without doing the same—and being very good at it, too.

I've had the experience of overseeing research programs to serve multiple customers. Some of whom were competitors with each other. And, and the way that I did that, you know-- And I'm going to be very specific about the names, just for the purposes of understanding, but it needs to be taken out. We did a lot of design engineering for both (Company A) and (Company B).

Okay.

And we had project leaders who worked extensively with each of those accounts, and they worked exclusively with one account or another. So there was a guy that worked the Company A stuff. There was a guy that worked the Company B stuff. And they were allowed to talk about sports, the weather, and politics.

Not religion and design! (*Laugh.*)

They were specifically constrained that they were not to talk about what was going on with their account to the other guy. Now, that had to come together at some point.

Umhm.

And it came together at me.

Umhm.

And so I knew what was going on both places, and I actually visited regularly both customers.

Umhm.

I had to draw compartments in my head of what I was going to talk about, what I could disclose, what I could know, literally, in a conversation.

Umhm.

When I went to (Company A headquarters), I sort of compressed and purged all this stuff to a holding spot in my brain of what we were doing with (Company B), and vice versa.

Umhm.

And so that's sort of how I think about this. I walk out the door and this part's gone.

Umhm.

And I walk back in and somehow it magically-- I have access again to it, but I, I just get rid of it for part of my life.

Umhm. What do you—so that's, I mean, being able to do that in the business of ideas, um, relies a lot on your experience, right? Because you are going to have intuition about what is potentially—

Where is the line, yeah.

--Important or not?

Yeah, and where's the line you cross in terms of what's really public and what's really private information. What's known and is knowable, versus what I picked up from other conversations.

Right, right.

It was-- That actually was stressful because I, I mean, the-- And, and how stressful it could get is if I were at an exhibition, I'd walk down one aisle and see the guys from (Company B) and two aisles over I'd see the guys from (Company A) and I'd have to switch modes.

Right. Did they know that you were working with the competitor?

I think they knew that I was doing that. Because of my position. I was in charge of all of Development.

So they would assume.

So they *had* to assume that I knew people at both places.

Right.

It was just, it was a very interesting situation. But-- And it told me that, in fact, that this is possible, to compartmentalize my knowledge.

Umhm.

And, and so that's why I expect people who do services for me to, in fact, do that.

. . . I was extremely cautious. . . . I stayed back from the line to be certain I didn't cross it.

Right.

Um, but what it did do, I mean, what it did require, rather, is a very specific and conscious force of-- I mean, I had to exercise real caution but real judgment. I had to be very aware. Any conversation I had with either of those customers, I had to be extraordinarily aware of what was being talked about, where my information was compartmentalized, because-- I mean, I gave the metaphor of pushing into the corner. In fact, it doesn't work that way, because all the information is all jumbled together. And where there were programs that were actually a little similar, I had to keep very cautious in a conversation about where it was going and how I was going to respond.

Umhm. Do you really think that it's possible for average Joes to, uh, exercise that kind of carefulness in their, in all their work?

Well, I think that's why we didn't let the project managers talk to each other.

Okay. Didn't expect that level of—

Yeah. I mean, they weren't getting paid for that, uh, for that level of responsibility.

Umhm.

And they may not have had the experience to be able to handle it well, and frankly there was no need for them to know.

Umhm.

Uh, and that made it easy.

It's part of what made it work.

Yeah, because there was literally no need. We made sure they didn't sit next to each other. We made sure that they kept development samples off their desk so there wasn't something inadvertent, and we just did it that way.

So that is an example of where you have consciously thought about privacy issues as "part of my work." I am a professional privacy person, in some ways.

This participant does a fine job of showing one of the many roles of selective disclosure and concealment in the corporate world. But he also shows how one's decisions regarding secrets work are influenced by self-knowledge regarding one's own capabilities. His ability to effectively manage other employees rests on his knowledge of what they are capable of, too. The trick is to provide them with experiences that will help them develop their skills and do their jobs while not jeopardizing the company.

The Anticipated Consequences of Disclosure and Concealment

In fact, experience plays an important role as individuals anticipate the consequences of their secrets decisions, whatever the situational context. The next woman, for instance, reminds us to be careful what secrets we wish to find out, having read some of her dead parents' letters to each other but drawing the line at reading their love letters. She can live just fine with the secrets revealed by some of their correspondence, but based on experience, she can guess the kinds of things that might be revealed in other communications. She knows herself well enough to know she does not want to see this.

You know, the girls have said, what do you want us to do with your journals [if something happened to you], and I said, well, you know, I don't really want you to read them. But my theory would be that if they did start reading them the way I started reading my parents' letters, they'd stop. I mean, it would just be boring and the little bits that were there-- I mean it's what Rhett Butler said when he emerged from the sofa after they had the fight, Ashley and Scarlet at the Wilkes's barbeque: "Eavesdroppers sometimes hear highly instructive things." Well, they do, but they're not always instructive in the way that you would like to be instructed. I mean, I'd prefer to have some of my illusions about people I'm so close to.

I mean, it was fascinating. And the one thing that made me stop was to realize that here was my father, who-- I mean, he used to tease my mother about having a temper and I guess she did, but it didn't seem anything like his, you know. And there is this letter where she was going cross-country with three of her friends-- This is in '48, for the summer, a bunch of school teachers. She had a fight with them in Salt Lake City and got angry enough that she came home alone on the train. And Daddy-- I mean, you know, he was being very sympathetic, but here's Daddy, Mr. Hothead, telling Mommy-- It was fascinating.

Kind of an interesting correction to an image, isn't it?

But the love letter ones were where you thought, okay, I'm out of here. I mean, you know, that's nice and it's nice to know, as we assume, they must have loved each other at one point. But they weren't being written for us. My sister still has them, but it's a difference in personality, I guess.

She doesn't mind that. It would be interesting to find out why that doesn't bother her or—

Or whether it would at a different point.

As seen here, part of our ability to live with secrets—and to know where we can and must draw our own comfort lines—depends on what those secrets might mean for our relationships with other people. This next person points out how selectively keeping secrets from others may be directed even at stakeholders who are as yet unseen and unmet. Here is a police officer reflecting on the matter.

And do people seem to be in any way overly concerned or concerned at all with their privacy in the kinds of cases that you're engaged in? You know, go ahead arrest me, do whatever you have to do, but please don't let my wife find out. Don't let my kids find out.

Well, to that point, we usually say, well, we're not going to tell anybody. It's up to you. You're a big boy and if you want to call somebody, call somebody. If you don't want to call somebody, then don't call somebody. We don't-- You know, especially you pick up guys for patronizing a prostitute or something like that, then they're all worried that their wife is going to find out. But, you know, we don't care about that stuff.

I mean—

I mean, we'll tease him about it just to have fun with him.

(*Laughing.*) It's so cruel.

There's nothing like a thirty-five-year-old tough guy crying their eyes out, you know what I mean?

Do you overtly try to get that response from them so that they don't do it again or—?

Oh, they're going to do it again. Who're you kidding? They're just going to be smarter about it.

Really?

Sex, there's recidivism. Nobody stops.

Nobody stops. It's like drugs.

Yeah.

Geez!

They'll just be smarter about it. They'll go to a topless place or something like that. That's all.

Right. And in the meantime, are you ever tempted to tell either a wife or a boss or somebody? Are you prevented from doing that?

Not prevented, but I don't think I'd do it.

It's sort of bad form, right?

Yeah. What's the point? Who are you hurting now?

The ways we manage secrets thus show not only our concern for ourselves, then, but also our desire to look out for other people. In this next story, another participant describes protecting some people's privacy by violating another's. As we see here, it is not only our own relationships, but also the relationships we want to see others have—or not have—that can drive our decisions.

I think that (*pause*) the ideal [amount of privacy] is where I have absolute control. Unless I've done something illegal and then, you know, then you lose certain rights. But I haven't.

Some people who have done something illegal, like former criminals? Or what do you mean?

Well I think that the laws that say-- you know, like the Megan's Law. Like if you, if you have been found guilty of an act of-- What is it, sexual aggression against a minor or an adult. Well, maybe-- No. Maybe against a minor. Then I think you lose privacy. I think that that's an important loss of privacy. I just don't feel that-- Because of the rate of the recidivism in that particular disorder, I don't feel that you have the right to maintain privacy, unfortunately.

And I actually-- Someone told me, you know, that the Chicago Police Department has a Web site of, you know-- They have the sex offenders, and it's always on the Web site.

And there was a guy in the next block. Not last fall, but the fall before that. A very nice, friendly guy. Lived on a block with a lot of kids.

And I just felt that I needed--

I did this. I--

And I thought about it a lot but, you know? It was just a little bit before Halloween and I thought, "You know what? I just-- I hate to do this, but I would rather do this than to have some child get hurt."

So I took the pictures and I went to visit every parent I knew on that block. I don't know all the parents, but I gave them the picture and I told them that I was sorry and I would never want to tell their children, but that I thought they should know. And that they should tell the other parents and-- You know? And--

Yeah.

You know, the guy doesn't live there anymore, you know. But--

I didn't want to do that. But, you know, he should go find a place to live in a block where there are not thirty children under the age of ten. You know, that's where he should live.

Yeah.

I think that that's appropriate. You know, he had a dog and he was very friendly to the kids and, you know, and I just thought "Oh, God."

I-- Once I wrote the letter, I just couldn't see not saying something to people.

Was everybody pretty grateful about that?

Yeah, they were. Yeah!

Again, through all these stories—including this last one, a tale of felt civic responsibility if ever there was one—it is the consequences for one's sense of self and for one's relationships with others that drive the storytellers' decisions about revealing these secrets

The same principle is seen in the following participant's reflections. He is an information technology professional in the securities business, talking about one of the biggest secrets in the workplace: how much money people get paid. He provides a fair amount of insight regarding the lengths to which people in this industry will go to keep control over who does and doesn't know certain things. But he also intimates the extent to which he personally goes to uphold and reinforce secrets—and the prevailing relationships in the organization—rather than risk challenging the status quo.

Do issues ever come up with how much access you have to [employees' information], what they feel is personal?

Yes.

What kinds of issues?

Primarily with the accounting department. Again, their information is sacrosanct, and we have no right to look at it. But then we have to fix a machine, so . . .

So what do they do to try to keep you from looking at it?

Threats.

Like, don't look in this directory?

Yeah. "Don't look there or you'll be fired." "If I found you in this room, I'd fire you."

Which must be just an invitation.

Not really. I know it's just posturing, and I also know that they have no idea what they're saying.

. . . Part of the problem with the trading industry is nobody knows what anybody else makes. And that is fundamental to the control of traders because-- The company wants to pay as little as possible and get as much as possible. So if you and I are traders and I know that you're getting a 60/30 deal—you know, 60 percent of the profits are yours and 30 percent go to the company—whereas I'm getting a 30/60 deal, and I'm making a lot more money than you. You know, last year I grossed ten million dollars and I only got three and you only made a couple hundred thousand. You know, you could make less than me, but earn more, personally. You know, that's fundamental, to make sure that I don't find that out.

So they're sensitive about you knowing that because—

Oh, yeah. The traders don't want us to know what they make because we might tell somebody. And the partners don't want that either. I mean, we might tell somebody. And the traders, of course, have a huge interest in knowing what other people make, but they lack any of the technical skill to pull it off.

It must be really hard to know these kinds of secrets that you can't tell because you know that people are so interested.

It's not hard at all.

You're never tempted to say, when you know somebody really wants this information—?

No. I mean it's-- You can't do it *once*. There's a saying that AA has that's really good. You can't unring a bell. And so-- Yeah. And there's the other issue of-- Usually if somebody's asking for that information, especially information that they're not supposed to have, there's a reason that they're not supposed to have it, and generally I tend to agree with those reasons-- Because I prefer to be consistent. So I'm not going to tell them.

It must be hard, like, if you know somebody's email and read and maybe they're going to be fired or something. Do you ever feel, like, a sense of, like, loyalty or, I don't know—

I'm an admin. We don't experience sympathy. No, and usually, like I said, I'm not going to give out the information unless I agree with the terms. Occasionally you do kind of feel bad because maybe they're getting shafted, but-- It's like a cop doing a wiretap, you can't say, "Wow! I really think this is wrong." You work to do something about it, but you still have to continue with the action.

I like to think that I'm collecting information for good reasons.

That would certainly make it easier to do it. It also makes it easier for this participant to keep his boss happy. The work of secrets undoubtedly includes the need to rationalize one's actions—or learn to live with them as mistakes. Of course, the better one is at the actual craft of secrecy, the less one will have to do the latter.

THE WORK OF SECRETS, PART II: SECRECY SKILLS AND TECHNIQUES

Through British spy, military, and action-adventure novels I became acquainted with the notion of "field craft." This term refers to the skills needed by these sorts of operatives working "in the field" in order to successfully conduct missions. Field craft makes great use of secrecy to provide a clear advantage for operatives.

Through field craft one strives to act in a decisive fashion using a remarkable range of skills to achieve one's mission-specific goals and still keep one's presence, location, identity, capabilities, knowledge, and intent as secret as possible for as long as one wishes. Field craft is also about finding out others' presence, identity, capabilities, and intent as soon as possible, since this kind of information can be critical in achieving one's own desired outcomes. And whether one is trying to keep, reveal, or find out secrets, good field craft also includes mastering appropriate (and usually covert) communication skills. Information acquired in the field is useless if it is not conveyed to the people who know how to use it.[35] In both proactive and reactive ways, field craft is thus the means by which one obtains and maintains the secrecy—and various degrees of publicity—needed to accomplish one's goals with as great an advantage as possible. It is also the means through which one tries to neutralize others' attempts to achieve this same advantage.

We tend to associate the activities of field craft with the territory of spies, SWAT teams, elite soldiers, and guerilla forces. We seem obsessed in the United States with stories that focus on these individuals and especially their skills. James Bond movies may well be so popular, for instance, not because of what is achieved in them or even because of the string of actors who play the main character, but because of the fascinating ways in which the spy gets his job done.[36]

Perhaps the appeal of these kinds of practitioners lies in the fact that they are merely more extreme, if fantastical examples of something with which we are all deeply familiar: the work of secrets, the tools one might use for it, the desire for personal secrecy as well as a few close intimates with whom we share important secrets, the attraction and sometimes necessity of finding out others' secrets, and the ways people in the States associate all this with personal power. In fact, we are all "operatives" to some extent, studying, using, and mastering the field craft of everyday life to greater and lesser extents, and with greater and lesser success.

MANAGING TANGIBLES AND INTANGIBLES,
INDIVIDUAL AND COLLECTIVE EFFORTS

At their most basic level, I am interested in the techniques and skills involved in the work of secrets in two respects. First, these must address the management of both the intangible and tangible forms of secrets. These forms range from the elusive, invisible information lurking inside an individual's head to the physical evidence of such secrets. Second, these techniques and skills also must encompass both individual and collective efforts at secrets management, the latter sometimes requiring quite complex, coordinated actions.

This first story is about managing both the intangible side of a secret along with the tangible signs of its existence. Here, a participant describes a familiar scenario and some excellent techniques for getting a friend to reveal something he may have preferred she didn't know.

(*Laughing.*) I guess our closest friends live around the corner. It's two daddies and they have two little girls who are really buddies and we're (*laughing*) talking-- I was talking with one of the partners and I said something and he kind of did a face. And I'm like-- [*makes a questioning, smiling gesture*]. And then I started pushing him, "What are you talking about, what are you talking about?" And finally he revealed to me that his partner had been married before and-- before they met and had their kids and stuff. And-- It was really funny. It wasn't too private, 'cause obviously he told me, but, yeah.

That's so funny you know, (*laughing*) it's just a real reversal of the way that it would have been before. Because before you would have hidden the fact that you're gay.

(*Laughing.*)

Whereas it is now like, "I was married before."

Yeah, he was really embarrassed (*laughing*).

Like so many stories about secrets, this is a story of the participant's success at secrets work as well as her friend's failure at it. He first unintentionally disclosed that he had a secret. Up until then, even the existence of the secret was secret. He then failed to conceal its actual content.

Of course, defining this as "failure" assumes this fellow truly did not want her to know it. An argument easily could be made otherwise. Perhaps what she's really describing is a very subtle, expert instance of someone carefully revealing a secret by getting the intended recipient to insist that he share it with her.[37] This is a story that reminds us how difficult it can be to tell who is more successful at their secrets work, then, as well as how dynamic the things that we do and do not keep secret may be.

Another tangible side of secrets work focuses on physical, material objects. These require similar attention if we are to manage secrets well. In this case, a husband reflects on factors that affect his ability keep objects secret from his wife.

So the things that I have that are private from Louise [my wife] are very, very few. So if I have something that I don't want Louise to know about, well, again, I have no place in the house that's mine, right? So the only place, like if I have a gift for her, I could maybe hide it in the garage somewhere and it's good for a while, but not, not 100 percent sure, certainly of a long period of time. In the back of my sock and underwear drawer because I have enough that I never get all the way to the back. Sometimes she goes in there and is doing laundry and she puts them in there. That's the only place I could put something that could be secure for a while. In the heat of the moment, if I need to write a passionate letter of frustration or whatever, you know-- I really don't need to send this when I'm done, but it's worth keeping-- so that would be in that category of wow, I don't want Louise to see this, so where do I put it? There are very few places.

In one sense, secret objects are actually double secrets—at least. Each one represents first the prima facie secret of what it is and the fact that it is connected to a given person, event, and/or activity—whether a gift or a letter, for instance. But these objects are also being kept secret *from* someone, which is yet another distinct secret linked to them. A secret object might also betray additional secrets, of course—acting as a hyperlink or portal into an entire chain of them. In fact, the more an object signifies and belongs to a multiplicity of secrets, the more carefully it must be managed. Its exposure could quickly lead down the path of discovery for all the secrets in which it plays a role.[38]

Secrets work must attend to both the individual and collective levels of effort, too. Here, I focus on several instances in which collective efforts are involved in the work of secrets, whether it's the work of keeping, revealing, or finding them out. These stories rely on individual efforts as well, of course, thus allowing for simultaneous reflection on both individual and coordinated instances of secrets work.

The first two examples are concerned with the collective efforts involved in *keeping* secrets. I begin with a participant who offered this observation when asked if he had a favorite hiding place for things he didn't want his family to see.

Yeah, I would say that the biggest thing that gets hidden in our house is gifts.

Umhm. (*Laugh.*)

Everybody knows where they are hidden and they stay away. (*Laughter.*)

Like many secrets, everyone must be willing to carefully avoid the presents in order to keep them as secrets—in this case, as surprises for later. In the same interview, this individual offered further insight on the collective, cooperative nature of secrets in his recounting his family's use of the phrase "too much information."

I've known people in my life who I have felt-- The joke at our house right now from the kids is "too much information." And there have been people I have felt that are just totally unabashed about what they are prepared to share. And to the point where, I don't want to know this. And, about as specific an example I can think of, I can think of one person that was just, you know, he had hemorrhoids and would give you the details. And that, as the kids would say, is too much information!

. . . A couple of years ago . . . We were in a bed-and-breakfast. We were all staying in one big room. And we told the kids, "Go downstairs for an hour."

Umhm. (*Laugh.*) Right.

Everybody knew what was going on.

Right. (*Laugh.*)

And, it was fine. They said "Too much information!" and then they ran away.

Relying on others to be tactful—to not discuss things we'd rather not know about or not ask about things we'd rather not spell out—is a collective form of secret keeping. Not asking and not telling can be a careful dance designed to keep certain things secret—whether a Christmas present, a coworker's medical problems, or our parents' sex lives. The skills needed to do this in spite of others' preferences can be quite sophisticated. The fact that this participant's kids are so adept at it hints at another essential part of collective secrets work, too: the need to socialize others so they can help manage secrets—both theirs and ours.

The following excerpt is about the sometimes collective nature of the work to *find out* secrets. This is our police detective talking about surveillance work. The sheer number of people who must work together well to pull off this rather ordinary procedure is quite remarkable.

I haven't ever actually talked to anybody who's engaged in surveillance, and I wonder if you can tell me, you know, first of all, why do you do it, but even more interesting to me is how do you do it.

Okay. Why? Because they pay me good money. Other than that-- It's a means of linking the players together. You might have-- You get some information from Source A saying that this guy has a Mercedes, has a Lexus, has two houses, a house in Boca. He's out all the time, doesn't have a job. Well, okay. Why doesn't he have a job? How does he get his money? So you start your research on him. You do the computer work, and it's amazing the amount of information you can get. And then you find out he's got bank accounts and how much is in those bank accounts, and he doesn't have a job. Now you start following him around and find out who's linked with him. Then you get, ooop, there's a known guy talking to him someplace. Then he meets with this guy, goes with that guy, hangs out here, doesn't work, doesn't do anything. Either he inherited all that money or he's doing it by other means. Sleeps all day 'til, you know, 1:00, 2:00 in the afternoon, and then he's out all night. The typical Mafioso mindset, but every ethnicity has it. So-- We're doing the Russians right now.

Are you really?

That's hard, though, because of the language barrier. That's the biggest—

Does anybody-- Would a detective try to learn another language in order to do this kind of work?

They could, but you have to be very proficient at it. That's the problem.

So, in other words, you're sort of stripped down to the level of just watching what they're doing rather than being able to understand what they're saying.

Right. Understanding what they're saying would get to the point if the investigation proceeds to a wiretap. But then you have to have-- We're unique. Our particular unit works closely with the Feds, FBI, ATF, DEA, and the IRS, and they have access to anybody that speaks any language in the world. So if you do a wiretap-- But that wire has to be maintained twenty-four hours a day, seven days a week. Somebody's got to be there listening and making sure they understand what's going on. That's helpful.

. . . Okay, then there is the actual surveillance itself and how you do that. So, tell me how you do that.

Well, you have about six to eight cars, single cars, and they're all cool cars. No police-looking cars.

You get to drive a cool car, huh?

Oh, yeah. Well, it's not that cool. That's just a term we use, cool car as opposed to a Ford Taurus, which everybody drives as a police car, or a Crown Victoria. So anything other than that, really.

Okay, so cool is non–Ford Taurus, non–Crown Victoria.

A non-police-looking car. And then you have one person, what we call as the eye, the person that's actually watching the target. So there's really only one person watching the target, while he's surrounded by, I'd say, like, five or six other people that are not in the vision of the bad guy. And then you rotate through that about every hour and a half, two hours so the guy that has the eye is fresh each time. And the other guys-- I'm going through like a couple of Clancy novels by the time, you know. You sit there and read. You do crossword puzzles. Some guys have portable TVs in their cars, anything to keep you going.

And what's the point of the extra five guys?

Well, when the guy moves, you can't have one car following you all the time. They're very surveillance conscious. So you rotate through. If you're going down the road, one guy's behind them and if you're still going down, say, the turnpike straight for a long period of time, you say, all right, I'm pulling off. The guy will pull off and then somebody else will move up for the eye. Or going through traffic, especially if there's busy traffic, somebody's got to be right on his bumper pretty much the whole way. And so you've got to just keep rotating through, somebody else on that bumper, so he doesn't get to see the same car for a long period of time.

There is something quite familiar about this description for anyone who watches U.S. television. Shows like *The Sopranos*—fabulously focused on secrets work, indeed—feature these and other collective techniques, too, but from the bad guys' perspective, of course. From either side of the story, what a remarkable coordination of efforts such secrets work entails. Clearly, good training in the group *and* individual level competencies needed for secrecy is essential for many kinds of criminal and law enforcement work.

Without a clear system of rules and regulations by which the State oversees the efforts of police and other court officers to find out people's secrets, this kind of activity easily takes a different, more nefarious path than it should. The structures underlying State-sanctioned secrets work are present in this next excerpt, too. Here we catch a glimpse of the collective, historical efforts involved in both keeping *and* finding out secrets of an even higher order—what are literally called State secrets. Here is an octogenarian recounting a job fresh out of college.

I'd typed some letters in French and that kind of thing before I got hired by the Signal Corps.

Okay.

. . . What we did-- You know when we left there we were required to swear that we would never reveal what we had done.

Oh, really.

Now that was-- I left in 1945 after V-E Day, so that was fifty-seven years ago. I think they have released people from that oath by now. But my brother especially took it very seriously because he was working on the real stuff. He was-- I don't, you know-- There are codes and there are ciphers. Ciphers are more complicated.

. . . What we did in the situation room-- You know, I don't think I'm, you know, breaking the law by telling you. All sorts of communicative, already translated and coded and decoded communications that may have been in plain English came on our desk. And we took notes on what the Afghan attaché in Moscow said to the Libyan consul in Moscow, this kind of thing. So we got all sorts of rumors crossing our desk and we were supposed to put together some picture of what the diplomats were thinking was happening. And once a week we would present, in a briefing, kind of, to whatever officers wanted to come to us.

After all this time, this participant is still worried about breaking an oath to never tell what she did. I have been struck by how secrecy can become remarkably second nature to professionals, whether attorneys, therapists, system administrators, doctors, cops, spies, or anyone else. The tendency to remain discrete may remain long after retirement or after formal agreements expire, too.

Finally, the collective possibilities for the work of *revealing* secrets are alluded to in the following story, in which a mom takes on the job of telling other people that her son is gay. The act of revealing difficult things on behalf of those we love is a fairly common one among participants, a way of trying to ease the burden that revelation sometimes entails.

I have a secret about my family that shouldn't be a secret that I just learned that I have to work on telling people. And I'll tell you what that secret is. The secret is that (Alex) is gay, and he told us this in December. So it's been very interesting. I have to-- I think this is-- It's both a secret and it's not a secret. And I have to tell people to make it normal and to make it normal for Alex and make Alex not have to feel like it's a secret. And yet he doesn't want to tell people because it's embarrassing for an eighteen-year-old, or for anyone to announce their sexuality because other kids don't have to do that. So what I've done—

But if he doesn't, then he runs the risk of being accused of hiding this from people and intentionally making a secret out of it.

Yes. Accused of hiding it. He would have to censor his talk, his talk about his social life. He would have to chance people being offensive and hurtful because, you know, everyone has things to say about gay people, and jokes they make and just little remarks, and it's just in everyone's cultural thing. Unless they've been enlightened or they know someone or they are gay, or-- And also for myself, I have to tell, because my friends have to know this. Because I want to be able to talk about my children as I always do with my friends. So, and I don't think it's been systematic. But it's just something that I've figured out.

How do you feel about feeling compelled to tell people? How do you feel when you tell them?

Feeling compelled to tell them is a good thing because it solves so many problems for me. I know what to do next, in a way.

In the context of doing the work of secrets, the value of "knowing what to do next" is not to be underrated. Indeed, this brief foray into thinking about the range of objects, evidence, matters, and numbers of people involved in the work of secrets only hints at the huge variety of tasks and knowledge involved in this activity. By looking closely at the techniques and skills of secrecy themselves, though, we can find out more about the nature of this kind of work and what it means to do it well.

A CLOSE LOOK AT SECRECY TECHNIQUES AND SKILLS

In order to look closely at the actual work of secrets, I combed a number of participants' stories, developing a list of the techniques they used or had used against them in the process of keeping, revealing, and finding out secrets. There is nothing generalizable nor representative about the stories I used for this exercise, much less the bits of information I ferreted out of them. Previously, though, I had extracted hundreds of interview excerpts and placed them into different documents that reflected some of my conceptual points of interest in this study. Because they seemed most relevant to the issue of secrets work, I chose to examine all the stories in documents I'd created with stories about "secrets," "hiding stuff," "domestic privacy" (because people first learn about secrecy and continue to gain extraordinary insight about how and why to do it here), and "privacy violations" (which included many examples of confidences that were broken and secret behaviors that were unhappily revealed).

I searched these stories for general rules, common practices, unique actions and reactions—for anything that seemed to be an example of what a person does in the process of keeping, revealing, and finding out secrets. I transferred my three lengthy lists of descriptive words and phrases onto Post-its then created three large mappings of these Post-it collections (one each for "keeping," "revealing," and "finding out" secrets). I clustered, reclustered, and subclustered them over a period of days so that I might capture small interrelationships between techniques. I then stepped back to see what higher level descriptors and insights might emerge across all of these actions.

Complete lists of the techniques I sorted under each category appear in appendix B. The lists include over 360 techniques used to do the work of secrets—many of them bundles of techniques, really. A small sample of the techniques used for keeping secrets includes, for example:

Do something when no one (who cares) is around to see you do it
   (dump Christmas tree next door)
Keep moving the evidence (e.g., a present; one's body to hide swollen,
   red eyes from crying)
Turn to next (blank) page in diary whenever dad comes in to say good
   night
Hide laptop in couch cushions

Before a party, put *Oprah* magazine at the bottom of the stack and *Bon Appetite* on top
Put things away the day the cleaning lady is coming
Roll up dirty underwear and put in bottom of laundry basket
Keep pornography in closet, in a box
Hide presents where receivers are unlikely to find them
Keep treasures in sock drawer in dresser

This is a sample of the techniques I catalogued for revealing secrets:

Use a code, known only to those with whom you want to communicate (close curtains at dinner time to tell neighborhood kids but nobody else)
Parents talk in code in front of kids (e.g., use big words, or spell or use second language)
Translate to a known language (diplomatic communiqués)
Use words others can understand (e.g., not "pothead," not big words for nonnative speakers and children, not medical terms, not another language)
Put a chair in the shoveled-out parking space (another code, in Chicago)
Wear a certain accessory (e.g., wedding ring, crucifix, yarmulke, headscarf, burka, Star of David)
Put arm around boyfriend, hold hands in public (gay man)
Wear headphones at work (don't bother me)

Finally, here are a few of the techniques used for finding out secrets:

Wait until they tell you (until Christmas, birthday, merger announcement)
Laugh and cajole in a highly interested but nonthreatening way
Give an art assignment
Get close—spend time and begin to trust and share stories with each other
Sleep with someone
Hang around a gossip/nosy person/insider seeking validation
Gossip
Ask someone who is likely to know or know someone who does (sometimes repeatedly—interrogation)
Snoop
Find other excuses to see/hear what you're really interested in
Drop in unannounced
Gaydar

Analysis of all these techniques and across all three categories of secrets work shows variation along a number of pertinent dimensions. Techniques are distributed across a number of continua, encompassing those that are:

· more passive versus those that are more active (withholding information is toward the more passive end, for instance, while lying is more active, and intimidation is more active still);
· essentially proactive (often based on setting up/avoiding or encouraging/discouraging opportunities for things to happen) versus more reactive (where individuals engage in an assortment of behaviors to respond to an event that has occurred);
· planned (such as rules for living and habitual practices) versus unplanned (spontaneous, in-the-moment decisions and actions);
· more defensive/protective versus more offensive/invasive (although this may change according to the perspective of various stakeholders);
· highly sophisticated and complex (involving an intricate sequence of actions) versus those that are extremely simple and yet still quite effective;
· legal versus illegal;
· more covert versus more overt;
· moral versus immoral (though again this assessment might vary between those who use these techniques and those on whom they are used);
· imposed on individuals only by themselves versus those that are imposed on individuals by others, although perhaps on behalf of the self;
· deeply personal and felt for years versus techniques that feel much more impersonal and barely worth mentioning.

In addition, there are techniques that:

· focus heavily on understanding, using, and manipulating objects and the physical infrastructure of the built environment;
· focus heavily on understanding, using, and manipulating people and the social-cultural, interpersonal infrastructure;
· focus heavily on understanding, using, and manipulating institutions, their services, and the rest of the political-legal-economic infrastructure;
· involve the knowing participation only of oneself, while others involve the coordinated, knowing participation of others;
· do not depend on judgment, performance ability, or any sort of nuanced execution versus others that absolutely do so;
· make an individual's discretion and singular contribution to the ensuing outcome clear, while others help deny or obfuscate the same.

The range of techniques in the stories used to inform this chapter makes clear the importance of a number of factors for success in the work of secrets. These include the importance of:

- observational abilities (the ability to use all senses to perceive exactly what is going on);
- knowledge of what is normal;
- good social judgment and the ability to determine the likely effect of a behavior or action on one's self, another, and/or a given relationship;
- performance abilities;
- analytical abilities;
- the ability to apply oneself systematically to the study of a problem;
- planning abilities;
- resourcefulness (using the expected, known, and available in unexpected, unknown ways);
- a mindset that embraces or actively rejects secrecy, which can be critical in helping one to achieve a desired goal (this includes developing the mental agility or constancy to achieve one's cognitive goals);
- the ability to do emotion work (Hochschild 1983) and adopt the correct emotional framework one believes one needs in a given situation.

One's capabilities across all these dimensions are relevant to many facets of secrets work. The ability to imagine potential scenarios, for instance—to envision various permutations of events that are both possible and probable outcomes of different situations—is remarkably important for success in doing the work of secrets. If one had this chess-playing-like ability—this cluster of abilities, really—one would then be better able to adjust one's own behavior and better manage secrets accordingly. A clear sense of how competent one is in doing this work is certainly critical in making informed decisions about what to do next regarding any potential secret.

CONCLUSION

Humans are not the only creatures who display remarkable talent in the work of secrets. The skills of the mimic octopus and the shape-shifting octopus, for instance, are simply stunning.[39] It is entirely possible that they actually learn and hone their secrets work over time, too. Nonetheless, there is something truly unique about the ways humans manage to selectively conceal, disclose, and expose all kinds of information. By the time I found myself reading about U.S. soldiers in Iraq who learn to notice slight, daily changes in roadside piles of trash—indicating the good possibility of a freshly buried IED[40]—I couldn't help but think what an incredible range of talents we put to work in so many ways in the management of secrets.

Indeed, the successful management of even the normal, everyday secrets of the participants in this study requires an extraordinary breadth of knowledge, techniques, and skill. The sheer amount of work involved in managing secrets is exponentially increased by the fact that the decision to keep, reveal, or find out a secret is done on a secret-by-secret—and person-by-person—basis, too. Secrets are thus an especially good place to begin seeing the detailed enormity of all the work we do to achieve privacy.

There also is no question that secrets are not only a focus of a rather amazing amount of work, but also the stuff of play. Important life lessons may emerge during the pleasurable activity of secrets, too, blurring the boundaries between what is fun and serious all at once.

We had a brotherhood. There was a cousin visiting and the boy across the road. I don't know whether that was when we were seven or we were twelve. But we wrote something. I think we pricked our fingers and sealed it with blood and put it between the baseboard and the wall just to the left of the living room door. (*Laugh.*)

What did that teach you about privacy?

That you want to keep some things secret. Because that was kind of a pact.

Similarly, like any other focus of play, secrets can easily reveal the fact that what is playful for one person—say, a doctor—might be dead serious for his patient.

I was mortified when anybody found out what I was really thinking about, you know. . . . When I was seven, I had my tonsils out, and at that time, they used ether to put you to sleep. And I remember after I woke up sometime, the doctors or whoever was there were kidding me about all the things that I'd said when the ether was taking effect. . . . And I had no idea what I had said but they wouldn't tell me. But-- Oh, boy, oh boy, oh boy. And I was mortified because I didn't want them knowing what might really be in my mind.

The game of truth or dare[41]—a game centered precisely on the revealing and concealing of secrets—is notorious for its capacity to instantaneously shift the frame from fun to threatening, particularly if one is on the receiving end of a turn. This riskiness is a great deal of its attraction.[42] What may be less anticipated, however, is that the effects of this game and the frame-shifting one risks while playing it may extend beyond the actual playing of the game itself. Here, a middle-aged woman reflects on an experience during her teenage years; it's another kissing-at-camp story.

We were all playing truth or dare, you know, and it's with the counsel-ors and it's the last day. We were about to go in. And somebody dared the counselor to kiss me, or French kiss me. So I can't remember if he [Frenched] or not, but we did kiss. And I-- So there was that. And I ended up kissing him a couple of more times before the end of the summer. And he kissed other, like, three of the other women.

You know that?

Because we talked about it.

. . . The confusing thing is that it was really nice. And-- But I didn't think about it. Though the three or four young women who were in that group didn't go back the next summer and the other people did.

Any time one engages in secrets, one risks the fact that even if they start out as a source of fun and play, they may later become a source of vague, troubling feelings—or worse—and an acute source of work.

This chapter has focused on the nature and extent of that work. To sum-marize, the management of secrets may require both individual and col-lective efforts, efforts that focus on both highly tangible and less tangible elements, and efforts that encompass an extraordinary wealth of skills and techniques—of field craft—that must be mastered in order to do it well. Decisions about what to do next with secrets not only depend on these factors, but also on individuals' moral claims, competencies, and imagi-nations in anticipating the outcomes of various actions on one's relation-ships with others.

This last and final excerpt provides a striking example of how all of these factors might come together. It is from a thirty-nine-year-old, trans-gendered participant. At the time that we spoke, many years after I had last seen her, she was about to undergo the final, surgical phase of her trans-formation.

So, what did your process look like? When did you start to have a sense?

When I was really little.

Really?

I just knew that something was wrong.

Something was wrong and you thought of it as wrong, not just different?

Yeah. Just something that-- You know, I just didn't fit in with boys and I wanted to be with the girls all the time. . . . And I guess I really didn't know what it was until, I don't know, like, when I was in high school or something.

So the whole time that I knew you and everybody knew you [back then], you knew this. You were living this remarkably dual existence?

Yes.

One in your head and your heart and another one on the outside.

Right.

How do you do that?

I don't know. I just kept myself really busy and the busier I was, the more I wouldn't think about it, and I felt like I could go on pretending forever. Then I think after I graduated [college], then it started to get bad.

Really? Is that because, all of a sudden, you weren't so busy anymore?

Well, I was really busy in grad school. I don't know what it was. Maybe I just hit the age where I just couldn't hide it anymore.

From yourself as well as from others?

From myself. I still kept it from everybody. I didn't tell my mom until the end of (1999).

I have an imagination. I also know what other people have told me about why they kept something like this quiet for so long from other people. What was your worst fear why you didn't want to tell anybody?

Being disowned. My mom and dad are pretty religious, and I didn't think they were going to take it very well.

How did they take it?

Pretty hard. My mom still isn't really too happy with it.

But she's accepting it?

She's accepted it. She knows this is what I have to do. And basically she hasn't told any of her friends at all. And then my dad-- I think my dad's actually taking it better than my mom.

Really?

Which is not what I expected.

So, whose uncle are you living with now?

My mom's.

Well, he must be okay with it then.

Yup.

Do you think your mom feels some kind of guilt somehow?

Yeah. I think that's her main thing. That she never even knew.

So do you think she feels bad that she couldn't help you through this?

Yes. I think that's what makes her feel the worst.

Well, I think that sometimes the primary parent often feels as if it was something that they did or didn't do, something, you know. There seem to be a couple of things that-- First of all, they're shocked that this person that they thought they knew so well, they don't know at all.

That was one thing with my mom. She just didn't know what to do. And then after I told her, she went seven months without saying anything.

About that, or didn't talk to you at all?

She talked to me a little bit because I was still living at home. But she didn't tell anybody and she didn't bring it up with me.

What did she do that whole time? I mean, who-- Did she talk to your dad?

No.

This is big stuff.

Just family, I guess. And I was going to a therapist that whole time, and finally I got her to go with me one day.

What was that like?

That was really hard. We sat there together and my therapist mostly talked to her, and she cried the whole time.

Oh, gosh. That must have just broken you to bits. I mean, you would think it's hard enough making this decision for yourself much less thinking that your decision is causing pain to somebody that you love so much.

And then we got out of there and she had finally-- She had said, you know, I haven't-- She hadn't told my dad at all and it was killing her to not be telling him. And she asked who should be the one to tell him, and my therapist told her that she should be the one. So I went away for that weekend, and then she told my dad and my brother and my grandma. And then I got home, and they all said I could keep going. I was in the doctor's office next week starting up hormones.

Wow. Now you have, one, two, three, four people that she told that weekend?

Yes. And then my grandma told my aunt, called my aunt when they got done.

How did you feel once they all knew?

I guess relieved and then scared, too. Just that everything was changing.

So fast. I mean, it was like boom, done. So this was something that you had really made up your mind was absolutely the right thing before you told anybody else?

Yes.

And did your therapist suggest that that was a good thing to do? To be 100 percent certain in your own mind?

I was sure before I even went to see her.

And does she have a specialty in sort of talking to people who—?

Yes. She has been doing transexualism for fifteen years, and she's moved away now, so-- I've been seeing somebody else, and she's not a specialist.

But are they good for you? Is this second person good for you?

Yeah.

. . . When did you start therapy?

(January of 2000), right after I told my mom.

Okay. And was that good, too, for you? Was that something that right away felt good?

Yes. Because I finally had somebody to talk to about it.

I've heard from some people who, depressives, who suddenly go on (antidepressants), that they suddenly see colors and they are suddenly so much happier that it's very disorienting. It feels good, but it's a remarkably disorienting experience for them. Was there any of that for you?

I think when I told, I think it lifted a huge burden. And then hormones were really stabilizing. I just felt normal all of a sudden.

Really? How quickly did that happen?

I think like the hour after I got the first injection. It was just all of a sudden-- He had even told me the calming effect that takes place with it, and then when I got through the injections and-- I had three injections within, like, every two weeks, and then I started an oral medication, and it's like what my mind wanted.

Wow.

And finally I had the right things in my body.

. . . What are the physiological changes that are associated with that? Other than sort of a calming effect. What kind of visible physical changes do you have now?

Breasts. The skin becomes really soft and body hair has been diminishing and-- My face began to, became more round. It just filled out. And then it kills a lot of the muscle in your body, or at least in your upper arms and everything, which I didn't have a whole lot to begin with. . . . It's taken a lot of that away.

Do you like the way that you look now?

Starting to.

Starting to? And how long has it been since you started the hormone treatment?

About a year. Over a year.

This is such an incredibly interesting thing because I've been spending so much time thinking about the body as the quintessential interface where the private and the public meet. You know? That is, the public persona is rooted in the visible features of your body and the

visible things that you do to your body. I was thinking that, how awful to have gone through so much of your life where the thing that the rest of the world judges you by, sees you as, is so different from how you think of yourself, how you would like to be seen by others, and the amazing conflict that that must create in you. So I would imagine that you would only be feeling more and more relief as your body starts to more closely match that internal, secret image that you have had of your identity.

Yeah, it does. I think I was mostly concerned that I wasn't going to look like I was a female and then when I quit [my job] . . . and moved down to [Miami] and started living completely as a girl, nobody's ever questioned it, so—

Do you think that's just Miami or do you think that's *you* not questioning it?

I think-- Everybody just assumes I'm a girl.

What about shopping? Shopping for girl clothes? That must have been something else. Do you remember the first time that you did that? I mean, I'm assuming that it was a long time ago that you first did that.

I think in high school when I'd finally gotten my driver's license.

Where did you keep them?

Everywhere. I hid them in my closet and all kinds of places.

Do you think that your mom—I mean, I'm assuming that most moms are the cleaners, launderers, all of that stuff. Do you think that she ever came across any of them?

Yeah. She had-- I had some underwear and she had-- She never went into my room at all, but before I was going back to college the first year, she found them in my room because she had gone in to look for something she wanted to make sure I had to take back. And she asked me about it and I lied to her.

What did you tell her?

I don't remember. She knew I'd never been out with a girl, so—

Jeepers. Did you worry that people would notice *that* and think, suspect?

Yeah. I thought-- I couldn't go out with anybody.

So now what kind of clothes do you like to wear?

I'm still in the shorts and, like, women's t-shirt kind of things. Because it's always hot down here. Now that I'm in (Miami), I'm two miles away from the water, so it stays cooler here, like 75 today. But, at home, it's still in the 90s. Skirts and two-piece suit kind of things that I bought when I was trying to get a job.

Well, it must have worked.

No, 'cause I never got the job.

Oh, no. Never mind. But it must still be a real treat to shop for clothes now. Is that sort of what it feels like? I mean, do you wake up in the morning and feel good?

Yeah, I just feel normal for once.

Oh, jeez, (Christi).

I never felt normal.

And the rest of the family at this point? How are they doing with this?

I'm not sure that my brother likes it too much. But everyone else seems to be doing okay with it.

Are you worried about people finding out about this, maybe even blackmail?

No. I think mostly I don't want people to know. Because right now, I'm just a normal woman to everybody and if they do find out, then everything changes, I think.

Do you feel-- I mean, it doesn't seem to me that this information would be relevant to a future employer. But it does seem to me that it might be relevant to a future spouse.

Yes.

Have you talked to your therapist at all about, you know, better and worse ways of breaking this to somebody that you might be dating?

Not yet. I still haven't ever dated anybody, so-- That worries me, that I'll have to tell. I don't think guys do too well with it. . . . I guess I'll come to that when it happens.

. . . I definitely don't want to tell anybody I work for. I know that if they do find out that I'm subject to being fired right away.

You know, I think the only grounds on which they could fire you now is for lying on your job application and your resume. And it's a very interesting question. Would you actually be lying?

Right. I see it as none of their business, and there's no reason for them to find out, now that my [name and] records are changed.

Right. This is your official name. This is what you did. This is what the records all say. And that's it. So there could be no legal cause for termination. Otherwise, what you get, you know, is discrimination based on sexual preference, maybe, gender, you know, any of those things.

They can't discriminate on sexual orientation anymore, but they can still discriminate on transgender grounds. We're not protected by law at all. So. And then they do-- You know, when they ask on the job application for any former name, then-- And if I don't put it down and then somebody finds out, then, you know, I'd be pretty sure to be fired on the spot.

And is that something you're prepared to do in exchange for not having to make this public.

Yeah.

The work of secrets is all here—from the kinds of effort involved in keeping, revealing, and finding out secrets to the skills, techniques, and decision-making factors it may entail over a very long period of time. The sheer number of moments in which this secret had to be managed and all the decisions that were made about how, precisely, to do that are incredible. Clearly, though, they were intricately linked to the relationships this participant had—and wished to have—with her self and with others.

NEXT

The ways individuals use their wallet and purse contents certainly show secrets work in action, too. In the next chapter, participants explain what they carry with them in their wallets and purses each day, as well as which contents they consider more private and more public—and why. It turns out that, like secrets, wallets and purses play a crucial role in helping people manage their privacy, especially as they selectively conceal and reveal just exactly who they are to the people around them.

CHAPTER TWO

Wallets
& Purses

WITH JAY MELICAN

Can you recall any specific instances from your childhood when someone taught you something about privacy and what's private?

I remember being a kid and sneaking when we were out at a dinner. And we were sneaking under the table and going through my grandmother's purse. And that, that got sounded out as private (*laughs*).

Did she get on your case about it?

Well, she was pretty gentle about it. I mean, I was six or seven. She was gentle about it, but also said that "if you want something in there, you just ask me." So it was sort of clear that there was a boundary that I just couldn't go into.

And so even now I feel funny about opening (my wife's) billfold. Although, I know exactly what's in there. I just don't want to open it up.

TOM, thirty-two-year-old married entrepreneur

Schwartz (1968) argues that society must create and reserve spaces and times of relatively unchallenged privacy if we want to interface smoothly with each other the rest of the time.[1] If anything is the quintessential, tangible example of "islands of privacy," wallets and purses are it. In the mobile, urban existence of the people in this study, these vessels perform just such a role. They are used to protect a variety of more and less essential, private objects while permitting their owners to more easily interact in public.

As seen in Tom's story, the prohibition against trespassing on these particular islands is taught to many of us at an early age. Internalized rules against the uninvited investigation of another's wallet or purse can persist for the rest of our lives, too.[2] Even when she has an excellent reason for doing so, for instance, this next participant also could not bring herself to go into someone else's purse, one that belonged to "a very modest, good citizen, a person who is self sufficient and takes care of herself" and who was slumped over on the sidewalk one morning.

So she's sitting there like this, sitting with her elbows on her knees with her head down. And I thought, that's not how this woman would behave in public. So-- And I was driving and I drove past her. As I was thinking about it, I thought, you know what? That is so much not how she would behave in public that I'm going to go back again. So I went around the block and came back, and by then she was lying on the sidewalk.

So I got out and I didn't know what to do. . . . I got her up. . . . But someone else, some ladies came out of the building and they were-- These nice ladies called 911 and, at the same time, two more women walked out of this apartment building. And one of them said to me, "What's going on?" And I said, "Ooh, this woman was lying in the street. She was walking and now she's lying in the street and I don't know what's wrong."

And this woman [who asked me that] was a nurse. And she-- And I hadn't started going through the purse. I looked at the purse so that I could see, who is this, and could I call someone? But before I just organized my thinking . . . this woman—[the nurse] who came out of the building—said, "She might be a diabetic. I'm going to open her purse and if she is, I bet she has a sucker in there. I bet this is a diabetic thing." So she opened her purse.

And I, you know, took the purse, but I couldn't plunge my hand into this woman's purse. . . . This nurse comes out, though—"I'm a nurse"—opens up, rummages around, touches everything, pulls out a wad of hard candy, and puts one in this woman's mouth. Opens her mouth and puts one in! And starts talking to this woman and touching her and--

Yep. That's what it was.

Nurses, doctors, police officers, firefighters—rescue personnel may very well take such boundary-crossing authority for granted. In fact, another participant, a former emergency room nurse, described her normal daily job as a string of tasks that would make many people stop short because of privacy norms. It was standard protocol for her to reach inside an unconscious stranger's mouth to remove their dentures, for instance—one of the first things she would do upon "meeting" them, in fact. It is an amazing testament to the power of socialization that the rest of us can be taught to think that the act of reaching into someone's purse is as unthinkable as reaching in their mouth to remove their false teeth. Instead, we may well stand back, indecisive, constrained even in emergencies by the privacy boundaries so thoroughly ingrained in us.[3]

Wallets, purses, and their contents are undoubtedly fascinating simply because they are such well-defined pockets of privacy. But if we were invited to take a tour through them, we might find that there are many more reasons to pay attention to them, too. Like secrets, wallets and purses are extraordinary windows to the self, so important for the basic process of identity management and, accordingly, so critical for the broader work of trying to achieve privacy. In fact, it turns out these "identity kits" (Nippert-Eng 1992) play a key role as individuals negotiate the boundary between what is private and what is public, what is for the self, and what is for others. In the process, they certainly reveal a great deal about the everyday need for disclosure and concealment—and the wealth of responses we have to that need. Here, then, is another fascinating place along the beach.

THE PROTOCOL

As I was designing this study, I thought of using participants' wallets and purses as elicitation devices. Past experience (Nippert-Eng 1992, 1996) taught me that one could learn a lot about some people from what they choose to keep in their wallets and purses. Moreover, manipulables—objects that can be touched and moved—can be extremely effective interviewing tools. Especially when the objects have clear and even special meaning, handling and looking at them can make it much easier for a person to talk about the most ephemeral concepts as well as the personal behaviors in which she or he incorporates those objects.

Accordingly, based on their earlier indications of availability and interests, about two-thirds of the study participants were asked to participate in a simple exercise using their wallets and purses. The contents of the forty-eight wallets and purses analyzed in this chapter belong to this representative subset of participants. Interestingly, no one who was asked to participate in this wallet-and-purse protocol—and who had her or his wallet and/or purse with them at the time of the interview—refused to do so.

Participants were asked to empty their wallets and purses and form two piles with the contents: a pile of items that they considered "more private" and a pile of things that they thought were "more public." They also were asked to explain why they placed the items where they did. If participants carried their wallets in a purse, the full contents of those purses were included in the inventory. Likewise, when wallets were normally carried in a briefcase or backpack—and when they had those with them at the time of the interview, too—the full contents of these larger vessels were inventoried, as well.

In this next section, we offer a close look at what people carried with them and which pile they placed it in. We look at the reasons people carry different items and the purposes to which they are put. This offers excellent insight into how individuals define "private" and "public" as well as the collections of objects themselves. The logic of what is selectively concealed and revealed to whom is further elucidated in this detailed and wonderfully taken-for-granted way.

"MORE PRIVATE" VERSUS "MORE PUBLIC": WHAT WAS IN THE PILES?

Table 2.1 is a comprehensive modified stem-and-leaf diagram of all participants' wallet and purse contents, as recorded by the study interviewers. It is organized by type of item and the pile in which a participant placed it. An individual participant is represented by a three-digit case number. This number functions as a tally mark in the diagram, but further allows the reader to map the entire contents of a given individual's wallet or purse throughout the chart.

A number of clear and mostly unsurprising patterns are evident among the items that participants characterize as "more private" versus "more public." Various forms of identification (drivers' licenses, student and work IDs, library cards, social security cards, et cetera) are evenly distributed between the "more private" and the "more public" categories. Sales receipts are more likely to be characterized as public, though credit card receipts and automatic teller machine (ATM) receipts—so frequently discarded on the floors of bank vestibules—are classified as "more private."

TABLE 2.1 Wallet and purse contents defined in terms of privacy

WALLET CONTENTS
total n=48

Identification	More Private	Debatable/Both/In-Between	More Public
	n=26	n=7	n=22
identification (card)	003		080
drivers license / state id	002 041 044 045 047 050 052 053 054 058 061 065 066 068 070 071 083 106	084 093	042 043 048 049 056 059 060 067 088 091 100 102
work/student id	002 046 047 050 052	055 084	041 042 060 062 066 088 091
library card	041 050 053 055 063 088	054 061 106	002 042 043 047 048 060 066 080
social security card	050 053 060 068 071 088		002 049
birth certificate	088		068
voter registration/id	041 047 048 106	055	002 042 068 071 102
auto registration			062 068
press id			051
organ donor card	046		
blood bank card			
lens implant id card			070
medic alert pendant		070	
cpr certification card	064		041
Troopers Lodge donor card			071
alumni association card			042

Membership Cards	More Private	Debatable/Both/In-Between	More Public
	n=7	n=3	n=15
membership card	041 046 050 053 063	056	042 068 102
coop membership card	070		043 066 068 071
museum membership card	070		066 067
zoo membership card			043 061
health club/gym membership card	046	106	047 048 081
son's YMCA card	070		071
hostel card			
professional soc/org member card			061
AARP/seniors org member card	070		068
WBEZ (public radio) member card			068
WTTW (public tv) member card			068
Costco member card			067 102
library carrel card		061	060
video rental card	002 041		042 047 052 062 067 071 080

Service Program Cards	More Private	Debatable/Both/In-Between	More Public
	n=3	n=0	n=9
AAA membership card	070		042 043 048 059 067 071 084 092
roadside assistance card	052 106		
Lexus card	052		
car warrantee card			068

TABLE 2.1 (*continued*)

WALLET CONTENTS
total n=48

	More Private	Debatable/Both/In-Between	More Public
Insurance Cards	n=19	n=7	n=11
insurance card(s) (unspecified)	102	058	081 092
expired insurance card		054	
health insurance card	002 003 042 045 046 048 050 053 055 060 065 066 067 070 106	052 061 068 084	043 056 059 062 071 100
medical card(s)	041	069	042
dental card			
auto insurance card	042 044 047 050	052 061	068 071
Rx card		061	042 066
Loyalty Rewards Cards	n=4	n=3	n=18
grocery card	041 053 055	083 106	002 043 048 049 052 054 060 062 065 067 071 088 100
frequent buyer rewards cards		106	048 052 059 060 067
frequent flyer card	046		042 049 056 062 071 102
Hertz Club member card			071
frequent diner card	046 055	083	048
college bar "Mug Club" member card			
Dave & Buster's card			088
Starbuck's card		071	
pet store discount card			002 046
Credit/Debit Cards	n=29	n=3	n=11
credit card	002 003 041 044 045 046 047 054 055 058 060 061 062 063 064 065 068 070 071 083 084 090 100 102 106	042 049	043 048 052 056 059 067 080 081
credit card case			
toy store charge/credit card		089	067
clothing store charge/credit cards	053		
gas charge/credit card	046 050 106		043
calling/phone card			067
atm/debit card	003 045 046 050 052 053 055 060 061 066 068 071 083 084 102 106		002 043 048 049 056 062 067
Money	n=16	n=5	n=16
money/cash	003 040 045 046 047 048 058 062 064 068 070 081 084 088 090 106	002 052 063 071	041 042 049 054 055 056 059 060 065 066 067 070 080
change		002 089	042 051 052
change purse			062
envelope (but not the cash in it)			070

WALLET CONTENTS
total n=48

	More Private	Debatable/Both/In-Between	More Public
As Good As Money	n=4	n=2	n=21
gift certificate/card			045 048
public transit card/pass		092	042 045 047 056 059 060 062 067 068 071 088 100 106
transit token	061		062
postage stamps			002 046 055 071
Kinko's copy card		052	046 061 068
museum passes	106		059
coupons			002 041 042 052 054 062
lottery tickets	041 102	092	
Checks	n=7	n=2	n=1
checkbook	044 068		
checks (blank)	058 066 070	093	
check for $5 (expired)		071	
check from mom	088		
rent check from tenant			056
pay check	064		
Receipts & Bills	n=17	n=4	n=14
atm receipts	041 042 045 052 054 068 093		043
credit card receipts	041 042 045 085		
sales receipts	046 060 065 080 081 088 102	002 064 083	002 042 045 059 062 067 068 085 092 100
restaurant receipts			043
business receipts		071	
blank cab receipts			045
mailed package receipt			068
dry cleaning bill	106		056
bill from therapist	002		
old parking tickets			042
movie/ticket stub(s)			049 054
museum admission button	088		002
boarding pass from trip			002
Financial Records	n=7	n=0	n=0
financial/expense records	003 085 092		
overdraft notice	085		
bank statement	002 050		
pay check stubs	044 062		

TABLE 2.1 (*continued*)

WALLET CONTENTS
total n=48

	More Private	Debatable/Both/In-Between	More Public
Keys & Access Cards	N=6	n=3	n=5
keys	040 068 070 084	051 064 092	
work keys			003 062
key card/access card/security card	003 050		081
work security card			049 062
parking card			056
Access Information	N=5	n=1	n=1
card w/ security codes passwords	046 061 071 100		003
card w/bank account numbers	106	067	
acct#/password for financial site	071		
Business Cards & Contact Info	n=11	n=8	n=23
business cards	041 088	057 085	002 041 042 043 047 051 052 055 056 060 064 066 068 070 071 100
participant's business cards		106	084
mother's business card	046		
father's old business card			046
husband's business card			042
son's business card			068
boyfriend's business card	066		085
friend's business card			
colleague's business card		002	046
friend's stepmother's b.card			
doctor's/therapist's business card	042 063 066	052	106
kids' pediatrician's business card			106
architect's business card			
cab driver's business card		002	
interviewer's business card	088		
Foster's card (class ring)	088		
b.cards with phone numbers on them	050 053 106		
boss' private cell phone number	052		
phone numbers	100	055 083	043
addresses, phone #s of coworkers			003
address book		070	
Alaska address	088		
tenants' phone numbers			
phone number of MD's billing dept			092
handwritten numbers		070	100
contact #s in case wallet stolen			054

WALLET CONTENTS
total n=48

Reference	More Private	Debatable/ Both/ In-Between	More Public
	n=13	n=3	n=13
calling card instructions			046
instructions for phone	052		067
train schedule			051
periodic table			068
to do list	002 040		003 085
grocery list	053		
list of books			041
datebook/dayplanner/calendar	050	052	003 070 091
folder of work stuff			003
notebook/notes	040 044 051 064 070	064	042 056 093
poem (written by daughter)		089	
letter from friend	003 051 066		
old travel log	070		
announcement of gallery show			092
funeral card	055		
set of Jewish blessings	060		
public school volunteer contract			068
fortune cookie fortunes			092

Stationery Supplies	More Private	In-Between	More Public
	n=1	n=2	n=10
blank paper			040 070
loose cards		089	085
Post-it Notes			002
pens/pencils		092	003 042 051 062 064 070
Cross pen	002		
work pens/markers	002		
drawing materials			040
paper clips	002		
bookmark			092

Accessories & Jewelry	More Private	In-Between	More Public
	n=3	n=1	n=3
hair accessories			064
comb	003		
hairbrush	064		042 051
barrettes		064	
earrings	002		

TABLE 2.1 (*continued*)

WALLET CONTENTS
total n=48

	More Private	Debatable/Both/In-Between	More Public
	n=9	n=3	n=9
Grooming & Hygiene Supplies			
bag of assorted toiletries	003	089	
makeup	002 051 064		
compact		042	058 070
lipstick	003	042	
lip gloss	002	042	092
lotion	002 003		
dental floss	040 051	064	062
Chapstick (lip balm)			058 064 070 093
mints, candy, gum	002		002 093
Band-aid (adhesive bandage)	003 042 051 064 070 085	064	
tampons		089	040 042 070
Kleenex (facial tissues)			092
napkins			064
wet wipes	044	064	
contact lens solution			070
glasses cleaner			093
hand sanitizer			
	n=3	n=2	n=3
Prescriptions & Medication			
medicine (unspecified)	058		
Tums		064	
Lactaid			070
Tylenol			070
Sudafed	051		
cold medicine			085
cough drops			070
Vioxx (Rx arthritis medication)			085
Rx anti-depressant medication	002		
prescription (written)	002	056	070
prescription for glasses			045
inhaler	002		
pill box	002		
	n=8	n=5	n=2
Photos			
photos	002 041 044 053 055 063 064 090	083 093	092
photos of family		059 061 083 091	041
religious guru photos	002		

WALLET CONTENTS
total n=48

| | | Debatable/ Both/ | |
	More Private	In-Between	More Public
Eyewear	**n=2**	**n=1**	**n=3**
eye glasses/sunglasses	058		003 044 062
contact lenses	044		044
eye glasses case		089	
swimming goggles			
Stuff for Kids	**n=0**	**n=0**	**n=1**
changing pad			063
diapers			063
clothes			063
Technology/Equipment	**n=3**	**n=3**	**n=4**
cell phone	003 058	089 092	
beeper/pager		092	092
Palm Pilot	045	064	
Palm Pilot case			062
camera			085
cassette recorder			051
Tools & Supplies	**n=1**	**n=0**	**n=6**
matches			051 058 064
lighter			058
batteries			051
water bottle			092
army knife			092
glasses repair kit	044		
plastic bag			092
sugar/sweetener			002 062 092
Other Tokens & Mementos	**n=5**	**n=0**	**n=0**
crucifix	063		
AA coin	092		
medal	090		
sea shell	053 060		
charms	060		
toys			063
nursing towels			063

Business cards are overwhelmingly categorized as "more public," with some exceptions made for cards of family members, close friends, doctors or therapists, and for business cards on which private phone numbers were written.

However, the most striking thing that the data reveal is that no single commonly carried item is decisively and without exception characterized as either "more private" or "more public." Money is considered "more public" just as often as it is decreed "more private," for instance. Not all interview participants consider their credit cards particularly private, either. Even ATM debit cards find their way into some participants' "more public" piles.

At one level, this is quite consistent with the simple fact that for these participants, very little, if anything, is inherently public or private. The classification of an object is rarely an attribute of the thing itself, but rather a function of how accessible a given individual wishes—and believes—it to be. It is an individual's relationship to the item and to the people with whom they might or might not share it that are most important in determining the item's classification.

This is not to say that "private" and "public" are a classificatory free-for-all in which every individual decides, in a vacuum, what is what. Cultural guidelines clearly exist about what is more and less private and public. These are taught to us from an early age and manifested constantly in legislation, litigation, and daily conversation.

At other points in their interviews, for instance, participants offered what amounts to a surprisingly short and consistent list of topics of conversation, behaviors, and things that they believe are generally private. By far the most prevalent two private matters are, as one person put it, "body and money things." But a more inclusive list includes: sexual matters, bodily functions (especially going to the bathroom) and nakedness, medical concerns, financial matters, religious and political beliefs, family matters, and displays of uncontrolled anger and disapproval. "Private" things also include objects that are related to all of this such as photographs, phone conversations, sex toys and pornography, diaries, personal computers, letters, underwear, thoughts, one's art and/or writing, personal hygiene items, medication, women's purses, and a variety of items that have deeply personal—but often hidden—meanings attached to them.

However, as participants themselves are quick to point out, conceptual guidelines about what is private or public are only that. It is our ability to categorically stretch, contract, and otherwise elaborate or undermine these guidelines that creates a range of possible private-public classifications for every item, in every situation, across individuals. Cross-cultural differences and historical changes in social expectations regarding both of these categorical contents further complicate the story, of course. Indeed, participants' explanations of their piling decisions reveal quite a bit about the consistencies underlying individuals' conceptualizations of private and public. The privateness or publicness of an object also manifested in how people described handling it, especially during interactions with others. Here is a closer look at exactly what they said on these matters.

TALK ABOUT THE PILES: IMAGINED SITUATIONS AND THE CONSEQUENCES OF ACCESS

There were two general patterns of participants' reactions to the sorting request. The first was a quick, decisive declaration of all contents as belonging to a single category—although the exact category varied. "Everything in my wallet is private," one person claimed. Another stated, "That's easy: it's all public." Of course, people typically reconsidered specific objects later on and declared their nature to be more nuanced than this. Comments like "Well, really, this is more private than this, but not as private as that" were common later on. Initially, however, people with this reaction were quite definitive in their generalized classification of everything they had with them.

The second response pattern to the protocol produced no immediate classification of the wallet or purse. Participants simply complied with the request and began a careful item-by-item sorting of the contents. They used the same self-referencing approach, too, where things were more private than *this* but not as much as *that*, but either explained their decisions as they went along or waited until after they completed making their piles to describe their thinking.

The actual working definitions of "private" and "public" that emerged and that guided participants' actions were quite interesting. People put things that they "care about" into the "more private" pile. These objects may be highly meaningful, personally—introspective signifiers of relationships or experiences. But this pile also included objects over which participants believe they must maintain careful control in terms of who gets to see and/or use them and under what conditions they may do so. There is a consistent and overwhelming belief among participants that it would be harmful for them—or for those they care about—if other people knew about or used this second type of private things. One person described it like this:

This is the private pile. And this is the public pile. And the way I would differentiate between the two is, I ask myself the question: Do I care if someone would see this or not? So that's how I decided to determine what went in what pile. So, I don't know. I have a lot of money here, and since I took out a lot of money for vacation, I would consider this private. But if this was a dollar, I wouldn't care, and I would put it in the public pile.

The "more private" category may include a remarkable range of items, then. It includes things that are personally, emotionally precious. It also includes things that might invite harm if one lost control of them. This might be anything that has significant exchange value or that might be traced back to a participant, for instance (revealing past and present identity as well as other information about her/him), as well as bodily objects like prescription medicine, make-up, or a hairbrush.

For the most part, the "more public" pile is made up of things that participants "don't care about." Participants may not care much about the actual item itself. They may not care if others know that they are carrying it. Either way, if someone saw these things or got their hands on them, the participant doesn't think it would cause any real harm to her or him or the people she/he cares about. In addition, people sometimes carry items in their wallets or purses that are for their own use but also for others' use—from candy to business cards. These items "for sharing" are also classified as "more public." The following participant touches on all these themes.

I put all my old receipts in the private pile. Basically I just throw them away. I guess they probably do have information, if I were more concerned with privacy, I wouldn't want people to be snooping in. But I don't really care that much.

So, they're a little less private than some of the other stuff?

I mean, they're going to become a little less private really quickly when I throw them in the trash outside and [they're] available for anyone who cares to look at them.

And then I put my various credit cards and bank cards in the private pile because they feel like things that I would want to protect from other people using. Like the IDs-- Unless someone is going to look enough like me that they're going to steal an ID, I don't feel like they need that same protection. But the credit cards and the bank card, I feel they need a certain protection. And some of them have PIN numbers associated with them that I don't share with anyone else.

… My social security card I keep in the private pile. Again, it is a number that is obviously used for public access to things, but it feels like not something I want everyone to know about.

... And this is a little, it's my traveling-- It's a little set of blessings so that if you want to say blessings over different kinds of food and you don't remember what the blessings are, they are all right here and I don't know why I have that. Oh, yes. On the back it has the prayer that you say before you travel, which I don't know by heart. It's nice to have. And I didn't-- It's private in the sense that it's something that I use privately, rather than-- I don't use it in exchanges with other people, but it's not something that I would necessarily feel like I had to hide from anyone. A pretty public prayer.

Note that this person's reflections were typical in both the criteria she used and the way she went back and forth between items, defining one item's privateness/publicness relative to that of another.

It need not be the entirety of an object that concerned participants during this process, though. Individuals frequently discussed objects in terms of their components and the multiplicity of their attributes. In this way, each *aspect* of a given object was considered and described as more or less private/public than the others.

This deconstructive analysis may have been crucial for the overall, summative assessment of the privateness/publicness of any item. A small detail or component of an item may have placed it in a different category than other similar objects. Even if it ultimately ended up in the same overarching category as those similar objects, it still might have been seen as slightly more public or private than the others it resembled.

Consider this example:

Okay. Here will be my private pile. Okay. On the back of this card I have the home address and phone number of one of my coworkers. And I was saying, ordinarily, I would consider this whole card—all of her personal information—to be private. I do consider her home address and phone number private. Ordinarily, I would consider her cell phone to be private, too, with the exception of the fact that she put it on the business card. So, since she put it on her business card, I would-- I would consider this to be public stuff. I'll leave that. That's sort of a category by itself.

Okay. I think pretty much-- Now this is [my university] ID, and ordinarily I would consider this to be public, except that it has my social security number on it, which makes it go over here [in the "more private" pile]. And the same thing for the driver's license. You really can't call that private, because you have to produce it for just about everything. But it has your driver's license number on there, which is useful information. All of this other information which people could use against you for, you know, use in order to steal your identity, is on there. So this is sort of in a category by itself, too, because it's actually private information, but you have to produce it every time somebody asks for it. So I don't know how to call that.

Because it must be protected, though, this participant knows what *not* to call it; it is definitely not part of her "more public" pile.

The criteria for sorting wallet and purse items into these two piles map nicely onto participants' more general definitions of "private" and "public." During their interviews, fifty-four people were asked the question "What does it mean to you if something is private?" Here is a summary of their responses. Note that a single response was coded into multiple categories if it focused on more than one aspect of the term. The total number of responses for each category of response appears in parentheses next it. See Nippert-Eng (2007) for a more detailed analysis of this data and examples of the kinds of responses coded into each category.

What does it mean to you if something is "private"?

1) only one person has access to it or it is shared only selectively
   $(n = 52)$
2) it is a thing that is mine, part of me, who I am, what I do, what I think
   $(n = 32)$
3) it is a thing that is not generally accessible for agreed upon interpersonal and/or social-interactional reasons
   $(n = 17)$
4) it is a thing that is inaccessible under legal, institutional, or professional codes (i.e., protected from others' use, interest, interference)
   $(n = 12)$

In addition, consider table 2.2. It is a list of all the examples participants happened to mention while discussing what "private" means to them. The number of cases in which each example was mentioned is indicated in parentheses.

Each element on this list has something in common with participants' broader definitions of privacy as well as the ways that they talked about the contents placed in their "more private" piles. That common element is the feeling that private things are, should be, or must be protected, most often because they are so closely associated with the self. Private items are close to who we are. This is a key reason why we develop an assortment of personal and shared practices to defend them so vigorously.

This is quite different from the ways people think about and treat things that are more public. Here is a summary of how the same fifty-four

TABLE 2.2 Comprehensive list of examples of "private" items

My name (1)
(Female friend's) age (1)
My phone number (1)
Where I live (1)
What I look like (1)
My hair color, length (1)
What books I read (1)
Purchase information (what/where
  I purchase) (1)
What toothpaste I use (1)
Color scheme in my house (1)
What's in my garbage (1)
What's in my closet (1)
What's in my freezer (1)

Financial information (3)
Bank account (1)
Passwords for accounts (1)
Bank card PIN (1)
Credit card number (1)
How much money you make (3)

Information on my computer (1)
Information in nondisclosure
  agreements (1)

The fact that I yell at my kids (1)
Being in an abusive relationship (1)
Interpersonal relationships: tensions
  about race and power (1)
That you were a drug addict (1)
Whether you're in AA or not and how
  well you're following your program (1)
Whom you've had an affair with (1)
Questions about your sex life (1)
Sexual things (1)
Mental conditions (1)
Why I don't have any children (1)

My reasons for making my art (1)
Your most profound fears, anxieties,
  hopes, dreams (1)
A feeling (1)
A thought (1)
An idea (1)

(An area of) my body (1)
My pubic region (1)
A beautiful woman (a beautiful woman's
  body) (1)
My image (as photographed) (1)

A (phone) conversation (2)
A meeting (1)

My lifestyle (1)
What I do (2)
My social interactions (1)
My economic interactions (1)
My physical interactions (1)
Enjoying Internet porn (1)
Going to the bathroom (1)
Giving birth (1)

A building (marked private) (1)
A piece of property/real estate (2)
A club (1)
My home/house/apartment (3)
A room (1)
The bathroom/toilet (1)
The shower (1)

Patient information (1)
Source of a quote (for newspaper
  reporter) (1)
How much money donors have
  contributed (1)

participants also responded to a question about this. (Nippert-Eng [2007]
contains further details on this, too.)

How would you define something that is public?

1) things to which anyone has access, including those over which I have
   no control
   (*n* = 41)

2) things I don't care about, including things about me that I don't care if other people know
   $(n = 9)$
3) things that we permit other people to access, including one's work and/or public personae
   $(n = 6)$
4) things that are accessible under legal, institutional, or professional codes (e.g., "by right" or "in the public domain"), including things that are owned by everyone/no one
   $(n = 20)$

Obviously, there is an inverted symmetry in participants' definitions of "public" that map directly onto the ways they defined "private." For example, one definition associated with "private" is "things to which only one person has access or which are shared only selectively." A corresponding definition emerged under the category of "public," too, that is, "things to which anyone has access, including those over which I have no control." One pronounced difference in this symmetry, however, is that the definition of "public" brought to mind legalistic definitions and references far more frequently than did the concept of "private."

Like the list of "private" things presented previously, the list of things mentioned while participants' tried to define "public" also is revealing. This list, seen in table 2.3, also is rather random, perhaps even accidental. It is nonetheless interesting to contemplate, particularly when compared to what came to people's minds when thinking about "private" things. (Again, the number of cases for which each example was mentioned is indicated in parentheses.)

If nothing else, this list differs from the "private" list in one respect. While both private and public things may need protecting, private things need protecting by the individual who wishes them to be so. If public things need protecting, it is more likely to be seen as the purview of the law, some public servant, or a system of professionals who are supposed to be responsible for them on our collective behalf.

This is quite consistent with Weintraub and Kumer's (1997, 3–5) assertion that

> at the deepest and most general level, lying behind the different forms of public/private distinction are (at least) two fundamental, and analytically quite distinct, kinds of imagery in terms of which "private" can be contrasted with "public":
>
> 1. What is hidden or withdrawn versus what is open, revealed, or accessible.

TABLE 2.3 Comprehensive list of examples of "public" items

Streets, roads (3)
Sidewalks (1)
Squares (1)
Public parks (3)
Parking lots (1)
Most buildings (1)
Government buildings (1)
Congress (1)
WPA (Works Progress Administration) (1)
Public library (2)
Public school (1)
Public pool (1)
Hospital (1)
Restaurant (1)
My grocery store (1)
Marshall Field's (department store) (1)
View of a house, garden, or lawn from outside the property line (2)
Public transportation (1)

Cultural things (1)
Theater (1)
Dance (1)
Music (1)
Symphony (1)
Art (3)

Public meetings (1)
Public debate (1)
Anything "in the public domain"/included under the Freedom of Information Act (6)
Companies' financial records (1)
Government records (2)
Knowledge/information available to anybody anytime (12)
Anything someone knows about you (1)
Color of my hair (1)

Your name on a check/in the phone book (1)
Social security number on driver's license (1)

Shared files (1)
Desk tops (1)
A note on a bulletin board (1)
Something on a bill board (1)
Standing on a rooftop and screaming out whatever (1)
Something about me that I wouldn't mind being published in a newspaper (1)
Publication on sale to the public (1)
Newspapers (1)
Magazines (1)
Records (1)
Internet and anything on it (4)

Things that are free (3)

Your presence in another country (1)
You, in any public space (1)
Anything you do walking down the street (1)
Everything that you do outside your home (3)
Your public personality (2)
Your work (1)
Things you do at work (1)
An actress taking off her clothes in a movie (1)
Driving your car (2)
Hitting a child in a store (1)
A public figure's affair and history of personal/professional conduct (1)
The abuse of anyone powerless to stop it (1)

2. What is individual, or pertains only to an individual, versus what is collective, or affects the interests of a collectivity of individuals.

In a way, then, public things exist regardless of who one is; private things are defined as such precisely *because* of who one is. Part of the reason we readily give away the more public things in our wallets and purses, for instance, is because they are so disconnected from our selves, our senses of who we are.

Yet another common aspect of people's talk about their piles was the way participants uniformly invented and ran various scenarios through their minds while explaining their classification decisions. Giddens's (1990) and Beck's (1992) observations on the importance and prevalence of scenario-running in the modern "risk" society were quite apparent here. Constant decision making, they argue, based on the probabilities of X or Y happening is the hallmark of such a society. The skills and practices of thinking ahead and guessing what is and isn't likely to occur were certainly present in these participants' comments. Individuals fabricated and talked at length about the different scenarios involving various items that they imagined (or "knew") might occur and how these scenarios might challenge or confirm their notions of the nature of an item. The consequences of intentionally or unintentionally permitting others access to wallet and purse items played an important role in the decision to label something in a certain way.

This is of course a key way in which fears about one's privacy make their appearance—and perhaps a way of generating them, too. Indeed, such imaginings often lead people to adjust their behavior. After considering and reconsidering what might happen to a given object, an individual may well have shifted objects from one pile to another as a newfound understanding became a source of concern. This is why most of the time, objects were shifted from the more public pile to the more private one.

A consistent element in participants' scenarios was speculation as to the different ways in which an object might be accessed. Participants may have considered up to six alternative modes in which, they imagined, some generalized other might interact with a given item. Someone might: (1) assume the participant has "this," (2) see this, (3) touch this, (4) take this, (5) use this, and/or (6) misuse this.

For example, this person begins by imagining her reaction if people saw what she has in her wallet. From there, she proceeds through all the remaining possibilities.

I don't think there's anything that I'm carrying in my wallet right now that, in some way, I don't let other people see. That there's nothing here that I don't use in terms of-- Like, it's either a transaction or it's an identification thing. So there's nothing here that is so private that I wouldn't want anybody else ever to see it.

At the same time, there are things here that, if anybody found my wallet, I would hope that they would just look at my driver's license to identify me and then return it to me, so they don't know everything else. Like, I don't think that people need to know about my voter registration, and I don't think that they need to know about who my doctor is at my health plan and what my health plan is. There's nothing else here that is private in the sense that-- I mean, I don't care if people know if I have a Visa card, and I don't care if people know if I have a debit card. What I would care about is if they took it from me and tried to use it.

During this process of scenario-running, participants also frequently reconceived of an object using different viewpoints. Three different perspectives on any specific object were apparent. First, the item may have been considered in its entirety, as a tangible object. Second, it may have been thought of as a multifaceted, multifunctional conglomerate of more public and more private attributes, features, and uses. Third, the item may have been reframed in terms of its information value only.

Thinking of an object in terms of its information value was an especially critical switch-point in this process. If, in the course of scenario-running, an object was cognitively transformed and reconsidered as pure information, the participant would usually take off on a distinct line of thought. Typically, she or he would think next about what might happen if (1) someone knew she possessed the object, or (2) the information accessed on, with, or through the object "got out." At that point, the reclassification of the object was highly likely and it would be seen as even "more private." For example, a credit card may have started out in the "more public" pile. Later, once a participant began thinking about the account number on the card, or the account and purchase history that could be accessed with it, it was moved to the "more private" pile.[4]

Our capacity to conceptualize objects as their informational value both reflects and contributes to what Smith (2000, 6) says has been a shift in Americans' concerns with privacy. Privacy, he says, is

the desire by each of us for physical space where we can be free of interruption, intrusion, embarrassment, or accountability and the attempt to control the time and manner of disclosures of personal information about ourselves.

In the first half of our history, Americans seemed to pursue the first, physical privacy; in the second half—after the Civil War—Americans seemed in pursuit of the second, "informational privacy."

These Americans certainly are. Moreover, to think of an object as information seems to quickly associate it more with privacy than when the object itself is considered.

Even after a couple rounds of careful consideration and reconsideration, though, the classification of an object may not be obvious or settled. The definition of an object as more public or more private is a dynamic and ongoing negotiation. The process is the antithesis of what Bowker and Star (2000, 135) describe as the kinds of "frozen" classification and coding work embedded in technological devices. Instead, participants readily change their minds about how they define any of the objects they carry should they suddenly learn or realize something new about it.

This is quite typical of the ongoing process of trying to acquire and protect one's privacy in general, of course. Individuals are constantly trying to anticipate where threats to privacy might come from, running scenarios and adjusting their behavior accordingly. Gina's story from the beginning of this book is but one example of this. It's a constant learning process, where experience informs endless adjustments in our understandings of how private/public something is or is likely to be.

This interview exercise certainly compelled people to closely consider each item that they carried with them and to share their reflections with the interviewer. In the following section we consider some of the most important themes that emerged during these conversations regarding the ways participants classified each item. Of special note are the issues of (1) the desire to exercise control over wallet and purse contents—and over some objects more than others—and (2) the audience for whom each item is carried.

THEMES OF CONTROL AND INTENDED AUDIENCES

CONTROL IS THE GOAL

A common thread in participants' comments begins with the idea that displaying and temporarily (sometimes even permanently) surrendering an individual item in one's wallet or purse is a relatively safe, normal, daily act. This is, after all, precisely why one carries many—if not all—of the things kept in one's wallet or purse. However, revealing any portion of one's wallet or purse contents can become quite a remarkable—and undesirable—event under two conditions.

First, any disclosure that the participant does not fully control is unwelcome. Participants want to choose when and how they share any given item, whether it is more public or more private in their minds. In fact, quite frequently when a participant says something like "everything in my wallet is public," what they really mean is that they would not be embarrassed if anyone saw these contents or knew they had them. However, they would be uniformly upset if someone tried to take their wallet or an object in it without permission. This individual vividly makes that point.

Okay. There's nothing private in my wallet.

Okay.

Everything that's in here I could, you know-- I've got a picture of my kids. That's the only thing that I thought about pulling out. It was kind of private, but I realized that every time that I open my wallet to use my credit card—which is, you know, a hundred times every day—everyone sees this picture of my kids, so it can't obviously be that. And in those instances I'm proud of it 'cause, "Oh, look at all these." You know—

Right.

But in terms of if someone said, "Can I go through your wallet?" I could care less. There's, you know, two credit cards, two bank cards, driver's license, a CTA [Chicago Transit Authority] card and an insurance card, a AAA [Automobile Association of America] card and two museum passes, and that's-- And, why, today I have a lot of money. I have forty-seven, forty-eight dollars. Normally I have about twenty-five dollars. And a couple receipts, and that's-- Anything else hidden back here? That's a, oh, um, my frequent photo card from Triangle Imaging.

Okay. And none of that stuff is private?

No. I mean these are all things that, you know, that people see all the time. I mean, I would be upset if I had, you know, to have to go and re-place this stuff. I wouldn't want anyone to steal it.

Right.

This is all "stuff" to me. Now if someone, you know, if-- Here again, if I'm sitting there handing my wallet to someone who says, "Can I see your wallet?" and I handed it to them. Fine. If I left my wallet in my car, and I have locked my car, and someone broke in my car, ripped the radio out, and went through my wallet, took all the credit cards, driver's license, took everything and threw them out on the seat, took the cash and threw the wallet onto the seat, and I came back and discovered that—I would probably feel, you know, that I was horribly violated, raped in some way. But how do I then--? You know, I just said that I could care less if you looked in my wallet. Here again, I'm giving you-- I'm letting you. I am controlling the situation.

The importance of control over objects—even if the objects themselves are not thought to be too private—appears in this person's reflections, too.

A while ago—recent history, from a couple months ago maybe—I went out with some people and-- My bag's filled with all kinds of stuff. And

I became very, very nervous because then I was in this weird situation where-- Actually, this is a totally good example. I felt like, it's not that there's anything private in there. Like it was my wallet, it was my keys, some maps. But the idea that it had spilled out--

First of all, I felt very out of control and that's a big issue, I think. So-- Okay. There was the first issue of all of my belongings were on the floor and people were going to see them. Again, it's not like I cared that people would see those, but they're, like, my things. So I feel attached to them in some way and it would make me nervous that anyone could see them because they were laying on the floor. That made me a little bit nervous.

Then I was maybe even more nervous by the fact that-- You know, if I had been alone or something, I could have just crawled around on the floor for a couple of hours, making sure I had everything. But I felt under some societal pressure to, like, not be on the floor picking up things. I think it's a little bit of an embarrassing situation maybe, so I wanted to get it done as quickly as possible. But then I was worried that I didn't get everything.

So I actually went home and I tried to, you know, do I have everything? But then I sort of drove myself crazy thinking about, like, what if there's something I didn't remember that was in there? It was an uncomfortable situation.

It was especially uncomfortable, perhaps, because if you can't remember if something was in your purse before it spilled out, how are you supposed to know if it is still under your control? There's no way to figure out if something private is still private, and there's no way to figure out, therefore, whether or not your privacy is still intact.

There is a second condition under which participants become actively concerned with what otherwise would be the unremarkable disclosure of wallet or purse contents. This is when an object reveals (or might reveal) an unusually large amount of information about participants, especially regarding their identity. The more a certain object does this, the more participants worry about it and the more careful they are in how they handle it.

During these interviews, identity theft and its consequences were heavy on participants' minds, and with good reason. Here is a woman, for instance, who suffered for years because of a case of identity theft that occurred a decade before most people—and most institutions—had even heard of the crime. It's a long story, well told, outlining in painful, escalating detail exactly what might be in store if one fails to keep the objects most revealing of identity under control.

You know your driver's license does have your social security number on it.

It does. You know what? Actually, they, um, here, they took it off.

Oh, did they?

Mm-hmm. I asked them to take it off.

You can do that?

You can now. But if you don't ask them, they put it on. Unless you've got somebody who has a clue behind the, the desk when you apply. And when it had your social security number on it, it had everything that a person needs to steal your ID. Absolutely everything. And that has happened to me before. I was a victim of identity theft.

Really? What, what happened?

Somebody used my social security number and my information to get credit. And what they did was they used my current address as their past address so it looked like I had moved. And they were able to get credit and they charged up--

They stayed at two hotels, the (Hilton) and the, the (Marriott). They got a car. They charged all kinds of things. And this was when-- This was back in the early '80s when identity theft had no name and people thought I-- When I told them what was going on, people looked at me like I had two heads. And it was a nightmare getting out from under that.

So did you lose your license or did somebody—?

No, um-- Somebody-- This was-- As it turned out, it happened to be someone that I know. . . . They didn't even have the totally, the correct information. But they had near enough information that they were able to use my, my stuff. They had my exact right social security number. So all the stuff that I was saying, people just looked at that as "Oh, well, that was the wrong information, so we'll correct it to be what this person is giving us."

Oh, my gosh.

It took me, I never did-- I ended up filing bankruptcy because some idiot lawyer told me to file bankruptcy on that, not realizing that once I filed bankruptcy, I accepted those debts as my own. Then, like, four years later, three or four years later, this same idiot was on Channel 2 news telling them that he didn't know anything about bankruptcy!

Because he was working for (Smith Legal Services) at the time, which was sort of like a, like a mill of lawyers. (*Laugh.*)

Right. Right.

And he was saying, "Well, you know, they have us doing all these, these, working in these areas that we don't know anything about, and I had bankruptcy and I really didn't know anything about that."

And this guy had almost destroyed me.

I had a condo, and the condo was going to foreclosure because after, behind this identity theft, I had lost my job. I had, you know-- I couldn't get a job anywhere else, because, of course, known as a thief or whatever. I had, I was trying to fight this at the same time. I was trying to get somebody to listen to me. Social security administration was not helpful. I went down the phone book and called every law enforcement agency that was in the *Yellow Pages*. Nobody cared. Everybody was saying it's not a crime against [me], it's a crime against the stores. And of course the stores could not care less because it was, like, $6,000. "That's not enough for us to get involved in any litigation." Or, you know, if that was the extent of their loss.

And then, like, the, I think it was the (Marriott) left me alone right away when they realized the difference in information. But the (Hilton) was just hellbent on getting me in as much trouble as possible. They got, they went to my job. I was an investment banker. They got me fired from my job. They just did everything in their power, but they didn't want to pursue [the person who really did it]. Well, first of all, they were convinced that I had done it. Because nobody had ever heard of somebody taking other people's identity. Of course *I* had to do it.

And you were, like, in your twenties at the time.

I was in my twenties. I was twenty-seven, twenty-six years old when that happened to me. Three days before my twenty-seventh birthday. You know, it was just a nightmare. I got fired and everything. And then, like, three gray hairs sprung up on my head. (*Laughs.*)

Oh, really.

I'm, like, great. I'm out of a job. All of this stuff is going on. And then I get three gray hairs. But, anyway. (*Laughs.*) It was like life was just kicking me in the butt.

But anyway-- And I was losing the condo because I-- Oh, the (Credit Union), when I was fired-- Well, that's who I was working for. Anyway, once I was fired, then they, they fought my unemployment. They said that of course I was fired for cause, because I had participated in some activity that was against the, the company policy.

I wasn't able to get, I wasn't able to get a job. I wasn't able to get unemployment [compensation]. I wasn't able to get anything. So I wasn't able to keep my house, get my mortgage paid, because, you know, I had no funds.

. . . I-- And then by this time, I was so just beaten down that I couldn't do nothing. I was just ready to die. I was just, I would just lay there. I wouldn't get up in the morning. I just wouldn't, you know. I was so devastated. And my mom, God bless her, would not let it happen. She was determined that I was going to survive. She took over and called the mortgage company, and, you know, made arrangements and she actually paid $8,000 towards my mortgage to get me, you know, to get everything back to where I could deal with it.

. . . But all of this was the result of somebody getting this information.

So was it-- How did you find out who the person was eventually?

As it turned out, it was my cousin.

Wow.

. . . And then the fact that it turned out to be my cousin made it even worse. Because they said, "She's not doing this without your knowledge. Your whole family is in on it." Which was insulting to us because we had fought with this problem with her for years.

. . . My mom was, my mom was out to save all of us. So she was not about to throw her sister's child into the street even though most of us at the end, you know, wanted her to just get rid of her, get her out of our lives so we could live in peace. But my mom wouldn't do it and actually, looking back, I thank God that she didn't do it because my cousin was in a car accident and died so early.

And in her last, her last few years, she improved her life and she came around and she was a much better person and she regretted all of the things that she had done. She had, she stopped doing the drugs and she just became a better person.

. . . It took me ten years, because, like-- This brings me to what I was saying about the stuff on your credit report. Ten years that stuff stayed on my credit report. . . . People were not, they were not going to remove that information. Even after they found out that it was a real crime.

After hearing one or two stories like this, sensible people start paying attention. Newspapers describe a plethora of these crimes, including situations in which victims suddenly find out that identity thieves (1) have been using their young children's social security numbers for years, (2) have taken out unknown second and third mortgages on the victims' homes, and (3) have even stolen their health insurance benefits and had expensive medical treatment under victims' names. Participants have developed a number of strategies that try to minimize the possibility of anything like this happening to them, accordingly. Selectively disclosing and concealing information like one's social security number—or any of the contents of one's wallet or purse—minimizes the risk of others taking advantage of us in just these ways.

One consequence of this is that the more fully an object reveals their identity—possibly including the identities of those whom they love—the more participants believe they must protect that object. Objects that are rich in identity information and/or are key to obtaining identity information from other sources—like drivers' licenses, checkbooks, and social security cards—thus receive special mention from participants as being "private, definitely private."[5] This next participant demonstrates this principle both in what she carries with her and in what she does not. She further demonstrates that this is at least one of the underlying causes of the universal worry of losing one's entire (highly identity revealing) wallet or purse.

My private stuff of course would be the billfold and, you know, the wallet, which-- I don't carry checks anymore. A friend of mine had complete identify theft.

Right.

So I pulled those out. But then there's the credit cards and the kids' pictures, which, I would be very sad if those were gone.

Right.

And, you know, all the miscellaneous stuff. There's cards, library cards, and I was a member of the union in (Nevada) for-- My union card and, um, the money. I don't care about that.

So, money is private but you don't really care-- Is it private or public?

I guess it's private because I need it to buy things (*laugh*). But public in the sense that it's not that big-- I never have that much cash on me. I mean, the credit cards would be a drag to lose but, you know, you cut them up and call the credit card company, you know. But as far as the money, I don't care if it's taken.

Um, so it's kind of caught in that middle ground.

What about the children's pictures, those photographs of the kids?

Yeah.

So those are definitely private?

Oh, yeah. I mean, I put all of this emotion into, you know, where (Kristin) was, how old she was. We have-- We don't just carry the portraits, you know, the snapshots from the studio. We have a picture of when she was, just turned one. We went to a pumpkin patch. We have, you know, sweet little ones that we put in there. Yeah, I would be sad if those were gone 'cause I don't have a copy. You know? (*Laughing*). So, yeah, I would feel that's private.

Okay.

And it would kind creep me out if somebody took the wallet and had pictures of my kids, you know. That's a bad feeling.

In other words, the decision to no longer carry checks is a result of the same concern this woman voices while contemplating the loss of her wallet with her children's photographs inside. Because checks have too much information on them and could too easily result in identity theft, she no longer carries them. Likewise, if a stranger got his hands on the whole wallet, including the kids' photos, he would be in possession of too much information. He would have too complete a picture of our participant and the life she leads. Losing the photos themselves might be "sad." Losing them while still in her wallet turns a sad situation into a scary one—but, interestingly, one she is still willing to risk, unlike the risk posed by carrying a checkbook.

This is a classic instance of a specific privacy fear and two common responses to it. It is not her own disclosure of her wallet contents, but someone else's *expo*sure of them that makes this person worry. The fear is rooted in the knowledge that loss of control over these objects—their overaccessibility—is not only possible, but also that she and/or her loved ones would be upset, perhaps even endangered were this to happen.

This participant adjusts her behavior as a result of this knowledge, but finds herself not quite willing to go all the way. She'll forgo the convenience of having a checkbook with her. But she is unwilling to give up the photos she carries with her. Like so many of us, she continues to indulge in something that she knows increases the chance of her privacy being violated because the alternative—having no photos of her kids in her wallet—is even less acceptable.

Constant vigilance and carefully handling wallets and purses is the common outcome for people who refuse to forsake carrying such treasured items. Making choices like this is one way in which we actually increase our daily privacy workload no matter how willing we are to make the trade-off. Young girls pay long hours of attention to this kind of privacy work in order to develop the unconscious awareness of "something's not right" if they leave their purses behind, eventually turning their attention to a much fuller range of purse-handling awareness. This next participant well describes one dimension of her approach to purse protection.

In public, I have to be touching my bag at all times. I feel very, very nervous that someone's going to steal it. It's to the point of almost clutching it at all times, which other people find amusing, I think. So, like, in a restaurant, if I'm at a table, the bag's always-- I keep the strap over my one knee at all times. At the movie theater, I keep it on my lap. On the bus, I keep it on my lap. Oh! And I always have one arm through the strap because—I don't know where this came from—but I feel that it's not good enough that it's just on my lap because someone could come and, I don't know, distract me. . . . So I want to sort of, like, know that there would be a physical reaction attached if someone tried to take my bag.

Has anyone ever taken your bag or have you ever seen a purse being snatched?

None of the above, no. Nothing. I've never been a victim of any sort of petty crime like that.

If others worked this hard to guard their purses perhaps they would never be victimized in this way, either. It takes a lot of effort to do so, though, and that may be exactly why others are more negligent—and easier marks for the opportunistic crook.

INTENDED AUDIENCES: FOR WHOM IS THIS CARRIED?

In addition to the issue of control, there is another theme common to participants' responses. This concerns the audience with whom individuals expect to share the items they carry. According to the ways they describe their uses, participants' wallet and purse contents belong to four groups.

First, there are things carried strictly for the self. These include both mementoes and certain items for the body. The former includes items such as funeral cards, poems, Alcoholics Anonymous sobriety medallions, souvenir subway tokens, and some expired membership cards and licenses. The latter includes products and tools for grooming, hygiene, and personal care, as well as prescription medicine.

Second, there are things that are carried both for the self and for displaying to or using on behalf of selected others. Photos of loved ones or past events, an infant's change of clothes, knives, and an army medal carried to prove service are included here. So are some expired membership cards, one's past and present business cards, as well as other people's business cards carried to distribute on their behalf.

Third, there are items that are carried not only for the self, but also for the express purpose of interacting with institutions and their representatives. Certain business cards fall into this class of items, along with more obvious transactional items like credit cards, ATM cards, drivers' licenses, and membership cards. Typically these are displayed or handed over in order to certify access to something or someone, used on a daily basis or as infrequently as once a year or less.

Fourth and finally, there are items that are carried for the self but readily shared with others. These are usually given away, in fact, to anyone who happens to ask for them. These are items like candy, tissues, bandages, and "spare" money, especially coins.

Of course, the reason and audience for whom a given object is carried can shift—over time or suddenly—as its apparent value and utility is situationally redefined. A license or membership card carried on a daily basis for institutional interactions may expire—or simply become unused because of a change in routine or geographical location. To continue carrying it may be a sign of its shift in value to that of a memento, an autobiographic signifier of self-identity.[6] A receipt—whether a cash register tape or ticket stub—also may be highly practical initially. Yet when these items linger, they begin to function as souvenirs of the experience and/or relationship associated with them.

In addition, something that is generally thought of as private and only for the self may be made available to others, too, if they want it, like a lipstick. But the expectation is that either nobody would actually take it if a participant were to offer it and/or that if someone did take it, the participant would not want it back. Like a mint, a tampon, condom, tissue, or "spare" change, it would not be lent and returned but "shared" by giving it away. In fact, participants might routinely choose to carry such items for just this purpose, fulfilling an important aspect of her or his identity, such as "caregiver" or "urbanite."

STEPPING BACK: A MODEL OF THE SORTING

Figure 2.1 represents an attempt to make sense of the most salient dimensions of participants' responses to the wallet and purse protocol. It combines the two most important distinctions that repeatedly emerged in defining contents that are "more private" versus "more public." These dimensions are (1) whether or not something is personally meaningful to a participant, and (2) whether or not an object might cause harm to the participant or those for whom she/he is responsible if she/he lost control of it.[7] The model is built on a dichotomous approach to answering these two questions, as this is the participants' repeated response mode as they asked and answered these questions of themselves.

The intersection of these two key dimensions helps explain the relationships between the kinds of objects that are placed into the "more private" and "more public" piles. In fact, this analysis further helps us map out the classification of objects whether a participant claimed that they were distributed across one, two, or three piles. Everything in one's wallet could be called "more private," for instance. Yet some things still may be more and less private than others, distributed within internal minipiles across several of the figure's corners. In other words, the overall framing (Goffman 1974; Bateson 2000) of the wallet/purse (e.g, "Everything here is private") does not negate further internal classificatory variation (e.g., "But this is a little more private than that").

The model also helps organize the ways in which the kinds of objects and the piles in which they are placed are related to the people and purposes for whom they are carried (i.e., for the self alone versus for the self and various others). Clearly, there is a tremendous amount of relationship work going on via the uses of one's wallet and purse. As we have seen, while everything is there ostensibly for oneself, plenty of objects may also be present to support the establishment or continuation of relationships with other people and even with institutions.[8] Privacy as well as these relationships are managed by selectively sharing some things with some people under some circumstances, but not others.

Thus, this summary heuristic captures the collective flavor of what we have learned from looking at what people carry with them and how they classify it. Naturally, each participant has a unique variation on what objects might go in each corner of this four-cell model. Moreover, many participants—especially those who carry only wallets—may have only two of these cells represented in their wallet/purse contents. They may carry only objects that are (1) meaningful to them alone and pretty harmless if lost, and (2) needed for legal-bureaucratic reasons. Indeed, some people—and here we are talking about exclusively wallet carriers—carry only a single

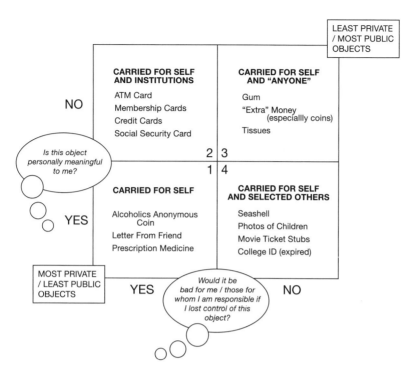

FIGURE 2.1 Sorting model for wallet and purse contents.

category of objects with them: those that are necessary for engaging in institutional transactions.

Nonetheless, our sorting model fully accommodates four cells or categories of objects. Objects in the bottom left corner (cell 1) are both personally meaningful and are believed to potentially cause harm if participants lose control of them. In the participants' minds, these items are likely to have significant implications for social status—whether stigmatizing (Goffman 1986) or glorifying (Adler and Adler 1991)—as well as obvious practical use to others. These are objects that are carried strictly for the self and this category constitutes the smallest group of objects represented in our study.[9]

Items in the top left corner of our model (cell 2) have no personal meaning to participants, yet if they lost control over these items, participants believe it could cause them harm. These things tend to have high practical value to anyone who might get their hands on them. Typically, they are used to access personal and institutional resources such as money (whether cash or discounts,) physical environments, and participants' financial-legal "identities." Thus, these are items carried in the wallet/purse for the purposes of the self and institutions. This constitutes the largest category of objects in our study.

Items classified in the top right corner (cell 3) are carried for the self and "anyone." These are the most public objects in our participants' wallets and purses. They are shared regularly with others, often because they have universal but limited use value and are quite inexpensive. Indeed, the symbolic value of sharing them outweighs the practical cost of doing so. These are objects that are neither personally meaningful nor threatening, in participants' minds, if they lose control of them. This is the one category of objects that is overwhelmingly absent for participants who carry only wallets, yet universally present for those who carry purses.

The objects represented in the bottom right corner of the model (cell 4) are those that are personally meaningful to participants, but thought to pose no harm if they are lost or inappropriately accessed by others. These are items carried for the self but also for sharing with selected others as social interactions warrant. These items have positive associations of some kind for the participants and may be used to authenticate privileged or special experiences and identities to others.

A final note about this model: the relative privateness/publicness of objects is distributed along a diagonal that starts in the bottom left corner and ends in the upper right corner. Objects that are more towards cell 1 in the bottom left-hand corner of our heuristic are the most private/least public items that our participants carry. Objects toward cell 3 in the upper right are the least private/most public. The contents of these cells—and their relationship to each other—reveal conceptualizations of private and public that are completely consistent with individuals' definitions of these terms as presented in chapter 1.

The objects in cells 2 and 4 (the upper left and lower right quadrants) follow the same logic, of course. However, these are both hybrid categories, being more private in some respects and more public in others. This is precisely why different participants appear to contradict or cancel out each other in how they define the objects found in these cells. They emphasize more of one side than the other, because the hybridity of the object allows them to do so. Two people may place the same hybrid objects in opposing cells, therefore, relegate them to a third "semi" pile, or leave them unclassified altogether, a recognition of a conundrum with no immediate answer. The following section focuses on some fine examples of this.

MONEY, CREDIT CARDS, AND BUSINESS CARDS

Money, credit cards, and business cards are among some of the most fascinating "hybrid" wallet/purse contents. They provide an opportunity for a closer look at the many qualifiers that can push a particular variation on a certain kind of object into one pile while another variation is placed in the opposite category. For instance, while the *amount* of money one carries may be deemed highly protected—private information, indeed—the currency itself may be classified as unquestionably public. In addition, the "platinum" status of a credit card may mean that this object occupies quite a different analytical space than does a "regular" credit card (Nippert-Eng 1996, 63–64). And a handwritten home phone number on the back of a business card may quickly put that in a different cell from cards that lack this additional information. The next section explores these kinds of qualifiers, identifying some of the key attributes that affect the ultimate framing or classification of these objects.

MONEY

Not surprisingly, nearly all participants carry money in their wallets and purses. In terms of exchange value, money sets the standard. Accordingly, one might predict that the money we carry with us would be among our most private of possessions. After all, our "hard-earned cash" is not something to be shared indiscriminately. It is something that, generally speaking, we carry strictly for personal use. However, it turns out that for our participants, money actually falls into that gray classificatory area somewhere between the public and private realms. It is characterized as "more public" by participants nearly as often as it is declared to be "more private." Here's why.

To begin with, money is in our possession only temporarily. One might think of one's money as "private, for the fact that I am using it and I need it." Yet participants generally are "not that attached to it."[10]

Oh, yeah, that, my cash. I forgot. That's kind of a different tune. It could go in public or private. It goes in private because it's yours and you're going to spend it on your own things. But when you spend it, you gotta give it away, so--

Money exists to be exchanged; it circulates. As we engage in everyday transactions, it passes through our hands and into the hands of others. As another participant puts it,

[T]he cash, I thought of as "public" because it's-- Cash is so fungible. It's mine to the extent that it's in my possession, but there's nothing "mine" about it.

In addition, money is issued by the State, and technically "it belongs to the government." It might be representative of our personal spending potential and we might use it for private purchases, but at the same time, it very much belongs in the public realm. As one individual astutely points out, the ambiguous status of money is clearly asserted on every American dollar bill:

What does it say on it? "Public and private tender"? I don't even know if it says-- "Legal tender for all debts, public and private." So money goes in both realms.

Moreover, most of what money enables us to do—many of the transactions in which we participate and during which we exchange money—occurs in what we would consider the public realm. Much of our daily routines take place out in public: buying coffee or a newspaper, paying bus fare, feeding parking meters. When we "go shopping," we go out and into the public world; money is often the buffer for our interactions there.

Numerous other everyday errands take place in and through the public world, too, even when they involve transferable currency in forms other than dollar bills and coins (e.g., postage stamps, prepaid phone cards, public transit tokens or cards). These are things that are as good as money and that could be used by anyone who got hold of them. Interestingly enough, they are more often characterized by participants as public than private. Perhaps this is because, even more so than money, these forms of currency are associated with the State and with public services.

The status of money is further complicated because some of the cash we carry with us, especially if it is stored outside the wallet, may be considered "extra" or "spare" money. It is clearly categorized as public for that reason. As she digs to the bottom of her purse, one participant finds:

. . . a coupon for Reynolds Wrap, 'cause I just went to the store. That's public. Some loose change that should be in my wallet. That's private. It's-- Actually, if it's loose, I'd consider it public.

Perhaps this is because, wherever we keep it, a subset of our cash-on-hand may be carried with the express intent of giving it away—to anyone, anywhere. Methodically emptying her purse, another participant puts it this way:

Let's see, I have my extra set of, my extra car key, and then change, and that's it.

So is change and the bills, are they both—?

Change is-- Change is kind of public because—

Change is public?

I'll give change away in a minute.

This is just one of a number of "earmarking" (Zelizer 1995) practices we saw, as people classified their money into different categories. Participants regularly make distinctions between bills and coins, for instance, often placing their paper money in the "more private" pile but their change in the "more public" one. Coins seem to evoke disposability, as in the phrase "spare change." Coins are trifles to our largely well-off participants. They are used to round off charges and payments, offered for the taking, and left behind at cash registers. For such individuals, "borrowed" coins need never be repaid. They are given to children as playful payment or trifling rewards. A coin spotted on the ground is just as likely to be ignored—or pointed out to a child—as it is to be picked up. Some dislike the inconvenience of carrying them, emptying pockets of them daily, and are happy to be rid of them whenever possible.[11]

Certain coins, however—like special bills—may be marked by more personal associations. We may hold them as souvenirs, even storing them with our expendable change, but with no intention of passing them on. One participant explains while enumerating his list of "private" wallet contents:

Um, change, a Canadian two-dollar Loonie piece, two-dollar bill, business card, phone card, company credit card stub, slip for a camera; got my credit card, more business cards, um, movie pass, personal credit card, library card, driver's license, and ATM card. I guess-- The Loonie is probably not transactional. We've had to take a lot of our vacations in Canada, so I'm just going to keep it there. I suppose it is different from the other objects in being nontransactional and being—and to the extent that it is noncommodified, has a noncommodified value—that, um, it is personal.

Even some paper money may be considered "extra," carried in order to be given away and therefore "more public." Separated from the "serious" or "significant" money, we may keep a small stash of "mad money" and/or "emergency cash," "just in case." A particularly independent eighty-year-old who uses a cane to walk physically segregates stashes of "private" and "public" cash in her purse this way.

Oh, that's public. And so are the loose dollar bills that I carry for tips. People keep telling me, "Oh, your money is coming out of your purse. Watch out!" I carry two or three [one-] dollar bills so I have them handy. Don't have to open up, don't have to unzip the purse.

. . . I don't carry a wallet now very often because they are, you know, it's another couple of ounces and I try to keep the weight [down]. Like, I have an envelope in which I have cash and I have-- I usually carry about $70 in that, including a little change with pennies so I don't get weighted down with more pennies. And in another envelope is a blank check and a $20 bill and $1 bill.

Okay. And so why $21?

Well, just because in case I need something big-- In case someone swipes the other cash envelope from me, say-- And I've still got enough with the $20 to take a cab somewhere and I've got a dollar in case I just need to tip somebody something or need something very small. And a blank check in case I've forgotten to bring one for someone that I will need a check for or in case something comes up.

The single most salient factor in determining whether money is more private or more public is the amount of money in question. Coins may be given away out in public and associated with it for that reason. There is another reason why smaller amounts of money are seen as a bit more public, though, also alluded to in this last reflection. Participants live with the fact that whatever money they carry on them might be lost or stolen. For urbanites, this is a reality. As a rule, they carry very little cash with them because of this, and then associate such small amounts with their engagement in the public realm. Fear of loss or theft is why a number of people make it a policy to "never have that much cash on me" and, for some, to think of everything they carry as more public—and loseable.

I only bring with me just enough money that I would need for the day anyhow. So if anybody did pick up my briefcase and go off with it, I wouldn't really lose all that much. I mean, I'd be pissed off, but it wouldn't be the end of the world.

In contrast to the publicness of the currency they physically carry on them, however—the bills and coins themselves—interview participants overwhelmingly indicate that *information* about the amount of money they have is another matter. "How much I have is private," as one person put it. "Other people" just "don't need to know how much I have with me." In fact, knowledge of "how much money I have"—or, more accurately, the knowledge or impression that one might have a significantly large quantity of money—is understood to be a potential liability.[12] The following participant not only reflects on this, but also on the situatedness of how much money it takes for it to be "significant" and, therefore, private—and in need of protection.

So, at what point does that [the amount of money you have in your wallet] become private?

Maybe when it reaches a point-- When it reaches an amount that would make me feel uncomfortable if someone saw. Where I'd feel maybe threatened if this was just laying out. So-- Gosh. I think maybe a five-dollar bill, I wouldn't care. But it also depends on the circumstance or where I am. You know, obviously, if I were in-- I don't know, in (Inglewood) and I had a five-dollar bill, I would feel more uncomfortable than if I were in Beverly Hills or something. But right now, I think I have about three hundred bucks, so definitely private. I wouldn't want anyone to see that.

This principle applies for the total amount of money that is available to people as well as whatever they carry on them. For the individuals in this study, what they have in their pocket is not the sum total of their resources. Thus, information on either of these amounts—what's in their pockets and what's in the bank—is in need of protection even more than any cash itself might be.

A variety of transactional artifacts in our wallets and purses may give away too much information about how much money we have—about how much we have just withdrawn from or have left in our bank accounts. Consider ATM receipts. These are most often considered private by participants who have taken a moment to reflect upon their status because sometimes "they have the account balance on them." While she classified the money she has withdrawn as public, for instance, one participant decides that her ATM withdrawal receipt is a different matter altogether.

I'll make the withdrawal [slip] "private." So somebody-- If I drop it when I leave the store, they don't see that I got four hundred bucks on me and mug me on the way out.

To the extent that money says something about us, then, it is considered "more private." The amount of money that we carry is private, as is our net worth. And the few participants who had any sort of financial records with them in their wallets or purses—including check stubs and bank statements—consistently characterize those documents as "more private."

This is part of an overarching theme when it comes to the private side of money, in which the informational or status value of money is considered the most important—and therefore most private—of its dimensions.

It's the nature of money as a physical object—the coins and bills we carry—that is less clear cut. Thus, it is primarily as an object—as opposed to information about that object—that money is a hybrid. This dimension of money is what subsequently produces the classificatory quandary expressed by so many participants.

CREDIT CARDS

For many people, credit cards, rather than cash, represent the chief physical means by which they interface with the modern economic system. Like cash, the nature of credit cards has both a physical and an informational side. And, like cash, this also places credit cards into a gray area—hybrids of the public and the private.

One participant, for instance, is quite consistent with others in describing the currency she carries as "more public":

[M]oney is nondescript and has nothing specific to do with me; and the [postage] stamps, the same way. You only use them to put them on things that are leaving you, so, you know. Um, they could be anybody's. You couldn't identify them as mine.

Yet the same participant characterizes her credit and debit cards as "private":

because they have to do with money. *My* money, in specific, specifically. Because people can get access-- You know, you hear about one little bit of information leading to another bit of information. People's identities being stolen and stuff like that. And they are enough of a hassle anyway that, just to replace them and go through all that phone calling and stuff when they are lost or stolen is something.

With a telephone call, stroke of a keyboard, or swipe through a machine, credit cards provide anyone with direct access to our financial resources and credit-worthiness, our trustworthiness. As such, they provide access to critical parts of our identity. Loss of control over access to our credit cards is a general cause for concern among participants. More often than not, the cards are characterized as "more private than public because they are things that I do not want the general public to have access to."

Yet, like cash, credit cards—and the information on them—are part of our public identities as well. As a result, their status is ambiguous. This participant put it well:

I've got all my credit cards, which-- That's a really weird thing because they're public because I use them in public and I give the number out to other people. But my number on it is kind of private. You don't want to just give that to anybody. I would say it was in the middle, maybe a little more public than private.

So while credit cards are strictly for our "own personal use," we expect others will see them and know that we have them with us. In this sense, just like money, credit cards as objects may be more public than the information associated with them.

Credit card companies provide a certain short-term buffer against the risks of credit card loss. We know that we can call up and cancel our line of credit should we lose our card or have it taken from us. Some participants are less concerned with the immediate financial and convenience implications of losing control of their credit cards, though, than they are with the longer-term implications for their financial reputations. This long-term threat is what makes credit cards especially private for some people.

It's potential for theft, potential for loss. I've got to have those and I work hard to have that credit rating where it is and we just cannot let those go. Even though I know legally I'm protected in some amount, those [cards] are taken care of very, very well.

Two of the main reasons why people fear identity theft are intimated here. First, as explained by the woman whose cousin stole her identity, financial reputations are difficult to create and difficult to reclaim if something goes wrong. But even more significant is another fact also introduced in her story. There has been an explosive increase in cases where miscreants steal and use just the information embossed on our credit cards, not the cards themselves. All of this can happen without any physical evidence that a theft or reputational damage has occurred until months later.[13] We may find out long after the fact that criminals not only purchased items using our card numbers, for instance, but that they also used them to open additional, unknown, and unimagined accounts in our names.

In some cases, protecting our credit cards may mean even more than protecting just our own resources and financial reputations. It also may mean protecting those of other members of our family.

One of these credit cards, I especially feel like I have to protect because it's a credit card that everyone in my family has the same card, so if I lose it or it gets stolen, everyone has to get a new card.

In fact, while our credit cards may need to be protected for their role in representing our financial reputations in institutional interactions, they may also take on more personal associations. Carrying them, showing them, being able to use them may be thought of as a significant symbol of one's identity.

I have my Platinum Master Card, which is totally clear. I owe nothing. I mean, we are out of debt. I worked really hard the last three months because we were almost $20,000 in debt in cards and shit and I just said-- I made a commitment to [my wife]. I said, I don't know how I'm going to do this, but I'm going to make enough money to get us out of debt. So I literally bought a car in the last few months. But we're clear. I mean, I've paid off our car. It's a good feeling. So we can get a more expensive car, that reminds me (*chuckles*).

Thus a credit card is an object that may be carried for display as much as for its value as a transactional instrument. This is also demonstrated by this proud mother of three. Here, the association of fond memories and family relationships with her personalized credit card also transforms the role it plays in everyday interactions.

Here's one that you might be interested in. It's a credit card, and you know how some credit cards-- I don't even know if they do that anymore. Companies, for security purposes, you could have your picture put on the credit card so that they could identify you. Well, instead of my picture, my husband went and got a picture of my kids put on the credit card, which is, I think, great. But it's, again, not only a picture of my kids but of a wonderful time. We were camping. And so I could see my kids, but also it reminds me of a wonderful time together with them. And also, then-- So you're paying for something with a credit card and people look at this and say, "Oh, wow, that's really cool. Are those your kids?"

This customized credit card does a wonderful job helping its owner walk the line between the desire for privacy and the desire for publicity, then. The key is the extent to which she feels in control of her ability to have both or neither, selectively, as she wishes.

Similar nuanced distinctions appear between instrumentality and personal meaning in the ways business cards are assigned to the "more private" or "more public" categories. Not surprisingly, business cards are among the wallet contents most frequently categorized as public. Even participants who declare their entire wallets to be private may find an exception in the business cards they carry, because:

Well, it's something that I specifically give to others and—including strangers, especially strangers. . . . [Also] there's nothing on that card that they couldn't look up either in the (company) directory or online on the (company) Web site and get. So I don't feel that's private.

Participants carry their own business cards—as well as others'—expressly for the purposes of publicity. The cards are used to endorse professional services and to extend business networks. One participant, who carries two wallets—one in each front pocket of his pants—dedicates the second exclusively to business cards for just this reason.

Here's one for a dog kennel—a cheap dog kennel. Here's one of a surgeon. Here's one of a bakery we go to sometimes. Mexican restaurant we go to. Healthy Food restaurant. Been there? Over in Bridgeport. Lithuanian on Halsted at about 33rd Street. John's Delicatessen: homemade sausage. That's over on West 47th Street, 4145. Pastry shop. Another bakery. This is the (Suki)—Japanese fine cuisine. Sometimes, so I can, so I know where it is. If somebody's talking about it, "What's a good Japanese restaurant?" I can pull this out. Vivo Fiesta is a nice Filipino restaurant on the North Side. Try that sometime.

Some respondents note exceptions to the general rule that business cards are "handed out to anybody." For instance, one respondent categorized as public a business card from his son (a doctor) because "I can't imagine any, any harm it would do to him if somebody had his business card." He had different thoughts about a second card for his son:

I think one of his has his pager or cell phone number on it. I wouldn't want to give that to anybody that I couldn't trust wouldn't misuse it. But just a regular business card that he hands out to anybody— that's already in the public domain, I would think, and not to be kept a secret.

This is a fine case of a common logic underlying the gifting of privacy to others. Restricting others' access to information that his son might wish to keep private not only protects the information, but also protects his son—and this father's relationship to him.

Business cards represent all kinds of relationships via the people they represent and even the circumstances under which individuals met. Overall, and regardless of why each one is kept, these cards form a collection of personal contacts. They are a sort of portable, unbound, and often badly organized rolodex. Each supports a specific relationship to a person, place, or event, no matter how dormant or active it is at a given time.

Participants may feel that a single business card could reveal too much personal information about them. But taken altogether, a *collection* of cards—the entire rolodex—could be even more revealing. If seen as a cohesive collection, one's business cards may be "more private" for this reason as well.

A pregnant woman who is carrying a pile of business cards from her midwife and from her other prenatal care providers, for instance, considers those to be "pretty private in some ways, because somebody could look through here and kind of figure out who I've been seeing." Another participant moved her doctors' business cards from her "more public" pile into a third, "semi-private" pile of wallet contents, too:

My eye doctor's card, my doctor's card-- And you know what? Actually, I would share this information if anybody was looking for a doctor or an eye doctor. I would share this with them. But when I think about it, then everybody knows who your doctors are. So that might move over here, too, to the semi-private thing. Because you don't want it, maybe don't want everybody to know that you're seeing a child psychologist.

Thus, the theme of selectivity continues to run through business card disclosures, too.

Finally, the business cards we carry may have intensely personal meanings for us. One elderly gentleman carries a business card from his former daughter-in-law now that his son has died. Deeply meaningful cards may be more aspirational, as well, or carried to help us to adjust to different kinds of life transitions.

My old business card's just kind of weird. It's almost like I value that one because I had these big, high hopes of coming here and being able to work and do these things part time while I went to school. And everyone knows that's not possible. And it's like I hung onto this one thing 'cause it was my phone number, and I have a hard time remembering numbers—even my own phone number—for months and months and months, and it was like my welcome-to-the-city-key kind of thing. This is it. This is how I survive in the city. For some reason, I think that that's why it's still here, because I can't even read our phone number on there very well.

Indeed, a mapping of the business cards we carry with us might tell us much about our identities over time: who we are, who we've been, and who we wish to become. Even if we carry very few—if any—of them with us, they can be telling features of our life journeys. Along with the rest of our wallet and purse contents, they function as material props in the everyday management of our much longer-term identity, too.

STRUCTURAL REASONS FOR IDENTITY DISCLOSURE AND CONCEALMENT

The wallets and purses of our participants are tool kits whose contents are used regularly and in very precise ways to facilitate the strategic disclosure and concealment of identity. They help their owners place, maintain, and sometimes challenge the line between what others do and do not know about them. They can play a critical role in managing the line between those aspects of identity that people choose to suppress and those they choose to affirm (Nippert-Eng 1996, 7, 55–60).

Identity is one of a number of concepts and practices the instantiation or achievement of which can be located along the private-public continuum. At one extreme, identity is "completely inaccessible" to others and to self. Here lies the condition of anonymity as well as an assortment of modern physical, psychological, spiritual, and philosophical crises about not knowing "who I am." At the other extreme, identity is completely accessible to self and others. This is the condition of being "fully identified"—completely known, as it were, "inside and out." Various degrees of partial identification fall in between these points—where identity is neither fully disclosed to nor fully concealed from anyone. Here is the territory of Simmel and Goffman, for sure, and where we most readily recognize the importance of concealing and disclosing as key components of identity management.[14]

Wallets and purses are filled with objects that are used in more and less conscious ways to support this activity. They help participants get through the range of daily tasks that are fundamentally about controlling identity, especially in the senses that Goffman wrote about (1959, 1966, 1982, 1986).[15] In other words, as identity *kits*, wallets and purses aid participants in controlling how much other people know about them in any given situation by allowing them to selectively reveal only the aspects of their identity that they believe others should or need to know.

Glaser and Strauss's (1964, 678) work on awareness contexts[16] endeavored to connect "the microscopic analysis of interaction" within a given awareness context to "the larger social structures in which it occurs." Similarly, we turn our attention now to the structural conditions that make it necessary to do this kind of private-public boundary (or identity) work today. While keeping one foot firmly grounded in the artifacts of participants' material culture, our analysis of what is in participants' wallets and purses and what participants say about them now focuses on the current political-legal-economic (i.e., institutional) situation. These are the key factors that constrain individuals' identity management on a daily basis, given today's economy of strangers.

TRUST AND REPUTATION IN AN ECONOMY OF STRANGERS

At a purely practical level, the primary function of wallets and purses has been to serve as containers for the currency that allows individuals to participate in a mediated exchange economy. They hold money. We have already seen that the nature of money—and its symbolic place in one's wallet—is not something to be taken for granted. Here, we see that the role of money in purchase transactions—and thus, a wallet—also warrants closer examination.[17]

Transferable currency (cash) is fading as the dominant form of transactional media in the U.S. At the same time, financial transactions more commonly occur between people who do not know one another. As a result of these two factors, wallets now must function as carriers of what Nock (1993) has called our "portable reputations." They help to establish an atmosphere of sufficient trust between parties so that cash-free transactions may take place between them.

Trust is a critical condition for even the most mundane of daily activities, including financial transactions. Basic trust provides us with a necessary sense of security (however illusory) that frees us from potentially paralyzing anxieties. Trust lets us "get on with the affairs of day-to-day life" (Giddens 1991, 40). Transactions in the U.S., for instance, are embedded in large, complex systems that we generally trust to bracket the potential risks and dangers inherent in any face-to-face financial exchange.[18]

As vendors, we require some assurance that our customers are "good for it"—that they are not deceiving us in their manner or medium of payment. If they are not paying us now in cash, we want to know that they (or their creditors) will pay us in full at a later date. Even when relatively small denominations of cash are involved in a financial transaction, our trustworthiness as legitimate, paying customers may be questioned. With only minor offense, for instance, a shop keeper may examine and test our twenty-dollar bill to determine whether or not it is counterfeit. In the other direction, and with the same lack of offense, customers examine their receipts and re-count their change. As purchasers, we need to feel secure in the perception that we will not be cheated, especially by being overcharged.

In small, established communities, trust of others hinges on individuals' reputations. Reputation—the collective perception of an individual's character (Nock 1993; Fine 2001; Schwartz 1987; Gamson 1994; Sennett 1992)—is shaped through repeated personal interactions and reports of those (real or alleged) interactions, the accumulated history of that person's dealings with other members of the group. A longtime neighbor can be trusted because we believe we know his character, his family, his past indiscretions and achievements and where he lives. In this sense, one's reputation is one's public identity, established under the scrutiny of family and community and affixed to the individual who remains within that community.

For the sake of transactions, the twenty-first-century American urbanite rarely has such a public reputation. It is unlikely that store clerks from whom our participants make many of their purchases know much at all about their families or personal histories.[19] In contemporary, complex societies—in what we term an "economy of strangers"—urban dwellers must regularly interact and conduct transactions with people whose reputations are wholly unknown to them. They cannot rely on personal relations between individual parties engaged in transacting business to establish the required condition of mutual trust.

Instead, our society "outsources" the establishment and maintenance of reputation (including the tasks of gathering the information necessary to build a reputation) to third-party agents (Shapiro 1987). These "institutions of surveillance" (Giddens 1990, 1991) then vouch for personal trustworthiness.[20] Even in smaller communities where people on either side of the retail counter are likely to know one another, these same institutional structures may demand of all parties that they behave as if they did not know each other. Even here, standard transactional practices and assessments of reputation may be enforced whenever familiar parties "conduct business."

In his historical study of emancipated young adults, Steven Nock (1993) argues that these impersonal, institutional methods of surveillance have developed in response to a variety of modern demographic shifts. These include higher divorce rates, longer life expectancies, growth and diversification of urban populations, a decline in the influence of the church, and an increasingly mobile population. At the same time, we have experienced a transition in American familial living arrangements. During the second half of the twentieth century, Nock notes, a sharp increase in the number of Americans living independently of family for significant periods of their lives has corresponded with a rise in the rates at which institutional credentials have been issued. These credentials, such as credit cards, identification cards, drivers' licenses, and educational degrees, serve as "portable reputations" for those without access to more traditional means of establishing their trustworthiness.

These are precisely the kinds of credentials whose signifiers our participants carry with them in their wallets and purses. These tools allow them to reveal their identities to strangers and to publicize (or allow access to) their reputations. In fact, they are *required* to carry such things and present them on demand to institutional representatives—by State systems regulating qualified drivers, by credit agencies and associated financial systems that monitor credit-worthiness, and by myriad other institutional systems for which our identities as contributors and authorized members must be confirmed.

In order to function in an economy of strangers, then, we are required to carry with us the means through which we can publicize who we are. This individual "burden of publicity" is one to which our participants have become well accustomed. As Nock argues, the need to prove who we are is the necessary cost of a contemporary American lifestyle. Unencumbered by our personal histories or by tradition, untethered by the bonds of family and community, instantly and incessantly portable, the modern American lives largely as a stranger, among strangers—at least part of the time—with all the advantages and disadvantages that entails.

WALLETS AND PURSES: A FLEXIBLE SOLUTION TO THE TWIN BURDENS OF PRIVACY AND PUBLICITY

The need to make oneself known on a daily basis, particularly in order to accomplish financial transactions, does not appear to be an undue burden for the participants in this study. No participant complained about needing to carry identification cards,[21] or of a system that demands independent proof of one's identity. Rather, it is the individual "burden of privacy"—the work needed to protect one's full or even partial anonymity—that is the focus of their attention and concern.

Wallets and purses afford remarkable flexibility in managing information as participants see fit. If they think that no one needs to know who they are or anything else about them, wallets can stay in pants pockets or purses, firmly closed and monitored for safekeeping. However, should participants want to purchase something, convince the seller to let them have it, and still protect their identity as much as possible, reaching into one's wallet for cash is the best choice of tender. Credit card exchanges protect personal identity less—especially if the card displays a "precious metal" reference indicating credit limit, a logo associating the account with a college, charitable organization, or retail corporation, or a personal or family photo. And finally, transactions that involve writing a check (typically preprinted with all kinds of identifying material) are even more revealing, especially when their use also requires the display and transfer of information from a driver's license or other photo ID.

For a variety of reasons—and especially when living among strangers—Americans cherish and are willing to defend their anonymity.[22] In these circumstances, they constantly weigh the risks of identity disclosure against the benefits of being able to function easily within the systems of an information-driven economy. While customary pleasantries may be willingly exchanged during the course of a purchase transaction, the safest, most risk-averse interaction is commonly perceived as one in which no identifying information is disclosed.

Yet often at least partial disclosure of identity is viewed as necessary in order to get through the day with the least amount of trouble. This is precisely the sort of commonly accepted tradeoff inherent, for instance, in the decision to accept the convenience of tollbooth "EZ Pass" technology in exchange for allowing one's comings and goings to be tracked via the same payment system. So is the decision many people make to input credit card and other information over computer Web sites, where the ease of shopping from a chair at home outweighs the risks they believe they run by not being able to see where that information actually ends up.

Compared to these kinds of interactions, participants generally feel more in control of their identities in face-to-face encounters. They feel better able to maintain a context of limited awareness by letting others know only as much about them as they feel they need to know.[23] In this sense, as one participant put it, protecting one's privacy means

keeping things about my life that I want to keep to myself, or to people who have a specific reason to know them for a good reason that I think is a good reason. Not giving people information that they don't need just for the sake of giving them information.

Unfortunately, the current number of unseen interactions in their lives has left participants perceiving a change in their abilities to control the disclosure of their identities. The digital technologies and systems with which we interface as citizens and customers are repeated sources of anxiety.[24] The sheer "amount of information about individuals that can be accessed by someone who's never had any contact with them" is a distinct source of alarm. These information systems are the direct cause of the sense that traditionally "private" information has now escaped individuals' control.

First, participants question how well secured their identifying information might be in such interactions. As identifying information is digitally encoded and transferred (or, in other situations, as it is spoken into the telephone, keyboarded into the Web page form, or sent along in an email message), people are aware that it might very well escape their immediate, physical control and protection. Second, once it is "out there," participants worry that one fact may be connected with others, because "you hear about one little bit of information leading to another bit of information." This may result from the concerted efforts of an unknown stranger—a hacker, say—or by way of a corporate-marketing or federal-agency-sponsored effort.

The end result is that participants fear the unseen and uncontrolled compilation of a more complete image of who they are, which is, as one person put it, "assembled in order to create a profile . . . for which the individual has not given authorization." The accumulation of isolated bits of information that they might have revealed with confidence for separate reasons in specific interpersonal interactions can, they suspect, lead to their identities being more fully known than they had intended.[25] As we have seen, the potential consequences of losing control over any "private" information—digitized or otherwise—can be quite severe. This is precisely why participants spend so much time trying to strike a good balance between what they do and do not allow others to know about them.

THE REFLEXIVE PROJECT OF THE (LATE MODERN) SELF

Participants pay attention to managing aspects of their identity not just because they fear that bad people and corporations might use this information in undesirable ways. The controlled concealment and disclosure of identity are processes that we direct toward ourselves as well as others. As Mary Chayko (2008, 31) puts it,

> As individuals and as groups, we are prone to constructing narratives for our lives; we like to view past events and project the future as episodes in

an overarching story. To bring order to seemingly unconnected series of events, to bring structure to our lives, we construct tales: of glory, of defeat, of progress, of togetherness.

Certain events, ritualized in American culture, provide us with opportunities to intentionally reflect upon and account for our own lives. They ask us to author, as it were, selectively edited autobiographies that present a certain image of how we think about ourselves and how we wish others to see us. High school reunions, first dates, job interviews, and professional conventions are among these "autobiographical occasions" (Zussman 1996; Vinitzky-Seroussi 1998).

Our wallet and purse contents certainly function as ideal props for such auspicious occasions. In their everyday use by participants we find the autobiographical occasion writ small. This is evidenced in everything from the roles wallets and purses play in daily purchases to the periodically necessary reorganization of their contents and even the flirtatious tour that the object of one's affections might take through them.[26]

Through what they choose to carry and not carry with them, participants support specific narratives of the self.[27] These objects—like the objects people put in their houses (Csikszentmihalyi and Rochberg-Halton 1981) and workplaces (Nippert-Eng 1996)—help their carriers tell stories about themselves to themselves and to others. Through their wallet and purse contents participants offer an account of who they have been, who they are, who they would like to be, and where their senses of self are more firmly—and fragilely—located.

This second function of wallet and purse contents has less to do with the direct political/legal/economic demands of everyday life and more with the widespread, social-psychological outcomes of these kinds of macrolevel, structuring dimensions of society. If "our status is backed by the solid buildings of the world, while our sense of personal identity often resides in the cracks" (Schwartz 1968, 752), wallets and purses are just these kinds of interstitial cracks. They are repositories of artifacts that reinforce both our more public and more private selves. They are filled with objects that are expressly for public interactions and frequently used to assert social membership and status. But they also are filled with things that are there exclusively for more private use, especially helpful in achieving a fuller sense of self. Accordingly, in this discussion we turn to those items that are carried more as mementos or souvenirs—reminders of other people, other times in one's life, and/or important aspects of self—whether or not they have obvious, practical, and transactional value as well.

In order to examine how these objects also may be used to prop up particular aspects of identity, consider the simple act of carrying a wallet or a purse with a wallet inside it. In the United States, a woman typically carries her wallet inside a purse; a man does not.[28] A man carries his wallet in a pocket, usually in his pants. Accordingly, a purse-toting woman or a purseless man, or a woman or a man extracting their wallets from the different places they are carried—all engage in recognizably gendered behaviors. A man extracting his wallet from a purse or a woman pulling a wallet out of her pocket may make this point even more clearly.

Moreover, as West and Zimmerman (1987) argue with regard to any gendered interaction, the wallet extractor is not only doing gender for her- or himself; she or he is also doing it for those who might observe them. The purse, the pocket, the wallet, and the systems and choreographies designed around them are visible symbols of an important component of the carrier's self-identity—her or his relative degree of femininity/masculinity. In this way, wallets and purses immediately disclose and support gender identity to their carriers and anyone who is watching.

In fact, various types of purses and wallets probably could be laid out along a continuum of more and less visibly feminine/masculine types, identifiable symbols of the different social types who typically possess them.[29] Yet it is not simply the styles of these items and the visible roles they play in daily transactions that reinforce gender identities. Their contents do this as well.

The choice to carry a wallet only, for instance, means that the tools it contains are likely to be more self-centered than wallet-purse combinations. Some wallet-only respondents, for instance, carried items such as business and insurance cards, grocery store loyalty cards, or physicians' phone numbers to facilitate carriers' roles as a parent or spouse. But this was largely the extent of wallet-only peoples' other-orientations in terms of the inventories carried with them.

Participants' purses, on the other hand, contained a retinue of objects that were there precisely in order to take care of others.[30] There is a publicness to these contents, an intention to share them with others that is missing from the contents of many wallets. Indeed, non-purse-carrying individuals frequently ask purse carriers if they will either carry something for them in the purse or if they can borrow or have something that is already in there. The orientation toward others, the nurturing of others, the worldview of building and maintaining relationships that is part and parcel of a "feminine" self is thus clearly manifested in the purse.[31]

The personal identity support work of wallets and purses doesn't end with the work of gender, of course. Myriad other objects support the active, daily construction of a specific self, many of which are disclosed to others on a selective basis. These objects link our participants' past, present, and perhaps future notions of who they are, constraining and supporting rich, cohesive narratives of the self.

While explaining his "more private" pile, for instance, this participant offers an example of one such wallet artifact that links him to his past.

My driver's license, my social security card's on the private pile, though I don't know why.

... There's only one thing that makes this at all interesting and private, and that's my signature from when I was probably nine years old.

Right.

And so I kinda like the object. It's not the number 'cause this number is on 800 million things. It's more-- You know. It's a trinket, I guess.

The card continues to serve some function as an institutionally required means of identification. It has taken on an additional role now, though, as an identity prop bridging his nine-year-old self and the person he is now. Note how it also serves as a prop for his conversation with the interviewer, as he tells this part of his story.

Even the exact *ways* in which we carry things can be private and important to narratives of the self.

I mean, actually, my dad always taught me to know exactly how much money is in your wallet and keep it organized and to arrange it in a certain way. He had this very kind of interesting thing about keeping your money in certain ways that he kind of ingrained into me and I do the exact same thing. So that's very private, actually, for me.[32]

Note that no one who looked in this man's wallet could possibly know this. This is not an activity engaged in for others. Even if someone else were to see his carefully lined up money, they would be unlikely to guess its significance—unless this participant chose to disclose it. These objects are carried this way as a silent, ever-present habit now, but they are also a reminder to himself of his father and their relationship.[33]

Photographs are perhaps the most obvious autobiographical props that people carry in their wallets. They work the same way that Csikszentmihalyi and Rochberg-Halton (1981, 69) argue that domestic photographs do: "provid[ing] an identity, a context of belongingness" to their holders. Many of the photographs we carry are "wallet-size" ones that represent (and thus help reinforce the significance of) transitional moments in the carrier's identity formation and solidification. Pictures of very young children reinforce a new role as parent, aunt, uncle, grandparent, or godparent. High school graduation and wedding photos reinforce the passage into a new stage of the life course, new roles, and a new way of conceiving of and acting out relationships to family. Similarly, photos of new homes, new cars, or an expensive, highly adventurous, or successful family vacation may all indicate new social statuses and interactional (identity) success.

The value of a photo as an identity prop may well extend beyond its personal use as a private memento, too. Photos are frequently carried for the express purpose of display—to be shown to others and to elicit conversations that further support the carrier in reinforcing some aspect of his or her identity (Nippert-Eng 1996). Countless other objects can fulfill this same function, though, as seen here.

I have a medal or a medallion that comes from the military. It's given to me by a high-ranking dignitary. I have a memento of the unit that I was operating with as well as the soldiers [who served in it]. And it's a tradition if you get these things and if anything happens, where you meet old guys from the unit—veterans or whatever—and you don't have that on you, it's traditional that you go out and buy them a drink.

(Laughing.)

So you'd better keep it on you at all times.

So pretty much everybody gets one for service and everybody keeps it?

Um, yes, but not everyone automatically gets it. It's an honor to get it 'cause it's given to you by a, usually a colonel, or general, in the service.

It's not just-- It's just a token to remind you of your service and the unit that you were affiliated with. And somewhat of a fraternity type of thing 'cause like I said before, you're fined without it. You gotta buy.

How often does that happen that you run into somebody?

Quite often.

As this story suggests, the absence of these sorts of autobiographically loaded objects may have as much meaning as their presence. What *does* it mean when we discover that someone's identity kit is relatively bereft of things that are expressly carried for personal or sentimental reasons? A number of participants would fall into this category, carrying with them only objects that are absolutely, practically necessary for engaging in institutional transactions. This makes for skinny wallets and light purses, relatively speaking, but because this is not "normal," it also can cause comment by interested observers.

One reason that people may not carry personally meaningful items with them is that thoughts and memories, without the support of physical props, are enough for these individuals. As this next person put it, he simply doesn't need photographic reinforcement of his memories, especially of one that is particularly sad.

So that's basically all that's in there. I don't have any pictures [in my wallet]. And many people have commented on that. And actually people have made the comments, too, like, "You're trying to pretend that you don't have a wife." You know, really weird stuff. Odd reactions. "No pictures of your family. Isn't that kind of cold?" And, you know, several people--

The whole object constancy thing-- I got passed, you know? I know they exist and I don't-- It's kind of odd. Actually, my mother gave me a-- The guy that I mentioned earlier—the twenty-year-old, twenty-one-year-old kid [a friend who killed himself]. [She] gave me a [large] picture of him. Also, a picture, like, the size for a wallet. It was almost like a hint, like, I could carry it around with me. I just find that stuff very bizarre, you know? It's weird.

And this was after he—?

After he passed away, yeah. She's given me lots of pictures and given frames and-- You know, I don't need any help in not forgetting.

In this respect, the absence of specific items in one's wallet may reflect a desire to ignore, deflect, or even suppress certain aspects of one's identity, of one's past. This individual is not denying this part of his past by refusing to carry pictures of his dead friend. He does not wish to dwell on the loss, though, by carrying the friend's image with him, everywhere, all the time.

Clearly, the narrative of the self is constrained by reality. But reality also permits—if not demands—a selective reading or reinforcement of the past and present. Numerous alternative autobiographies may be woven from what has happened and who one has been in one's life. As people use wallet and purse contents to reinforce who they are in this way, then, here again we see the process of selective identity disclosure and concealment. This time, however, the audience is more about the self, as well as others.[34]

In fact, institutional, "mandatory" items carried in one's wallet and purse might be all the identity anchors some individuals need. Especially if institutional sources of identity are privileged and perfectly fulfilling, the carriers of only practical, minimal wallet and purse contents might find these are the only pegs they need on which to hang their senses of self. More interstitial reminders of identity—even pleasant ones—are just not necessary.

Following this line of thought, what might the meaning be of more extensive identity kits? Given what we know about general perceptions of the threat of identity theft and about the efforts to which so many of our participants will go to protect their anonymity, why do some people carry wallets that are so thick, purses that are so weighty that they not infrequently send their carriers to the chiropractor? Why take such risks—especially when the stuff they carry is so personally meaningful and often irreplaceable?

Tables 2.4 and 2.5 present four individuals' complete wallet and purse inventories. These figures provide examples of both minimal and extensive wallet and purse contents for two women—one a scientist (minimal) and the other a human resource manager (extensive)—and two men who are both machinists (tool and die makers), one with minimal and one with extensive wallet contents.

TABLE 2.4 Examples of minimal (modern?) identity kits

A. Thirty-year-old female scientist	B. Fifty-year-old male machinist
Married, no children	Married, two teenaged children
Works "all the time"	Works "all the overtime I can get"
"everywhere"	
	Pocket and billfold contents
Purse, including wallet contents	
Cash	**Pocket**
Checkbook	Cash
Driver's license	Three respirator training cards (two just
Health insurance card	expired)
Credit cards:	
Visa, Mastercard, Macy's	**Billfold**
Cash card	Car registration
Video rental card	Driver's license
Library card	
Price club membership card	
Keys (two sets)	
House, office, and lab	
Car	
Stamps	
Calculator	
Brush	

TABLE 2.5 Examples of extensive (late modern?) identity kits

A. Forty-year-old female HR manager
Divorced, one child
Works 9–5, never more
In therapy

Purse, including wallet contents
Cash
Business cards:
  Three self
  Three boyfriend
  Jacuzzi repairman
  Psychiatrist
  Gastroenterologist
  Hematologist
  Endocrinologist
  OB/gynecologist
  Ex-husband
  Insurance agent
  Director of facility at other research
    center
  Associate re: problems of handicapped
    in industry

Driver's license
Insurance cards (two)
Two calling cards
Employee identification card
Mortgage rate card
Car rental card
Credit union membership card
Two video rental cards
Library card
Cash card (ATM)
Two notes with PIN access numbers
Three raffle tickets

Women in Science membership card
Town residence card
Radio station movie card (for discounts)

Two address books (changing over)
Pens
Calculator

Hairbrush
Emery boards
Sewing supplies
Cosmetics
Tissues
Nail polish

Earrings
Hair clips
Perfume
Hand lotion
Sweet'N Low
Medication
Bandaids
Empty film container

Checkbook, containing:
  Cashcard
  Letters from boyfriend
  Business cards
  Car registration
  Bandaid
  Two receipts for building supplies
  Philosophical notes to self (reflections
    for the day)
  Directions for playing back answering
    machine

Keys, all on one key chain:
  Office, car, two houses' worth, luggage
Six sets of keys for employees

Seven photos
  Six of child
  One of coworker's child

Notebook and pad with lists of things to
  do and buy, cards and love letters from
  boyfriend

Library course schedule (for employees)

Thesis manuscript from a friend's
  daughter whose funeral service she
  attended two weeks earlier, cowritten by
  friend and recently deceased daughter

Two books
  Parapsychology
  Mystery
Victoria's Secret catalog

An apple

TABLE 2.5 (*continued*)

B. Sixty-year-old male machinist

Married, two grown children

Works 8–4, never more

Previously in therapy

Wallet contents

Cash

Business cards
  Medical emergency
  Surgeon
  Friend who sells houses

Phone numbers
  (And address) of coworker in jail, but no
    plans to use it
  Friend, now employee here
  Auto mechanic
List with coworkers' and families' work
  and home business numbers
Health insurance central office
"Garbage busters" to report illegal
  dumping

Four car registrations

Social Security card

Two health insurance cards

Credit cards
  Discover
  Sears
  Mastercard (union sponsored)
  Firstcard

Employee identification card

Three blood donor cards

Credit union card

Two video rental cards

Union membership card (IBEW)

Two CPR certification cards

Store senior citizen discount card

Radiation worker training card

Respirator training card

IBEW pocket calendar card

Receipts for tools

NFL season schedule card

Bandaids

Photos
  Chinese man and baby (left in credit
    union, placed "found ad" in paper, never
    claimed, can't throw out)
  From magazine: photo similar to pet dog
    who died
  Four of married daughter
  Five of younger daughter
  Two of daughters together
  Self and brothers
  Two of self and wife
  Niece
  Father and mother
  Mother and grandmother with ex-
    girlfriend cut out
  Wife
  From magazine: four of Piper Cub
    airplane interior, two of exterior (plane
    he learned to pilot in)

Notes
  Sparkplug numbers for car
  Spelling of retiree's name
  Credit card numbers
  Calculator serial number
  Dimensions for lumber
  Coworkers' baseball pool pick
  Reminder for car oil change
  Spec on resistor to purchase
  Diagram for sink unit
  Gas grill dimensions
  Directions on how to read resistors
  Electrical formulae
  Lawn mower engine serial number
  Two from daughters' childhoods

Card with father-in-law's death notice
  (years old)

"Garbage" (a few receipts to throw out)

One implication of these inventories is that clearly a great deal of variation exists in terms of the sheer volume of objects that individuals carry with them. Yet if we believe the claims of modernity theorists and contemporary cultural theorists, those with few wallet and purse contents may well represent not only those who are more content with traditional, institutional sources of identity in their lives, but also a dwindling portion of the population ("electronic wallets" and PDA substitutes notwithstanding). This is because in a materialistic culture, where the need to attend to the self is increasing, the size of our purses and the thickness of our wallets may be expected to do the same.[35]

In the past, people like Georg Simmel (1955) and Rose Coser (1991) set the stage for contemporary sociologists' attention to the link between the modern condition and the exponential increase in attention to the self that we find in late modern life. Anthony Giddens (1991, 52–54), for instance, argues that as "[t]he reflexivity of modernity extends into the core of the self . . . the self becomes a *reflexive project*" (italics in original). Not only does the self need to be "routinely created and sustained in the reflexive activities of the individual" in late modern life, he argues, but "a person's identity is to be found . . . in the capacity to keep a particular narrative going."

Richard Sennett (1998) echoes Giddens, but further argues that it is increasingly difficult today for people to create and keep that narrative going. One's sense of character, he argues, is found in a cohesive life narrative or account of what one has accomplished and committed to over a lengthy period. He claims that traditionally character has been so thoroughly embedded in workplace institutions and careers as well as marriage and community that the decimation of these institutional sources of identity has led to a widespread problem: the current inability of many people (especially men) to develop a true sense of who they are. In order to reclaim their character, Sennett argues, individuals now have to seek meaning, continuity, and a sense of self elsewhere, especially outside the workplace.

Daniel Pink (2002) addresses these same factors, but argues they have led dissatisfied workers who seek meaning and self-fulfillment in their lives to reject the conventional workplace. Instead, he sees them choosing "free agency," inventing their sense of who they are through self-employment, consulting, (voluntarily) temporary and part-time work, and the running of microbusinesses in which "my size fits me." In this model, families and leisure can be healthfully blended together with work, too.[36] As a set of self-defining practices and locations outside the traditional institutions of the past, free agency itself is evidence of a growing need and desire to engage in identity work.

In fact, Ulrich Beck (1992) argues that today people have the opportunity and incentive to withdraw from a number of traditional, institutional sources of identity, including marriage, the family, the church, and formal education in addition to the corporate workplace and career. The conditions of late modernity, he writes, encourage us to want to make decisions and to construct our selves and our lives as we wish. As a result,

> Each person's biography is removed from given determinations and placed in his or her own hands, open and dependent on decisions. The proportion of life opportunities which are fundamentally closed to decision-making is decreasing and the proportion of the biography which is open and must be constructed personally is increasing. Individualization of life situations and processes thus means that biographies become *self-reflexive*; socially prescribed biography is transformed into biography that is self-produced and continues to be produced. (Beck 1992, 135)

From the outside to the inside of participants' wallets and purses, from the stuff they carry to the ways they carry it, surely this is one location in which important aspects of self are re-presented—whether these are aspects of self that one wishes to never engage in again or the most precious, most desirable parts of all. These material "souvenirs" are present for the self and for others—drawn forth whenever participants wish to share certain pieces of who they are and/or challenge others to do the same. Thus, participants manage the private-public boundary in this way, too, carrying a selection of items that are strictly for themselves along with things that are also for others. In this way—and through the stories they tell that incorporate these items—they actively work to suppress and support a carefully edited, highly selective sense of self.

CONCLUSION

Each time one opens one's wallet or purse, the sound of the ocean may be heard. There is room for agency, for individual preferences, practices, and other idiosyncrasies even in these small islands of privacy. But those preferences and the identity work associated with them are always enacted within the broader constraints of the social structural and cultural expectations of our time. Personal privacy—how much we have, how we try to achieve it, and how much we succeed or fail at this—is continuously bracketed by these broader realities.

Wallets and purses are such useful items, then, because they allow participants to negotiate with great flexibility a number of the daily tensions that are part and parcel of the modern condition. First, there is the tension between what is intensely private—requiring a great deal of attention and protection—and what is almost mindlessly public—surrendered for inspection or given away without a second thought. Second, wallets and purses help individuals negotiate the tension between the freedoms of anonymity, on the one hand, and the advantages of positive identification, on the other. Third, wallets and purses help individuals manage the tension between the need to interact with and be oriented toward others in their daily lives and, at the same time, the need to be inwardly oriented and concerned with the self. They assist in meeting the societal need to interface in predictable, role-specific ways with others—including society's multiple institutional systems—as well as the culturally mandated need to be a unique and dynamic self in progress. Fourth and finally, wallets and purses also help us explore the tension between the more purely practical and the more purely symbolic meanings of material culture—the physical stuff of our lives—as individuals try to create a more desirable private-public boundary. Clearly, the practical value of an object does not preclude it also having enormous symbolic value.

In an economy of strangers, none of these tensions are going to be resolved soon. Certainly, the need to make one's identity selectively accessible while keeping others from knowing any more than they must will only increase as systems that allow both for convenience and for silent and undetected identity theft become more pervasive. Wallet and purse inventories thus allow people to better manage the resulting individual, double burden of modernity: the burden of publicity *and* the burden of privacy. One need only forget one's wallet at home to realize the extent to which many of us rely on it to meet both of these sets of expectations and just how much of our daily privacy work takes place along this part of the beach.

NEXT

If the consequences of unmitigated access to individuals' identities, wallets, and purses can be severe, so can the outcome when others have unlimited access to us via information and communication technologies. In the next chapter, I continue to look at the ways participants try to achieve privacy through the ways they try to manage the demands for their attention that arrive via various communication technologies. Selectivity remains the name of the game here, too, as participants develop an assortment of piecemeal systems to better manage their accessibility to others.

CHAPTER THREE

Cell Phones & Email

If I needed to contact you during the day, how many numbers would I have to call before I got in touch with you?

So, if you are a patient?

Not exactly, no. The question doesn't vary according to—

Sure it varies, depending on who you are (*laughing*).

> BILL, forty-three-year-old father, husband,
> physician, and research program director

Zerubavel (1979b) claims that "the regulation of the modern person's social accessibility" is a central feature of daily life. It certainly is for the participants in this study. Trying to control who can reach them, when, how, and for how long is a persistent theme of their day.

Managing social accessibility is a vital aspect of achieving privacy, one that focuses on the privacy of one's time, space, thoughts, and actions. The behaviors associated with this dimension of privacy thus provide another excellent vantage point for learning about selective concealment and disclosure—in this case, concerning one's presence and availability. In this chapter, I explore this facet of privacy by examining participants' expectations and practices regarding communication technologies and the requests for their attention that arrive through these channels.

I think of social accessibility as a combination of reachability and responsiveness. It is a function of one's receptivity to others' requests for access. The remarkable range of accessibility participants must—and might—give to others is an important constraint on how they manage this particular dimension of privacy. Based on our relationships, there are customary, role-related expectations for making ourselves available to others. We constantly assess whatever islands might be established in response to these expectations, negotiating the shape and size of the territories in which we can flat-out deny contact as well as those from which we carefully contain it or even welcome it without exception (i.e., the island, the beach, and the ocean, respectively).

Accordingly, individuals actively work (consciously or otherwise) to accomplish a given degree of availability. They try to make themselves available at any given time to only select others (and sometimes to no one), even though any restriction of access may be temporary. Overall, the desire and need to be available to some people at some times is balanced with the simultaneous desire and need to deny access to others.

Managing one's accessibility takes multiple forms, whether the goal is to increase or decrease one's availability to any specific other. Goffman (1959, 138), for instance, describes one fundamental and highly dynamic way in which individuals control their social accessibility: scheduling. Through scheduling, he argues, one can sequentially accommodate different social roles, audiences, and ways of being.

> By proper scheduling of one's performances, it is possible not only to keep one's audiences separated from each other . . . but also to allow a few moments in between performances so as to extricate oneself psychologically and physically from one personal front, while taking on another.

Zerubavel (1979b, 40) further describes the ways scheduling helps us manage private and public roles.

> By providing some boundaries along which the private and public spheres of life are segregated from one another and to which the association of person and role is confined, the temporal structure of social life has be-

come indispensable to the regulation of the modern person's social accessibility, as well as to the maintenance of the partiality of each of his various social involvements.

Separating aspects of one's life by separating the times in which one engages in them is certainly one way in which individuals manage their accessibility to others. In earlier work (Nippert-Eng 1996), for instance, I described a lengthy list of behaviors that "segmentors" engage in on a daily basis so that they can place a strong boundary between the worlds of home and work. This includes making good use of scheduling so that the people who belong to either realm have minimal presence in the other. Early morning or evening phone calls from workplace associates are discouraged, as are daytime calls from family. Weekends are work free, as are vacations. By providing transitional space and time, even segmentors' daily, scheduled commutes help them place and keep a boundary between the social, mental, and physical worlds of home and work. The schedule thus helps organize life in predictable ways for these folks.

Yet other individuals work equally hard to blur the home-work boundary—to integrate the realms and selves of home and work. The idea of scheduling interactions with "work people" or "home people" such that they take place only in certain times and spaces has little application to their lives. They regularly bring work and workmates home and family members and domestic concerns and objects into the workplace, for instance. They certainly take phone calls wherever they happen to be from people others might associate with work *or* home. The transitional function of their far less predictable daily commutes is much less pronounced for them, too, of course, since their social accessibility and mental and physical worlds on either end of the trip are so similar.

An April 11, 2005, report from the online journal *Consumer Affairs*[1] describes another group of people who also choose not to restrict their accessibility along more conventional lines.

Fourteen percent of the world's cell phone users report that they have stopped in the middle of a sex act to answer a ringing wireless device, *Ad Age* reported.

The highest incidence of cellular interruptus was found in Germany and Spain, where 22 percent of users interrupted sex to answer their cell phones; the lowest was in Italy, where only 7 percent reported doing so. In the U.S., the figure was 15 percent, the magazine said, citing a study conducted by BBDO Worldwide and Proximity Worldwide.

"People can't bear to miss a call," said Christine Hannis, head of communications for BBDO Europe. "Everybody thinks the next call can be something really exciting. And getting so many calls proves social success," she said. "It fulfills a fundamental insecurity."

For some people, in other words, success in managing one's accessibility means that others can reach them anytime, anywhere, no matter what they're doing—or whom they're doing it with. The scheduler's psychosocial transitions that Goffman talks about are either irrelevant for them or perhaps achieved in a truly superior fashion.

In order to understand the basic organizing principles underlying such a wide range of approaches to accessibility, I draw here on a special subset of interviews. Some study participants were asked to respond to an interview module dedicated to detailed inventories and explanations of the ways they use various communication technologies. While everyone in the study commented on these matters in some way, only thirty-three individuals were asked to fully complete this section of the interview. These were people who I believed had the desire to discuss these things and had expressed a willingness to spend enough time on the interview process in order to do so. Incomplete inventory data were gathered for an additional eight participants who nonetheless answered a majority of the pointed questions about communications technologies. No one who was asked to participate in this part of the interview refused to do so, and everyone was remarkably articulate about their practices and experiences with these matters.

Focusing on participants' uses of communication technologies reveals two main dimensions to the privacy/social accessibility problem they face each day. The first concerns the ways in which the relative distribution of power manifests in the general question of who is supposed to be accessible to whom and in what ways. The second concerns the ways in which new communications technologies—especially mobile ones—increase and intensify power struggles over accessibility. Both aspects of the privacy problem must be understood in order to fully grasp the logic and cleverness of participants' responses to it.

THE PROBLEM, PART I: POWER, AGENDA SETTING, ATTENTION GIVING, AND ATTENTION GETTING

Because privacy is a fundamentally social phenomenon, conflict over how much privacy one may have or how private or public something should be is rather inevitable. When discrepancies regarding privacy translate into active social conflict, the role of the relative distribution of power across individuals becomes readily apparent.[2] In terms of social accessibility, the distribution of power plays a crucial role in the ways people understand and try to manage others' demands for their attention. This balance of power largely accounts for whose agenda will prevail at any given time.

Lukes (1988, 34) argues that the ability to set agendas is a critical dimension of power. Agenda setting is about the ability to decide what will and won't be allowed to get people's attention as well as the ways in which that might happen. From this perspective, power is very much about deciding the extent to which something—or someone—will be more or less accessible to others. This includes, incidentally, the agenda-setting process itself.[3]

Interruptions reveal the link between power, attention, and agenda setting. Interruptability is a key measure of how much privacy one has. We saw this earlier, for instance, in participants' definitions of privacy. It is an important aspect of privacy especially for the working mother-wives in this study, for whom this dimension of privacy is especially fragile. (See also Nippert-Eng 1993, 2009a.)

The principle is the same as that proposed by Barry Schwartz (1975) regarding waiting. Waiting symbolizes one's relative powerlessness in any given situation. Those with power do not wait; those without power do. Similarly, those who lack power are eminently interruptable, while those with power are not. In fact, the relatively powerless keep others from interrupting superiors while staying constantly available—waiting—for interruption by them.

During an interruption, one person's agenda directly supplants another's for a given period of time.[4] This makes interruptions specific instances in which one person exerts power over another in a very immediate, behavioral sense.[5] When a pattern emerges of one person interrupting another, each act of interruption, like each incident of waiting (Schwartz 1975, 132–52) confirms and perpetuates the actors' social status relative to each other.

Normally, the powerful's privacy—which at least partially translates into the ability to pursue one's agenda and pay attention to whom and what one wants, in the way one wishes to do so—is protected from interruptions in at least two ways. First, the powerful acquire a variety of people, technologies, and other barriers to reduce interruptions. These ensure that only certain demands get through: those that must have the powerful's personal attention. Such high-level demands then actually confirm and further the powerful's high status.

In addition, the powerful are protected from interruptions through their right to disattend certain people and events. Another person's demand must be noticed before it can interrupt us. Further, the more we think a demand requires our own personal attention, the greater are its chances of becoming an interruption for us, rather than someone else. In this way, role and status expectations that direct us to notice and respond to certain demands by certain people result in differing amounts and kinds of interruptions for role occupants. Wherever they are, the more powerful learn it is "not my job" to manage mundane requests for help, especially when these requests come from relatively powerless people.

If the powerful lessen interruptions by failing to notice and/or respond to others' demands, this is complemented by others' failures to direct their demands toward the powerful. The less powerful may not feel entitled to ask for their superiors' attention or to intrude upon their "more important" concerns. Subordinates may have simply learned to go to other subordinates with their problems. As a result of all these factors, it may not even occur to an interrupter to approach a more powerful person with her or his concerns.

In other words, the allocation of privacy—how inaccessible one is to others and, accordingly, how much one can follow through on one's own agenda rather than somebody else's—is a clear measure of one's status and power in any given situation. Subordinates are easily identified as the people who are most visibly and actively responding to others' demands, that is, those whose privacy is constantly intruded upon. In a fuller hierarchy, those on the bottom interrupt each other and those in the middle. The people on the top are interrupted least and it had better be absolutely necessary when this happens.

Layered onto these expectations of who should be accessible to whom are related expectations regarding who will give and who will get others' attention. In his analysis of attention-giving and attention-getting roles, Derber (1979) puts it like this:

> Social dominance is institutionalized face-to-face through an organization of roles in families, workplaces and politics which permits those of higher status to claim attention as their due and requires lower-status individuals to seek and accept less. (41)

> [These institutional roles] can be characterized as attention-getting or attention-giving, depending on whether the actor is expected to give or get it. . . . The allocation of these roles is a function of power, with the great majority of attention-getting roles assigned to dominant groups and attention-giving roles to subordinate ones. (21)

Derber argues, then, that status relations are also fundamentally about the distribution of attention getting and attention giving across the social hierarchy. Those of lower status are expected to give attention to those of higher status in accordance with their superiors' wishes.[6]

In other words, in this interactionist grammar, setting and pursuing personal agendas are the signs of powerful people. Constantly being interrupted and having to respond to others' demands for attention signify the presence of social inferiors. Finding oneself engaged in any of these behaviors has undeniable symbolic significance, hammering home one's position in the status hierarchy.[7]

This is not to say that people always recognize interactions around struggles like this as expressions of power. Michel Foucault (1995, 1990) demonstrates throughout his work that the power of the State manifests in mental and behavioral expectations that often are not recognized as mechanisms of social control despite their effectiveness as such. Likewise, Zerubavel (2006) provides overwhelming evidence that the State and other powerful entities within families, workplaces, and other social groups express their positions in the power hierarchy through the things individuals are directed *not* to notice, talk about, question, or remember. This is precisely the locus of much of Karl Marx's life's work, of course, particularly as he and his colleagues tried to shatter the "false consciousness" and mistaken materialism and consumption ideology of the masses.[8] In other words, as Lukes himself might argue, it is in the things we do not think to attend to—but which nonetheless structure our lives in quite practical ways—where we may find the most effective expressions of power.

In fact, participants' strong reactions to violations of their privacy are often an implicit, gut-level acknowledgement of what these incidents say about their power and social status relative to the intruder's. For instance, when asked to discuss any especially annoying or distasteful violations to their privacy that occur in public, participants repeatedly mentioned a fairly small number of everyday urban events. These include people engaged in loud cell phone conversations, drivers blasting distasteful music from car stereos, couples fighting and adults being abusive toward children in public, people using loud, foul language, and anyone engaged in a variety of bodily functions in one's proximity such as snoring, smelling badly, urinating, or engaging in sexual activity.

The intrusiveness of such mundane events is not limited to their specific sensory impact on these participants for the duration of the encounter. Rather, it is also the symbolic message of such incidents that bothers participants.[9] By derailing witnesses' own agendas at these times and places, such self-centered, ill-mannered intruders demonstrate that they do indeed have power over those around them, no matter how fleeting.

We may respond with a variety of informal sanctions, from scowling or yelling at offenders to talking about them (loudly) with other offended witnesses or even to retreating out of the public realm altogether, to more private, more controlled settings.[10] The latter makes particular sense. If people behave well and keep themselves to themselves—or interact with us only in welcome ways—then being out in public, so very accessible to others, is just fine. If others behave badly, though, retreating to a less accessible lifestyle—say, keeping mostly to one's apartment, SUV, or suburban neighborhood—may solve the problem quite effectively.

Of course, one other possible response is to ignore such intrusions. Compared to a rural or suburban visitor to the city, a seasoned urbanite may hardly break stride when these things happen. Just as the powerful are free to ignore anything that they do not believe requires their attention, city dwellers may well ignore such things after a while—along with anyone or anything else that they do not think warrants their attention.

When asked if there was a time in her life when she felt her privacy was being violated, for instance, one participant offered this story.

When I first moved to (Boston), I got flashed[11] three times in, like, six months. And finally I said-- I was telling this attorney that I was working for—we were walking down the street—and I was telling her about this. And she said, "You know what your problem is? You look at everybody. Quit looking at everybody." I mean, it's just typical. And I realized that I didn't have that (Boston) shell around me. I was, like, really looking at people as they walked by.

And these are people who are looking for people who are looking.

Exactly. And they flash you if you do that. And I quit looking at people after that.

And you didn't get flashed anymore.

Right.

By denying them her attention, this participant removed the incentive for the flashers to give her their own unwanted, visual brand of it. What she finally did, in other words, was reduce her accessibility to the flashers. In the process, she releveled the playing field, reestablished control, reempowered herself relative to them, and regained her privacy.

The connection between privacy, power, agendas, and the giving and getting of attention is a close one, then. Zerubavel (1979a, 1979b, 1985), for instance, discusses "private time" as time during which one is relatively inaccessible to others. It is the privacy of one's time that allows an individual to establish and follow through on a specific agenda. During private time, one may pay attention to what she or he wishes to, in the ways she or he wishes to, and does not have to attend to what others would like her or him to do.

This simple principle is not so simple in practice, however. There are moments when clear boundaries may delineate private time or space for us, even within social realms where we are normally subordinate to others. Time in the bathroom, the doctor's office, or on a prayer rug may all signal privacy to some people—though not to one's toddler, the nurse, or the mullah, perhaps. One's wallet or purse may signal the same.

Yet there are many more times and places where the extent to which one should or should not be accessible—and to whom and in what way—is much less clear. At these times, the struggle for privacy may more clearly be seen as a struggle over power. The more equal the distribution of power in any relationship, for instance, the more likely there will be a constant if sometimes latent tension between multiple parties' differing desires for attention at specific times, in specific ways, and regarding specific things. And anytime that one individual's distinct, personal agenda plays against another's—as one individual's relative, situated allocation of power meets up against another's—some very complex rules and attention-management techniques may come into play.

This is at least part of the symbolic interactionist context from which participants interpret the demands for their attention that arrive via communication technologies. But today's communications technologies perturb daily life in ways that add to these more general accessibility issues. These effects can make the quest for privacy even more elusive for many people—superiors and subordinates alike.

THE PROBLEM, PART II: ICTS, RELATIONSHIPS, AND THE GROWING DEMAND FOR ATTENTION

In order to fully appreciate participants' responses to the problem of accessibility, one more set of constraints must be taken into account. By now it should be clear that managing privacy is fundamentally about managing our relationships with others. When we choose to make ourselves more and less available to others—to defend or set aside our personal agendas and to give others more and less of our attention—we are actively engaged in relationship work. Through each act of (in)accessibility, we establish or end, defend, challenge, and/or change the nature of a given relationship. The detailed choices we make each time we do and do not make ourselves accessible resonate across the history and possible futures of the relevant relationships.

The fact that one must work to achieve a given degree of social accessibility—and, thus, a specific kind of relationship with another person—is nothing new. Yet the nature of that work has been altered today by the extent to which individuals' requests for each other's attention can be separated from their physical copresence (Couch, 1996). The more this is possible—especially when requests can be made remotely but still in real time—the more the management of others' communiqués becomes critical to managing the individuals themselves and, of course, our relationships with them.

Today's explosion of information and communication technologies (ICTs) and their widespread adoption by so many people have exponentially complicated this reality. Kenneth Gergen (1991) has offered what is perhaps the most seminal work on this to date. Today, he argues—largely because of communication technologies—many people engage in far more relationships than the average individual would have had at any previous point in history.

In fact, Michael Schrage (1997, 1) perfectly captures the importance of these technologies for relationships. When it comes to information technology, Schrage tells us, "Whenever you see the word 'information' . . . substitute the word 'relationship'" to more fully understand its uses and its consequences. Claude Fischer (1992, 268) concurs in his excellent social history of the telephone, arguing these are indeed "technologies of sociability." But, he notes, expanded sociability is not all positive: "a key drawback of the home telephone is that very same expanded sociability. To have access to others means that they have access to you, like it or not."

The number and kinds of demands for attention that we are likely to receive at any given time, in any given place, are much greater when these technologies are in use than when they are not. Mobile communication technologies not only facilitate this burgeoning request for attention, they add another twist. They let others outside our immediate physical grasp reach us, but they also let them do so in what have been traditionally and especially interstitial places and times—where and when, for most of history, it would have been very difficult if not impossible for this to happen.[12]

The implications of this for the sheer amount of privacy and relationship work that we must do are staggering. Simmel (1955) was the first to point out that the modern sense of self is defined by memberships in a unique and diverse "web of group affiliations." One implication of this is that the modern individual's social territory is likely to include a larger number of more diverse social relationships than those that are possessed by members of premodern social groups.

In fact, Gergen (1991) argues that today—in what some call the postmodern society—the relationship landscape has virtually exploded. It is not simply that we have more relationships demanding even more attention because of our technologies, either. Rather, our contacts with others are scattered across far more channels of (often instantaneous) communication than ever before, too.

Now, we still need to manage the demands for our attention that come from traditional face-to-face encounters, posted mail, and desk and kitchen phones that were once answered in real time or not at all. But we also have to deal with demands that arrive instantaneously from all over the world. These relentlessly direct us to "pick up" and be online no matter where we are, or at least retrieve the pile of demands waiting for us later on in an assortment of electronic repositories.[13]

Accordingly, for the participants in this study, the problem of achieving privacy, of controlling one's accessibility, agenda, and attention, has taken on new urgency. And while the story of social accessibility has always been linked to the story of technological accessibility, the nature of success in the former now undeniably relies on a new kind of success in the latter. Chayko (2008, 93) summarizes the result, noting that mobile technology in particular

> allows us to make and "juggle" many social connections, as numerous so-
> cial ties and networks are established, offering almost limitless opportu-
> nities for social connectedness. But it places substantial responsibility on
> the shoulders of the individual—the "portal" for all this connectivity—to
> manage and coordinate these networks.

Thus, the capacity of today's communication technologies to exponentially extend our social territories simultaneously increases our need to pay attention to the management of that territory. Each relationship requires a certain amount and kind of attention. As Derber (1979) points out, expectations for attention—both the giving and the getting of it—are greatly infused by a variety of social norms.[14] One set of these norms has to do with the nature or type of the relationship—current and/or potential—and what this means for the allocation of attention. But other factors influence these expectations, too, such as the more personal desire of one member in the relationship for a certain amount and kind of attention from another.

A general principle, though, is that if an individual fails to provide the minimal sustainable amount and kind of attention, a relationship will either fail to take root or it will transform from what it has been into something else, and possibly even terminate.[15] Depending on how well one manages the entirety of one's relationships, one's social territory will expand, remain the same, or shrink as one tries to stay as inaccessible and inattentive as possible to some people and as accessible and attentive as possible to others. Thus, the same people who use a filtering device to happily cut off any relationship with a spammer or telemarketer may also buy a collection of cell phones on a family plan to establish a "hotline" of constant accessibility between children and parents.

Regulating one's attention is especially important when it comes to relationships that one values highly, including, in the U.S., one's relationship with oneself. Westin argues, for instance, that the reason a person lays claim to private space and has rules of territoriality and trespass is "to promote individual well-being and small-group intimacy" (1967, 9). In this regard, the entire purpose of private territory is undermined by intrusions into it. Westin argues (1967, 9): "If persistent enough, these intrusions certainly may bode ill for the self and for any small group."[16]

At the very least, these intrusions may take the form of interruptions, whereby others' agendas do indeed become our own, at least temporarily. The negative effect that these pose for the self and group is not just a function of the practical effects of interruptions, either. It is also because of the symbolic message they convey, that is, that the interrupter is more powerful, more important than the interruptee, who is not only not permitted to do what she or he would like with her or his space and time, but must at least partially accommodate the intruder's agenda instead. This grates on the nerves of a number of people, including the following participant.

I get so damn many phone calls that are information seekers. Mostly companies trying to sell you something or trying to get you to sell something of theirs, and that's very intrusive. It's an intrusion on my privacy in the sense that one of the things that ought to be private is my time and my concentration, and they break it. They break into it. And that's the category into which I put telemarketers, sales people, survey research organizations, spam, and junk mail. They are taking something of mine. They're taking my time and my intellectual concentration, and I don't like that.

Even calls from friends feel intrusive to some participants, who feel overwhelmed by the sheer volume of others' demands for their attention.[17] Imagine what it is like for the children reported on in a June 7, 2005, article in the *Guardian*.[18] No longer limited to their victims' face-to-face accessibility, school bullies are showing remarkable savvy as they send or threaten to send a variety of abusive and embarrassing messages to their victims, their victims' circle of friends, or the friends of the bullies. Camera phones, texting, blogging, posts on Facebook and other electronic media forms are all used to instantly, broadly, effectively intrude on and influence victims' ever-growing social turf.

However, for these study participants, telemarketers—a different kind of bully, perhaps—are guilty of the worst intrusions on self and family. There is a remarkable intolerance for them and the companies for which they work. They are responsible for some profound adaptations in phone-answering behavior, too. In response to a question about whether she could identify anyone who had seriously threatened her privacy, one person put it this way:

Telemarketers. I just get furious.

Right. So do you think about your privacy?

Yeah, at that point I get very annoyed. . . . If I'm doing something and I have to get up to answer the telephone and it's one of these telemarketers, I get furious. Or if it's somebody asking my opinion on something or other, oh, I mean, I just really get annoyed. And usually I'm in the middle of something and I don't like to be disturbed. And for what?

Right.

They're invading my privacy when they call.

Another individual explained the rationale for her dislike this way:

I try to answer the phone because of my mother. [She's elderly and lives alone.] I never know if there is going to be an emergency or something, so-- Then I get all those harassing commercial calls, you know.

. . . And I particularly felt it when my daughter was young because, you know, you never can leave a child alone when they're, you know, really little. And I would be giving her a bath or something and then the phone would ring and I would be in this quandary. So I would scoop her up from the tub and carry her dripping across the room to a phone. And then it would be somebody, you know, trying to sell me insurance or something.

It just irritates me beyond belief.

A number of participants say that because of telemarketers they rarely answer their home phones these days. Any call may be from a telemarketer, and that's reason enough to just not bother anymore. Some participants say that *most* of the calls on their home phone are from these salespeople.[19] As a result, these individuals now let all home phone calls go to voicemail or their answering machines, where they can hear who it is before deciding whether or not the person or the situation deserves a response. Others may pay for caller ID and always check the display to see who's calling before picking up. One participant describes the transformation in her phone-answering policy, comparing it to her family's approach prior to the advent of telemarketing.[20]

Would you say that privacy is problematic for you right now?

Oh, yeah.

Why is that?

Very much so.

Well, I think it, that it goes from little annoyances, you know, like spam in your email box to, you know-- Unbelievable, the telemarketing, you know, that just besieges my household every single day, you know.

I mean it's-- I would love to do a study on stuff like that if I, you know, could because it's just horrendous. It literally does change your behavior, you know, we don't answer the phone. I think as a cultural category, that's a great one, right?

Yeah.

Because when I was young, I remember my aunts, right? And the behavior on answering the phones was always very interesting, you know. And a phone call was kind of a, important, special thing. You would not not answer the phone when someone was calling unless it was, like, in the middle of a seder. My family was Jewish. And so if it's, like, a holiday or something like that, you wouldn't answer the phone. But even that helped to mark the importance of it, you know. "It's an important thing to answer the phone and answer it in a certain kind of a way," and, you know, et cetera. "And the only time that we don't do that is on very special holidays."

Right.

So. And they were the same [rules] as television, too. Like, you can have television but, you know, certain times you don't have television. And that [rule] would be broken. It was a big deal. During the Six Day War or something like that.

Yeah.

They actually had television at the dinner table then and-- Like, you know, at my aunt's house. And that was never done before. But Walter Cronkite-- You know, everyone paid homage to Walter, and if he had something important to tell you, you were going to listen.

But I think the phone has-- Now it's this pest in my life, you know, so there are just wholesale blocks of time where I won't answer the phone.

I rely very heavily on the voicemail system to filter out that kind of stuff. Where you develop the behavior pattern that if you do answer the phone—

'cause you need to because you're waiting for somebody you care about to call (*laughing*), you know. You answer the phone and if it has that delay—

Yeah.

—you just hang right up.

Right.

And all of my friends and family know that they have to be on it. They have to say something immediately or they may get hung up on (*laughing*).

The delay to which this participant refers is caused by the fact that a telephone solicitation is frequently initiated today by a computer dialing the phone number. If a potential customer answers the call, a salesperson who monitors the computer-initiated contacts tries to quickly come on the line in order to speak with her or him. As a result, there is often a delay of a second or two between the recipient's "Hello?" and the live solicitor's reply. This delay has become a signal to many savvy participants that they've been had—again—by these awful intruders. What they do next ranges from hanging up immediately, as with this participant, to waiting to find out who it is and then hanging up (politely or abruptly) or even beginning to game the solicitor.

A number of people commented that now that these calls are initiated by computers, they are even more insulting, an even bigger violation of their privacy than before. The intrusion into the private time and space of their home, forcing them to stop doing what they're doing in order to respond to a machine-driven demand for their attention is just "over the top." The company doesn't want to waste the time of someone on their payroll, but it's perfectly fine to waste the time of the person they call? To ruin their meal, their time with their kids, their train of thought? As they stand up to these soliciting bullies, then, people have taken up a number of strategies to reset what is seen as an absolutely unacceptable balance of power distributed across their communication lines.

It's a relatively rare individual or family who manages to turn the whole spamming and telemarketing phenomena into a game, but those who do seem to defend and strengthen their social territories in the process. These are people, for instance, who acquire and selectively distribute multiple email addresses in order to track, study, turn in, and boycott those who send them spam.[21] They are also people who try to keep telephone solicitors on the line as long as possible without intending to buy anything from them. And, of course, people like this:

Have you heard any interesting or normal everyday things that either you or other people do to protect privacy at home?

Well, once we found out that you don't *have* to take calls from telemarketers, we don't take them. Once you get them to admit they're telemarketers, we have no problems.

Once we were watching *The Wizard of Oz* and got a telemarketing call just at the spot where Belinda says *Begone from-- You*, you know, *you have no power*, and the phone rings. Any my husband answers the phone and says he was selling blah, blah, blah. And my husband says, *Be gone from here, you have—you have no power. (Laughter.)*

That's so funny.

It was hysterical. It was the moment.

. . . That telemarketing call was about as funny as they get. Another thing we have, the kids had a book where you press the button and it makes little sounds. And it was a witch or an eel from *The Little Mermaid*, and it cackled. And (Junie) says, "You want us to buy what?" June, she was, like, eight at the time. "You want us to buy *what*?" And then she hit this button and it went (*cackles*). So telemarketers are really on our shit list. They really don't get treated kindly.

These kinds of shared, humor-filled experiences undoubtedly strengthen family bonds, especially since they manage to turn the tables so effectively on the intruders. The telemarketers are now the recipients of the *family's* demand for attention. In these power struggles—over each party's right to pursue its own agenda—the family doesn't just hold its own. It comes out on top.

Attention-getting forays into our social territories may have other subtle and long-lasting effects on the ways we set up and experience our territories. It is not simply that we have more relationships demanding more attention because of these technologies. Rather, the diverse nature of how we have to manage those relationships has increased, too. Demands for our attention appear in multiple ways and sometimes in multiple locations within even a single technological channel, such as when an individual possesses multiple phone lines or multiple email addresses. Those demands may not only come in thick and heavy, every day, every minute, but others are interpreting the ways we respond to them as direct indications of what we think of them.[22]

Communication technologies' unique capabilities have allowed us to complicate two further and interrelated aspects of daily life through which we regulate our accessibility and our attention. First, these technologies are well suited to blurring any subterritories we may have created between and within our social worlds, however unintentionally. The result is a breakdown of the traditional segmentation of roles, social networks, and personal ways of being that many people have long relied on in the U.S. to help regulate their accessibility—and their attention.[23]

Gergen (1991) argues that one of the effects of these technologies is that we become aware of the multiplicity of selves, of the many identities of which we are capable. This presents a bit of a problem when communications with others evoke or demand different identities and ways of being than those that we are actively engaged in at the moment. Depending on the nature of a contact, we may find ourselves required to instantly transform our current frame of mind in order to accommodate whatever mentality is mandated by a newly appearing request.[24]

The effect of a communiqué that instantly appears in a different place can be quite jarring at first. This was certainly the case for the segmenting individuals I studied whose "work" and "home" selves were distinctly embedded within specific times and spaces. Meyrowitz (1985) found a similar effect, too, in his study of the distinct identities, social groups, and interactions associated with specific times and places prior to the advent of television. In both cases, though, we found that cross-realm communications gradually chip away at the social-psychological walls separating social worlds; more integrated lives and identities result.

Thanks to our use of communication technologies, many more individuals may be experiencing both of these effects—the discomforting, cross-realm conflicting one and the boundary-challenging, possibly identity-merging one. People associated with one aspect of our lives are now suddenly requesting our attention with increasing regularity in all kinds of places and times other than those in which they traditionally might have been expected to appear. This is not limited to cases of "cellular interruptus," either. The result is that numerous boundaries are far less certain today and rules about one's accessibility across them are no longer so obvious—or easily assumed.[25]

One participant describes a common manifestation of this problem: a boss who won't leave her alone outside the office. The variation here is that he quickly (and unfortunately) learned to call her boyfriend's cell phone whenever he wanted to reach her during "nonwork" time.

So is there somebody, though, on a regular basis that you just don't want contacting you from work?

Yeah. My boss.

Actually, I got a cell phone not too long ago and I sent out the number to a very select group of people and I said, "Under absolutely no circumstances do I want (Neil Wright) to know that I have this cell phone."

And these are people at work?

Yeah, these are people at work. And they totally understood. And one of the guys actually came up to me and he said, "Hey, I have a cell phone now, too." And I said, "Don't worry, your secret is safe with me." This is, like, the unwritten law that everyone knows that if you have a cell phone, you do not give it to this man because he will abuse it.

I mean, at one point-- He has (Ryan's) [my boyfriend's] cell phone number. So he thinks that it's mine. So on a Friday night, maybe, like, three or four weeks ago, we were at dinner and Ryan's cell phone rang and it was Neil calling for me. And I was just so-- I was so pissed. I was like, "Don't call me." And I specifically told him several times. I said, "This is not my cell phone. This is Ryan's cell phone. Do not call me on this cell phone." And he just ignores-- I mean, he's very selective about what he hears and he reads, and so he just chooses to ignore it.

All it takes is a few people to selectively ignore one's wishes and we quickly discover that mobile technologies especially can make managing our accessibility a very personal burden, requiring a more personal solution than ever before.[26]

This is happening in part because each individual seeking our attention has her or his own ideas of where and how these lines should be drawn. This includes individualized preferences about not only how much access and attention we should give them, but of the forms that our accessibility and attention should take, too. Informing each of these individualized preferences are marked changes in related practical expectations about things like the sheer number of responses we should be prepared to make (or demand), the speed of those responses (our own and others'), and the plethora of preferred response modes that we are all supposed to manage.

What emerges is a picture of what can be a daily, extremely personal, and constant juggling act. It's a never-ending and dynamically situated problem of whom and what to pay attention to, when, and in what way. The scope of the problem encompasses our face-to-face and physical engagements, as it has for quite some time. But now it also includes those that occur in the ever-larger, increasingly compelling, more virtual spaces of our lives.

Of course, as Rob Shields (2003) points out, no virtual encounter happens without it simultaneously being embedded in a physical one. In fact, as Gergen notes especially in his essay "The Challenge of Absent Presence"

(2002), the demands and opportunities for our attention that appear via communication technologies compete directly with and often supplant the giving of one's attention to things happening within one's physical presence. Indeed, Chayko (2008, 181) argues that "the younger among us may not even experience a sharp distinction between online and offline phenomena, and it would not be unreasonable to speculate that in time the online-offline distinction may fade entirely." Certainly, the more the playing field is defined as including everyone who is mentally present— whether they are physically present as well or must be accessed using the technological device in one's hand—the more complicated the whole attention-demanding balancing act gets. Thus, the ongoing negotiation of who matters most and least in any given moment demands ever more of our constant attention.[27]

Table 3.1, "Number of self-reported communication technology access points for each participant," presents information on the number and kinds of channels participants used at the time of this study. It shows how individuals today need to navigate between a number of telephones with different locations and numbers, email accounts, beepers, pagers, instant messages, and text messages. The average person in our subset had five technology access points through which they could be reached any given day—three telephone numbers and two email accounts.[28]

An individual's multiple access points—and the channels to which they are attached—become stitched together to create worlds of persistent access. The effect of this on daily life can be daunting, if not overwhelming. As Gergen (1991, 75) puts it, "In effect, the potential for new connection and new opportunities is practically unlimited. Daily life has become a sea of drowning demands, and there is no shore in sight." Or, as one participant put it,

I'm a slave to my cell phone because people can reach me anywhere, anytime. I started hearing my cell phone ringing when it's not ringing. It's really freaking me out. I really want to pitch it.

This is the overall context of the remainder of this chapter, then, where, for at least some people, daily life—and the problem of achieving privacy—includes (1) a burgeoning number of demands for their attention, appearing across an increasingly diverse communication landscape; (2) a marked increase in the number of relationships they have or might have with the people making those demands; and (3) a shrinking set of shared rules, expectations, and practices for how to manage all of this.

In addressing this reality, the issue of power and its agenda-setting dimension comes to the fore: how much weight do we give to our own ideas

TABLE 3.1 Number of self-reported communication technologies access points for each participant

Case #	Total Phone Numbers	Home	Work	Mobile	Other	Beeper	PDA	Total Email Addresses	Personal	Work	Other	Other	Total Access Points
30	5	1	2	2				3					8
40	2		1	1				2	1	1			4
41	2	1		1				2					4
42	2	1		1				4	2	1	1		6
43	2	1		1				1					3
45	5	1	3	1				2	1	1			7
46	2	1	1					2					4
47	5	1	3	1				1					6
48	2	1		1				1					3
49	3	1	1	1				1					4
50	2	1	1			1		1		1			4
51	3	1	1	1				2					5
52	5	2	2	1				2					7
53	3	1	1	1				1					4
54	3	1	1	1				1					4
55	2	1	1					1					3
56	3	1	1	1		1		3	1	2			7
57	2	1	1					4					6
58	4	1	1	1	1			1					5
59	2	1		1				1					3
61	2	1	1					2					4
62	3	1	1	1				2					5
65	3	1	1	1		1		2					6
66	3	1	1	1				1				1	4
67	2	1		1				1					3
68	3	1	1	1				2					5
69	2	1		1				1					3
70	2	1		1									2
81	3	1	1	1		1		12					16
84	3	1	1	1									3
85	2	1		1				2					4
89	2							1					3
92	2	1		1		1		1					4
TOTAL	33	91	32	28	28	1	5	8	63	5	6	1	1	159
AVERAGES		3	1	1	1	0	0	0	2	0	0	0	0	5

of what we want to do—and when and how we wish to do it—versus other people's ideas of what we ought to be doing? Clearly, this begs the question of how difficult it might be for an individual to figure out what, exactly, she or he should pay attention to at a given moment. Should it be the baby one is bathing or the person on the other end of the ringing telephone? The individual on the office phone or the one on your cell phone? The person who wrote you the first email of the day, the author of the most recent one, or the one whose demand is most easily answered? Should it be any of the two hundred unread messages you've just seen on the computer in your hotel's lobby while on vacation or should it be the family waiting for you at the pool? The report that needs writing or the constant stream of IM questions that keep your subordinates working? Your pager or the patient waiting in the examination room? The list of options is seemingly endless.

The actual process of assigning priority to the very different demands for one's attention is rather mindboggling—and very likely to get any of these participants into at least a little trouble no matter what choice they make. It is also well outside of the scope of this book. Rather, here I limit myself to acknowledging the difficulty of the process and pointing out that this is precisely why developing techniques, strategies, and practices to manage these demands is so important.

THE SOLUTION: PERSONAL SOCIOTECHNICAL SYSTEMS FOR ACCESSIBILITY AND ATTENTION MANAGEMENT

Communication technologies have enabled a wide variety of others to challenge the privacy of our time and space and to try to supplant our agendas with their own in remarkably profound ways. They have allowed the demands for—and directions of—our attention to expand exponentially. Yet these potentially power-destabilizing technologies are also an important part of participants' arsenals for responding to these challenges. Given often nonnegotiable expectations to use these technologies, individuals empower themselves by using them in particular ways. They *manage* demands, not merely respond to them willy-nilly. This allows them to better balance their own and others' agendas as well as manage multiple demands for their attention in a more reasonable fashion.

For individuals who find themselves subordinated to others' agendas and demands for their attention, this may well mean engaging in efforts to relevel the playing field. The way they do that is twofold. First, they actively use these technologies—and other resources—to try to increase their ability to determine how accessible/inaccessible they (and the things about them) are to others. Second, they also try to better control the *ways* in which they will and won't be accessible to others. Participants' foremost desire is to possess the discretion to respond to others' demands in ways that make sense for them. To put it simply, their goal is to give their attention to whom or what they want, when they want, for as long as they want, in the ways that they want to do so.

In order to achieve this kind of demand management, each individual in this study draws on a dynamic system of resources. Through these systems, people, rules, devices, services, and practices are used in ways that (1) help the recipient filter what are perceived to be an overwhelming number of potential and actual technology-delivered requests for her or his attention; (2) shift responsibility for responding to unwanted requests away from the recipient; and (3) minimize the amount of effort the recipient expends on undesirable communiqués. Each component in the system may help achieve any or all of these outcomes, particularly when used in a coordinated fashion with other system elements.

The components of these systems fall under the following (by no means mutually exclusive) categories: (1) people, (2) rules and strategies, (3) practices, and (4) devices, features, services, and applications. The first category includes people such as personal assistants who screen and process calls on behalf of the recipient. Children and spouses as well as friends and employees may be called upon to do this.

Individuals also may be used as the basis for sorting what messages should be attended to or not. If an email or phone message comes from a certain person, for instance, that may be a signal that it should be attended to. If it comes from another person, it may be a signal that it should not. This can be highly dynamic, of course, as a recipient may not want to talk to a particular person at a given moment or duration of time, yet generally would be willing to do so—or vice versa.

This leads us to the second category of tools to manage demands for attention: rules and strategies. These include things such as a policy of answering all telephone calls because every one could be an opportunity for a growing business or a policy of never answering the phone "cold" without first checking the caller ID readout; interpreting a mispronunciation of one's name as a sign of an unknown, undesirable caller and therefore a signal to hang up; never giving out one's cell phone number; or never answering the work line after 5:00 PM. Similarly, participants have rules like "never read emails on which one has been copied," "never look at what has been targeted by the spam filter," "never use a particular email address to conduct business," and "never give an IM address to a nonwork person." Rules regarding the tone of one's response abound as well, of course, ranging from "keep it short" to "always be pleasant."

Whether or not people always follow such self-imposed rules, these guidelines typically result in a third set of tools to help manage others' demands: specific practices, including those that become habits. For example, one might have given out a cell phone number only to close family, and so now one never hesitates to answer it. One might always turn off one's cell phone before any scheduled meeting. One might listen to voicemail messages at the same time each day such as in the morning, after turning on the lights, putting away one's coat and purse, and starting the coffee. One might return obligatory calls from extended family only while driving home from work. One might check a cell phone for messages just before lining up to board the plane, then again after touchdown. One might check email every ten minutes or so whenever one is at one's desk, or try to battle the "compulsion of proximity"[29] by only checking every three hours.

Systems for this kind of attention management also rely on a fourth category of tools: a variety of devices, features, services, and applications. These include things like a computer, a landline phone, a cell phone, a Blackberry-type, bundled device, email, IM, a PDA, a pager, caller ID, privacy manager software, voicemail, buddy lists, "receipt requested" and "urgency" email features, a multiline phone connected to two or more lines, phones with different ring tones to signal different callers, signal blockers, and even services that turn all messages from multiple sources into email that can be accessed from one address or electronically vocalized (read to the recipient) over the phone.

With what is quite possibly a unique permutation of all of these kinds of resources, each individual tries to manage the activity of triaging and responding to the demands for her or his attention. What results is a dynamic (flexible and ever-changing) sociotechnical system used to deal with the problem of accessibility and attention management. Individuals use this emergent system to try to (1) get others to put their demands in certain forms, (2) get others to contain their demands to certain times and places, (3) make sure certain others can reach them while certain others cannot, and (4) receive and respond to the number of demands with which they are comfortable. All of this is designed to try to level the playing field, reequalizing the power distribution between those who use communications technologies to issue demands for recipients' attention and the recipients themselves.

KEY POINTS OF INTERVENTION

These systems are used primarily to manage or control demands at two points in the demands' journeys. The first point in the process occurs in the channeling of these demands down specific technological pipelines prior to the actual receipt of them. The second point in the process occurs after receipt of the demand, when it has already gotten the recipient's attention. This is when we see individuals actually responding to individual requests, dispensing with each one as they see fit.

CHANNELING: PRERECEIPT MANAGEMENT OF DEMANDS

Before a specific demand even reaches them, participants try to sort these requests into various channels of communication. Through more active and passive ways, they direct people to use different lines of communication to reach them. They follow more general as well as situational guidelines as they allocate people to these different channels.

Consider this participant, for instance, a consultant who frequently but not always works from home. He describes the specific ways in which he allocates people across his system of email, IM, a home phone, and a cell phone, granting access in specific ways and denying it in others in order to better regulate his attention. It's a good example of how participants draw on the full breadth of their communication systems to better control the demands others make on them.

I have to say I'm fairly new to using it [instant messaging]. I literally had never used it until eight months ago. Um. And the group of people I use it with is still very small. It's like a total of maybe ten. So we all, I think, use it in a very similar way.

So those are other consultants?

Yeah. Or coworkers, people I am working on jobs with, or whatever, but—

So how do you find out that they have instant messaging?

Well, you just tell them. It's like, "This is my instant messaging address, add me to your list."

. . . So do you give somebody your email address and your instant messaging address at the same time?

No. I only give out that [IM] if we have some sort of established relationship. And as we go. I think, "Oh, if this person IMs me it would be good." I don't usually right off say, "Hi, I have this IM address and that's how you should get to know me."

Do people do that to you? Do people—

I think I have seen that a couple of times, maybe. But, it's the whole, like, what do you put on your business card? A lot of people want to put everything. They put their home phone, their babysitter's pager, whatever. That's exaggerating. But, um-- And their IM and all that.

But, um, I like to-- I used to not even want to put my phone on my business card. It kind of depends on your job function. I would just write that in if I needed it.

So I treat IM much the same. I'll add it if I think I need it, but by default, email is the only thing I give out. It's like-- discretion-- for my address and cell phone.

I never give out the home phone.

Never?

No. 'Cause it's like, with a cell, it's like, there's no reason. And what I do at home is that I, like, leave the cell phone in the basement when I don't want to hear it.

You don't turn it off?

No, I mean, there is no reason. Because if I turned it off, I'll forget that it's off the next day. 'Cause I don't look at it, I just pick it up.

So anyway, I leave it in the basement so it doesn't wake me up or anything.

But if you give them your home phone-- You assume if people call you at midnight on the home phone, there's some emergency.

So it's okay for people to call you at midnight on the cell phone because you aren't going to hear it anyway?

That's right.

Do people know that?

Or if I happen to be working late, you know, then I'll pick it up. But-- They know it if they need to know it.

The key here is that it's the participant who gets to decide whether or not they do.

Efforts to allocate different people to different communication channels often focus on the issue of how directly we want someone to be able contact us. Three factors seem to underlie decisions about this issue of directness and, therefore, the precise ways that participants want others to reach them: (1) who the sender is; (2) what the precise reason is she or he might be trying to reach them; and (3) how attentive the participant is in monitoring each of her or his communication channels. (This last is important because this is what creates a fairly predictable level of availability for any given channel.)

In fact, these three factors lead to a hierarchy of preferred and less preferred channels for each sender and/or situation. Recipients may engage multiple phone lines and multiple email accounts as well as an entire smorgasbord of access points that cross multiple technologies to increase their demand-organizing and responding options. When used strategically, each channel can be used not only to better schedule the things and people one attends to, but also to provide a recipient with a sense of how important a certain demand might be, simply because of the way it arrives. Marshall McLuhan's (1965) insight that "the medium is the message" takes a very practical turn in just this way. By reserving a particular channel for communication with the most important people in their lives, for instance, or for the most important situations, participants know that when that channel is activated, they should respond to it as quickly as possible.

Once a demand has been sent down a particular channel, it may be further filtered before reaching the intended recipient. A child, spouse, or assistant may answer the phone first. A spam filter may assess email first. A cell phone may identify the sender's number and either display the sender's name or initiate a certain ring tone to signal a demand's arrival. A domestic phone service may block the call if it does not recognize the sender as a "white-listed," preapproved caller.

Figure 3.1 illustrates how such a system might work for a typical person in this study across the five channels commonly reported (i.e., cell phone, home phone, work phone, plus work and personal email accounts).

As shown in the diagram, a demand may be filtered one or more times after entering a specific channel. Afterward, if the demand continues on its journey toward the recipient, it may then be relegated into any number of holding places (e.g., a special spot on a desk for message slips, a chair, a refrigerator, an email inbox, a spam box, an answering machine or voicemail, the mind of a husband who monitors a couple's joint email account, or the mind of a teenager who listened to the answering machine messages upon arriving home from school). Here, the accumulated demands await the designated recipient's attention.

In general, the more discretion a channel provides in terms of concealing one's availability, the more participants like it. The ability to conceal availability is a function both of the actual technological features of the channel and the kinds of use patterns an individual establishes around it.

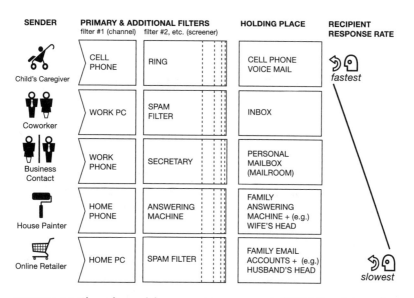

SENDER	PRIMARY & ADDITIONAL FILTERS			HOLDING PLACE	RECIPIENT RESPONSE RATE
	filter #1 (channel)	filter #2, etc. (screener)			
Child's Caregiver	CELL PHONE	RING		CELL PHONE VOICE MAIL	fastest
Coworker	WORK PC	SPAM FILTER		INBOX	
Business Contact	WORK PHONE	SECRETARY		PERSONAL MAILBOX (MAILROOM)	
House Painter	HOME PHONE	ANSWERING MACHINE		FAMILY ANSWERING MACHINE + (e.g.) WIFE'S HEAD	
Online Retailer	HOME PC	SPAM FILTER		FAMILY EMAIL ACCOUNTS + (e.g.) HUSBAND'S HEAD	slowest

FIGURE 3.1 Channeling and the pre-receipt management of ICT-delivered demands for attention.

As a result of both, users can exert a certain amount of control in any given situation as they seek to respond quickly to certain demands, but to put off others as they wish, too.

Toward this end, quite a few participants choose to reserve a specific communication channel for the most important people in their lives—or for the most important matters. Because of the highly personal and direct nature of the channel, cell phones were the commonly preferred channels reserved for this purpose. Cell phones and their features are inherently designed for an individual, able to be taken almost anywhere, and commonly carried close to the body. It allows the most ubiquitous, direct access to an individual. It is also a fashion, coming-of-age, and status accessory that has set new standards for conspicuous consumption (Veblen 1994). In the States, it is thought of as a highly personal object for all these reasons.[30]

Many participants had a difficult time envisioning, much less recalling, anyone but themselves ever answering their cell phones. Its association with only one specific individual means that people are rarely tempted to pick up, much less use, another's mobile phone—unless directly asked to do so. Cell phones are like wallets and purses in this respect. The following person's responses to these questions are typical, for example.

You said that the admin does not answer your cell phone.

No.

Does she ever?

Not ever.

Not ever. So does anyone ever answer this phone other than you?

No.

One reason cell phones *can* be so personal—and people so protective of them as a direct link to them and only them—is because cell phone numbers are not yet available on public listings, especially to telemarketers. Indeed, it is the availability of a telemarketing-free cell phone that has allowed so many participants to simply redirect important others to call them on their cell phones, leaving their home landlines for those unwelcome sales calls—and any unanticipated but welcome contact from others. Commercial policies of publishing landline numbers but not cell phone numbers are precisely what has allowed individuals to take this systems approach to reacquiring telephone privacy in the age of telemarketing.

In fact, because of its function as a nearly direct link to them, participants themselves frequently limit the number of people to whom they give their cell phone number. This "white-listing" strategy—preselecting who may have direct access to you and, therefore, your cell phone number—was a common tactic to control the privacy of one's time and space even though the phone might always be on, with you, and answered without hesitation.

When do you usually answer this [your cell] phone?

If it rings, I answer it. Because if it rings, I presume it's someone-- My husband or whoever's taking care of the kids has a very important reason for getting in touch with me.

And would there ever be a time when you wouldn't answer it, even if you're nearby?

No.

No? And you never listen to messages?

I don't even know how to. Its entire purpose is for me to be able to make an outgoing call if I really need to, to have it with me if the car breaks down, or for someone to reach me if the kids are in the hospital.

As we've already seen, a common reason for not giving out one's cell phone number is the fear that individuals would "abuse" it, that is, use it in a way that the recipient would not like.

Who typically has electronic or telephone access to you?

Telephone. Because I have a cell phone, everybody has access to my cell. Not clients, but coworkers have access to both the cell phone and the phone.

Not clients?

They wouldn't. No. The only reason I don't use the cell phone with clients is just because someone could abuse it, or be calling at two o'clock in the morning.

"Abusing" a communication channel typically means someone uses the channel in a way that challenges the social, temporal, or spatial boundaries with which a participant tries to organize her or his attention and agenda. Abuses of communication channels are therefore seen as violations of one's privacy, something to be avoided if at all possible. As this next participant shows, one's cell phone isn't the only number participants selectively withhold from others in order to prevent just this kind of occurrence, though—and clients and telemarketers aren't the only perpetrators we worry about, either.

And who has access to that [work] number? Do you give that out only to work-related people?

No. Not at all. Who has it? My sisters. Probably three friends. If I'm involved with anybody— That's about it. I don't like my parents—although I have good relationships with them—I don't like them to be able to contact me whenever they want. So they don't have that number.

Do they call you at home?

Yeah, they call me at home. But they don't have *this* number. I worked here for over three and a half years without giving them so much as a dime of this life. Because my mother calls both of my sisters at work several times a week.

. . . I talk to my sisters—and they do have this number—and they call me and say "Oh God, Mom's really pestering me. God!" . . . And it's really small stuff. You know, like, "Are you coming home for dinner? Do you want the broccoli or asparagus?" The moment the question pops into her head, she has to call.

This limiting strategy is not restricted solely to telephone channels, either. It can be seen in email and also through instant messaging.

Well, the two things I use heavily are email and instant messaging. And instant messaging-- Chris and I talked about this a little bit, how it's-- Do you use it?

I have used it. I haven't used it in a long time actually.

But it, um. It can be as disruptive as the phone, but I feel it's how you set boundaries around it. Um, I mean, you can block people and so on. I've never had to do that. It's like, 'cause-- The key distinction for me is I use IM only with business contacts. I never had a personal contact to instant messaging. Um, now it's much like-- I have separate email addresses for personal and work, and most purely social contacts don't have the work address, 'cause the distinction is important, the separation.

For you?

Uh, huh.

You make that conscious decision to—

I do have a lot of reasons. One is like, during the day, you kind of have to be more focused on work. Reachable, but you need, um, for the other stuff to have higher priority during the day.

By excluding anything except work-related matters from a certain email account or using IM only with work-related people, it makes this "focusing" task much easier. These practices afford this individual more control over the appearance of others' demands in the middle of his work day.

Allocating different people to different channels is thus an important way in which participants try to counteract the boundary-blurring potential of otherwise ubiquitous accessibility. It helps reimpose spatial and temporal boundaries around what and whom they pay attention to—and when—in an attempt to regulate the selves, social networks, and practical tasks that might otherwise be activated at any and all times. Of course, not everyone may appreciate participants' attempts to place certain boundaries around them, particularly if it means rejecting their own preferred ways of getting in touch.

Channel Conflict

When people fail to align over their preferred channels of communication, conflict may well ensue. From minor annoyances to unmasked power struggles, contests over who does and does not have control, who will and will not bend in a relationship may be seen here. Individuals described employing a variety of tactics, occasionally subversive, to condition others into using their preferred channels of communication—in the ways they prefer them used.

Refusing to use a particular channel, for instance, is a very effective way to get others to use yours. Here is an office assistant:

Like I said, I'm a phone person. Even when they send me emails through the system, I don't normally send them an email back. I will pick up the phone and call them back and discuss it with them. . . . Now, no one emails me. (*Laughter.*)

And here is a mother, another email resister:

Okay. How many times a day or a week would you log onto your email account?

Maybe, if I remember, every week or so.

Uh huh.

I really don't log on as much as I should, and I have been yelled at by my son. Yes. (*Laughing.*) It is a good way of keeping in touch with people, it's just that it's so easy-- to not turn it on.

Uh huh. I understand that. Are there ever any times when you don't return email messages that you receive?

Uh huh. (*Laughing.*) Oh, yes. Yes.

Is there a pattern to that? Or—?

My son says that there is a pattern. It is so easy to just put it off. I will do it later. I will do it later.

Uh huh.

Or if-- He got desperate and he just finally picked up the telephone and said, "You didn't pick up your mail." And I hadn't. And that was it. I just hadn't. I just hadn't even opened it. So I know that I've got to do better.

Or not. What she does in the future may mostly depend on just how much her son pushes her on this—or just how badly she needs to reach him should he start refusing to answer the phone.

In fact, refusing to use or develop reliable accessibility via a certain channel may be a great way to make others' demands more manageable. The office assistant mentioned previously, for instance, not only has to pay less attention to email than others do in her institution, but as a result of this, she gets asked to do far less than others do, too. Making or taking a separate phone call to communicate with her is a disincentive for others to place any more demands on her than they absolutely have to. Whether people like workplace assistants or the mothers of grown children, individuals who spend much of their lives dropping whatever they're doing to support others' agendas may find it quite empowering—or even essential—to disattend entire channels of communication.

This sort of conflict should not be reduced to mere interpersonal preference, though. The previous two participants were both over sixty years of age at the time of their interviews. Given the extraordinary importance of habits in effectively managing others' demands for our attention, it should be no surprise that they might find it difficult as well as undesirable to adopt and effectively monitor entirely new communication channels. If someone has gotten along fine their entire life with one phone at home and one at work, for instance, it *should* take some serious convincing for her or him to willingly adopt and monitor a cell phone as well, much less log onto a computer and babysit an email account or two. The effort required to establish such habits must be driven by a strong need to do so.

Here, another senior describes a similar situation in which her son's generational focus on and enthusiasm for the computer is at odds with her own view of the same.

Does anybody else that you know of have access to the documents or databases that you might create on your computer?

No. But of all of them-- Maybe my son. My oldest son has used it.

Okay.

He has the most-- He knows most, I guess. He's in charge of everything.

Right. So did he set it up for you and everything?

He's from (St. Louis). Unfortunately, he did, he helped me. Well, I have a young lady here who is helping me with the computer, so she has helped me. But he would have most of the information.

So he set up your email account?

Unfortunately, he did.

Okay. Why do you say "unfortunately"?

Because-- I think that he signed me up for things that I haven't learned to use yet.

Right.

So they're still there and he is harassing me about them. "Mom, you're not doing so and so" and "Mom, haven't you done so and so?" So I think that is why it's unfortunate.

If he hadn't done it, he wouldn't know I wasn't doing it.

As many people have found out much to their chagrin, it's hard to keep any secrets about your computer use—or disuse—from your system administrator, maybe especially if he's your son.

Corrupted Channels

Occasionally communication channels become corrupted and no longer serve the function they once did. As we have seen, answering the home telephone before telemarketers became rampant was a far different experience from what it is now. Because of these solicitors, this communication channel has certainly lost at least a measure of directness and privateness for everyone in this study. It has been corrupted. The home phone's function—as well as people's interactions with it—has changed accordingly.

Any time an "intruder" appears within a specific channel, it can remind us of our preferences for that channel. Here, one participant recalls a story about her relationship to instant messaging and the bind she finds herself in when a family member begins popping up there.

Have you ever monitored someone else's computer use? And this also includes friendly monitoring, like instant messaging, you know, when you're looking online to see if somebody else is online.

No. I so don't care about that. In fact, I find that really irritating—that someone can find out if I'm online and send me an instant message that I have to respond to. Actually, the only person who does that to me is (my niece) and I can't very well not reply to my niece, so-- And I'm working, and then I get these messages from her and that's really irritating. Luckily, she's the only person that does that to me.

If the channel becomes corrupted to the point where the annoyances and intrusions associated with it outweigh the benefits of using that channel, it can foster such a negative reaction that the channel may be abandoned altogether. People who have no landline at home because of telemarketers and use only their cell phones fall into this category. So does the following person.

Okay. Now, do you have a beeper?

Not any more, thank God!

Why did you hate your beeper, or not want a beeper?

Well, general principle: someone can get you; you can't get them. You know?

It lets you know there's something that's going on, but you can't do anything about it.

[Then there's] the noise, you know.

And then, just, I think-- Specifically, when I had it for two years doing another type of job-- When it goes off, it means something bad just happened and-- It's not like beep, beep, beep, "Hey! I've got a $50 free gift certificate for you."

It's all bad news.

And this one:

Would you like to have a beeper?

Absolutely not!

Why not?

I hate those things. In fact, I do. You know, this is part of this privacy thing. I don't like to be called, beeped, or whatever, I guess, unless somebody really has something to say.

In fact, I don't like to receive emails so I turned off this automatic email [notification of delivery] thing. So people get very upset that I didn't read their email they sent five seconds ago.

Right.

Because I pick it up whenever I feel like it, and it could be twice a day.

All of these individuals have either abandoned or modified their use of a channel because of the ways others were using it. Telemarketers and, somewhat less so, e-marketers are seen as the most nefarious forces corrupting participants' communication channels. People adopt service providers and software specifically because of their spam filters, as well as caller identification, privacy manager, and voicemail services to screen out these demands for their attention.

The impact of these services may be unexpected, too. Here, a school nurse is unable to reach sick children's parents because her phone number is blocked on a caller ID display. It is labeled in a way that has become synonymous with telemarketers.

Who typically has electronic or telephone access to you while you're at work?

Oh, well, that's interesting. Um, telephone access—anyone could call. You can dial directly from outside. The weird thing though is that it's an (internal) school phone, and all the school-- What I've been told is all the internal caller ID numbers are blocked.

So if I call someone at home, it doesn't say "School Nurse, (Orland Park)." It says "Call Blocked," which makes me sound like, seem like, a salesperson. And I'm not. I'm calling because your daughter just threw up on my shoes and she needs to go home.

So that issue is awful. That's not my privacy. It's others' privacy, and kind of like, the things they have in place to try to maintain it.

And I've tried with telecommunications [the support department] to get that undone, but they claim it's not, it's just not possible.

But if I call within the school, my call to another school phone, it'll come up on the school caller ID as "Nurse (Joan)" or whatever. So they know.

Without a doubt, most parents would want to be instantly available to take a call from this woman. Yet the very device that is supposed to give them *more* control over their accessibility is actually giving them less.

This next participant describes a similar situation in which his furious attempts to thwart telemarketers and other solicitors nearly backfired on him, too. His caller ID fails to give him complete enough information to regulate his accessibility as accurately as he'd like. While he wants to deny access to solicitors, he definitely wants to pick up for an old, now famous friend.

You don't screen calls?

Well, now I do. I just look on the little screen. You know, and if it's Viet Now or some other charity, I don't do it anymore. I used to be good about it. If people wanted, you know-- They'd say, this is Viet Now or this is State Troopers. This is our one-time-a-year donation. But do you know what? It's bullshit. It's not one time a year, it's three or four times a year. And I told them, I said, look, man. I was giving money to you every year three or four times, so this is not one time a year, and I'm done. And with all that—the Police Lodges, there's Lodge 41, the State Troopers

Retirement Fund, I mean it's just a giant fucking scam. But I was real-- I thought, I want to be forthright and help these people, but-- I don't believe it anymore because 99 percent of the money does not go to anybody other than the greedmongers who are running the charities.

... [N]ow we have caller ID, so we always know who's calling.

Does it have—?

Except for our snooty friends, who have private numbers.

Right.

It's like, (Mills) called me from New York a couple of weeks ago now and, you know, it came up "private number." And I thought, well--? And [after I picked up] then he says, "Howard *who*? Howard-- I can't--." I said, "It's Stern, Howard Stern. And Robin Quivers." He hangs up. And so then I listen to the show and he does this whole thing about Howard Stern. He had written this bit, but he could not remember the guy's last name. (*Chuckles.*)

Caller ID isn't used merely to thwart solicitors. This next participant and his wife—an architectural engineer married to a lawyer, both of whom practice from home—use caller ID along with a two-line phone system dedicated to their businesses. Caller ID lets them withhold their attention for strategic professional reasons.

I have five telephone numbers.

Now, if it's okay with you, if we can go through each of these five telephones and figure out how you use them and how they play out. So your first one, what would that be?

Well, the primary one that I use is my office phone. The office phone has two lines. The first line is for general calls. The second line is a rollover line. Or, you know, with special clients, in situations where there's an emergency, I will give them the second line so that they-- so that I know it's a significant issue that they're calling about and it doesn't get fended off into electronic hell and I don't get back to them until a couple hours later.

When would be the situation when you wouldn't answer it?

Well, you know (Catherine) represents-- is a criminal lawyer. She gets a lot of phone calls, collect calls from prisoners. And they're very expensive and they almost never are any-- There's almost never a conveyance of information; it's more of a psychic need. So we don't usually take those calls. Unless there's a specific reason to take the call, we don't take those calls.

Occasionally you get into a situation in litigation where there is an advantage to not getting back to somebody right away, too. So she'll use discretion in answering opposing counsel's calls. Answer them right away if there's something that you think you can take care of right away. You delay if you think that there's an advantage to delay.

And otherwise—of course, sales calls—which are intrusive and which we get a lot of.

Like the systems every participant has developed to handle unwanted phone calls, spam has also led to some unexpected outcomes regarding email management. These include not only legislation and litigation and spam filters, but also the complete abandonment of email channels as individuals swamped by spam migrate out of them. People may create and use "false" channels, too, where email accounts are used (like some cell phones) only to initiate communication, like transactions. Incoming messages are never read in these accounts and the addresses are never given out to anyone whose correspondence matters.

With false channels, what appears to be a two-way channel—the existence of which can be sold to marketers who will then try to get the recipient's attention—actually is not. Individuals who allow others to leave telephone messages but never listen to them or who list telephone numbers that they literally never answer also demonstrate the concept of a false channel. One participant has an answering machine for people to leave messages, yet he "never" listens to them. He says he does this so that people will leave him alone. "Unless they get to leave a message," he says, "they'll just keep calling." He simply deletes all messages without ever playing them back. The same principle guides the following fellow's strategy:

How many email addresses do you have?

(*Cracks up, laughing.*) Considering the amount of free reign that Yahoo has in terms of creating email accounts, I think I have, like, seven, um. The amount that I use consistently, however, differs a lot. I am able-- I use my (university) account almost every single day. I check my Yahoo account, like, every single week, um, my main Yahoo account. And then I-- Then the other accounts are either, like, dummy accounts in order to collect spam or they're just accounts that I used for different sorts of projects that I don't use anymore.

Giving out entirely fake email addresses or phone numbers is just one step away from these kinds of false channels. They all can be valuable tools for managing one's privacy.

RESPONDING: POSTRECEIPT MANAGEMENT
OF DEMANDS

Responses to telemarketing and spam show that not everyone uses some form of filter to first screen out unwanted calls or email. One participant's spam may be another one's delight, especially when scanning for discounts and deals is a major motivation for logging on. In fact, in some situations, participants choose to accept all demands for their attention. They would worry more about what they might miss than what they might get.

Sometimes people don't try to screen calls, for instance, because it's just not worth the effort to do so. This may be especially true because of technological limitations in their communication systems and/or social expectations for their more constant accessibility. Sometimes the rationale is more specific: the fear of missing an important request for their attention.

One of the jokes we've got right now—because Polly's waiting to hear back from colleges and universities about interviews and admission stuff—is that everybody answers every call. (*Laughs.*) No call will go unanswered! (*Laughs.*)

In this case, the policy of answering all calls is likely to end upon this daughter's college admission and acceptance. The following participant, however, seems to have a much longer duration in mind for the system he's created to handle work-related phone calls.

Last night, when I called the number on your card, I got somebody else. Is that a way that you manage your schedule, by kind of filtering calls to you?

No. She answered the phone. Sometimes I answer the phone, but my assistant was there to answer the phone. But I'm glad you called.

She'll handle—?

She just answers the phone. And I don't screen my calls, no. . . . If someone wants to get at me, I want to know that. For good or for bad.

So you don't use the voicemail?

Oh, sure. Voicemail. For the odd hours. But, no, I don't avoid calls.

That's interesting. I think a lot of people use that.

I don't. I'm not a lot of people.

This is not to suggest that such decisions come without a cost, however, or that their wisdom is always readily apparent. The following individual also tries to answer all calls, yet has developed a pronounced negative reaction to the ringing of the phone as a result.

Oh, here's one thing that I was-- I still regret it, but I don't know if I would do it any different. When I had my business, people would use my home phone number and I felt that it was a really valuable asset to be able to tell people that they could always reach me at home. So it was a really good sign, too, but it made me dread looking-- Like even still today, a year and a half later, I would really rather not get phone calls. So I guess that's really a privacy issue, in a way, but I'm trying to start thinking of it differently, you know. Because phone calls usually are good things.

Yeah, how do you get people to reach you?

No, no, no. It's just—

(Laughing.)

—it's just, no. It's just that my brain got turned around wrong, really, because I just started to dread the phone calls because I was just overwhelmed with them for years and years and years. It was just too much. And, you know, I didn't get on-- I didn't start using email regularly until the last year because I didn't want one more way that I would have to check constantly to find out who wanted what or what needed to get where kind of thing.

. . . Do you do things like just, you know, let the machine pick up most of the time so you don't have to answer it right then?

No, that's really rare. Um, the only time that I will do that is if I'm, you know, totally unable to come to the phone, you know, if I'm in the shower or something.

And yet still you dread it.

Yeah, well the problem for me is that the dread of what it might be is, could be, more than the dread of [what it actually is]-- This is the deal right now, and that's just the way my personality works. I'd rather just get it over with and deal with it than just be worrying about whatever.

Whether a point of pride or just practicality, some individuals don't want to use filters on their email accounts, either. It's not because they like spam. Rather, they are afraid of important messages being accidentally siphoned off and being prevented from responding to the requests of people to whom they do wish to be available.[31]

For whatever reason, these participants' strategies to reduce the demands for their attention focus on minimizing how much attention they give to others. While many people use the one-two punch of channeling and filtering first, then selectively granting different amounts of attention to those who actually get through, other participants may rely only on the latter to control their accessibility. This person is quite aware of her attempts to minimize time on the phone, for instance.

Do you ever feel as if your accessibility through telephones, computers, and other electronic devices are a problem for you?

I'm really not paranoid about it. I think it's more of an annoyance. And now that you mention it, the phone has always annoyed me. One of the joys in our house in Wisconsin is that there are no phones. If we have to communicate with someone, we walk over to their cabin. And to me, that is the greatest gift—to not hear the telephone ring. Because what happens is people don't communicate with you unless it's important, if they need it. It's amazing, when you don't have all those ways of communication, how rarely you need to talk and so—

So you don't feel overwhelmed by all the ways people can get a hold of you, just annoyed?

Um, I don't really give people the opportunity, and I'm quite gruff. You can ask any of my friends or (Dave's) friends. And, you know, they call and they get Dave, that's great. But if they get me then they're really brief or I'll pass them right onto Dave. I rarely sit and chat. So I get annoyed. And I do feel it's a real intrusion.

As we see here, one of the most effective and interesting ways of giving individuals only as much attention as one would like is to get other people to respond on our behalf. Participants frequently report a communications division of labor in the home as well as at work. This is designed not only to accommodate each person's preferred mode of communication, but also to ensure that there are reasonable coverage and response rates over the entire system of communications in use. Different household members' willingness to talk, type, initiate, respond, schedule their time, or be interrupted can all be assets in figuring out this division of labor at home.

However they do it, though, once demands have been received, the general behavior is that of participants adjusting their responses in order to further allocate attention as they wish. The following individual describes some of this process regarding email messages.

Do you ever not return messages?

Sure.

Good.

Wait, that's on tape. (*Laughs.*) Um, sure—I do *not*.

(*Laughs.*) What types of messages would you not?

Well, this is really silly. Unwanted social ones. Um, I've heard from-- Like on our high school Web site, I'm on my Web site. I went to put in my email address and I first heard from two people that I knew in high school who I don't care for (*laugh*). And so that's just a really silly example but—

No, it's a good example.

Then I delete a lot of, sort of the-- We get a lot of sort of just random consumer ones, and I just delete them immediately. You know, they want you to go click on whatever, and stuff like that.

. . . Yeah. The junk mail I delete. (*Baby talking in background.*) Most of it I give maybe about a second or two of eyeball time, and then I delete them. Even a second or two actually seems long. It's like a split second.

Among our participants, email generally is the preferred mode of communication. It allows demands to be easily organized and held in waiting and provides the best cover for hiding one's true availability and awareness of another's demand. It makes it especially easy to prioritize what to respond to at any given moment—and often minimizes the effort necessary to respond altogether.

For all those reasons, email permits individuals to better balance the power distribution between all communicators. It not only helps participants manage others' demands for their attention, though, it also allows at least some of them to feel better about making their own demands on others. The following individual taps into all of these themes.

. . . What I like about email, even email from people I don't know and why I prefer it to contact people I don't know-- You know, this job involves a certain amount of cold contact. I prefer to do it by email because I like to have—and I like other people to have—the freedom to respond on their own schedule.

Uh huh.

A phone ringing says you must talk to me now. That insistence. And even with caller ID it's-- You asked if there's anybody I'd rather filter out and that's certainly true. You know, I only pick up the phone when I know it's some kind of solicitation when I'm in the mood for a fight or something. You know.

But I often don't pick up the phone when it's my closest friends also. I mean, I don't tell them later that they've been screened, I just say I'm not going to be a great conversationalist right now. You know. Could be in the middle of the afternoon, it's not, you know [a good time]. Maybe I'll call them back an hour later, whatever, but--

And then of course you're saying "*Now* I'm ready to talk" and, you know, "You'll talk on *my* schedule."

(*Laughs.*)

And so the phone always involves that for one of the parties. But email has that advantage of being a kind of "time customizable" thing.

For a variety of reasons, then, email has proven itself to be an enormously important tool in managing accessibility and relationships for a number of participants.

Okay. What do you use your email account for?

What kind of communications?

Um, just-- Huh. I use it actually, um-- A substitute for telephones. 'Cause I don't like to chat on the phone and also I find it's very hard to concentrate on the phone. So when I have a free moment, I'm more apt to send an email to a friend or to my sister or whatever. If I call my sister, it'll take an hour. If I email her, it will take two minutes.

Right.

And it's just much better for the relationship. (*Laugh.*)

At least she believes it is, for now. In fact, while participants have distinct preferences for the specific system tools and ways that they use them at any given time, those preferences may well change. Systems are reconfigured and adapted to new household and employment situations, new technologies, new expectations for how we are supposed to respond to others' demands for our attention, and changes in our own comfort with different levels of accessibility. It is their very dynamism as well as their creators' cleverness in responding to changes in their daily lives that make these systems so interesting.

The following participant discusses one quite common way in which the dynamic nature of the system may be seen. Here, the rules for answering the phone and getting through to her are changing because there's a new baby in the family. Fortunately, her husband is a "phone person," and her movement away from that device is offset by his orientation toward it.

Where is your home phone located? In the kitchen?

Yes.

Okay. When would you be likely to be near it?

All day, because it's cordless. (*Laughing.*) It tends to go-- As you can see, it's on the table with us. So it goes with me. If I go upstairs with him, I might put it up there. If I go down in the playroom with the kids later in the day, it goes down with us. Just so I'm not running around and leaving him alone, and I get phone calls a lot.

Okay. Who answers it usually?

Myself, 95 percent of the time.

And if somebody else answers it on your behalf, what would the general rules be for what happened next?

Well, the rules are changing, but now in the evening. (Doug)-- I'm either putting him down or I need to not talk to anybody (*laughing*) for awhile, so he's running interference now. I guess they've accepted the rule now and the evening is becoming "She can't come to the phone right now. (*Laughing.*) Who is this?" So, yeah.

. . . Doug's somebody who can't not answer the phone.

Yeah.

Sometimes we're having a conversation or—either the baby or whatever—he'll just go, "Just a second" and "I'll get it." I'm like, let the machine get it when we're actually having a life moment or whatever.

Without question, expectations for communications technology are a significant part of the current challenge for participants as they try to achieve balance in their accessibility. Yet these technologies and the ways people use them are also part of what are often ingenious—though not always successful—responses to this challenge. Whether there's a new baby in the house or a phone-friendly teenager leaves for college or a new Blackberry replaces one's laptop, the entire system is in a potential state of flux.

Like all the issues involved in managing one's accessibility, even the issue of how much one cares about it can change over time. Participants' response systems tend to morph in numerous ways, becoming more and less effective, simpler and more convoluted as new components are adopted and old ones are replaced. Sometimes this happens because components have remarkably unintended consequences on participants' abilities to manage their accessibility. Any of these components can backfire, worsening the very problem that they were supposed to address, that is, letting important people and matters get to the recipient as quickly as possible while keeping the others at bay.

Sometimes this is because individuals never understood how a device or service—or their system—works. Sometimes it is because a component functions exactly as the designer and purchaser intended, but it is dysfunctional for a specific user in the context of the rest of her or his system. When one participant's husband gave her voicemail for a Christmas gift, for instance, it unintentionally caused her a great deal of extra stress. It replaced her answering machine—along with her ability to screen calls in real time and to be visually notified of any messages she might have received via the answering machine's blinking light.

Through these systems, individuals try to reset the balance of power between themselves and any others who might request their attention. Participants try to develop systems in which others' desirable (or at least tolerable) demands for their attention get through while the undesirable demands are blocked or quickly dispensed with. In this way, individuals simultaneously attempt to manage the relationships—or potential relationships—that they have with others, whether those are of a parent/child, employer/employee, seller/buyer, expert/inquirer, or any other nature.

A seventy-four-year-old widow perfectly captures the way these systems are meant to work in helping one to manage one's accessibility and attention.

Do you have an answering machine or is it voicemail?

Answering machine.

Okay, so you can hear when other people are leaving a message?

Yes.

Do you ever use that to screen calls?

Sure. What's the point in paying for it if you're not going to do that?

Right. So you would screen out, like, telephone solicitors and things like that.

And I also have caller ID. If it says incoming, no number, whatever, I don't answer unless I really want to, to see who it is.

How about on your cell phone? You said that people can leave messages. Do you retrieve the messages?

No, I don't. Until I come home. When I am out, I am out. I don't want to be bothered, so I will not retrieve a message when I'm out.

It is enough that you can reach me at home. When I am out, I don't want to be reached unless it's an emergency. And then I figure that whatever it is, they can just wait until I either contact them or when I come home.

Uh huh.

When I go shopping, I'm shopping. When I go to a concert, I don't want a call. I don't want to sit there and forget that I have turned nothing off and have it go off. When I come to church, I don't want to be disturbed.

Okay. And then when you come home, do you have any general guidelines for how you respond to or handle messages that come in on your cell phone?

I will listen to all of them and then I will pick the ones that I-- that are important, that I consider more important than the others, and then I answer them in that order. Not in the order in which the person may have called me.

Okay. And how about at home, what guidelines do you have for dealing with the messages that come in at home?

Same way. If a call comes in, and it's not something that I feel is very important, I mean, I will not respond until I have taken care of what matters.

"What matters" may be another message someone left, or it might be something needing her attention right there, in her cozy urban home.

"SENSORY OVERLOAD" AND THE "URBAN MODE OF LIFE"

Because communication technologies add an extra and competitive layer of social territory onto what already exists at a face-to-face level, these technologies can bring anyone closer to the experiential equivalent of a hustling, bustling, dense, heterogeneous, large-as-life[32] "city life," regardless of her or his geographic location. These participants certainly describe daily (communication-rich) experiences that are remarkably consistent with Wirth's (1938, 1) "urban mode of life"—which he prophetically and specifically states is not confined to the experience of living in cities.

In addition to Wirth, scholars such as Simmel (1950a)[33] and Goffman (1959, 1966, 1982) have written extensively on the ways individuals must adjust to the potentially overwhelming nature of the public urban experience. Their descriptions resonate surprisingly well with the psychological state of "overload" and resulting adaptations that Milgram (1970, 1462) wrote about, too.

> [O]verload . . . refers to a system's inability to process inputs from the environment because there are too many inputs for the system to cope with, or because successive inputs come so fast that input A cannot be processed when input B is presented. When overload is present, adaptations occur. The system must set priorities and make choices. A may be processed first while B is kept in abeyance, or one input may be sacrificed altogether.
>
> City life, as we experience it, constitutes a continuous set of encounters with overload, and of resultant adaptations.

For Milgram, urban living poses a serious attention-regulation problem. It is a stimulus-overrich environment. Failure to develop protective "norms of non-involvement"—that is, adaptations—to this environment risks serious consequences, too, "impinging on role performance, the evolution of social norms, cognitive functioning, and the use of facilities."

Milgram (1970, 1462) identifies six ways in which people try to manage or prevent stimulus overload and the endless distractibility of the city. These usefully collapse into three classes of adaptations. These have to do with (1) filtering, (2) avoiding responsibility for, and (3) minimizing personal responses to environmental stimuli.

These adaptations are precisely what one participant learned to do as she adjusted to life in Boston, for instance. In order to avoid being flashed, she got better at figuring out what she should and should not pay attention to, avoiding and minimizing her response to the flashers who might be in her vicinity. Her new way of being further reflected what Milgram calls the "ultimate adaptation":

> The ultimate adaptation to an over-loaded social environment is to totally disregard the needs, interests, and demands of those whom one does not

define as relevant to the satisfaction of personal needs, and to develop highly efficient perceptual means of determining whether an individual falls into the category of friend or stranger.

This chapter supports many of Milgram's descriptions of how people respond to urbanlike environmental demands on their attention. Although these study participants already live in and around a major metropolitan center, communications technologies seem to have further urbanized daily life for them. They specifically identify these technologies as an important contributor to their current feelings that there are too many things and too many people competing (or potentially competing) for their attention every day. The experience of overload is often alluded to in their interviews, as are the specific activities they engage in to cope with it.[34]

Communications habits in particular show evidence not only of the development of the "ultimate adaptation" of those living in an urban mode (i.e., quickly figuring out who is friend or stranger and dismissing any claims from the latter) but also of its corollary. This, Milgram claims, is the prediction that "the disparity in the treatment of friends and strangers ought to be greater in cities than in towns." In the next chapter especially, we will see that participants often show great disparity in their treatment of friends and strangers. Here, though, we see this in the fact that an entire communication channel typically is reserved for the closest of relationships, while another (perhaps even a false one) is available for strangers. An assortment of other options are used for everyone in between. Moreover, in the often overwhelming richness of everyone's technology-delivered demands, these participants are very quick to use automatic filters and hang up on or delete messages from strangers—quicker, perhaps, than their relatively demand-deprived "rural-like" counterparts with a single phone to monitor and very few calls during the day.[35]

Thus, individuals walk a fine line when trying to control their accessibility through communications technology. This next participant is keenly aware of this fact. In this last excerpt, he provides a beautiful overview of the ways in which controlling one's privacy—in the home and over communications technologies—can affect one's life. One may cut off one's accessibility to others, but such choices have consequences. One's dislike of intrusions, of a loss of control, can easily take one to a place not only of privacy, but of isolation.

Um, we just bought a TeleZapper.

Oh.

As seen on TV. Because it is tiresome to continue to get phone calls.

How does that work—do you have to pick up?

No, actually what it does, it senses if a computer has dialed the number.

It does? Okay.

And then it sends a signal back that tells the computer the number isn't in service or has been disconnected. And it only does that for computer-dialed numbers. It apparently can sense by the way that the call comes in.

Hm.

That's-- And I didn't buy it. They [my family] bought it yesterday. Because we're tired of those calls.

Because you were getting a lot of calls, huh?

Yeah, and they tend to come at dinner.

Hum.

Which is-- And so, everybody now knows: "Remove us from your list," that's the key phrase.

Umhm.

Um, and I think that has been an invasion, um, from my perspective.

Umhm.

It's unsolicited, and I haven't reached out. I mean, if I get a call from church, asking for my help for something, that's not an invasion because I have, I joined there, and I have expressed an interest in doing things.

Umhm.

Um, or if I have friends that call, there's no invasion associated with that. I mean, frankly, no matter what the topic is.

Hm.

Because I've extended the number to them, and there's a permission associated with that friendship.

Umhm.

And, in fact, if it's a time when we can't talk, I'll say I'll call you back in forty-five minutes if that's fine. But there is, it does feel like an invasion to me when the unsolicited call comes in to sell me something goofy.

Right.

Um, uh, I think spam email has the potential to greatly diminish the value of the Internet because it's painful to have to go there every day and wipe out fourteen ads of messages for Viagra or mortgages.

Right, it becomes a barrier, and you don't want to use it because of that.

Yeah, right, and I don't much like that.

Hm.

Um, I think a car alarm is an invasion.

Right.

When it sits in front of the house and goes off all night.

Umhm.

Um, that's invading my auditory space.

Umhm.

And I don't like that. I think there are avenues of invasion into the house that we have less control over than we'd like, or I have less control over than I would like.

Umhm.

And, um, that said, the house is still the place when I can exercise the most control.

Umhm.

I can pull the drapes.

Umhm, right.

I can choose not to answer the phone. I can turn up the stereo and not hear the other thing if I wanted to. I mean, so there are ways to deal with it all.

Um, the sad part of that is all those ways make me more isolated.

Hm. Because you can do that?

Well, if I exercise all those options, then I have closed myself off to things like seeing the trees. If I'm worried about somebody looking in my house, and I pull the drapes, I don't see the outside world.

Umhm.

Uh, and so there are some prices that are, um, substantial, and that I'm not prepared, in a broad sense, to pay fully, at those prices.

Umhm.

We went four and a half or five years without any window treatments on our-- Across the front of our house there was a big living and dining room combination. And we just put some little sheers on there, one-half way up right now. Largely because it looks better from the inside.

Umhm.

But now that closed off the outside.

Right.

Um, because I still want to be able to see outside. And it's bad enough that we're on the second floor and I just can't walk out onto a deck or something.

Okay.

So there are some penalties to be paid.

Stories of mistakes made and lessons learned in the "struggle to achieve a balance between privacy and participation" (Westin, 1967, 11) abound for these participants. Rather than simply giving up, though, for the most part—and in spite of a palpable sense of frustration—most of them seem to be holding their own. They do so in the ways that people usually do: by taking the resources at hand and putting them to work as best they are able in order to address the problem. In the process, they reveal much about the current problems, solutions, and tradeoffs of managing social accessibility in an information and communication technology-saturated world.

CONCLUSION: TECHNOLOGY AND PRIVACY

Technology[36] provides an entry point from which we can uncover what is socially problematic. It gives us a place from which we can see what a social group takes for granted as well as its more contested terrains. Technology is itself a kind of hyperlink that can take us into the assumptions and practices surrounding it.

This characteristic of technology persists at least in part because of the way it functions as a prosthetic.[37] Technology allows us to extend our senses, our reach, our influence, and other aspects of our selves. It does this by extending our physical capabilities (including our presence) over time, space, and social networks of relationships.

These two interrelated characteristics of technology mean that as new and more powerful technologies are made—and older ones are abandoned—we bring them with us into experiential realms and daily routines where they did not previously appear. As a result, cultural concepts and expectations become juxtaposed and linked in new ways with specific times, spaces, people, objects, and activities. In the process, we not only find new challenges to our previous understandings and experiences of the world, but we also discover that much of what we had taken for granted was and is largely socially constructed, however reified it may have become.[38]

This chapter has focused on the ways this process is played out regarding privacy and the challenge of managing social accessibility. Changing technologies, expectations, and the habits that incorporate them mean that the need to attend to the problem of social accessibility is highly likely to persist in the future. The need to personally attend to this aspect of achieving privacy certainly will not go away.

This is not only because of practical problems like where to focus one's attention given all the people who want it and who can now knock on one's electronic as well as physical doors. Gergen (1991) believes that the very concept of self is becoming defined more thoroughly by relationships because of these changes, too—relationships that are ever increasing in number as well as importance.

> In this era the self is redefined as no longer an essence in itself, but relational. In the postmodern world, selves may become the manifestations of relationships, thus placing relationships in the central position occupied by the individual self for the last several hundred years of Western history.

Our ability to manage those relationships via the management of our accessibility may take on even greater importance in the future, accordingly—whether it's in response to the phone ringing, an email or text message arriving, some new and currently unimaginable technologies, or the person sitting next to us who is competing with all of these.

NEXT

Managing the accessibility of one's information, identity, and sociability face-to-face, in the neighborhood, is an equally important and difficult privacy challenge. From the moment the doorbell rings to putting out the trash, walking the dog, or getting a bit of yard work done, managing one's privacy and one's relationships with neighbors—and anyone else passing through—is up next. Given the nature of participants' urban homes, it is another fascinating opportunity to look at even more locations along the private-public beach.

CHAPTER FOUR

Doorbells & Windows

How would you define something that's "public" compared to something that's "private"?

Sort of, my analogy would be the exterior of my dwelling versus the interior. The exterior is completely public. Anyone can walk up to it. Anyone can view it. I choose when I draw the shades. I choose to whom I open the door. When someone comes in I choose how far in my dwelling someone goes and may see. So, that's sort of how I would choose-- how I would define the opposite. It's the places where I legally, morally, legitimately cannot have control over access or viewing.

> DAVID, forty-seven-year-old husband, father, and engineer

David's metaphor builds on a classically American perspective. Outside the house is public, but inside is private. Outside we have little control over our accessibility, but inside we have a lot. One's home, after all, is one's castle.

What about the castle perimeter, then? What about that remarkably interesting space we create around the edges of our homes? Surely, here is another fabulous beach and another great place to explore the work of privacy.[1]

In the United States, what goes on inside the house is generally agreed to be private. Our legal system is founded upon this principle. As Alderman and Kennedy (1997, 25) write:

> The home is sacrosanct under American law and has long been protected against unwarranted government intrusions. It was the general searches of colonists' houses that prompted the Framers to draft the Fourth Amendment two hundred years ago. In the 1990s, courts are still quoting William Pitt's impassioned plea for the inviolability of the home: "The poorest man may in his cottage bid defiance to all the forces of the Crown. It may be frail—its roof may shake—the wind may blow through it—the storm may enter—the rain may enter—but the King of England cannot enter!"
>
> Indeed, the law even recognizes a certain zone of privacy around the home that we can reasonably expect to reserve for ourselves. That space, along with our house, is protected by the Fourth Amendment. Under the law, this area is known as the "curtilage." To most of us, it is known as our yard.

Because of this legal foundation, for instance, the historical standard has been that the State may only enter one's home—physically or electronically—if its representatives are invited in or if there is overwhelming evidence that something criminal is going on inside. Without question, participants shared this perspective at the time of their interviews. They certainly viewed the home and yard (if any) as private property, subject to criminal trespass laws.

Despite its legal standing, of course, whatever happens in the yard is more public than whatever happens in the house. Some of the things happening inside may not be as private as the law might suggest, either. Anything that someone can see, hear, or smell from the street or the interior spaces of a building, for instance, is obviously not nearly as private as one might wish. It does not matter if it occurs within the bounds of private property. Physical accessibility—visual, auditory, olfactory, and tactile variations—makes people, creatures, objects, and activities socially accessible, too, and an open invitation for any potential witnesses' engagement.[2]

This is one of the reasons why there is such a potentially contested terrain waiting along the borders of our homes, every day. It's a wonderful vantage point from which to see both boundary conflict and resolution. Here is where people try to control not only what they will make available to each other, but also what they notice, draw attention to, and even choose to remember from whatever they might have seen and heard in others' homes. It is a great place to learn more about how we define what is public and what is private, as well, and what we do with hybrid objects and behaviors that turn out to be more problematic than we might have thought.

In this chapter, I look at the doors, windows, trash, mail, yards, cars, kids, and dogs that not only help define the private-public boundary, but are themselves key instruments through which we try to manage our privacy. In fact, the perimeter of the home is a fine place to realize that accessibility is not just about the selective accessibility of an embodied self. As we saw in the cases of objects that betray secrets, in the things in our wallets and purses, and with participants' communication devices, accessibility is also about controlling objects that are strongly linked to the self. Sometimes such efforts focus on our own objects. But sometimes our work is focused on others' accessibility and the objects and activities we associate with them. In this chapter, we'll see how this results in a rich variety of attempts to control others' possessions and behaviors in addition to our own.

I begin with the object that Simmel (1997, 170–73) has identified as "the image of the boundary point," by which "the bounded and the boundary-less adjoin one another, not in the dead geometric form of a mere separating wall, but rather as the possibility of a permanent interchange."[3] Enter, the door. Or not.

WHEN THE DOORBELL RINGS

What do you do at home when the doorbell rings?

Look out of the window to see who it is and if it's a car I know, I'll buzz them in.

If it's somebody that-- And if it's somebody that on that particular day I don't feel like seeing, I'll just pretend I'm not home. And a couple of days later: "I came by your house." "Was my car there?" "Yeah." "Oh, you know, sometimes I go with so-and-so and so-and-so."

I'm usually always at home. It's terrible. It's like saying I just don't want to have anything to do with you. Not now.

But I'll look out of the window. If I see a car, I'll buzz them in. If not, I'll just go and sit down.

And don't knock on my back door because I will not answer it. There's a peep hole and if I move a curtain, you'll see me. And if I don't want you to come in that means, darn, you've seen me move the curtains. So I have to let you in.

In the simple act of someone ringing a doorbell, the problem of social accessibility once again rears its head. Screening phone calls may make some participants feel a bit guilty in terms of hiding their actual physical availability to answer the phone and respond to a caller's request for attention. But for most of these same people, failing to answer the door when one is home and physically capable of doing so is truly grounds for a stricken conscience. A diminished, possibly lost relationship awaits if the caller on the doorstep sees evidence that the resident *is* at home, doesn't appear hindered in their ability to answer the door, and yet still makes no attempt to do so.

Avoiding consequences like these leads to a rich array of behaviors in participants' responses to a knock on the door. Like the ways we manage demands for attention that arrive via communication technologies, here we also see numerous strategies, filtering mechanisms, and rationales. These include never screening and always answering the door if one is home; answering the door only if one is expecting someone; using windows and peepholes and intercoms or talking through the door to find out who it is before opening; moving to a place that has a doorman or that is relatively physically inaccessible to most people and vehicles; and actually hiding in one's own house to prevent those at the door from seeing if one is inside.

Participants' goals here are similar to when the phone rings, too. The first goal is to determine whether or not one should bother answering the door, given the likelihood of the caller being someone one would like to see. The second is to decide how much further attention one should give the caller, depending on a variety of factors including other demands on one's time. Even if the caller is someone we like but not someone we wish to see at that moment, for instance, we might choose to keep our presence in the home entirely secret—like the preceding participant—thus avoiding the social obligation one might feel if the individual knew one was actually available.

Here are some fine examples of how participants describe their response to someone at the door.

What do you do when the doorbell rings?

It hasn't rung often, but I know it's nobody I want to talk to. At this stage of my life, people do not drop by unannounced. So I ignore it sometimes. Um, or I will sometimes open up the window and stick my head out and look down on the street and say, "What!?"

Oh!

I can't see who's there because there's an awning over it [the door]. And usually by the time I get the window up and get my head out, whatever neighborhood kid it was is gone. (*Laughs.*)

This next person describes a slightly more complicated set of considerations guiding his choice of response. He uses the fairly sophisticated yet common device of deductive reasoning in the process, too, based on prior patterns of visitations that occur at different times of the day.

What do you do at home if the doorbell rings?

For the most part, I know if somebody's coming over. It's fairly rare for someone to come over without calling first. Really quite rare. Because if it's one of my neighbors, it would be one of my neighbors in my building, most likely, who would just ring my doorbell to ask me a quick question. And in that case, they're already in the building and they're ringing that bell outside the front door and I know it's that bell. So if the doorbell rings and I'm not expecting anybody, I'll-- If it's during the day, I'll presume that it could be UPS and it usually is. If it's getting later in the afternoon, I might be more likely to look out the window and see if it's somebody collecting signatures on a petition or something. Because I'm really not interested in dealing with that because they never just want a signature; they always want money. And I'm not giving money to people at my door and that always makes them mad. But I don't get too much of that. I really don't.

The next participant has the equivalent of a phone-answering secretary to handle most of his requests at the door:

What do you do at home if the buzzer rings, from downstairs or—?

Oh, there isn't a buzzer from downstairs, there is a house phone.

Okay, what do you do if the house phone rings?

I answer it. Unless it wakes me up and then sometimes I just growl and yell and maybe struggle out there and by the time that I get there, there's nobody there. And then I either go back to bed or call the doorman and say, "Did you try to call me?" Yeah.

So in general, usually you are expecting somebody when they arrive.

And the doorman and the janitors mostly know that I'm a late riser, so they are wonderful about not bothering me early in the morning.[4]

Rather than well-trained staff, the following person relies more on technology along with the spatial distance between his home and the building entrance to fulfill this screening function.

Do you have a doorbell?

Um-hm.

When the door bell rings—

But it's not at the street. There's this gate.

So first you have to—

Very rarely do you get a doorbell ring other than somebody that's got a package for you. But, it's like, the buzzer at the gate rings the phone. Which is a really good system. It's way better than-- 'Cause you don't get all those solicitation people, which I absolutely hate.

It's a privacy issue?

Yes. In your face.

The door-to-door—?

I really dislike that stuff.

So, did that used to happen at the old—?

Yeah. It's not the subject matter, it's just they're doing this unsolicited thing.

There's only one-- The Sierra Club people are always interesting. So when they came by—and they were always interesting people doing interesting things—I'd talk to them.

The distance, the gate, and the communication channel are "a really good system," of course, because filtering mechanisms are supposed to do exactly this—let you make yourself available to talk to the interesting (or essential) people when you want to and keep the rest away.

Yet another approach that lets you talk to whom you want to talk without risking social embarrassment is to have no filter at all:

What do you do at home if the doorbell rings?

Answer it.

Always?

Always.

. . . even if it means inconvenience and the sure knowledge that sometimes this is not going to be a welcome event.

What do you do at home if the doorbell rings?

Roll my eyes.

(*Laughing*.)

Run down the stairs and answer it.

The number and kinds of constraints at work on participants' doorbell answering responses are varied, of course. Their choices about what to do and their subsequent choreographies at the sound of the bell are adjusted accordingly. If there is or is not a peephole, if it is or is not easy to see through, if there is or is not good lighting, if there is or is not a working intercom, or if one lives in a friendly, crime-free neighborhood or not, for instance, may very well alter one's door-answering behaviors.

Constraints like these limit the options people have if they want to make themselves selectively available to others at the door. This next participant feels her presence inside the home is given away before the bell even rings. Accordingly, she always answers the door when she's home, with one common exception: when it gets "too late" on Halloween.

What do you do at home if the doorbell rings?

Well-- Buddy, lay down [*to dog*]! I mean, the dogs started barking before you even ring the bell.

Right. Right.

So in that instant, you know, we have to deal with the dog first. The dog-- Come [*calls to dog*].

The dog doesn't listen to me, as you notice.

Uh huh. (*Laughing*.)

Gerald-- He'll go "down" with Gerald, and he won't with me. No. Sammy [second dog], I'll get him to go "down," and then the minute I turn he's (*whispers*) sneaking up again. I attribute it to male-female thing. (*Laughing.*)

(*Laughing.*) Could be.

So, so-- I mean, we have to, I mean, we have to answer so we have to go to the door because the dog's gone crazy and blown it so I never have the opportunity to not, really, to not answer it. Although, like, Halloween is coming and you know we stop answering the door, the doorbell, at a certain hour on Halloween.

Right.

No matter what happens, we turn out the lights and everything. There.

For the most part we-- I think that anybody that comes I'll at least, you know, speak to them. We get a lot of solicitations and stuff and we always listen to what they say. And we say "no" a lot.

(*Laughing.*)

But it's not alarming. I don't feel that we're overburdened by that.

Halloween is a lovely opportunity to examine the obligation to be socially accessible to whoever shows up at the door.[5] It is a stark exception to everyday life in some ways. Yet, as this resident implies, participating in trick-or-treating festivities may simply amplify a preexisting social norm in which we are expected to answer the door when someone knocks—and, in general, not to feel overburdened by that obligation.

Participation in Halloween is so much of an expectation in the United States that clear—but totally informal—neighborhood protocols have emerged to signal a desire to be excused from this ritual. For example, residents who don't want to be part of Halloween may be expected to turn off the porch light and draw the curtains or move to another part of the house to hide any interior lights. In addition, parents may make a special effort to remind children of any infirm or distraught neighbors so that these "excused" individuals are not bothered by demands to answer the door or give candy—or suffer the material consequences of nonparticipation. Children may still feel free to make up their own (creepy) stories about the individuals who are too reclusive—too inaccessible—that evening, of course. Yet they may quickly spread the word about anyone who is especially generous that night, too, those who make themselves exceptionally accessible both with the treats they hand out and the ways they do it.[6]

Of course, if trick-or-treaters don't buy someone's attempt to excuse themselves from the festivities, the person trying to claim inaccessibility is liable to hear the doorbell sounding incessantly anyway. Worse, she or he may wake up to smashed pumpkins and eggs on the front step, toilet paper around the trees and telephone cables, and/or a shaving-creamed mailbox. Trick-or-treaters are especially effective in reminding us that privacy—inaccessibility—is socially gifted, after all, and that techniques directed at one's physical accessibility can be acute reminders of one's social accessibility, too.

Urban houses invite queries from all kinds of people who might be looking for a high-density residential area in which to do door-to-door business—not unlike the trick-or-treaters of Halloween. This often forces participants to attend to the work of accessibility in a way that living high on top of a mountain with relatively inaccessible roads does not. In the city, one never knows when the simple social courtesy of answering the door could invite a most undesirable relationship with perhaps dreadful consequences.[7]

This is another reason why we see here strong support for Milgram's (1970) prediction that strangers in urban settings will be treated less kindly than those who are known. Shortly after moving in to her family's new house, for instance, someone knocked on this participant's door late at night. They weren't expecting anyone, and immediately the dog was growling and barking at the door, "going wild, which is great."

And (Steve) goes to the door and looks through the peephole and sees it's a young guy. So he says, "Who is it?" and the guy mumbles something. So Steve says, "I can't understand what you're saying, what do you want? Who are you?" And the guy mumbled something again. And I'm saying, "Don't open it. And don't even crack the door." So we've got this hook thing, lock where the door can open a couple inches but it won't open beyond that. So Steve flips that around and cracks it open. And I would not have opened it at all.

Right.

We don't know them, we don't expect anybody-- sorry. And, and the guy-- And I guess (Hanna) got her muzzle in there and was barking ferociously and the guy said, "This doesn't seem like a good time," and just turned around and left. So we don't know who he was, what he wanted, whatever. But it's just like, you know, when people get mugged a block or so away, is this a home invasion? I mean that thing is not beyond possibility around here, so—

Right.

You know. And nothing happened with that incident but it reminded both of us that something could happen.

Uh huh.

And after that we-- I, you know, got Steve to agree that opening the door even slightly isn't a good idea.

This family's adjustment in their door-answering behavior is a perfect example of how anyone might change their behavior in response to a new—or newly honed—privacy fear. As a result, the family has lessened their degree of accessibility. But their sense of security, of privacy, and of being in control over who has access to them has increased.

Not all strangers are thought to be threats to one's physical well-being, of course. As a range of participants described the ways they respond to the doorbell, I could not help but notice the repeated reference to Jehovah's Witnesses.[8] Here is a sampling of comments that include remarkably consistent views of these evangelicals.

#1
What do you do at home if the doorbell rings?

Ahhhh, if I'm not expecting anyone, I go and check to see who it is. I will not open the door for Jehovah's Witnesses, sorry. I respect their right to practice their religion, but in our neighborhood they are really tough and they come in groups of eight. (*Laughing.*)

#2
What do you do at home if the doorbell rings?

If it's a Jehovah's Witness, I don't answer. Or if I do, I will tell you "no" and close the door. They are the only people that I'm really rude to.

Right. Do you get a lot of that around here?

Yes, I do. As yesterday-- And I just-- She said she wanted to discuss things with me and I said, "Not with me" and closed the door.

Uh huh.

They'll get you at bath time. (*Laughing.*) Oh, yes, when you're taking a bath. And ring the bell. And you really don't know who it is. If I see them, nine times out of ten, I don't answer.

So can you see them from this window?

If I'm sitting here. But if I see them in the area, I will then be very aware of that-- that they're here in the area. And when the doorbell rings, I will probably look out to see. And if I see them, I won't answer.

#3

Okay. What do you do at home if the doorbell rings?

Go answer it. We're on the second level. You enter on the first level. The second level is where the kitchen and dining area is, and there's a little porch, so we have an intercom system, but you go out and kind of look down and kind of conduct your business. If you don't want to talk to a Jehovah's Witness, you can say this is a bad time and close the door, and that's sort of it.

For a striking number of participants, Jehovah's Witnesses are perceived as annoying but categorically recognizable and physically harmless strangers at the door. Their periodic presence is somewhat expected but definitely perceived as intrusive. They appear on participants' doorsteps, unpredictably and uninvited, and make demands not only for residents' attention but also for their money. It is seen as an invasion of the privacy of one's space, one's time, and one's peace of mind. To approach one's door with an agenda of religious faith—for many in the United States, still an extremely private matter—makes the violation that much worse.

Jehovah's Witnesses are the precise face-to-face equivalent of telemarketers. Yet there is no face-to-face equivalent of an answering machine that lets one camouflage one's availability from a person at the door and still go about one's business. Thus, these strangers in particular elicit a remarkable range of accessibility-managing behavior, most of which is designed to avoid any contact with them.

These behaviors include those of otherwise highly competent and lovely people who literally hide inside their own homes when they know a Jehovah's Witness team is coming to their door. Compelled by a socialized, almost Pavlovian response to answer the doorbell, these kindly people—in this study, all women—betray an inner struggle. On the one hand, there is the desire to follow proper etiquette and at least be polite to the person on the other side by answering the door. One would not want the evangelist to feel insulted or demeaned. On the other hand, residents dearly wish to avoid interactions with these people who are, after all, intruding on them. Participants are left pretending they are not home, hiding to deny these callers access without causing, in these women's minds, unforgivable offense.

Of course, no pattern of behavior holds for every individual. There are still those who, like people who always answer their phone when they're home, perhaps just find it easier to welcome everyone who comes to their door, including Jehovah's Witnesses. As this next person suggests, however, even when individuals give them donations, it may be done out of guilt for the selectivity with which she sometimes greets them and sometimes dashes out the back door instead.

What do you do when the Witnesses come to your door? Do they come a lot?

Uh, you know what, it usually happens possibly, maybe once every two weeks.

Wow.

I just go to the door and open the door and say, "No, thank you" and give them a donation and let them move on.

So you actually give them a donation?

Sometimes I'll give them a donation because most of the times when you open the door, they'll put their literature in your hands. So since they hand it to me, it cost them money just for the paper.

So you feel like you have to give?

Just give them a small donation. But that doesn't force you, me to read all their literature.

But do you feel sort of forced to give that donation?

You feel uncomfortable not giving and you know-- Then this other is a time I'm running-- And I may look out the door—and they can't see me—but I'm running out the other door because I don't have time to stand there and say, well, you know, whatever. A long conversation. Blah, blah, blah.

Most participants' reactions to the doorbell seem to be guided by the desire to attain a certain degree of social-psychological comfort while maintaining the ability to respond differently in different situations. The concept of "backdoor friends" also reflects this principle. In the States, the front yard and the front door are more public than the back yard and back door to one's house. Houses "face" the street. Driveways, sidewalks, and walkways of other kinds provide wayfinding clues for those leaving the more public space of the street for the private space of the home, providing a transition to the threshold of the house. Once inside, the front door typically opens into more formal, "receiving" spaces, too.

Back yards may not only lack such planned transition space, but typically are more personalized than front yards, and perceived as more private. Back doors tend to open into the more personalized and private garages, kitchens, and similar workspaces of the home, too. This is why it is a sign of relative intimacy and comfort for a visitor to be in the back yard, rather than the front, or to use the back door rather than the front to enter one's house. Good friends, neighbors, and any others who regularly drop by may well be told to "just come around back" when they drop by. Such familiar visitors may even be admonished for coming to the front door and ringing the bell "like a stranger"—as if they don't know the resident well enough to move past such formalities.

For many people, then, the front and back yards and doors provide another avenue through which accessibility along the house perimeter is managed. The front door and yard are more like the publically listed home phone, while the back door and yard are like one's cell phone. Like one's system of phones, the degree of emotional comfort and flexibility offered by these spaces well supports controlled accessibility. It reveals the intersection of the more physical and social elements underlying privacy especially well. We see this theme also in the ways participants think about and use their windows.

WINDOWS

Is your home a private place?

For the most part, yeah. I think because I can filter out the calls that come through. If somebody comes into the building, they have to ring the bell, so I know everybody that's coming in here. Although I can't see them. I can lean out the window to see because we're on the first floor, so, you know, I can pretty much control who comes into this environment.

Windows are also part of a system individuals use to control accessibility in a variety of ways.[9] Here, in combination with curtains, a clever mom uses them as a signal to neighborhood kids.

[W]hen the kids were growing up, and I have three, this [house] was great for them. There were-- There's sixteen houses in the immediate area. There were forty-eight kids. Um, privacy went out the window.

Right.

We used, we'd have to-- And I always believed in having the family eat together whenever possible. And somebody was always ringing the doorbell and-- you know, another kid or something. And I used to close the drape and say that meant "Don't bother us, we're having dinner."

See, they knew. They didn't bother us and then when we finished, I'd open it and okay, it's a free for all. But that is how I handled the privacy issue and getting my kids to eat and sit down in one place and so forth.

The resident in this next participant's story seems to have been using his windows to signal his accessibility/availability, too—but in ways the participant finds less than comfortable.

I know it's hard to resist looking in other people's windows when you're strolling around.

Oh, yeah.

Were there ever any times when people seemed uncomfortable with it, or surprised?

You know, there have been. The few places over in, kind of, Wicker Park-- ... It's more of a modern style, huge windows. And they do kind of look like they're in a fishbowl. And there was one guy, I think it was closer to (Doug's) place, that had, like, an exercise bike—

In the window?

It was on, like, the lower level. And this whole window kind of ran, like, two, three stories up. And I'm like, why would somebody just, you know-- I am not, like, flashy enough to go and "I'm just going to work out and show everybody," you know. I'm like, forget it. I'm hiding. So I thought that was kind of-- I mean, I didn't see an actual person on the exercise bike or using the weights or anything like that. I just thought that was kind of strange.

... He didn't have any curtains?

Didn't have any curtains. I'm like, *some* kind of treatment-- privacy-- *some*thing!

Windows are logical tools for residents wishing to advertise themselves. They're good for more literal signage, too. In my neighborhood of Hyde Park in Chicago, signs displayed in residential windows range from posters for residents' newly authored books and political campaigns (the older and more sun-faded one's signs for Barack Obama, for instance, the more one's neighborhood cachet), to holiday decorations, to tags declaring the presence of home security systems, to "neighborhood watch" signs. In the past, they also included the following, which were part of a larger system of neighborhood protection:

There was a campaign here, which began many, many, many years ago. In fact, we used to have signs in the window for kids saying this is a safe house. If you have a problem, you can ring the bell. Blow your whistle and ring the bell.

Like the signs freshmen put up on their dormitory room doors (Nathan 2005, 23–27), such signs tell anyone passing by—neighbors, emergency response personnel, strangers—something more about the residents than they would know otherwise. Thus, the signs are a way in which residents increase their accessibility to others via the information they convey about who lives there, similar to the ways we presume to know things about drivers based on their cars' bumper stickers. Because windows allow people to see out as well as in, they are logical places for individuals to put things that they wish to physically control or protect but also display to passersby.

In part, then, it is windows' two-way nature that lets them function as such great visual tools for residents trying to control their level of privacy/publicity.[10] But the only reason this works is because we seem so drawn to looking through them—from either direction. If windows are commonly used by residents to control their physical and social accessibility, they are also a source of vulnerability that increases this challenge.

Windows are a point of vulnerability in maintaining one's privacy in two ways. First, and perhaps most obviously, a window is not a door. It is much more easily broken and a building is more easily broken into via a window than a door. People forget to close and lock windows far more than doors, too. From this perspective, windows are a security problem, potentially leading to unexpected and profound senses of privacy violations among participants. In some urban neighborhoods, break-ins are not uncommon, with consequences that range from loss of valuable objects to this most extreme case:

We have a neighbor, she's three houses down, and I've been told that somebody got in through her back window. You know, the same style house as ours. Left it opened. And she was raped. Everyone has been told, discretely. We were told within a week of moving in because no one wants this to happen to anyone else.

It makes perfect sense, then, that people who are especially concerned with security may elect not to have windows at all. As the following attorney shows, they may at least want one or two windowless offices. These may be used selectively, as needed.

Because of the nature of some of the cases that we have—we're doing, actually, class-action litigation against tobacco companies—there have been instances where we thought that we were being bugged. So that's why we have people sign confidentiality agreements. That's why sometimes we have meetings in inner offices, because if they were in the offices with the windows then, obviously, conversations could be bugged more easily.

Sounds or sights—even smells—may provide an undesirable source of information to outsiders. Based on these clues, others may be enticed to try to gain physical access to the inside of the room, too. Good smells, for instance—bacon frying, bread baking, an apple pie fresh from the oven—may entice unwanted people to visit. Bad smells, however—especially dangerous ones—may also cause individuals to "visit," or at least call professionals to investigate what's going on. After smelling an overwhelming presence of natural gas, for instance, one participant had his wife call 911 while he forced entry into a neighbor's locked home and rescued the older, disabled woman he knew was inside.

Participants are remarkably sensitive to one simple fact about windows: people love to look through them—in either direction. When we are inside our homes, we are drawn to looking outside for a host of reasons, whether aesthetic, daydreamy, soul-refreshing ones, or those having to do with security. When we're outside, we're equally drawn to looking through windows and to seeing the insides of homes, in particular—whether by accident, because of nosiness, or, again, due to simple security and safety issues in the neighborhood.

This is what our species does. We look—wherever we can, whenever we can, at whomever and whatever we can. The only time we don't is when we specifically decide not to, sometimes because others have trained us that way. Otherwise, we simply expect everyone to look at whatever might be seen. Accordingly, we try to control what that is, whenever there's something we really don't want them to access in this way.

At home, I do have blinds, like I said, and as soon as it gets as dark outside as it is inside, I close them. I myself like to look into peoples' houses when I'm walking down the street. Who doesn't? Fascinating stuff. And so I know that the impulse exists, more or less. With socialized people, less probably. So I do [have blinds].

Not that everyone is always attentive to this simple, predictable way in which they might better protect their privacy, given others' simple, predictable propensity to violate it in this way. So many participants have stories in which they suddenly realize how oblivious they were to the ease with which other people can see inside their homes. Caught up in the drama and space of their own lives, they become heedless of just how available sounds and sights are to people on the other side of the glass.

What do you do if you want privacy from your neighbors?

Close the blinds. (*Laughs.*)

I was bathing (Peter) in a tub on the counter sink, the kitchen sink, the other day. And when we left for (Thanksgiving), our diagonal neighbor— we saw her while we were loading up the car for Thanksgiving—and she said, "I saw the most beautiful thing the other day." We had been at a movie and so I said, "What's that?" And, "I saw you bathing your baby in the sink. I just watched. It was so sweet. He was splashing around and—"

And we're like, "Lovely."

And we got out in the car and we thought, "Okay. Close the blinds." (*Laughing.*)

(*Laughing.*)

The neighbors are watching. What we're doing.

... It reminds me of *Rear Window* with Jimmy Stewart. Because you can just see what's going on. ... And this woman is really sweet and it cracks me up. I didn't care that she saw me bathing (Peter), but it makes me think. You know?

Yet window treatments and what they do and do not let others see are not an all-or-nothing thing for a number of participants. With their window-covering choices, some people choose to have their homes fully visible or fully closed off to anyone who might happen to look in. They typically alternate the accessibility of their homes' interiors throughout the day and night in this more dichotomous fashion.

A number of these urban dwellers select partial window coverings, though, which remain in the same position twenty-four hours a day. This design choice allows them to feel more connected to the world outside, with a number of people remarking how fully drawn drapes or blinds make them feel cut off. Some feel as if this emits a message of unfriendliness to the neighborhood, too. Window treatments that cover only the bottom half of windows are the preferred choice here. These provide a more constant level of accessibility to onlookers, although they, too, grant only selective access.

After moving from a more suburban location, for instance, this next person was initially struck by the level of visual access windows provide to city dwellers. But it wasn't until she and her husband changed something inside their house that she understood exactly what this meant. Her response was not to deny complete accessibility to onlookers, but to make sure some things would be off limits.

When we moved in, we had all the mustard drapery kind of '70s stuff. So we took that down and actually just hung, like, a sheer fabric halfway— kind of like café curtains with some found fabric that I had. Kind of this off-white, so you could kind of see in, but you couldn't see the activity that was going on in the living room.

And we painted it, like, I don't know, it was kind of a celery green, kind of a lighter green with a grayish tint to it.

And once we did it, neighbors kept walking, you know, on their walk, and they're like, "That color is so beautiful!"

You know? It's just like, oh wow, I guess they can see in.

That must have been strange.

It was strange, but you know I do it all the time, you know (*chuckles*). Somebody's got their lights on and I'm walking around, you know. You kind of have that voyeur kind of quality. You just want to see what's going on in other people's lives.

So did you think about changing the curtains when people said, "Oh, that's a great green"?

No, it just kind of took me-- . . . I was more concerned with what they could see. Like, okay, if I'm walking into the living room in my pajamas, who's going to see me?

So did you start thinking about that every morning?

Actually (*laughing*), we actually went out and looked. It was like, "Okay, are these, thick enough?" [My husband's] like, "They're fine." So it was fine.

Oh, that's great, so you sent him out, and you walked out in your pajamas?

No. (*Both laugh.*) Actually I said, "Stay right there," and I went out and I was looking to see what could be discerned, if at all. But you couldn't see anything, so. (*Laughing.*) It was all good.

So it's like, yeah, I'll have an appearance of being open. But I'm, like, halfway, halfway.

Yet the problem with windows isn't simply that others might be able to see things you don't want them to see. It's also that if you look through them, you might be able to see things that *you* don't want to see, either. Overall, participants' stories include a fair amount of attention to what Rosen (2000, 18) calls the "injury caused by being seen." Because of the presence, positioning, and visibility of windows, those who are forced to observe others also may feel as if their privacy has been invaded. If our neighbors' uncontrolled knowledge of us makes us uncomfortable, so does our uncontrolled knowledge of them.

This next individual, for instance, would be happy not to have found out all he knows about his neighbors via their combined windows.

So for this neighbor that you see into their living room, do you wish that you couldn't?

Yeah.

Really? Is it that (*laughs*), do you see things that you wish you didn't see or is it kind of, just, like—?

I don't know. I-- Yeah, I would rather not see into their living room. I mean, I'd rather not know if they're watching TV all time. Which they are. (*Laughs.*)

Can you see what they are watching? Are there, do you have curtains on your side that you could draw?

Yeah, I suppose we could, but um-- They're on the south side of the house and that's where our lights are. We have to leave them [the blinds] up. We see their seventeen-year-old go out on the roof and smoke. (*Laughs.*)

Do they know she does that?

No, I'm sure they don't.

Does she know that you can see her?

Yeah, yeah. He.

Oh, he?

Um, I wish we didn't. I mean, I wouldn't—

Squeal?

I don't care if he does. It's just so nuts.

Discomfort easily results when the activity one sees is that of an unwanted secret. It binds the conflicted secret-keeper to the secret-maker and those from whom the secret is withheld in unexpected and undesirable ways.[11] It's made worse in this case because this participant is quite friendly with this teenager's parents.

The next participant discusses the similarly unwanted ability to see the behavior of people outside her window. In this case, it's that of a train conductor and his passengers, who may well be engaged in a persistent (yet failed) attempt at boundary play. It is their observation of her as well as her forced observation of them that is disturbing to her, all because of the proximity of her apartment and the placement of a window right next to the train stop.

Can you see what people are doing? . . . On the El [elevated train] platform?

There's this conductor. Like, he can see what we're doing. Like, if he's going down-- And sometimes he comes to a complete stop, hangs out by the-- Waves his hand at the window. It's waving. He tried to talk to us. I don't know. Sometimes people [passengers] can see in because they're stopped. And a lot of times, they do stop. Not necessarily because the conductor is hanging out talking to us, but they just do.

. . . So they'll actually yell stuff at you?

There's one specific conductor. He tries to have a conversation.

This woman, a consultant, works from her small apartment. Her home office is a tiny room with this one, small window—the only source of natural light and her only weapon against claustrophobia. Covering up the window is not an option, though she definitely dislikes that this conductor and a bunch of passengers can see her on a regular basis—and even try to communicate with her.

It's no wonder that participants go to great lengths to gift privacy to others by not looking in their windows. Here is a sampling of the ways so many people responded to the same question about how they and their neighbors "respect each others' privacy." The centrality of windows in their answers is striking and makes it even clearer that, as with other forms of privacy work, managing windows is about managing relationships.

A chief way in which participants report respecting their neighbors' privacy is by trying not to look directly into their windows. They hope that others will reciprocate in all this not-looking, thus making it easier for everyone to maintain good relationships. However, they also realize that people often do look, and so they must do something about that. The most common response is to put up window treatments that enable residents to selectively allow outsiders to see what is going on inside.

What do you and your neighbors do to respect each other's privacy?

Close our blinds. Except we didn't have blinds any place [at first]. Um. Let's see. Something for privacy. There are other things we do just to be good neighbors, but it doesn't have to do with privacy.

OK.

Um, I mean-- When we first-- We went a long time without blinds and we sat in this dining room and we had people that would walk by and *stop*. We'd be having dinner, they would stop and just look at us.

That's bizarre. (*Laughing*.)

Yeah, that's really bizarre.

Yeah. (*Laughing*.)

I mean, yeah, you really feel like you're in a fishbowl. And, you know? (*Laughing*.) So the blinds really made a difference, but it was weird. Why would somebody do that? We're just having dinner. Give us a break. (*Laughing*.)[12]

In addition to putting up window treatments, there are three more popular adaptive choices for residents trying to protect their privacy. The first is to alter their behavior if they think outsiders can see in. The second is to simply decide that the outsiders can't see them. In the third adaption, participants decide that even if outsiders can see them, they don't care— at least, not enough to change either their behavior or others' abilities to see it.

This first example of these other strategies in action is a wonderful reflection on how attitudes about what one needs to control and how one needs to do it can shift over time. What might have been an unthinkable risk regarding privacy a couple years ago has shifted significantly for this person.

I know you've talked to me before about, you know, walking around in your apartment with your blinds up.

Well, yes, I am comfortable talking about that because I think that's an interesting point-- is that with privacy, there's something that-- I think that if I am able to maintain anonymity with it, I'm just much more comfortable. So in the sense that, like, I have this apartment here and I like to keep my blinds, well, exactly as you see them here, which is-- I kind of like the balanced look of this, which is exactly halfway up, so that--

And so across the street, there's a hotel and lots of people often looking out the window because they're tourists looking at the street below and lots of things. So when I first moved here, I was always going into, like, the little hallway to change my clothes and do all sorts of things. And then as I've lived here more and more, it's just gotten to a point where I just think that's ridiculous. And I either have just said to myself, well, they can't see me, or I don't really care because they don't know who I am.

And I can't say that I would be comfortable standing close to the windows without any clothes or doing something, you know, that one wouldn't normally do in front of windows. But, I mean, I actually think I sort of have a threshold, which is about the halfway point, and I'm comfortable up until that point walking around, like, as *you* would walk around in a room with all the blinds closed and the windows shut and the whole thing.

But I've become very comfortable with that, I think because-- I mean, as I said, it's just like those people never know who I am and also, because it's a hotel, I also kind of assume they don't even live in this city. And I think all of those factors add up to the fact that it just doesn't bother me so much.

But, you know, at the same time, I'm not comfortable walking around without any clothes in the locker room in the gym because then it's like, they see your face. There's something, I think, attached to your name and your face that makes me uncomfortable. But seeing a silhouette or something, you know, from one hundred yards away, kind of doesn't really bother me.

But I think that's a new development for me. Like, I never would have been that way two and a half years ago, as I said, when I first moved here. I wasn't that way, and I was always going in the other hallway. And then it just became a hassle.

The tradeoff between the inconvenience posed by more fully protecting one's privacy and the practical advantages of acceding at least a little bit of it is well illustrated here. This next participant also admits full knowledge that people outside his apartment might have been able to see what he was doing on one occasion. Apparently, however, he was having such a good time in the moment, he was perfectly willing to take that risk rather than refrain from what he did.

Can you think of any really funny invasion of privacy that you remember about . . . while somebody was at home?

Ummmm. Well one was I was at home alone, right? I'm washing dishes, which I was not known for. This was when I was living in [my previous apartment] and I got washing the dishes. And I don't really make a lot of dishes because I don't know how to cook and so I eat out a lot.

And I started, you know, making this mass of bubbles and so I, like, you know, I had to take a shower anyway so I just, like, plunk! I grabbed a bunch of them and put them on my head and shaped a little mohawk. And then I grabbed some more and I made a beard. And I was going to take a shower anyway, so I was in my birthday suit. And so I gave myself a little, like, a loincloth.

And I'm sitting there in this foam loincloth and foam beard and foam mohawk and I hear laughing. And I look and it's my girlfriend. And she's been watching me for, I don't know, she said, like, five, ten minutes. And-- because there was music on, too, so I was dancing around a little bit with this foam beard and this foam mohawk.

And I hear laughing. I'm like, ooooh! And I duck down. I'm like-- (*laughing*). And I kind of could tell it was her laugh after the initial, like-- And when you live in the city, you get used to people looking in your windows and it's not something you want, but-- You get used to it. (*Laughing.*)[13]

Participants clearly exhibit a range of inhibitions in their behavior around windows. However, it's also clear that there is a range of rewards at work here that also might encourage us to not attend to our privacy as fully as we might—such as convenience or the freedom to think about or do enjoyable things. Positive incentives, along with simply becoming desensitized to one's surroundings, helps explain the ability of individuals to become used to and therefore oblivious to their visibility via windows. It is an illustration of the basic adaptation behaviors that allow so many people to adjust to—and become rather oblivious to—the daily constraints on their privacy.

This last person comments on the ways this manifests in car behavior as well as within the home, relative to windows—and the occasional, startling realization that brings her attention back to it.

I think that people think that when they're in their car, they're in this zone of, you know, invisibility, and no one can see them. Seeming-- I am thinking that if someone is able to look outside themselves in this instance, they probably would never, you know, putting on their makeup, eating the way they eat, um. You know, singing at the top of their lungs. Do they have any concept of "Yes, I could sing perfectly"? And every once in a while I find myself thinking that way when I'm doing something in front of a window in my house at night and I realize that they can see me outside. I can't see outside, but I-- "Oh, my God!"-- But someone can see what I'm doing inside!

The ways we handle our trash also show the tradeoffs we are willing to make in securing our privacy and the ways we can become desensitized—and resensitized—to our actual accessibility.

TRASH

If I buy something, I have it delivered to my sister's house. I have it delivered at her house, take it out of the box, leave it [the box] at her house, and get a bag and take it [my purchase] home.

I even burn stuff. I put it on the grill and burn it.

What gets burnt?

Credit card bills, old credit card statements, my medicine refills. You know, they give you the little pamphlets, I burn those. Light bills, gas bills. I burn everything. If I don't shred it? I have even shredded it and then burned it.

Because it shreds a certain way and if you get so many pages, you can put it back together. I did that, too, to see. I'd just shredded a whole lot of paper in different colors and it's easy to put it back together, if you have the time. But that was just something I wanted to see if it could be done, and I did it. So then I started burning it.

I put stuff in another trash bag and then another trash bag and tie it up and put some water in it. I did that one last night. I was shredding some of my pamphlets from the doctor. I shredded them, I tore them up, and then I put it in a bag, put it in the sink, let water sit in there, swoosh it around. And I finally drained the water and threw it in the garbage.

Participants in this study show an acute, fairly new sensitivity to being mindful of their garbage and what it could reveal about them. Not everyone is as motivated as this person—who grew up in public housing and learned early in life to protect anything and everything that you might not want seen by others. There, even the box from a purchase could attract miscreants to one's home. Better to leave it far away from one's own doorstep.

Even if they are not so extreme, many participants nonetheless exhibit a similarly analytical approach to their trash. They spend a fair amount of time deciding which trash is and is not worth the effort needed to protect it from the nosy and nefarious, then disposing of it accordingly. The fact that so many people are now able to be so articulate about what may have once been a simple, thoughtless act—throwing out the garbage—is a reflection of the fact that this is not so simple or thoughtless any more.

Participants report that, for the most part, they did not pay much attention to their trash previously. Like anything else, one must learn to pay attention to the implications of trash for one's privacy. Now, training people on what to do with garbage has become a formalized point in a number of workplaces—and not just in highly secure ones that may have long had rules about what must be burned, shredded, or thrown out.[14]

We got a new person today and one of the things that I was telling her was-- We were making a copy of something and the copy machine jammed. And I said, "Don't just toss anything away. What you need to do is you need to think, 'Is it something that if it was out in public I would care that anyone saw it?'" So-- It was instructions on how to use the phone. And she looked at me and she said, "No, absolutely not."

And then there was another document that went through and it jammed. And I said, "How about this? Would we be able to throw this away?" And it was basically a list of all the different cases we worked on and their file codes, and she said, "Ummmm, well, it looks harmless enough." I said, "Yeah, it looks harmless enough, but you have to think, do we want anybody knowing on the street that we're working specifically on these cases?" And she goes, "No." And I said, "Right, so we're going to shred this."

So those are some instances where at work, I'm always thinking about the privacy issue.

Participants' lack of attention to trash has changed owing to a number of factors. These include a combination of voluntary and mandatory recycling efforts and new pricing structures that charge extra for certain kinds of garbage or penalize people for putting the wrong kind of garbage in the wrong kind of receptacle. In addition, there is a growing awareness of the ways information contained in trash can violate clients' or other individuals' rights, setting up businesses and institutions for litigation. Such information can be used to commit industrial espionage or personal identity theft, as well, also resulting in increased attention to the garbage.

For some people in this study, moving to the city also had a profound impact on how much attention they gave to their garbage. Their trash quickly became redefined as far more public than they previously thought it was—or would like it to be.[15]

I remember one time, the first time this ever happened. Well, every time this happens to me. In Chicago, you, you know, live in a city built of alleyways. And all your garbage cans are in alleyways. And the street life-- It's their God-given right to go through these alleyways and go through garbage cans.

And I remember the first time that I pulled out of my garage and sort of looked around and there-- Photographs that I had thrown out that were sort of laying in the street. And bank statements that I had thrown out. And I just felt sort of horribly violated.

Yeah.

Not because-- I guess because somebody else glimpsed my "private life." So I went out and bought a shredder and then, you know, anything that I didn't want anyone to see this, was shredded.

But it's still-- You know, it happens. You couldn't even-- I mean, I don't go out and see the, you know, box of frozen potatoes and freak out. It's just weird to know that someone was going through your garbage. To me, that's weird.

OK. I wanted to ask you about—

And I don't think it's weird that someone goes through the garbage. I think it's weird that someone goes through, you know, leaves it out there, and then someone *else* saw your stuff.

This next person echoes the effects of an urban awakening in how they now handle their garbage.

[W]hen we were first married and we were living in our first apartment, someone got a hold of our, um, phone—like MCI—calling number and charged I don't know however many hundreds of dollars on [my husband's] work phone.

Right.

Which we didn't have to pay for, because they figured it out pretty quickly.

Yeah.

But that was-- Somebody pulled it out of the garbage, and we didn't tear it up or anything. And we did end up getting a paper shredder soon after because there's a lot of, you know, documents that go through our house.

Yeah.

. . . We lived on a system of alleys when we lived in (Bucktown) before we moved, with people pawing through our garbage cans constantly.

Yeah.

There was no privacy out there. Everything was open to, um, you know, anyone who wanted to take it out of the garbage can.

Right.

So in that sense, I would say that's sort of a privacy thing.

So did it upset you to see your stuff, like the garbage that you threw out, strewn all over the alley?

Ah, what-- Especially what annoyed me more than anything else was, um, the fact that we went to great extremes to separate our garbage. (*Laughing.*)

Yeah.

For recycling. For recycling. And then all those people would come through and mix everything up. And I still don't understand how Chicago ever recycles.

I don't. I go through the routine, but I kind of know that it's for nothing.

Right. So anything that I-- I got to know what people were looking for while they were going through the cans, so anything that I thought would be the least bit of interest to them, I just laid on top.

Talk about trying to selectively manage the accessibility of things. In fact, participants' increased attention to their garbage has resulted in a plethora of new behaviors. These largely fall under the category of secrets work, beginning with the process of deciding what should and should not be a secret.

Participants describe their trash as having both secret parts and far more public ones that they absolutely do not care about. Accordingly, the desire for selective concealment and disclosure not only leads to participants sorting their trash, but also to treating the emergent piles in very different ways. Some receive far more attention than others. Like many of our most sacred wallet contents, the focus of their attention is on the parts of their trash that seem potentially most harmful.

One of the interesting facts about trash is its private/public hybridity.[16] It is a hybrid first in the sense that particular items or objects in the trash are seen as more and less private/public than others. The most private ones are those that are the most protected and subject to the highest degree of secrets work, such as receipts . . .

This is a receipt. . . . Actually it's an unusual receipt, it has the full account number of my business Visa card. So I would never throw this in the garbage unless it was ripped, you know, into a thousand little tiny pieces. 'Cause I'm paranoid about that.

. . . and any other financial information.

Someone gained access to my checking account.

Right.

And I'm sure it was because I had thrown out some cancelled checks. I shred all that stuff now.

Uh huh. You know, people laugh at me but I do, too.

Um, the credit card offers-- Yeah, I either shred it or burn it.

Or anything that, for instance, this system administrator thinks is "useful."

Of course, I shred anything that has a number on there that could be used.

So you have a shredder?

No, I rip it in a way that-- and then I throw them in different garbage cans. Like when someone, like, someone gives me a log-in name and a password. I'll, like, rip it three times in the middle and put one in one garbage can and one in another garbage can, just to separate-- Because I know one of the ways that you can get this stuff is you go in the dumpster and you go and you look through.

This selectivity occurs at work and at home, then, as well as in public places.

What about trash here [at work]?

We should be protective about that. I try to shred things. That's, like, just kind of going through my head. What are the odds that someone is going to pull this document out of the trash that might be sensitive to this one person somewhere else? Nobody even knows that I would have access to that information. I mean, we actually had an incident, just last week. We're doing work for a major company, and we had some early prototypes that had to do with household activities and cleaning, things like that. The proto we had, it didn't look like much, just scraps of some sample materials. Well, it got left in a cardboard box on the floor. Gone. Everyone's theory is the garbage people thought it was trash and threw it away.

Because it wasn't recognizable as anything?

Right, and people are wringing their hands, like should we worry about that? I thought, well, if we were that client, I would be really worried because anyone who cares about that client or competitor or whatever, if they're really going to get sneaky, they could go through their trash and they know anything in their trash says what this company is doing. Well, nobody knows that we're working for that client. So, it's so far out of context, why do we need to worry about it?

I feel that way about a lot of the information at home. Credit card information? Yeah, okay. When I destroy credit cards, I cut it in two or three and I throw it in different trash cans. That one is going to go out this week and that one will go out next week. I feel quite confident that it's covered.

My wife is much more protective about all of our old bills and everything else. I'm like, people don't care that much. For the most part, all of them, they've changed them so they generally don't show credit card numbers, the expiration date.

My wife has a bag—you can't tell on tape, I'm showing a bag the size of a probably half-filled, sort of, outdoor garbage can—of just papers that she's collected.

She's always sent things in that pile. A few weeks ago she had a fire. She didn't even get through it all and burned them all and that was her way of doing it. Okay, it's good. Is it worth an hour of your time? I don't know.

Naturally, conflict over what belongs in the "secret trash" category is likely, in part because of a particular aspect of the decision-making process. To begin with, one person's secret trash may indeed be mere garbage to another.

I know of other people who rip up their mail and shred their mail to the point of absurdity. My mother is one. And some others. And, there's very eccentric behavior surrounding privacy. . . . But, you know, I have noticed that some people don't rip up their mail, for example, into little bits. No one's ever commented on my ripping of my mail, but you spend time in other people's houses and you see them maybe throw something out, things that I would not just throw out. In a whole package! And that surprises me.

This is not only because of different experiences that lead people to take their trash and what it might reveal more and less seriously. It is also in part because the decision-making process about how to treat trash inevitably includes the need also to decide whether or not a participant is willing to do the extra work that would be required if she or he actually defined part (or all) of the trash as "secret." Here, the tradeoff between the ease of not protecting something and the risk of that decision coming back to haunt one is easily seen. This first individual hasn't yet reached the point of being willing to expend more than minimal effort on the matter.

My mother-in-law shreds everything.

Yup, there's shredders around.

Again, the only reason I would shred is for identity theft, and I'm too lazy to do that. Although I would not put credit card offers into recycling. I would not do that. I think that's foolish.

This next person, too, draws a line around what he's willing to expend effort on, and also minimizes that effort. To do so, he uses various categories of trash themselves to help protect the one that is most secret.

I tend to rip all my junk mail in half and I do not recycle credit card offers, to use these examples. I'm not all that worried about it. You know, you hear horror stories about people's identities but—

You never had anything like that happen?

No, I haven't and, um, maybe I'm not as careful as I should be, but, um, I just think that when you start being real worried about that kind of stuff, I'm not sure where you stop. You know? So, I just, I rip them up. They're usually in the garbage. Coffee grounds and other really sickening garbage-- You know, I think that, well, if somebody is willing to go through this and to reassemble a credit card offer to steal my identity, it's probably worth more to them than it is to me.

(Laughs.)

Let them have it. Good news. . . . But there's somebody here and another editor, for instance-- His wife wanted to get a shredder. A paper shredder. And that seems to me to entail a little more effort than I want to make for my junk mail.

The category of trash that is not entitled to quite so much effort includes anything thrown out at home for this next person—despite having bought a shredder for just this purpose. She refrains from domestic shredding despite the additional facts that (1) her mother clearly taught her the importance of it, (2) she does, indeed, have a healthy fear of what people might learn from the trash, and (3) she participates in active trash protection at work.

Do you think that the responsibilities that you associate with work demand that you give attention to issues of privacy?

Well, with the bills and everything, yeah. But, you know, not so much, not so much at home. At home I don't feel so worried about my privacy. Now, when we throw things out, I'm very careful about what we throw out. In fact, I bought a shredder. Um hmm. But I don't do any of that. I do, I bought the shredder, but I haven't opened it. My mom used to take scissors and cut up every little piece of thing that she threw out. She would cut it up into pieces that are like this big. Because she didn't want her private information out.

In the end, whoever is most concerned with secrecy is generally the one who will have to exert the most effort to make sure that whatever they're most worried about is sorted out and selectively destroyed. That may mean shredding anything with one's name on it, for instance.

Would you say privacy is problematic for you now?

I-- Any piece of mail that comes into the house, I don't put our name--
either my name or Steven's name, which are two different names-- they
don't go into the trash at all. . . . So it's a little bit of work, but I don't
think it's a problem.

So you shred all mail, not just the credit card statements?

I shred everything. They say that with identity theft, you don't even
want them to know your name. . . . I'm just following suggestions.

Taken altogether, then, garbage is spread across the private-public continuum, emerging as a hybrid category that has many subcategories.

Garbage is a private/public hybrid in a second sense, too. Like credit
cards, money, or business cards, participants often define various components of a single piece of garbage as more and less public. Specific, selective behaviors to protect the most private bits emerge as a result of this.
Along with credit card numbers and financial account information, names
and addresses are among some of the most common parts of trash to be
singled out for secrecy behaviors.

This next individual is not only sensitive to leaving labels on magazines
in public places, for instance. His concern with the disposal of a variety of
other extremely "private" items is also apparent, including his Christmas
tree.

[W]hen I get credit card issues or something like that, I usually shred
the paper in my hand, tear it up. And when I'm actually here at Star-
bucks and I'll be paying bills or doing stuff like that, anything I throw
away in the trash can that has an address and stuff like that, I'll tear up. I
have a tendency in some places when I'm reading a magazine that when
I'm done reading it, I'll just leave it there. Because at a place like this,
you can leave it and someone else will pick it up. But if I have a mailing
label on it, I take that off. When I'm throwing out a magazine in a place
like this and I don't think it's a kind of a magazine that anybody else
would really want—like an electronic network kind of magazine, a trade
kind of magazine—I'll black out my address on it.

I used to be concerned about pill bottles, but I've gotten to a stage
where I don't care. But I did have, at one point, you know-- You know, I
was throwing out-- Like I said, I'm treated for chronic depression, so I
take some medication for that. And I thought, "Do I want everybody to
know this?" But I thought, God, they'd have to be really curious to open
garbage bags and do all that kind of stuff.

A secret thing that I do that you didn't mention, but it's like talking about putting boxes at someone else's house and stuff? Okay. We live next to (this apartment building), which is a very large, multi, like, probably five hundred units or something like that. And we're next door to that. Okay. At Christmas, when we have a Christmas tree?

Uh huh.

If we put it out by our trash things, the scavenger retrieval charges us so much money to do it. But next door at the apartment building, they have sort of a general contract. So at the dead of night, we sneak our Christmas tree out and shove it next door. And if we have anything like an old piece of furniture that we want to get rid of or something like that, we take it over to the apartment building, like, in the early evening when their staff is gone and put it there. So it's not so much because we-- Well, we want to hide that we're throwing it away. We don't want to hide that we once owned it. Okay? So it's not like a new box for, you know, something. We're doing it because we don't want the extra charge on our scavenger service.[17]

This participant not only shows the first two ways in which the hybridity of trash results in specific trash-management behaviors, that is, some items of trash are much more private than others and some *parts* of items are much more private than others. He also introduces a third sense in which trash is a private-public hybrid, seen across a more spatiotemporal continuum. Here, the nature of garbage seems to be redefined over time and over space. It moves from being more private—within the confines of one's home, for a given duration of time—to being more public, out there, on the curb, and waiting for pickup at a later time.

Christmas trees on the curb are, in some ways, a sad and slightly jarring sight precisely because of the speed at which they make this classificatory transition. One minute they're in people's living rooms, an almost sacred centerpiece of relationships, children's fantasies,[18] and holiday festivities. The next minute, they're profane cast offs, lying out in the cold with their orphaned bits of tinsel and no longer of any interest whatsoever.[19] Only the trail of dry pine needles left behind gets any attention, perhaps from whoever's wielding the vacuum or whoever steps on them. Christmas trees move from the realm of the private, even the intimate, to the most public realm there is—garbage, on the street—in but a few (apparently sometimes furtive) moments.[20] In the case of this participant's tree, of course, it moves from the realm of the private to the more intense realm of the secret to that of the extremely public in this same span of time. In the case of this next participant's receipts, the trajectory feels a bit more direct.

I put all my old receipts in the private pile. Basically I just throw them away. I guess they probably do have information if I were more concerned with privacy, I wouldn't want people to be snooping in, but I don't really care that much.

So they're a little less private than some of the other stuff?

I mean, they're going to become a little less private really quickly when I throw them in the trash outside and be available for anyone who cares to look at them.

In Chicago, even the trash cans themselves are public property, and the city is careful to stamp that information on every one of the receptacles used by private homeowners. This emphasizes the fact that the moment one drops something in an outdoor trash can, it instantly becomes more public. Trash may be at its most intimate at the point of creation, then, traveling from a bedroom or bathroom wastebasket along an ever more public path of receptacles and toward the city dump, recycling center, or an ocean barge. It is fascinating to consider whether or not an individual might have an increasing or decreasing sense of worry about what a piece of trash might reveal while traveling along that path.

MAIL

From a privacy perspective, trash isn't the only item that routinely embarks on a journey of potential concern. For people who are worried about anything that has their name on it, the mail is an obvious focus of attention. In fact, items received through the mail are the biggest "secret" components of trash according to these participants' sorting and protecting behaviors.

A former military intelligence officer now employed as a mail carrier explains how mail and trash might be linked in the following story. It is no wonder some people seem so worried about the former when it becomes the latter.

Is there anyone else here, maybe, where you think you know more about them through seeing their mail than they might want you to know?

Several of them that I deliver to. I wouldn't bring that to their attention.

Yeah.

But there's certain things that are evident. You can tell by the person's handwriting, by the correspondence style, who sent the stuff to him. A lot about what their ideas are, what their business is about, even some of their personal details. Yeah, you can read a lot into some people's mail. If they are reading their mail.

But you *can* tell a lot through the mail. And being in the military, you're screened to reduce the mail, garbage, everything.

What do you mean?

Um-- In the military-- I guess I can share that, it's nonclassified. A person who is in a high classification is trained to observe a lot about people. One of the things is that "make sure they know nothing from your trash." You want to find out something about a person, look in the garbage can, what's there, and read the mail.[21]

(Laughing.)

"Oh, the person has gone to Timbucktu" or somewhere. "They have plans to beat up Mr. Smith" or something.

Yeah.

And this is pretty sick. But these are things that you take for granted. Other people pick up on them and we lose our privacy because we don't pick up after ourselves.

Interestingly enough, trash and mail are linked in another way. Like the broader category of trash, mail also has a distinct public-private hybridity about it. There are more public and private items within the daily pile of mail. There are more public and private parts to a single item of mail. The envelope boasts information that anyone can see, for instance. However, the envelope conceals information that no one else is supposed to see.[22] There is a spatiotemporal aspect of mail hybridity, too, as these items travel from their time and place of origin to their destinations. In fact, Smith (2000) makes a compelling case for the importance of privacy (and politics) in early postal legislation in this regard. It explicitly made it a crime for anyone other than the sender or the intended recipient to intercept and read mail during its vulnerable (public) period of transit.

This doesn't do a whole lot to reassure urban participants who may have curious or meddlesome neighbors. It turns out that a hallmark of a "good" neighbor, in fact, is someone who doesn't mess with one's mail. When answering the question "What do you and your neighbors do to respect each other's privacy?" a participant responded:

When packages get delivered to the wrong place, people bring them over and, you know, they're not opened or whatever. . . . You know, no-body's opening each other's mail.

Uh huh.

But I think we'll try to get things promptly to the right place if the mail comes to the wrong house and things like that.

The expectation—and hope—that neighbors will respect the privacy of each others' mail is precisely what underlies this next participant's outrage and continued bad feelings with one of his neighbors.

Because it's a condominium, we have to have meetings where we, you know, we're sitting face to face with each other. A lot.

It's sort of public knowledge in a condominium: this is how much we pay for assessments. This is what everybody owes to the condominium building. And these are decisions that are being made having to do with them. That I think is public information.

But one of the things I mentioned very early on that I think is private are financials, so that comments were being made like, "Oh, I see you're driving this kind of a car. You must have money." But you don't know anything about the car I'm driving, how I got the car, where I'm driving the car. You know, it's a rental car and I'm getting it for my business. So you don't know anything.

I have a place where I think my privacy was being invaded. At one point, when-- and this was-- I had an unemployment period between one position and before I started at (Smith). It was very hard for us to pay our assessment fee every month completely and on time. So we were really strung out, and there was anger in the condominium building, for good reason. I never doubted that that was a problem.

At one point, I think, the guy below me really, in my mind, crossed the line in this, being public information, and our privacy in how we dealt with it. They had every right to want me to give the money and to ad-dress it that way. But I get (this) magazine. I always have. And at that point it came with a brown wrapper on it, and it was left on the window ledge with a bunch of other stuff that didn't fit through the mailbox. And he wrote on the wrapper, "What about your assessment fee?" On this brown wrapper. And I still have it in a file because that was just so incredibly offensive to me that anybody would do that.

It's one thing in a meeting, and it's one thing even in a letter to say, "Where's your assessment? We're going to take you to court," you know, blah, blah, blah, all that stuff. But that was a personal, you know-- Uumph! And I really, really resented it.

And, as a result of that, that's colored my opinion of this family ever since. That was thirteen years ago.

But what happens when the mail carrier is the invasive person? In 2007, Chicago was reported to be the city with the worst mail delivery service in the United States.[23] It was not only the speed at which their mail was delivered that upset people. Numerous stories also reported residents being outraged with the poor, unprofessional service of their local mail carriers. It's bad enough to have neighbors who are second guessing all kinds of things about one's life and violating one's privacy regarding mail. What if one suspects the mail carrier has a similar frame of mind?

What is the worst invasion of somebody's privacy at home that you've heard of or that happened to you?

Well, we have this wonderful mailman named Julio. Julio just told me that he put a bid in for a new spot. The old mailman that we had was-- He was nice, but he was very flirtatious, kind of in a creepy way. But not creepy *really*. But, you know? It's like the mailman actually is somebody who knows more about you than you ever want anybody else to know, really. You know what I'm saying?

Yeah.

. . . And *this* mailman is darling, but he's much more-- You know, he-- He's more polite, you know. It's just not his way to be too formal over something.

. . . My friend Sally, when she was unemployed for awhile . . . she was around the house a lot. And she got to know *her* mailman and she was *really* freaked out.

I think that the mailman is really a person who has way more information than really you want somebody that's creepy to have.

Yeah.

. . . Like you were asking about should priests have background checks, should so and so, whatever? I don't know, mailmen are getting-- . . . They get a lot of information about people and sort of-- I don't know that I'd say that they should have a background check, but-- They like their privacy too. But I don't know. It's a vulnerable spot.

It is not only the face-to-face contact that these women had with their mail carriers that worried them, then. It was also the carriers' access to very complete information about their lives that bothered them, and the very little control they had over that.

In fact, even when postal workers are doing their jobs exactly as they are supposed to, they might know more about us than we wish they would. Listen to what one mail carrier said happened when a letter could not be delivered properly nor returned easily to its sender.

Can you think of, like, any stories or examples about somebody you know, of something that they wouldn't want you to know or wouldn't want public?

Yeah, like that one letter I was telling you about where I opened it up. [It had been sent back, marked "return to sender."] But I had to open it because it had no [specific] return address on it.

(*Laughing.*) Yeah.

I opened it to find out who had sent it out, yeah. And I read it and then-- Like I said it before, it was a love letter.

(*Laughing.*)

AND, it went to a married person. Reading it-- First two lines, there's all this intimate stuff, and then it goes on to say this person's married. "I know you're married, but we had a wonderful time."

(*Laughing.*) Was it tempting to just put that one in the trash to, like, save everybody the embarrassment?

Yeah. I wanted to. I wanted to throw it away then. And I should have-- let the person believe that it'd got picked up on the other end and the person didn't decide to write back or it got lost in the mail.

So I know more about that situation, you know-- And so any time I see that person, to spite me, I remember that letter.

(*Laughing.*) Yeah.

But I never, never divulged.

Do they know that you know?

Oh, no. Well, they know somebody opened the letter to get it back.

But they don't know who.

They probably have an inclination that it was done on their route.

Yeah.

But-- So obviously, they don't know who, actually, to reroute the letter back to. But somebody had to do it or else it would go in the trash.

Yeah.

But before we throw it in the trash because of lack of information on the letter, we have to try to return it where it belongs.

Empowered in circumstances like these to see the most private parts of our most private mail, postal workers remind us that even the kinds and parts of mail that we think are most protected may not be. It depends on where the mail is in its journey.

But what about the reverse case? What about items that we are raised to think of as public that also turn out to have a more hybrid status than we thought? Besides our trash cans and mailboxes, one other item routinely found curbside proves interesting in this regard: cars. Specifically, private cars parked on a public street.

STREET PARKING

Our neighborhood is not-- It's civil. Sometimes. The immediate neighbors are polite generally, but it's not overly friendly.

When is it not civil?

Well, you know, when my son gets mugged three blocks from home. And it's happened twice.

Wow.

So, it's not civil. It's not civil when the great Chicago tradition of marking out a parking space in the winter occurs, particularly if one, or someone, did not shovel the space. I find that to be-- I extrapolate that to the character of the city.

It's become-- right, it's become such a-- Now in the news, where the mayor has said, "This is what people in Chicago do," and then—

Yeah, "We are rude."

Have you ever saved a parking spot?

No.

No. Do *they* save them? Do you have a street where they save them all the way down? In some neighborhoods they just, both sides, like all-- A lot of the people do it.

No, it, it's not that bad, no.

Umhm.

There's a very pleasant woman next door that does it and laughs about it.

Have you talked to her about it?

I haven't talked to her about it, but she just laughed about it. "It's time to get my chairs out," and she gets them out.

Oh, she said that.

Two inches of snow last winter, and she had the chairs out!

Um. Have you ever removed somebody's chairs?

Uh, I've walked close to several and bumped them over.

(Laugh.)

Very, very sort of, on the edge of aggressive behavior, for me. (*Laughter.*) I have not removed them.

Hm. I've had-- I'll tell you that I did know someone-- I knew this old couple who had-- The husband was handicapped, and they had left their parking spot and tried to come back. And someone had put chairs, you know, where they [the handicapped man and his wife] normally park. And I was so angry. And they didn't feel like they could move the chair. And they were worried about their tires getting slashed, and all this kind of stuff.

Yeah.

But, it's a, what a bizarre trespassing of, um, public space.

Yeah, I mean, it's really strange.

Thus goes Chicago's well-recognized tradition in the winter. In order to park one's car, an individual shovels the snow out of an appropriate-sized space (or waits until someone else does), then claims that portion of the (very public) street as one's own. One does this either by keeping one's car in that space until the thaw or by putting an assortment of semidisposable, "private" household items in its place whenever one moves the car. Those new to the city soon find out that, should anyone else attempt to move the items from the shoveled-out parking space in order to use it, they can expect retribution—usually in the form of property damage to the usurper's car. Houses with deeded parking spaces go for much higher prices, accordingly.

Of course, this excerpt makes it clear that there are at least two people involved in this study who think the parking space squatters are the original usurpers, treating the public's property as private and insisting others do the same. There are assorted rationales for squatters' behavior, leaving them feeling perfectly righteous. The primary ones include (1) the argument that if one uses one's labor to transform the nature of something, one now has a moral claim of ownership over it; and (2) that in times of (parking) scarcity—as every urbanite knows—it's each person for her- or himself.[24]

What is so fascinating about this is that it taps directly into the fact that even the nature of something as public as a street may be, in fact, a classificatory hybrid, subject to change, perhaps according to the weather.[25] And if the wintertime privacy of the street appears to be gifted here—by the mayor and the (intimidated) neighbors—so, too, is its fair-weather publicness. Both classifications require some well-recognized, symbolic-interactionist work, though, in accordance with the outside temperature.

Streetside parking is not the only place we find the privatizing of public space. Lofland (1998, 12–14) argues that a variety of small pieces of the private realm, that is, "bubbles," may intrude into public space, such as when couples or groups occupy public parks and the like, sometimes reserving such space for private events. This also reflects the fact that the borders around private and public realms are "protean, mercurial in nature," as she puts it. Indeed, Lofland points out that as a result, the boundaries between these different kinds of spaces can be a source of as much conflict as any other contested classificatory terrain.

Street parking plays another important role in participants' work to negotiate the boundary between what is private and what is public, however. Like yard work, dogs, and children, a parked car on the street can greatly increase people's accessibility to each other.

Do you feel like you know your neighbors now better or less [than before]?

Less than.

Really? . . . Why do you think that is?

Because it's this whole, it's a-- . . . Okay. If you walk somewhere, you still may meet somebody. But, if you drive, or if you-- The difference is we parked on the street there and so you had to walk to your car and you might run into somebody. Here, it's this garage, in a cloister, and the car's sealed up.

So potentially you would never see anybody?

Right. And you often don't.

Thus, parking on the street creates opportunities for interaction—and/or resistance to it—that parking in a private garage does not.

YARD WORK

The same is true for yard work, of course. Though one's yard is legally private, the visibility and audibility of whatever happens on it makes anyone or anything going on in the yard—even the length of the grass—accessible to the public. In many gated communities, for instance, neighborhood boards insist on a variety of rules that mandate the appearance of one's yard and the activities that can take place there. Strict rules about the sizes, shapes, styles, and colors of mailboxes, the leaving of trash at the curb, and parking on the street, complement an assortment of other rules regarding (no) clotheslines, (no) visible working on cars, and (no) grass above a certain height, as well as literally dozens of other ordinances for things such as noise, pets, posting signs, socializing, and yard sales. (Actually, these may have to be garage sales, if they're allowed at all.)

Yet things needn't be so formalized. Simple peer pressure among neighbors may suffice to keep some level of conformity across the yards in some neighborhoods—something this participant happily rejects.

I think also this particular neighborhood, as people go, are pretty tolerant. . . . In this neighborhood, conforming is not a value, whereas in another neighborhood, I think it is. In some other neighborhoods, it is.

. . . When we first moved into this house-- We lived here for a couple of years, and I didn't even notice that I had a lawn. And my mother-in-law said to me, "Well, don't your neighbors complain about your lawn?" And I said "No. What's wrong with-- ? Well, first of all, what's wrong with my lawn? And secondly, no." And she said, "Oh, they would in (Glenview)." And I thought, well, that's why I don't live in Glenview, I guess. I didn't even know that. And I knew not to live there.

There are places, in other words, where one's private property might feel like anything but—and where one's theoretical classification of something might be quite different from what happens in practice.

Keeping the lawn trim and tidy requires that someone pays attention to it. Like walking to a car parked on the street or barbecuing in the back yard, landscaping and gardening presents a common opportunity for participants to interact with neighbors and even strangers. They may have to work hard at it if they refuse to do so.

So, when you're cooling out, you might go to the yard, do neighbors ever stop by or wave?

Well, sometimes. Depending on if it's in the evening. It all depends. Because one of our neighbors next door, he lives by himself, but if he's around, we'll chat. Our other immediate neighbor, if it's, say, a holiday, I'll see her more because sometimes we'll be out grilling at the same time. And our neighbor who's a little older and lives further, I see her more when we're driving, just going to the garage, because she's retired. See her waving. But most of the people, as I said, they're older, and you just don't see them out that much. Except for my neighbor on my right. I think he's a little younger man agewise.

So he's out more?

Well, I see him more because he cuts the grass and grooms his hedges and my husband will chat and get together and prune. It's just a nice relationship.

In fact, a number of participants look forward to the spring, when their yard work means renewing friendships with neighbors that were put on hold over the winter.

DOGS

Unlike some garden work, most city dogs need to be attended to—including walked—every day, year round. The opportunities they present for boundary work may be minimized by severe weather, but they are never entirely eliminated.

I've lived here for nine years. And I know a lot of people here. And it takes nine years to know people in the neighborhood. It takes nine years and a dog—

(Laughing.)

—to really get to know people even on any kind of basis at all.

. . . Maybe because I've always lived in sort of developing neighbor-hoods where there is a crime problem, but I think that people are very reticent to share much of anything about their lives or, you know, or whatever. . . . It took me several years to even get to know that, um, people lived here, much less know their names and spend any time with them, so—

How did you manage to meet those other women?

Um, I'm sure only because I have a dog. I know the one at the corner, you know. She would just see me walking the dog over and over and over. And she didn't have a dog at that time. But she, she would drive by and say hello but, you know, first you do the, you do the eye-contact thing, and then at some point you start nodding or saying hi.

. . . The woman across the street, I had heard of her, heard that she was, you know, there—whatever. Again, I'm sure it's from walking the dog. If it wasn't for the dog, I wouldn't know anyone at all. Not a soul. (*Laughing.*)

Yard work attracts passersby and creates opportunities for interaction or avoidance in the area immediately around one's home. Dog walking, on the other hand, takes participants to the perimeters of other people's homes as well as out to parks and other public spaces. In this way, dogs help foster additional interactions by raising the neighborhood visibility of their owners in a way that may even surpass the effect of children. This may be particularly true since dogs seem to be relatively easier to identify as individuals and are routinely seen in predictable places and times, thus making it easier to identify as well as engage their owners. Indeed, dogs seem to regularly invite conversation from passersby when "civil inatten-tion" would otherwise be the rule.

Another participant boasts about the extensiveness of his neighbor-hood network, for instance, and unequivocally attributes it to his dog.

Well, I really actually know almost everybody on the block. I know who they are. You know, let me put it this way. I bet you that I know more people on the block than anybody else on the block. And I know them more than anybody else on the block. Do I know them well? No. But, um, but I do know more people because of the dog.

Thus, dog walking sets the stage for owners' episodic needs to draw the private-public line to a degree that non–dog owners do not have to. Each walk is a series of moments in which the owner can expect to be predict-ably and unpredictably engaged in various ways and in which she or he will have to make a decision about how to respond. Typically, the dog walker's response is welcoming of at least a limited form of connection with the people they meet. (A number of participants suggest that if people want to be left alone and remain unfamiliar with their neighborhoods, then "They shouldn't get a dog.")

In the case of mutual dog walkers, especially people who take their dogs to parks each day so both species can have more sustained socializing time, the connection can become that of good friends. Typically, the exchanges focus on information about the neighborhood.

Last night, somebody told me that their kids had been held up by-- and you should know about this. The kid is eighteen or something, and he and his girlfriend were held up at gunpoint in front of their apartment at (this corner).

Oh, my God!

At 1:00 AM. And then someone else said, "Yeah, someone was held up on my street (one block away from there), 10:00," much earlier, in the past two weeks.

Ten o'clock?!

And it came up because we're out there with our dogs. There's just a huge group of us at about, between nine and eleven o'clock [in the eve-ning], really.

The value of dog owners' routines to the entire neighborhood is not lost on the following participant.

What do your neighbors do, if anything, to interact, recognize, and create a healthy public life with each other?

We've got neighbors who walk the dogs every day and greet everybody as they walk their dogs. They're kind of the ones that hold the neighbor-hood together.

In addition to dogs' effects on our accessibility during walks and play sessions, they—and other creatures—remind us of the physical accessibil-ity of our yards, too. Sometimes that accessibility stretches into the house, a fact that can lead to events either threatening or amusing.

When I lived in the apartment down the block, my landlord and neighbor lived upstairs and they were perpetually saving animals. Um, so it-- They had family in (Nebraska). They'd always be coming back from Nebraska, and that almost always meant some wounded, injured animal found on the roadside would also be coming home with them. They had a series of crows that were nursed back to health or allowed to die while being doted upon in the backyard.

And there was a squirrel that they befriended, and his name was (Swirl). And Swirl was raised from the time he was sitting in the palm of your hand, and in the upstairs apartment and so forth. Well, Swirl grew up and Swirl had absolutely no fear of human beings and Swirl would let himself into our house and our kitchen on a regular basis. You would walk into your large pantry and there would be Swirl, like, chowing on Wheat Thins, you know.

(*Laughing.*) Right.

And you would say, "Go away," and Swirl would be looking, "Ha, ha, ha," (*laughing*) and sort of flip you off, you know.

Right.

And then you'd swat at him and he'd jump on your shoulder and, you know-- So a lot of people could be insulted by something like that. Like, that you would let your pets run wild.

And the upstairs dog would come down and-- Our front door, because we didn't lock it most of the time, all it needed was a nudge to get open. So the dog upstairs would come down and spring our dog free and then they would play together. Only—

Uh huh.

—we had the better end of that deal because our dog is a champion countertop stealer.

Uh huh.

There are many loaves of bread—

(*Laughing.*)

—a chicken that was thawing. You know. Stories that-- Things that were fun. The only thing that we had to say was, "Our dog can't open the door. It's your dog that opens the door and springs our dog free." But um--

I think pets can be weird that way, you know. Certainly if my dog was breaking into someone's house who didn't have a pet—

(Laughing.)

—they would see that's a grotesque invasion of privacy. It's really okay when you both have dogs, though. Well, you know. They're just dogs.

In fact, if dogs increase our accessibility to others in a number of ways, they also decrease it in one respect that particularly stands out: warding off home intruders and safeguarding our persons when we're out walking. Dogs are so valuable in helping to secure one's home and person, in fact, that people even pretend to have dogs in order to deter anyone who might be thinking about breaking in.

I don't have a dog, although I've thought about getting one of those little electronic things that barks when you ring the doorbell.

Yeah, that's smart.

Now, I have had-- Of course we've had the thing to pretend that there is a dog in the backyard. We've done that.

Uh huh. "Beware of the dog" sign?

Uh huh. And we've done that.

Others put out dog dishes—with water and sometimes food—and even leave an occasional pile of poo in their yards to further the illusion. Thus, people strategically publicize (make more accessible) the (alleged) presence of a dog outside of the house in order to increase their senses of privacy and security (inaccessibility) inside of it.

Dogs are local characters (Milgram's [1970] "familiar strangers," perhaps) who invite connection and increase the possibilities of interaction among the humans they encounter. They are also extremely efficacious at discouraging interaction, though. It is precisely this dual dimension that defines dogs' roles as assistant managers of our privacy, helping us to negotiate our selective accessibility to others.

CHILDREN

Pets aren't the only less-than-fully-socialized creatures who regularly create opportunities for people to negotiate the private-public line. As one participant noted, "Kids cross boundaries and create linkages even their reluctant parents might not." This excellent observation was made in various ways by the people in this study, and in reference to completely mundane situations as well as special ones, like Halloween.

Older, "empty nester" participants were especially sensitive to this, reflecting on the effect of having children of various ages living at home, before, during, and after they did so.

Are there things you do to make sure that you do see or talk to somebody [in the neighborhood] once in a while, or is it all by chance?

Most of it by chance. Because most people-- If I had small children, it may be different, but most of it is by chance and most of us are out working on something. Maybe in the garden or my husband is cutting grass and talking to the neighbor down the street or whatever. So most of it is by chance, basically because we're all older.

How was it different when you had small children?

. . . It's a lot different than when they were older than it was when they were younger, because you got to know the kids they played with. Their parents might come out on the porch and sit just to chat with people in the neighborhood.

In fact, children are especially good at creating "sidewalk life" (Jacobs 1992) for the entire community, in all kinds of spaces along their household perimeters. Another participant describes how this happens in her apartment complex.

Do you think other people who live here seem to interact a lot or know each other?

I think it's-- You know, you can have kids here, so I think obviously the families with kids get hooked up, you know, through the kids and through doing something with the kids. They do, the management tries to organize activities, like, you know, like yesterday for Halloween they had, like, a party for people with kids and stuff like that. But, like, I wouldn't go. They wouldn't give me any candy.

(Laughter.)

So, I think, you know, I think certainly because there is this townhouse aspect to it that you do, you know, see more people outside. So you, you know, get to know more people rather than just living in a midrise apartment building.

Well, there's kind of this shared courtyard.

Yeah.

Does that feel communal? Do people sort of use that?

Well, you know what's tough is actually-- They don't have an actual playground here. So what happens in that courtyard in the summer is like, it's, well, whatever you call it, the pathway is a wide pathway. Kids use it for, like, foot races, or wear their roller skates and, you know. And then the management yells down, because it's like, "Hey," you know, "Don't work up the bricks with your skateboards" or whatever.

Not all children draw people out into the yard or common play areas. Infants and teenagers do not have nearly the effect that toddlers and primary school children do on the interaction patterns of study participants. Young, independently mobile children are the ones who more or less force adults to engage in boundary work along the household perimeter, perhaps beginning with the design of spaces and objects to support—or inhibit—their interactions.

Consider the following example of designing for increased accessibility between two neighbors' yards—and between the families who use them. This individual reflects on the amount of interaction in his neighborhood in general, and with one neighbor's family in particular.

There's not a tremendous amount of necessary overlap and interaction and yet there's more than you would suspect in most neighborhoods. . . . Um, the neighbor in my backyard, to give you an example, just built a fence which is higher than the average fence. However, he has two little kids and I've got two little kids and we both have dogs. And we like each other, right? So he put the gate between his yard and my yard and made the gate climbable by little boys, right?

. . . So these little boys-- My boys used to climb up on this playhouse and jump over the fence. There used to be just, like, a chain link. And he replaced it with a solid wooden fence. But right in the middle of-- Right in the middle of my forsythia bushes where the kids are always playing anyway, there's a gate that can fully open or be climbed over. It's designed to be climbed over.

Contrast this intentional effort to permit and even foster accessibility and the boundary-blurring effect of children—this participant's children, in particular—with this next design effort, built to do the opposite. Both approaches clearly take into consideration children's propensity for not recognizing boundaries.

Is there anything while you're outside that you do to protect your privacy and let people know that now's not a good time?

Yeah, we have a fence. (*Laughing.*)

Okay.

Now, you know, I've talked to people going back and forth. And the kids in the neighborhood, if we're watering, they want to run through the sprinkler—But, yeah, we have a fenced-off area.

Okay. Do people respect that or do you have problems with people—?

When we first moved in we had a lot of stoop sitting, but that kind of disappeared.

Right.

That hasn't been an issue. Um, and the fence pretty much keeps kids from running up on the lawn during dismissal time after school.

It's no wonder the following participant is considering a similar move to better ensure the private nature of her yard.

Since they have begun to demolish the highrise buildings and there's a Section 8 housing problem,[26] they are now putting those people, and I guess that sounds terrible, into the quieter neighborhoods. And they're coming in with children that receive absolutely no discipline. They have no respect for people's individual privacy.

And the children trample your lawn, tear up your flowers, play on the pathway, and throw things on the front porch. So there is, there is a difference. So the area, we have very-- We're getting a very strong block club, and we're trying to work with the parish [people] and with the disruptive children, to try to work together to settle this. So it's for the most part, it's pretty good. We don't have any more than they have in other places.

. . . If it doesn't get better, I would then put up the fence that I've threatened to.

The wide pathway, the climbable gate between yards, and the fences whose purpose is to keep kids out are all examples of infrastructural privacy work. These design elements, intentionally added onto the perimeters of participants' yards, constrain the boundary options of less-than-fully-socialized creatures.[27] They are used in differing ways across a single individual's curtilage, too. This depends on a number of factors including the customary front yard/back yard distinction, the nature of specific neighbors and regular passersby, the presence of wild or domesticated animals, and any community ordinances regulating such boundary markers.

In a country where the notion of private property and the value of privacy, fences, doors, and locks dominate homeowners' mindsets, finding ways to selectively encourage interaction among neighbors seems to be a constant design challenge. Outside, given the relatively safe, urban settings of these particular study participants, at least one may count on the presence of sidewalks and streets. There is usually a bit of yard as well. Such shared space functions as a remarkably important stage for the private-public negotiations of study participants—whether it's a parked car, yard work, grilling, dogs, kids, or anything else that brings them there. Here, the true privacy challenge becomes clear: to encourage interaction when one wants it, about the things one wishes to interact about, and to discourage interaction whenever one wishes to do that, about whatever one would like to avoid.

THIS FUNNY LITTLE DANCE

What do you and your neighbors do to respect each other's privacy?

Well one thing is we have these backyards that are just chain-link fence, and they're really small backyards. So, like, if I sit on my porch, I can see what's going on—my neighbors to the right and left of me. So we say hi to each other, but you also kind of respect each others' privacies, also. So you don't necessarily stop and talk to them unless you get indications that they're also willing to talk. So it's kind of this funny little dance of how much you talk to them, for example, when they're out in their backyards.

Of all the difficult work involved in negotiating the private-public boundary, some of the most sophisticated happens during face-to-face interactions among urban neighbors. In high-density residential areas, achieving the right balance between privacy and publicity can feel like a constantly moving target, requiring all the social skills and knowledge we possess. This is a dance, indeed, where numerous factors influence every successful step—and misstep—that might take place.

One problem is that there may be no clear, shared understanding of where even longtime community members fall on the scale between intimates and strangers. As we have seen, our disclosure and concealment decisions rely heavily on the nature of our relationships. With neighbors, each potential conversational topic, each behavior that one might or might not permit them to witness, each of the neighbors' actions that we might or might not acknowledge in order to gift them privacy is just such a decision. Sometimes we make these decisions with very little to go by in the way of relationship guidelines.

The problem is that granting or denying the wrong degree of accessibility—perhaps only one time out of many otherwise successful encounters—can lead to endless difficulties with one's neighbors. Does that person over in their yard want to be left alone right now or is he looking for conversation? If you say something when he wants privacy—or don't say something when he wants to talk—you run the risk of being a "bad" neighbor, especially if you keep making the same mistake.

For study participants, part of the enjoyment that comes from having "good" neighbors seems to come from the relief of having settled into a mutually acceptable and pleasurable understanding along these lines. Even with these individuals, though, the dance never really ends.

What do you and your neighbors do to respect each other's privacy?

I think that people monitor and are a little tentative in the ways that they interrupt one another when they're outside. Um, although it happens a ton. Like I said, um, I can't imagine going out into my backyard and be gardening and seeing my neighbor, (Drew), in his garden and not saying something to him.

Right.

Although it's happened. If he's passing to his garage and on his way out, he's not going to, necessarily, going to interrupt me or talk to me, you know, every single time. But if we're both out there, we'll definitely find fifteen minutes to hang over the fence and talk or whatever. If we're both outside and mowing our lawns or something, we'll hang out or just shoot the breeze for a bit.

If the neighbor is someone whose signals are too difficult to read, the job is that much more difficult.

Is there anything that you do, you or your neighbors, to kind of respect each others' privacy?

Well, I have this thing where, um-- We have this new yuppie couple that moved in on the corner. It's, like, different because their house is oriented different than the old shack that was there and everything. I felt really bad one day because I heard a noise and I looked up. And it was all sort of coming together, and I realized I was looking at her on her deck. I was in my yard and she was on her-- I don't really-- It's sort of like you pretend that there is a wall there even though there isn't a wall.

Yeah.

So I felt bad because I was looking at her and then I did it. Then I just [looked away]--

So then afterwards I thought, "If they don't have that weird code that I have, then did she think that I snubbed her?" You know, I really don't know. So, but, it's just sort of hard because you want to be able to be friendly to people, but you don't want to invade their space.

. . . We were looking at each other. I should have said, "Oh, hi," you know, or something. But it's, like, I looked down and I was, like, embarrassed.

I guess she didn't say hi, either.

Right. No, she didn't! No.

The dance isn't just about trying to figure out what other people want, either. It's also about trying to let your desires be known—and prevail—without actually offending anyone. Avoidance is a logical reaction to neighbors who put us in awkward boundary positions.

Are there neighbors that you would consider nosey?

. . . One of them, I thought, actually was quite nosey. I forgot about him.

What would he—?

He just sort of seemed to always be there. You know, every time you'd leave, leave the front door of the place, he was out there walking his dog, and then, you know, have a question for you, or something. I mean, just always, he was everywhere. Yeah. Watching.

. . . You wouldn't see him until you got out there, so you kind of-- . . . Just have a very short conversation with him and stuff. But I would definitely-- There were times when I would see him and I would just walk on the other side of the street. You know. A little bit. I mean, just sometimes.

Thus, careful avoidance techniques—making eye contact or not, closing one's blinds or not, crossing to the other side of the street or not, denying access without letting someone know you're doing it intentionally—are an important part of one's neighboring arsenal. These allow one to minimize one's accessibility to certain others at certain times, while granting it to others at other times and still remain a member of the community in good standing.

The importance of recognizing and using such privacy mechanisms should not be underestimated. They preserve tolerable living conditions even among individuals we would rather not be associated with. The following participant understands this surprisingly well, even though his usual avoidance techniques were not quite up to snuff for one encounter.

How about your neighbors?

Hate 'em.

Current ones or all of them?

Hate 'em all. (*Chuckles.*)

(*Laughing.*) What is the neighborhood like? Busy? Do you know other people?

I live in, ah, not, like, a highrise apartment building, but it's sort of-- The entrance that I use-- There are six apartments, two per floor. But there are also two other entrances in this building with a big kind of corner. There are probably eighteen, a dozen or eighteen units in all. If I-- I don't know anybody very well. I know-- Excuse me. I know the woman who lives upstairs from me because she introduced herself. . . . You know, "If you ever need a cup of sugar" and all that stuff. But-- And we've gotten each others' mail. No details.

(*Laughs.*)

But that's as close as the relationship gets. There's another lady, uh, who I know lives on the second floor. And there's an Alice that's above me.

And another one, whose name I don't know, lives on the first floor. Who brought a plate of cookies to everybody and-- I don't know if everybody in the whole building, but certainly on our staircase. Last Christmas. Which-- She is somebody who I've never seen before.

Did you eat the cookies?

Did I eat them? Yeah. I stored them in my favorite place (*laughing*).

I thought it kind of odd. Because this seems to be something that people do for people who they know. But to have a knock on your door—and you're not in a house where anybody can knock on the door—and when you open the door, "Here's," you know-- I'm in my living room (*laughing*)-- "Here's these cookies." It felt very awkward to me. They were good, but I didn't thank her afterwards or anything. I said thanks at the door, but I was like, but what now?

(*Laughing.*)

Do we have to be friends? Do we have-- ? There was this kind of Seinfeld thing. You know what I mean?

Indeed, bringing cookies or a cake to neighbors—either to welcome them or to extend holiday hospitality—is a ritual that a number of participants mentioned. It is clearly part of a code, a recognition of the relationship that exists by virtue of proximity and that the baker hopes might be a friendly one in the future.

 Getting the boundary "right" with one's neighbors may well change over time. Events shape and reshape specific relationships. Our own privacy preferences change. Neighbors themselves come and go, too. We change the kinds of work we do to be accessible—or not—in response.

About your relationship with your neighbors, you said that you don't know most of them but over the past ten years you've gotten to know a few?

Well, I really actually know almost everybody on the block. . . . I want to know who my neighbors are but, but I wouldn't say that I know anybody very well except for my neighbor (Sally). But we used to be much friendlier. But she has a baby now and her life is totally, totally different than, you know-- There's all that stuff that goes along with it. And there's some weird stuff that happened a couple years ago, you know, before the baby, that it's just sort of like-- I just felt like I needed to step back a little bit.

Like what?

Oh, we had a fight about a garage sale. It was very stupid.

(*Laugh.*)

I had a garage sale here one year and she and (Janine) brought their stuff over. And, I mean, it's a big pain in the ass and a lot of work. So then the next year we were going to have a garage sale and it was going to be at Sally's but-- And we did have the garage sale at Sally's. But sometimes-- She was really mad at me for it, and I couldn't really understand why. There was just a bunch of stuff that really didn't make sense and I just sort of felt--

. . . I don't feel like she puts her cards on the table ever and that's fine, but I just don't feel that close to her. You know what I mean.

Yeah. Are there any of your neighbors that you consider nosey?

I think I'm considered the nosiest person. But I have this old lady who lives a couple doors down, and she is always very-- And these bushes in front-- And there were a couple years where, that I grew the bushes high because I was just tired of people looking in my yard. I just needed a little-- You know what I mean.

Uh huh.

She was really not cool with that! She really felt like I should be cutting my bushes. She's always out cutting her bushes. So she is nosey in that way but I don't think--

And the nanny next door now, "Where you going, (Kara)?"

(Laughing.)

No matter what I'm doing, "Where you going now, Kara?" *(Laughing.)*

(Laughing.) **What do you say?**

I usually say, "Oh, I'm going to go see friends." Like, she asked me when I went out for a few minutes-- She had the baby in the pool. "Where you going now Kara?" "Oh, I'm just going to have lunch, I'm going out later, I have an appointment and then I'm going to see friends. It's Tuesday night, you know." She knows I go out to see girlfriends on Tuesday night. I go to an AA meeting and then I go out with some girls afterwards.

Yeah.

And she always says "Where you going now, Kara?" *(Laughing.)*

(Laughing.) **She's probably bored.**

Poor thing.

Thus the dance between neighbors not only changes across individual encounters, but also over time, as relationships shift, our own desires for privacy and connection change, and new actors are introduced onto the scene.

The importance of historical changes in the expectation for privacy across neighbors and neighborhoods should not be forgotten, either. A seventy-eight-year-old woman who grew up in the South describes her sense of privacy when she was younger, for instance.

You were not able-- You were not free. There were so many restrictions as a black. So that would invade your privacy, in that there were things that you couldn't have and places you couldn't go.

Uh huh.

And that invades your privacy. You were always in the limelight, I guess. Like when I visited with my cousin, when I was talking about it from the end, in the picture. She taught in (Erickson City). That was in-- Well, it wasn't too long ago. But anyway, when she was in the southwest part of (Tennessee) and after 6:00 PM, we couldn't go down the back, to the main street. If we forgot something after dark, we had to go in the back door of the store to purchase it. And if she was-- She always rode home every night with her mother, and we would go down the back street to take the mail, the letters, to the train to post it.

Uh huh.

And that is sort of an invasion of privacy, a definite invasion of privacy.

Uh huh.

Because you couldn't go in the front. And that, of course, as growing up in the South, you couldn't go in the front part of the theater. You were always in the balcony, so you had to go through a side door. And when I went to high school, I had to ride a public bus because there wasn't a high school for blacks in [my] town. So I had to go from one county to the next. And I could stand in the old drug store. I couldn't sit. The whites could sit, on the bus. So that is an invasion of privacy because then you are not a person as such. You are a member only of a race, or a group, and that's an invasion of privacy.

Uh huh.

It's that kind of thing. I couldn't go-- There were places I couldn't go.

What about-- You had mentioned that a lot of people mistook your father for white?

Yes.

Do you feel like that invaded his privacy? Or your privacy?

Oh, yes. Oh, yes. Because of the reaction when they found out that he wasn't.

Uh huh.

He ceased to be a person. As long as they thought he was white, he was a person. But when they found he wasn't, he ceased to be a person. We could come from something that he would never be called "Mister."

Uh huh.

He would be called by his first name but not "Mister."

It sounds like part of what you're saying is that privacy, at least back then, privacy was a right only given to real people, which were by definition white.

To whites. Yes. White, yes. Blacks were not. They had no privacy. And it was the same way with-- A white person could come to your home and come in the front door, but you couldn't go to the white person's house and go in the front door.

No.

You had to always go to the back. And they didn't go to your back.

In the case of African Americans in the U.S., the master status of race has been constructed and maintained at least in part via a denial of even the most basic forms of privacy granted to whites. Schwartz (1968, 748) has argued that "to be subject to limitless intrusion is to exist in a state of dishonor." This is an all-too-accurate summary of much of the history of African Americans' daily life in this country, with undue interest shown in one's parentage, residence, presence, posture, comings and goings—any and all aspects of one's daily business. Chicago in the twenty-first century affords a level of anonymity among neighbors—including those, now, of differing races and ethnicities—that simply did not exist a few decades ago.

In order to understand more fully the difficulties of interacting appropriately with neighbors, Albert Hunter's and Lynn Lofland's work on urban communities is useful.[28] Hunter (1982, 230–31) argues that there are three levels or types of social order in urban communities—the private, the parochial, and the public. Each order guides individuals' decisions about what to expect of others and how to interact with them. Lofland (1998, 10–11) builds on Hunter's insights to argue that

> the private realm is the world of the household and friend and kin networks; the parochial realm is the world of the neighborhood, workplace,

or acquaintance networks; and the public realm is the world of strangers and the "street."

Hunter and Lofland thus argue that interactions within one's home, with one's neighbors, and with strangers out in public are guided by different sets of expectations. Each realm has its own rules—including, I would argue, those about where and how we expect the private-public boundary to be drawn.

The idea that people belong to different social/moral orders and that this is what drives our interactions with and expectations of them in urban settings is quite correct. However, this does not mean—as Lofland suggests—that urban *spaces* may be classified as "public" or "parochial" or "private."[29] Rather, the joy, tragedy, security, danger, and, above all, the challenge of living in urban neighborhoods stems from the fact that all three of these social realms may exist simultaneously in any given physical space.[30]

Urban space is defined by a "this *and* that" nature; it is not a collection of mutually exclusive environments at all.[31] In urban neighborhoods, for instance, a stranger, a friend, and a spouse all may be present on the same sidewalk at the same time. We expect them to be. Thus, the challenge of urban living and especially urban sidewalk life is not for each individual to figure out "What kind of space is this?" (i.e., "What moral order dominates here?"); instead, it is to develop the ability to quickly sort out everyone encountered according to the relationship one has with each of them. This is what then tells you how to interact with anyone you see, based on the expectations and rules of interaction associated with any given order/ relationship.

In fact, thinking in terms of categories of space rather than the specific relationship one has with a given individual distracts us from another important influence on one's privacy expectations in the neighborhood: how difficult it can be to classify relationships with neighbors. Hunter and Lofland treat all neighbors the same, for instance. "Neighbors" are placed in "the parochial realm" of "the neighborhood." They are distinguished from the "strangers" of "the public realm" and the "kin and friends" of "the private realm."

This tidy cordoning off of neighbors from other categories of individuals simply does not reflect the reality expressed by nearly every participant in this study. Almost every individual reported having neighbors who were complete strangers, those they recognized as "familiar strangers" (Milgram 1970), neighbors who were friends, and even those who were "good friends." A number of participants live next to family members, too, making these kin their neighbors as well. "Neighbors" are present in every moral order identified by Hunter and Lofland, that is, not just the parochial one.

From a privacy perspective, then, interacting with neighbors can be quite a selective endeavor. We would expect different privacy expectations to apply to different neighbors, depending on the relationships one has with them. Those expectations change not only according to idiosyncratic preferences and patterns between individuals, but also according to broader shifts in whichever category one places a given neighbor at a given time.

Another way of thinking of the challenge of living in an urban neighborhood and achieving privacy there is suggested by Lally's (2002) work on "collective ownership." In her work on computers in the home, Lally argues that the very same object—a family computer—may be experienced in different ways by the people who use it. Anyone who has sustained interaction with an object, for instance, can have a profound and legitimate sense of ownership over that object—and it can be quite different from anyone else's.

Likewise, depending on their experiences with it, individuals in urban neighborhoods can have very different understandings of and relationships with the exact same space as well as with each other.[32] This is especially true given the degree of sustained interaction that they have with the neighborhood and with specific other people in it. The same person who is an aloof stranger to those living on one side of the street may be the dearest and most reliable of friends to the neighbors who live on the other side. The dog walker's neighborhood and relationships with neighbors can be quite different from those of an individual with no dog, a private garage, and a habit of driving everywhere. They can be quite different from those of the avid gardener, too, the childless hospital resident working nights, and the family with three soccer- and baseball-playing, churchgoing, art- and music-class-attending primary school kids.

Why does the multifaceted nature of the urban neighborhood and urban participants matter for a study of privacy? Because it sets up the ways participants learn to interpret and respond to what they experience there. From the ways they answer their doorbells and use their blinds to the ways they react to seeing a neighbor in their backyards, this understanding of neighbors and the neighborhood sets the stage for privacy work along the household perimeter.[33]

Perhaps dozens of times a day, each person in the neighborhood must decide which realm the others fall into—and to what degree. As we've seen, this is a highly dynamic process in which even the classification of a given neighbor may change from moment to moment, week to week, or year to year. During each encounter, one must further act on each decision one has made in a way that results in a satisfactory private-public negotiation. (In cases where one is not yet able to classify the individual, this may mean feeling compelled to act in a sort of "worst-case" scenario—meaning, "I'm going to assume this person is a stranger who means to do me harm if I give him the opportunity to do so.")

The urban neighborhood is a highly social environment, in other words, and thus requires a continuous stream of choices and effort on the part of a resident.[34] One may adopt a blanket policy of refusing to "dance" as much as possible. One may throw oneself into "dancing lessons," of a sort, working to acquire superb interactional skills—and perhaps a dog—along with a wealth of relationships. Or one may work to acquire a willingness and ability to live with the outcome of being an adamantly bad dancer, possessing less-than-adequate talent and living with the sense of isolation—or overaccessibility—that might result. Only one alternative remains: identify and move to a more comfortable place, where others have the same definition of the dance and similar skill levels, requiring neither radical change nor compromise in order to feel personally at ease.

"GOOD" NEIGHBORS AND "GOOD" NEIGHBORHOODS = "GOOD" PRIVACY

Do you like where you live? Do you like your neighbors?

It's a nice neighborhood where if your garage door is open, somebody will run in and close the door. And everybody got your phone number, so they'll call and say "Your garage door is open."

MARGARET, seventy-three-year-old retiree

* * *

Have you ever lived somewhere where people did not respect each other's privacy as much as you would have liked?

I would say up in (Michigan). We had a-- We moved into a very well established older neighborhood with very, uh, very longstanding residents, who were just, sort of, the traditional busybody. We'd get a call in the morning, "Did you know your basement light was on last night?"

DAN, fifty-six-year-old executive

When it comes to neighborhoods, it would appear that one person's treasure is indeed another person's trash. The degree of privacy one feels from the door outward—the degree to which participants feel in control of how accessible/inaccessible they, their families, and their affairs are to those in proximity to them on a daily basis—is a remarkably important factor in assessing how "good" a community is. In fact, a "good" neighbor, building, or neighborhood seems to be as much a function of how problematic they make one's daily privacy as it is the result of anything else.

Auditory privacy is as good a place as any to begin teasing out the impact of successful and unsuccessful privacy negotiations with neighbors. Here, a guitar player discusses his views on the matter.

Do you have any electric [guitars]? Has anybody ever complained about noise?

They haven't complained, but it's a concern for me.

For you?

For me. Yeah. The neighbors haven't bugged me. On, and on occasion they have. And (Mandy) upstairs has moon chimes. Huge aspen chimes on her back porch. They're, like, the size of that pole. They are so loud. I had to train myself to sleep again when I moved into this apartment.

'Cause they go all night.

Uhhh huh. It's unbelievable. It's like being at a cathedral. And now they don't bother me. She's been there for eight years, so I assumed that everybody else in the building had gotten acclimated to it—so I guess I, you know.

You could at least try? (*Chuckling.*)

It's not right for me to kind of be the new guy. "Oh, can you unscrew this huge pipe organ that you got hanging from your porch?" Well, it made me furious for a while. Really, really quite hot. Furious. Aside from that, I don't feel disturbed all that often. And that makes me, depending on how my mind is working at the moment-- If I'm playing loud music I sometimes think, well, I can't hear them, they probably can't hear me. And other times I think because they're not playing loud music, and maybe I shouldn't either. (*Laughs.*) You know.

(*Laughs.*)

And I do like playing the music and, you know, it's on. I mean, it's not blaring, but I had it on at six thirty in the morning. I don't really stay out late, so it's not midnight or ten thirty. I sometimes think in the morning and I do turn it down. I have a bunch of guitars and most of them are acoustic but there's one electric guitar that I sometimes play. Well, you know, I sometimes turn it up louder than I should. And I'm a pretty good musician, so it's not like I'm practicing, like, "practicing." I think if it's loud, I should try to be pleasing, you know. I shouldn't play obnoxious stuff. You know, if I turn it up above, like, three or four, then play all the things you are going to hate—

(*Laughing.*)

—or something, like, everybody's going to like (*makes frustrated face, chuckles*) if they can hear. But, yeah, there is a certain-- On one hand there's a self consciousness and desire to be polite. On the other hand there's a totally irresistible urge not to play Mozart.

This awareness of a need for self-restraint, to adjust the degree to which one conceals and discloses so that a mutually agreeable private-public boundary could be maintained between neighbors, was expressed repeatedly by study participants. It was completely absent from the following individual's childhood home in a public housing project. Note how quickly his reflections turned to the issue of auditory privacy, too.

I wonder if, while we're going through these questions, if you could contrast your current situation to the Taylor Homes,[35] because I think that would be very interesting. Is it—the neighborhood you're in now—is it a lot different than that?

Yes. Oh certainly, yes.

Would you say where you were, did it feel pretty busy or quiet when you were home?

Which one?

The Taylor Homes.

Um, it was busy in the sense that everybody was outside. Either just standing around or selling drugs or just talking with people or something like that.

That seems like it could be kind of a nice social situation.

It could be except for the very, very bad influences inspiring the social situation. But I really didn't participate. I didn't really participate in the social situations at the Taylor Home. But it could also be very extremely loud. Sometimes there was a kid who was crying because his parents were beating him up, or there was a, there was this guy who was yelling out-- or there was some guy yelling out to his girlfriend without him using the concept of a phone (*imitates yelling*), that sort of thing. That just drove me nuts. There were the occasional gunshots. There were the-- There was always the presence of rap music somewhere—probably one reason why I don't like that music right now, because it's just-- You know, there was always some guy who turned down the treble and turned up the bass to its maximum level. You know, he didn't really want to hear the words. He didn't really want to hear the-- He didn't want to hear the melody. He just wanted to hear the beat, you know, and that-- And unfortunately, once it bleeds through the walls it starts to get more and more dissonant. So instead of your "boomp, boomp, boomp." You know, just a-- It just really, really bad in terms of—

Generally the kind of quiet neighborhood you're in now is more comfortable?

It's a lot more comfortable, yeah. I mean, I was a lot more comfortable inside the dorms at UIC. I lived in-- But even then, there was an El train right next to us. I didn't hear it because I was so-- Because over in the Taylor Homes I was also right next to an El train. So it was just part of the surroundings.

Participants' stories about "neighbors from hell" are stories about people like these, who uniformly do not reciprocate regarding auditory and other dimensions of privacy.

Do you think that there is such a thing as a right to privacy?

I sure do! (*Laughing.*)

Why do you think that?

(*Laughing.*) It is just part of your right to live your life the way you want to live it.... You know, it's funny because I am pretty leftist in a lot of my political views. Um, and particularly as far as guns. You know, I don't think anyone should have guns at all, ever. But a little teeny part of me sympathizes with those people on those ranches in Montana who want to do their thing (*laughing*), and I don't want anyone to bother them.

Uh huh (*laughing*).

You know, one little part of me says "Yeah, I understand that."

Un huh.

I just want to live my life the way I want to live it.

In fact, one of the things I just thought of now that I find very difficult to deal with is the condo association, and if I had it to do over again I would never, ever, ever live in a condo because by default, um, other people in your building get to know what you are doing in your life. And in a situation like ours, since it is only a three-person condo-- I absolutely despise one of the families. (*Laughing.*)

(*Laughing.*)

I mean, I have nothing but contempt for them. They have made my life miserable for fifteen years, and it irks me to even know that they need to know every once in awhile that I am in town or not in town. They have invaded my privacy so many times that it's been unbelievable. And I despise them for it.

Well, what kinds of things have they done?

Well, as I said, we are in the middle of a three, three-floor condo, and we manage ourselves more or less because no condo assoc--, management company wants to manage us because we're too small. And so therefore we have to make joint decisions. But the people below us, when they were married—and they have two teenage daughters—just gave out keys to their apartment to everybody. Their daughters are very, very wild. They brought in enormous numbers of unknown teenagers streaming through the house. They took a mattress down in the basement and were screwing around, literally. They had-- The parents finally put a stop to some of that, went out of town and had their daughters stay with somebody else. Well, their daughters stayed with somebody else, but they gave the keys to their condo to their friends. They turned the bathroom faucet on in the tub, and they never shut it off. It overflowed the tub, and water went through the ceiling, flooded the entire lower level of the house. We had to call in the police and we're-- In my life I have never had any contact with the police except in relationship to these people. Noisy. And their noise just spilled out, back yard, front yard, side yard, neighbors complaining, everybody. And yet their, my-- I am bound to them by this building. And I despise it! (*Laughing.*)

(*Laughing.*)

And they have invaded my privacy! In my whole life, I just want to block them out.

In fact, participants' past experiences with awful neighbors uniformly influence their present views of how satisfactory their current level of privacy is and whether or not a given degree of accessibility is over or under the acceptable limit. The desire to be nice, fear of retribution, the knowledge that one is bound to one's residence and one's neighbors for possibly a long time are all reasons for tempering one's own behavior and remaining more flexible than one might want to be about intrusions into one's own privacy.

Worries about one's overaccessibility to the wrong kinds of people permeate the following participant's reflections on her neighborhood, too.

In fact, I was just thinking the other, the last day or two, how some people actually have their gate locked so you can't even get into the house, up to the front porch, you know what I'm saying?

Uh huh.

So what that requires is you have to run an electrical line down to the front door so someone can intercom in kind of thing.

(Laugh.)

... And then you have to have a mailbox, blah, blah, and I just, you know. I don't know how that came out. I guess because (Sam's) bike got stolen, so then I started thinking that everything, everything is, is vulnerable. And the dog had disappeared. What if they start stealing my-- ? Oh, because I bought this clematis that I planted today. But that was sitting on the back porch on the, you know-- I've had a lot of stuff stolen in my life so--

Nothing's been stolen off the porch. The furniture and the grill are both chained down, literally chained down.

... These people nearby-- ... Their porch furniture is visible from the street. They have a cable, and I thought maybe I should do the cable thing.

Yeah.

And the grill-- Again, a lot of money sitting outside.

... So have you been thinking more about those kinds of things since Steven lost his bike?

Yeah, I get more paranoid.

Extra accessibility is not the same as *overaccessibility*, of course. Throwing parties for neighbors and attending parties at others' houses down the street may be going above and beyond the accessibility norm for some participants. Yet it is a common, enjoyable way in which individuals help obtain a more comfortable kind of private-public boundary in the neighborhood.

We actually have several friends on this street. We're in a group of five graystones that are all attached, ah, so there's sort of a big front yard in front, somewhat subdivided into little yards, but not with any fence.

Uh huh, okay. Ah, do you do anything with your neighbors either formally or informally to interact or recognize that's your neighborhood in some way?

Ah, when we moved in one of our neighbors had a bake party to welcome us.

Wow.

And invited people up and down the street. That was a lot of fun.

Where was that?

It was at their house. It was at one of the other five graystones. And then we met a lot of neighbors. There's one neighbor down the street who tends to be the social organizer for the neighborhood and has parties, sort of neighborhood parties for people. She has a Halloween party every year. Um, there's another guy, the guy next door, who we can see in through his living room. They have a New Year's Day party every year. We are invited to another open house up the street this weekend. So it's fairly—

So do you go to those?

Yeah.

You think most people in the neighborhood do?

A lot of people do.

Yeah.

I mean, there's probably a group that tends to want to get together and probably a group that doesn't, and they're self-selected.

The socioeconomic and ethnic diversity of many of Chicago's neighborhoods and the different kinds of neighborhoods participants have lived in throughout their lives led a number of them to comment on how different norms of privacy and engagement could be. This individual currently lives in a predominantly African American neighborhood.

Have you ever lived somewhere where people didn't respect each other's privacy as much as you would have liked?

Yeah, downtown was really, really noisy. We had a couple of prostitutes in the SRO [single-room-occupancy building] next to us, and that was horrible. Did not like that at all.

Yeah.

I mean, we would have to turn the fan on, the air conditioner, just to white noise it, you know.

Oh, God.

Yeah, I felt that people were more disrespectful up there. They threw a lot of garbage around. Um, they stole things. Well, that's happened in our neighborhood, too.

Right.

There was also-- I've noticed there was a lot more heckling there than on the South Side. It's interesting. I find it more respectful in an African American neighborhood, it's friendlier. People say "Good morning."

Yeah.

"How are you?"

You know what I think? It's that Southern-- It comes from the South.

Yes, it does.

Southern formality that African-- 'Cause, I mean, most African Americans in Chicago came from the South.

And, yes, (Casey) is from the South. He's from (Georgia). And when I'm down there, you know, you do change your manners.

Yeah.

You say "good morning," "good evening," "how do you do?" You never walk down a neighborhood street and pass someone without greeting them. Ever. It's considered hostile, actually.

... "Civil," I guess, is the correct word for it.

Have you ever lived somewhere where people didn't seem to work at making a certain level or kind of public interaction and recognition that you would have liked?

Oh, God, yes! In New York. Ohhhhh man, voom! When I lived in (Queens)-- I lived there for ten years.

Yeah.

There was a whole group of people across the street who never introduced themselves. I never knew their names and I saw these people every day.

Uh huh. That's weird.

It's bizarre. And in Manhattan I think it reaches its height, you know.

Uh huh.

Um, people just-- It's just like they don't want to know.

Uh huh. I know. New York is a great place, but it's distancing.

Oh, it's great. It's really got that-- (*laughing*). Give me my space, back away.

In general, participants are looking for neighbors who strike the right balance between noninterference and care—whatever that means to them. The past can provide either the gold standard or a negative standard against which privacy in future homes is measured. Another individual who grew up in public housing briefly described her childhood in these terms.

I wanted to ask you just about what it was like to, when you were living in the projects because it relates a lot to privacy. I've talked to some other people, you know, that had that experience, and they described a place where they couldn't, couldn't get any privacy. Did you have that experience?

You know what? It *was* that kind of experience. And when I think about the days that I spent in the, in the projects-- Talk about invasion of personal space, physical space, you know. Talk about invasion of your, just your, violation of your, of your whole person. From just every kind of point, you know, your, um, angle. Because I remember, well, for one thing, you know, people would feel free to look in your window to see what was going on in your house. And not just children. And the, the, the case workers or whoever was there felt free to come, to look, and they would come into your house unannounced, too.[36]

The ability to control one's accessibility in the home and prevent people from looking—and even coming—in was especially limited here, of course. In many cases the State was not only the perpetrator, but it also withheld the means to control the intrusions. The participant's only eventual response to all this was both simple and extremely difficult: leave.

A number of participants confirm that moving house is both a long-valued and common response to the feeling of not having enough privacy in the U.S. Intrusive neighbors are a great motivation for moving. So are *others'* intrusive neighbors. Stories about them, and about how they made people feel, can become part of the family lore that informs kin's decisions about what to look for in future neighbors and neighborhoods.

The following individual, for instance, says he is happy to straddle the worlds of anonymity and connection that are afforded by his urban neighborhood. He has many neighbors he doesn't know and has no problem with that. This middle-aged man helped justify his delight in where he lives now by recounting his grandmother's comments.

My grandmother grew up in a really small, little town in Indiana. She said you opened up the back door and everybody in town knew that you had done it. She talked about how she wanted to get out of that so bad when she got older. I mean, where she grew up. But at the same time, my grandmother knew everything about anybody that lived next to *her*. You know, if they opened up their back door, she knew about it. And she never saw the inconsistency in her hating it in the one place and her actually doing it all the time in another place.

In other words, it need not be our own past experiences that provide the standard against which we judge those of the present.

CONCLUSION

At different times in our lives, we look for different things from the world around us. Single students living on low incomes have expectations about their residence and neighborhood that might be different from those of married couples with young children. Partnered older men with a dog may have different ones still, as might an octogenarian widow living alone.

In addition to other autobiographical factors, life-course constraints like these result in wide variation in what constitutes a "good" neighbor. Is it someone who doesn't even notice that you have a cellar, much less a light left on? Someone who will not only notice, but call? Someone who will ring your doorbell and use that information as an excuse to beg a slice of cake and a chat? Someone who will notice that the bulb has gone out while you're on vacation, grab your spare keys from her kitchen drawer, replace the bulb, and neatly sort the mail piled up by the door before leaving? What is crossing the line for one neighbor, or at one point in one's life, may be quite welcome from another neighbor, or at another point in one's life.

People feel they have good privacy when the things they want to be private are as private as they want them to be, in other words. It's an idea that infuses the notion of the good neighbor and the good neighborhood. For some, it may not be far from the following individual's description.

It's an old-fashioned neighborhood. That means that there's some family or friendship connection between myself and most of the people that live around me.

When I lived in (L.A.), it was more like anonymity than (*laughing*) privacy. Well, I didn't know anybody, nobody knew me, you know. It wasn't that they were respecting my privacy. It's that they didn't care one way or the other what I did (*laughing*).

And did you enjoy that?

Not particularly, no.

Why not?

Because I like being part of a community. And L.A. was at that time a community of transients.

What do you like about being part of a community?

Well I like the fact that I know everybody that I live around, basically. I know all the people that are on my block. I know the kids, I know the-- you know, maybe know their families going back. Or their friendships. I know where they went to school. I know, you know, I know that they like the Sox, that they're Democrats, you know. I know a lot of stuff about them.

For others, though, at least at some point in their lives, the sense of big-city anonymity and the freedom that goes with it may be just what they're looking for.

For most study participants, there is a fine line between that rewarding sense of being connected to others in their neighborhood and still feeling as if they have good privacy. Given the simultaneous presence of family, friends, and strangers that permeates urban neighborhoods, successfully negotiating the private-public boundary requires a great deal of social knowledge, skills, and dexterity. This can be seen in how we answer the door and manage our windows and trash, how we think of our mail, park our cars, manage the perimeter of our yards, and engage our neighbors in conversation. These behaviors reveal recurrent themes from the other case studies of this book, too, including the private-public hybridity of objects, actions, and spaces; our different practices around things that are more and less private; the management of social accessibility through systems of objects, people, services, rules, and habits; the connection between the successful management of privacy and the successful management of relationships; and the overall importance of selective concealment and disclosure for our success in achieving privacy.

Violations,
Fears,
& Beaches

What would you say is the funniest invasion of someone's privacy that ever happened to someone you know or you yourself while this person was at home?

Oh, I've got a good one. It involves an animal. I lived with this group of friends. Not friends, coworkers, in (Georgia). My very first job, newspaper job. And there was one woman who was very active in a church group but so hypocritical. So, she presented herself as, um, not using the word "virginal," but, you know, as a very prim and proper lady. And we were in the Deep South, where that matters. (*Laugh.*) And she was dating a guy on the desk at this paper and—

Uh huh.

—and they were having a relationship. And, um, and he often stayed the night at this house. And so her church group came over to talk to her and kind of bring her back into the fold. 'Cause she stopped being active in the Young Life or, whatever, Young Christian Life group. And while she's meeting with them and they're seated—three or four of them on the couch and the chair, and she's in another chair—her cat came out of the bedroom with a used condom in its mouth—

(*Gasping.*)

—and traipses across the room in front of all of them. And she just about died. (*Laughing.*)

You know, I kind of think it's all karma.

BRIDGET, thirty-four-year-old reporter

Achieving privacy in our daily lives is work. Sometimes the nature of that work can be most unexpected. To always selectively conceal and reveal as one might wish means anticipating the most unlikely of scenarios, given the endless constellations of actors, actions, and objects that might result in a violation of our privacy at any given time. The difficulty of the task means that we can pretty much count on an inexhaustible supply of stories like this one.

A close look at participants' efforts to achieve privacy reveals that much of it is driven by the fear of one's privacy being violated. In the U.S., our attempts to control accessibility cannot be fully understood without also trying to understand this. Thus, exploring the nature of privacy violations and worries further frames what it is, exactly, that participants are trying to accomplish with their daily privacy work, whatever the particular form it takes.

What does it mean to have one's privacy violated? What factors help account for the range of experiences we might have when this happens? Why are some people so worried about privacy violations and why do they spend so much energy trying to prevent them, while others are much more minimalist in their approaches?

PRIVACY VIOLATIONS

Consider, first, the nature of a privacy violation. Recall that privacy is a condition of relative inaccessibility. Study participants operationalize this as the condition in which the things they want to be inaccessible are as inaccessible as they want them to be, relative to specific others, at specific places and times. If the level of access exceeds what we believe it is or was—or should be/should have been—a sense of violation occurs. Thus, stories of violations are stories in which people find out they do not or did not possess the selectivity they desired regarding the accessibility of their private matters.

Our mortified cat owner, for example, would not have been opposed to *some* people knowing there was a used condom in her bedroom. It was obviously fine for her lover and herself to know this. It was probably fine for the cat to be aware of it, too. Her feline companion may even have been present in the room while this object went from "new" and "highly valued" to "used" and "garbage." It was not fine, however—not in the least—for her Christian friends to know about any of this, later on. Accordingly, it was when someone else—in this case, her cat—disclosed this information to people she did not want to know about it that the violation occurred. That the disclosure happened while she was present only added insult to injury.

As we can see here, too, stories of violations are also stories about the tacit expectations and assumptions underlying our privacy. They reveal the kinds of taken-for-granted thinking and acting that constantly inform our privacy work. We might assume, for instance, that by restricting certain activities to the bedroom when no other person is present, these activities will remain private—especially from future visitors who stay in the living room. If we live alone (or, to be more exact, if we are the only human in the house) we might also assume that once we throw something in the trash or drop it behind the bed, no one will look for it. We certainly wouldn't expect anyone to retrieve and actively display it to company sitting on the couch.

Yet once something like the previous story happens, we might quickly realize the flaws in all these kinds of common assumptions and behaviors. We may choose to adapt accordingly, letting our fear of a similar violation happening again lead to corrections in our assumptions as well as our practical behavior. (Some of the parents of toddlers in this study, for instance, no longer keep certain things under their beds, either.)

The following anecdotes cover the range of smaller and larger violations routinely reported by participants.

I had a yearly visit to the gynecologist a few weeks ago. And I was sitting in a clinic with all these people. And the nurse was coming out and yelling people's names to come in-- and yelling their names really loud in the clinic. And I found it so-- jarring-- and such an invasion of all the patients' privacies that everyone had to know that they were at the doctor today, at the gynecologist. And I just-- I was horrified. And I almost left because I didn't want my name called out. And I wasn't there for any reason but to have my annual physical for, you know, my pap smear and stuff. And I was horrified.

* * *

Briefly, today, I was on the bus and there was an older man that was sitting next to me, and he just struck up a conversation. And he said, "I betcha I can tell you how old you are." And I felt like he said that so loudly that other people were looking at me. And I guess I felt really kind of self-conscious about it. So I guess maybe that would be an instance.

So you just were self-conscious because you didn't want people around you to know how old you were.

Right. And I didn't want people to know something personal about me. And here's this person that I just met! I mean, I said two words about, "Oh, it is really warm in here," and he starts up this conversation and wants to know if I would like him to guess my age. It was kind of odd.

Right. Can you think of a time when you saw somebody else doing something in public that you thought was private and therefore inappropriate?

I guess, again, on the bus-- There are so many strange things that happen on a bus. Maybe it's because of the close proximity of things. But, just recently, I saw a woman breast feeding on the bus and I thought, whoa! Too close for comfort, you know? There's a time and a place for that. I mean, she had a towel or something covering her breast, but still. At one point, she had to move it to allow her child to get under there and so there's a moment where you thought you were going to see a bare breast on the bus.

* * *

A couple of weeks ago, we were at Applebee's and this young guy was behind us-- a younger, Hispanic guy was behind us. And another lady was sitting on the other side and we were sitting on the left side. And this guy, he cursed the whole time we were sitting there eating. And it was always "mf" this and "b" that. And it was like-- I turned around, like, "That's inappropriate. I have a six-year-old here." He was like, "Aah, aah--" It was, like, *okay*. And at the end of the dinner, the young lady that was on the right side of us got up and said, "I apologize. People shouldn't do that type of thing. I feel sorry for his mother." He's like, "You feel sorry for my mother? Aaah, aaah, aaah." It just went on.

Is there any time you can remember where you felt that somebody totally invaded your privacy at work?

Yeah. Last week. This guy, Craig, who's a dick, came over. And I had some food on my desk. And he picked up some and started eating it. Like, right in front of me. And I looked at him like, "What the fuck are you doing?" We have a desk, or a table, rather, that we put food on for everybody, when we bring something in. If it's on your desk, it's your food. I almost bit his hand off.

* * *

I had worked at a job before where I was sitting across from this one lady who was just-- You could not shut her up. She would always be telling all of her personal business. And, you know, you would say, "Okay. Well, so-and-so, I have to, you know, finish this report now. I have to finish whatever." And she would still be talking and talking and talking about her personal business.

* * *

Do you know someone who is engaged in some kind of behavior in her/his workspace that others define as too private or personal and therefore inappropriate?

Sure. Um-- I'm sure there's plenty of that going on. One of the best examples would be-- I mean, the whole sexual harassment stuff, you know, trying to ask you to go out and-- I mean, that's the easiest comes to mind, that you would just say "Agh." One of the-- We had a (director) in (L.A.). A father of twins. Total oddball. The kids were, like, four or five, and he had a desk calendar that took up most of his desk. He would mark every month when his wife was menstruating.

Oh, my God!

That was-- We (the office workers) were like, okay, you're obviously ill equipped to deal with women.

That is so—

It's a complete violation of her privacy.

Right.

How thrilled would she be to know that the entire L.A. office knows when she's menstruating? And then, why did he feel the need to let you know-- to mark that? To *mark* that? To show that he can't deal with her then? You know?

So where was this calendar?

On his desk.

And he wrote it out.

He marked the date and (the staff) had to come and pull up the chair and sit with him while he edited their reports sometimes. (*Laugh*.) But everybody is sitting there. Yeah, he was eventually was forced out of that job and went to Oshkosh or something.

Uh huh.

But I don't know what he's doing now but-- just so wrong.

Yeah.

So shocking and wrong.

* * *

There's actually a funny family story from later about my father walking in on my brother and his fiancé in the shower.

I think you told me this before.

I'm sure I have. It didn't stop the wedding. They've been married for six years now.

But my dad knocked on the door. And my older brother said, "Yeah?" meaning "Yeah? Who is it? What do you want?" And my dad thought it meant, "Yeah. Come on in."

Oh, God.

So he walked in. And they felt that was quite a violation of their privacy. (*Chuckles*.)

* * *

[S]he found the birth control pills, which were in my purse. Talk about privacy. I had put them in my purse so that she would not see them. She says, "I went in your purse to find a comb." And you know how the Ortho drugs were in a little-- She said, "I thought I was pulling a comb out."

You know, she is a vicious intruder.

... Yeah, and she told me that I was just a piece of used merchandise. So I would have been, what? Nineteen? Nineteen or twenty years old. She said, "You're just a piece of used merchandise." And I went up and took a shower. Privacy again. And cried and cried and cried and cried.

... It was typical of her. She had done things like read my journals and would say, "Well, I was cleaning in there and it fell off the bookshelf and opened to that page."

Well, first of all, she never has cleaned the house. EVER. NEVER has cleaned the house.

... I think one of the ways I've learned to be a lawyer, learned to put a logical argument together ... was that I had long talks with my father about that there was something seriously, seriously wrong with my mother. That's the terrain where I dealt with it. I don't feel like it was the last straw because to acknowledge it was the last straw would be to have to acknowledge you didn't have a mother, and I wasn't-- I was way too young. I wasn't ready to do that. That took me until I was thirty to be able to do.

So there were these constant invasive, controlling, demeaning-- You know, we call her Vulture, The Vulture, because she eats souls for entertainment.

There is quite a range in the emotional impact of these very different kinds of violations. Yet they share at least one element in common: all privacy violations stem from a framing mismatch. In each of these stories, the individuals' expectations or understandings of how private something is and who should have access to it in what way turn out to be different from the degree of privacy/accessibility that actually exists.

Accordingly, one way of conceiving of privacy violations is as a function of the goodness of fit between what an individual believes about how private something is (or should be) and the potential for alternative definitions of the situation. Privacy violations are made possible precisely because of the sociosubjective ways in which an individual envisions and enacts privacy, on the one hand, and the simultaneously socially gifted/withheld nature of privacy, on the other.

Figure 5.1 captures the analytical elements of this relatively straightforward process, based on the theories of social constructivists such as Peter Berger and Thomas Luckmann (1968), Alfred Schutz (1973), and Schutz and Luckmann (1973), and the basics of frame analysis as put forth by Gregory Bateson (2000) and Erving Goffman (1974). The upper left-hand triangle

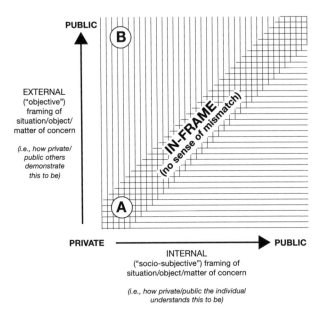

Legend within figure:

PUBLIC

B

EXTERNAL
("objective")
framing of
situation/object/
matter of concern

(i.e., how private/
public others
demonstrate
this to be)

IN-FRAME
(no sense of mismatch)

A

PRIVATE ————————————➤ PUBLIC

INTERNAL
("socio-subjective") framing of
situation/object/matter of concern

(i.e., how private/public the individual
understands this to be)

FIGURE 5.1 A frame analysis of privacy violations

of the chart represents the experiences of privacy violations. (The bottom right-hand triangle represents the experiences of what might be termed publicity failures—not the subject of this book but certainly related to it, as they also stem from this framing mismatch.)[1]

To elaborate, consider point A on this figure. It indicates a situation in which an individual's framing of something as fairly private is quite in synch with others' understandings and/or demonstrations of it. I may think, for instance, that a phone conversation I'm having with my girlfriend is pretty private—a shared secret, in fact—and that everything I tell her about my new boyfriend is just between us. As far as I'm concerned, now only my boyfriend, my girlfriend, and I know about these things. Call after call, nothing happens to challenge my definition of the situation, which is that I have a secret and I've shared it extremely selectively with only two other human beings. I am, in other words, happily "in frame," in control, and with my privacy intact.

However, at some point in the future, I may find that my understanding of the situation was horrifyingly wrong. In Goffman's (1974, 347) terms, I may be forced to "break frame," suddenly realizing that I am quite off the mark in my understanding of what has been going on. In fact, I may very well discover that not only is my framing of the situation different from—and indeed, incompatible with—someone else's, but that her or his framing actually trumps mine. This other individual may have relatively greater power than me to define the situation—given the social, political, legal, and economic possibilities—and my view, my desires, may have been overridden by theirs. I may find out just how low my status is, relative to this other person, and how little control I actually have over what I thought was this very private matter.

My girlfriend, for instance—let's call her Linda Tripp—may have been secretly taping all my conversations with her. She may have then given those tapes to someone else who shared their contents with yet more people. The next thing I know, subpoenas are being slapped into my hand, my apartment, my computer, my closet—everything—is being searched, and shortly I'm testifying in front of Congress. Everything I do and have been doing—including what are uniformly considered extraordinarily private behaviors by these study participants—is being investigated and exposed, recorded and distributed via every known form of media to the world.

The moment I grasp the magnitude of what is happening, of course, it may well be the experiential equivalent of a tsunami. Here I was, thinking I was having a nice, private time, fooling around on my beach blanket with my boyfriend and giggling over it with my girlfriend. And then, with no warning whatsoever, I am in way, way over my head, drowning in a sea of unwanted accessibility. Far from quietly sharing forbidden, dangerous, and thoroughly enjoyable secrets with my new boyfriend and my trusted girlfriend, my most private of private objects, actions, thoughts, and emotions are wrenched from me, exposed to the entire world for as long as the Internet endures.

That would be, say, point B on the chart.

Note that what would make this such a profound violation is the huge differential between the individual's framing of the situation and the other-imposed reality that suddenly becomes all too clear. In fact, nothing in the real world may have changed between the time the victim did whatever she was doing and the ensuing denouement. It is only the eventual correction to what turns out to have been the individual's misapprehension of how private things were that triggers the realization of a violation.[2]

Consider the implications of the following participant's reflections. A medical doctor, he ponders the very nature of a violation of one's privacy. Here, he discusses the way in which completely different realities or framings of the situation may come together in the operating room.

The student versus attending is a serious issue, and it's degrading in a sense that there are students, third-year students or even second-year students, who have never seen a patient before. Third-year students are just learning to see, ah, residents. No one tells you when you're seeing a resident. Is that okay?

So *60 Minutes* did a piece on this where they actually set up physicians at Harvard. What they told the attending physician is that "We would like to do a segment on resident training. So could we see a surgery performed by residents, can we film it?" "Sure, come on in. They are great surgeons, and we'll allow you to film it." And what the segment was really about was that they had never told the patient that it was a resident doing the surgery instead of the physician that they thought was doing the surgery.

So it goes beyond-- I mean, there are things that I think people would consider an invasion of privacy. I mean, if you get to a court of law-- and this has happened. Women who have had gynecological surgery done take their physicians to court. "I was unconscious and he did a bimanual exam on me."

How unethical is that? Well, in fact, the woman may think that it's an invasion of privacy, but it is a required part of the surgical procedure.

And not only-- You know, this is something that people don't know. Not only did the surgeon do it. The medical student does it. The resident does it. Everybody does it. I mean, this is--

You know, these things that people consider very, very private are part of medical procedures. And it's a very strange world that, that, you know, we are trying these things [in court].

Yeah.

And what is a "private" thing during a surgery?

So, for example, when you're doing a hysterectomy-- Okay? A transvaginal hysterectomy. I mean, this is a transvaginal hysterectomy. Everything is coming out through the vagina. I mean, it's not-- I mean, what was very, very private is no longer private at all. And there are people in there you have never met. You know, rotating people. Like, I assisted with transvaginal hysterectomies when I was a visiting student from (Nevada) in (New York). No one's ever met me. No one knows that I'm going to be there.

So are these invasions of privacy or just medical treatment?

What do you think?

I think it's medical treatment.

As this doctor points out, though, for the lay person, common, necessary, professional protocol may be seen in quite a different light. For normal patients, suddenly finding out just how exposed, how accessible one was to complete strangers—or worse, physician *friends* whom you know socially—could qualify as an individual's worst privacy nightmare. And yet it would be completely unremarkable for a professional.

In fact, people in precisely the same situations can exhibit quite a range in the experiential impact of any given violation. Three factors seem to contribute to a violation's experiential outcome for a given victim. First, there is the extent to which the individual's understanding of the situation is in synch with the broader reality of it. (On figure 5.1, this is the difference between the locations of point A and point B, for instance.) The surprise factor in the discrepancy alone means that the greater the distance from the diagonal in figure 5.1, the greater the experiential impact of the violation might be on the victim.

Second, however, and layered on to the magnitude of this framing discrepancy, are the practical consequences of the violation for the victim. These may be virtually anything, but the more complicated, expensive, and protracted the response to a privacy violation turns out to be, the more profound the experiential impact may be for the victim. Again, the greater the distance from the diagonal, the more undesirable these consequences are likely to be.

Third, and, again, layered onto these two previous factors, are the symbolic consequences of the violation for the victim. Once more, the greater the distance from the diagonal, the more undesirable these consequences tend to be for the victim. As we shall see, this is especially true if the violation threatens one's core sense of self, often a function of being forced to reenvision the self relative to others and the relationships one has with them.

Stories from study participants suggest that this third, symbolic dimension of a violation may be the most important element of all in determining the experiential impact of it.[3] Jack Katz (2001) provides an insightful explanation as to why this might be. He argues that strong emotional responses—such as those we might experience in response to egregious privacy violations—indicate situations that are extremely important to one's sense of self. These responses—whether they make us laugh, cry, or explode in anger—betray our felt knowledge that the ways others see us matter deeply when it comes to how we see our selves.

Moreover, Katz argues, emotionally charged scenes are a product of our making sense of our selves over a much longer time span than the duration of any particular incident. We instantaneously assess the meaning of what's happening to us now within the context of how we have thought of ourselves in the past and how we'd like to think of ourselves in the future, too. Thus, it is our in-the-moment interpretation of what others' actions say about us—relative to them, and given how we see ourselves—that can lead to strong, almost uncontrollable emotional responses in any situation.

Katz's analysis of road rage suggests this may be especially visible in instances when we believe someone else thinks that they matter more than we do. When we define such a situation in this way, the other person's behavior is seen as flaunting and denigrating to our selves. The situation cuts instantly to our core sense of self, our relationships with others, and our past, present, and future, all at once.

Privacy violations are perfect for fostering just these kinds of reactions. First, and if nothing else, a violation of our privacy hammers home the fact that we possess privacy only when others gift it to us. Violations make it clear that our desires depend on and are subordinated to those of the potential privacy givers and withholders around us. As John Donne reminds us, no man (or woman) is an island. We may happily operate under the illusion that this is not the case, particularly if we are normally privileged to have a great deal of control over our privacy. However, a sudden violation of one's privacy demonstrates in no uncertain terms that one clearly is not an all-powerful being. We are subject to others' agendas and abilities to carry them out as well.

Second, however, is the fact that privacy violations also remind us that privacy is seen as an entitlement for any respectable citizen in this country—an empowering symbol of one's good social status. When others deny us privacy, they also deny us status. If we believe we have been denied privacy/status unjustly, the situation is that much worse.

Accordingly, extreme emotionality—outrage over the injustice, the disrespect that has been shown—may accompany the realization of a privacy violation. Practical consequences aside, we are forced at these moments to confront a certain demonstrated lack of control over our own lives—perhaps over things that are extremely important to us—as well as an equally undeniable lack of social status, relative to the violator. Why should this person's idea of how public/private this thing should be—their definition, their agenda—trump mine? Why should they have more control over my private things than I do? What does that mean about me—especially if they're allowed to get away with this? Does this mean they're actually more important than I am?

These violations can threaten our very core, then, challenging the way we see ourselves especially via the ways we now know others see us. Add to this the shame of having been victimized,[4] and a violation may be hugely felt, no matter how small it might seem to others. The more unjust one feels the act is, the more likely this will be the outcome.

It is their symbolic meaning, in other words, that may make the smallest things instantly blow up in our bodies and minds, as in the case of road rage. It is their symbolic meaning that also may leave these things relegated to the mere raising of an eyebrow, a shrug, and whatever response (or even nonresponse) might be required by the laws of physics. Thus, the same dynamics that lead us to sometimes experience privacy violations as utterly devastating also mean that there will be violations that do not have nearly so much impact. From outed secrets and identity theft to flashers, telemarketers, and noisy neighbors, a violation of one's privacy may be perceived as a gigantic commentary on how little the perpetrator thinks the victim matters and how little power the victim really has over her or his own life. But a violation's effect also may be limited to however surprising (educational?) it was initially and whatever its practical inconveniences might be. It may be annoying, but certainly not a big deal and no threat to one's fundamental sense of self.

Recovering from violations, incidentally, is the process of getting back "in frame." The goal of the process is for personal and external views of the degree of privacy to be in synch and for the practical and symbolic consequences of the violation to be back under control. There are endless roads to achieving recovery after a violation, but they draw on three categories of action: (1) adjusting one's understanding of how private something is (so one is more accepting of what happened and/or so that one is not taken by surprise again); (2) adjusting one's privacy-related behaviors (in order to prevent future violations); and (3) forcing others to adjust their behavior (as recompense for—or prevention of—any particular privacy violation). In many cases, some variation on all three strategies is used in the recovery process.

The following stories indicate just a few of the ways these themes may appear in individuals' recovery stories. The first emphasizes recovery by adjusting one's definition of just how private something is.

Giving birth is a rather private, personal experience. You kind of have to do that in public at the hospital. People going in and out of your room all the time.

That's a great example.

And after a while, you don't really care all that much. But it is certainly very strange at first, since you're usually only partially clothed.

Oh! Oh! Here's a good example, now that I think about it in that sense. With my first child, I had a caesarean, and this is a good example of that.

You know, I was in the hospital for, like, a week afterwards and, by that time, you don't care who sees anything, which is a huge, huge difference from when you first go in, especially if it's your first child. So, by that time, I absolutely didn't care about anything. And one of the final days before I left, some resident was sent in to take out my stitches. And they make you wear these hospital underpants that are, like, see-through. They're not even hardly underpants. So it was funny because he found that very embarrassing, and I couldn't care less. I was like, "Fine, take them out. Here you go." And he's like-- He didn't even want to look. It really cracked me up that I had come that far in a week that I couldn't care less about this stranger taking out stitches right above my pubic hair.

The next story is an example of changing one's behavior in response to prior violations, so as to prevent more of the same kind.

Well, my [phone] number is unlisted because my wallet was stolen about seven years ago and, you know, I knew right away and cancelled all the checks and all of that. But then a couple weeks later, I got notices—they got nine checks and they used them—since I got notices from Marshall Fields and there were a couple checks bounced, and from Circuit City, another check bounced. And so they were able to use about eight or nine of the checks. And I didn't lose any money, but it was just a huge hassle to figure it all out with the bank. It was like a catch-22 situation. I don't need to go into that. But then about six months later, um, somebody opened a cell phone account with my name and used my home number. And after that I think decided to have it unlisted so that, um, I would have more control over who got my phone number.

Finally, this last story focuses on recovering from a violation of one's privacy by forcing others to change their intrusive behavior.

The apartment that I moved out of, the guy on the first floor, everything that happened in my apartment he went back and he told the landlord. If three people came over there, he would tell how many people came up, how many people come up in the week. And I think that-- Because I could hear their phone conversations. So I'm sure they could hear my phone conversations. So they didn't respect anybody's privacy.

Right. Did you do anything about it?

Yes.

What did you do?

I told the landlord that if Mr. (Krane) tells on one more thing that happens in my apartment that I was going to cut him. I sure did. I told him he needs to mind his business. He should worry about what's going on in his apartment instead of being worried about what's going on in mine.

Did the landlord do anything about it?

He told him not to say anything else to me.

A single strategy may be all one needs to get back into frame. Where that doesn't work, though, and where the threat or sense of violation continues to grow, various permutations of all three options may be used. Institutions, social networks, and the built environment can be remarkably important constraints and resources in the recovery process, too. Any of these can make it easier or harder.

Success in recovering from any particular violation does not seem to be correlated with how much one worries over future violations, though. Some people's fears over what might happen next to their privacy never go away, despite any temporarily diminished or heightened state of concern. Others seem to merely take whatever precautions are convenient and simply refuse to overworry about what the future might hold. In order to better understand individuals' attempts to achieve privacy, this range of responses also bears closer examination.

PRIVACY FEARS

Do you worry about your privacy or the privacy of the people that you care about?

No.

No. Why not?

I guess because it hasn't been invaded, or I haven't felt that it's invaded. You know, you didn't worry about terrorists before 9/11, either.

TOM, twenty-nine-year-old teacher

Certainly, the meaning and importance of privacy is clearest to study participants when it has been violated. The more severe a privacy violation experience, the more articulate they tend to be on the matter, too. Thus, individuals' privacy-related fears offer another excellent opportunity to further explore how we think of and "do" privacy, especially regarding the privacy matters that matter most.

In essence, privacy fears are concerns that one will be caught out of frame at some point in the future, believing that more privacy prevails—or should prevail—than actually is the case. The worry is that, should a mis-apprehension of this kind occur, one would be left coping with an assort-ment of undesirable pragmatic, symbolic, and emotional consequences. Because these consequences may range from the merely annoying to the deeply threatening, the feelings associated with privacy fears can range from the mildly worrisome to intense, acute distress.

Privacy fears fall into two basic categories: "general" and "specific." Both are rooted in the same underlying concern. In the first category of "general" (or nonspecific) privacy fears, an individual worries that she or he—in fact, all of society—will not have as much privacy in the future as they should. These fears are not specific to the individual's situation, per se, and typically are not associated with any one event or its repercussions. A particular event may be singled out for attention, but it is its place in a sequence of events that matters most—the precedent it might set, for instance, or the events that preceded it and allowed it to happen in the first place. These are fears of a corrosive environment, in other words, in which one believes that one's privacy will decline through a highly undesirable socio-cultural-political-legal-economic shift.

These kinds of fears are rooted in an individual's worry about being caught out of frame because of the difference between the degree of pri-vacy that individuals believe *should* apply to a situation (usually because it *used* to apply to it) and the degree of privacy that seems as if it will apply, in the future. Such fears have personal implications, for sure, but the privacy one fears losing isn't "personal," per se. It's the social level of privacy—the condition that everyone shares—that is threatened.

This form of privacy fear is associated with an erosion of the classic lib-eral tradition and basic civil rights, as well as the daily interactive norms of civil society. Sometimes the government is the identified as culprit. The George W. Bush administration was regularly singled out by participants as posing an exceptional threat to privacy for U.S. and other citizens, de-spite the extraordinary degree of privacy—indeed, secrecy—the admin-istration granted itself. Sometimes regular, "normal" people themselves were blamed by participants for this deterioration in privacy—being all too willing to give it up for some additional convenience, a 10 percent discount, or the belief that someone was doing something to get even for the 9/11 attacks on the Twin Towers. But even more frequently, cor-porate America was identified as the unforgivably intrusive party, ever more worried about the behavior of its employees (Lane 2003) as well as its customers (see Cavoukian and Hamilton 2002, Chesbro 1999, Garfinkel 2000, Kassanoff 2001, and McKeown and Stern 1999, for instance), and willing to violate everyone's privacy in endless ways to assuage its own concerns.

Reflecting on the relationship between consumers' loss of privacy and their futures *as* consumers, for instance, one participant offered this interpretation of where he sees us going:

You'd be amazed . . . maybe you wouldn't be amazed, at how many people I ask and they've only heard about cookies in the last week or two. They never knew that any Web site was getting information on them.

—or was tracking, or that when you fill out a form, that they track you. I would guess there are still far more people than not who don't know that every network card that you use to attach to the Web has a unique address that can be tracked. And, you know, if you filled out the registration card when you bought your network card, somebody's database has got your name and address and your network card ID and can match it with your name and address from shopping.

. . . Speaking of tracking, I use a Gillette razor. I use a Track II razor, which is the double blade. They have a newer version, the Mach III or some such thing.

The triple-blade thing.

Right. So a couple months ago we went to Sam's Warehouse Club, and I bought some Track II razor blades. Two weeks later in the mail I got a Mach III razor jointly labeled by Sam's and Gillette in the mail.

They somehow got your purchase on file through Sam's, who sold it to them, probably.

Probably.

"The following people have purchased Gillette products this week."

No. The following people have purchased *obsolete* Gillette products this week, older models.

What do you think about that, as a member of Sam's?

Well, I don't particularly like it. On the other hand, I save seven bucks that I-- See, it's the tradeoff.

Getting the new razor.

Getting the new razor. Now the razor blades are 30 percent more expensive because they have three blades instead of two. I mean, even buying them at Sam's. But-- I'm not real happy with it. But on the other hand, I knew when I joined Sam's that when they swipe my card at the cash register before they'll check me out, they're going to know exactly what I'm buying. And I've known for a long time that Jewel and Dominick's [grocery stores] and-- The (local store), I don't think knows because I don't think the (local store) is smart enough to figure it out. But they [Jewel and Dominick's] know what you're buying.

. . . But they are selling your information to other companies.

They are selling it or they are selling prepaid labels to Gillette. There are multiple ways to do that. I mean, they could call Gillette and say, "We have five thousand people this week who bought Track II razor blades. Do you want their names on a mailing label?" I mean, I'm probably giving them more credit than—

It would be a way of maintaining their database, right?

They keep control of the database that way.

Right. . . . To control the database. . . . And now to track individuals' behavior.

Well, it's become possible.

Because of the data.

Because of the data. Didn't used to have data. Didn't used to be able to put the data together. You knew so-and-so bought-- Okay?

Now we've got Sam's out there, now we've got . . .

Now we've got Sam's. Now you've got all the credit card companies that have collected data on a number of people in the family, what their ages are, what their incomes are, the mortgage records are now online. And people can go in and mine that data to find out what's the typical profile of a person who lives at (Oak Park). What do those families look like? What kind of cars do they drive? How many times does Federal Express deliver to them?

What do you think about . . . companies that have databases where they have suggestions for you based on your past consumer behavior? So these are—

Like Amazon.com.

. . . Late at night, I worry about what that's going to do to us as a species and I don't have pleasant dreams as a result. I mean, we are being trained to be more predictable, and I don't think that's good, personally or as a species.

A combination of personal experiences and reading and talking to other people has thus led to this participant's concerns about a loss of privacy—and related aspects of U.S. culture. He sees producers' and consumers' behaviors and choices in particular as being fashioned by businesses using the personal data that they are collecting.[5] Along with others, he believes all that privacy we give up and all that information we give over to corporations won't even result in anything good for us, as consumers. Each specific observation is linked to another, then, informing his overall, general sense of worry about the future of privacy, individuals' freedom of choice, and daily life in the U.S.

At a deeper level, though, this kind of perspective reflects a fundamental concern with the diminishing of the self. The individual is increasingly subordinated to the growing importance, privilege, and power of corporations and their stockholders. For other participants, of course, the culprits may be George W. Bush, Dick Cheney, the FBI, the police, and/or even a "tyranny of the majority," in which enough voters can become frightened enough, threatened enough by something to further strip away individuals' privacy through formal and informal sanctions.

Privacy concerns may be much more focused and personal, however. This is what we find in the second category of "specific" privacy fears. Here, individuals worry about making a specific mistake at some point in the future over a particular matter. People fear being personally caught by surprise, believing that they have more privacy than they actually do—that the accessibility of some thing that they believe is under their control actually is not. The undesirable consequences associated with these fears are distinctly personal and explicit, too. Accordingly, these are the kinds of fears that result in specific behaviors, designed to prevent the dreaded violation from happening. Karen, for instance, a twenty-seven-year-old teacher, offers an example of these preventive behaviors and the kind of thinking—and experience—that led her down this path.

Have you ever taken any measures or adopted any practices to specifically, intentionally protect your electronic privacy?

Well, I've pretty much decided I don't want to buy anything online anymore. I have bought things online, but I've decided--

You know, it's funny. No one I know went through an ordeal-- Well. I went through an ordeal with an ATM machine. . . . My ATM pin number was stolen and money taken from my account. . . . I used an ATM at a convenience store and then, you know, after talking to the bank and after actually reading a bunch of stuff online about ATM fraud, their tips are "Don't use an ATM machine that's not connected to a bank." It doesn't need to be your bank, but it should be connected to a bank branch. And not to use those ATM machines that are just sort of on the street or in another location. So, as a result of that, that was about four months ago, four and a half months ago, I've stopped using those.

And-- I don't know when I basically decided, if there was something that actually sparked this, but I just don't think that I want to put my credit card on the Internet anymore.

So what would you say is the most important thing you've learned recently about privacy?

I would say that you have to protect it. That it's not going to always be there. That if you want it, you have to be thinking about it. I think I've come to realize that through this ATM fraud thing, you know, and the way that it happened.

Privacy worries may or may not lead to behaviors specifically designed to address them. It is quite common for participants to change nothing about their behavior even after becoming educated about what might go wrong and beginning to worry about it. Moreover, even when we decide change is desirable, we may only adopt some preventive behaviors; others may be seen as excessive or unrealistic and therefore rejected. At times, the practical and cognitive consequences of trying to prevent potential violations of one's privacy may seem simply not worth it. For example, Jim, a twenty-six-year-old musician, discusses some of the changes he might make but does not, and why.

You know, sometimes people in the building sometimes will put a newspaper in the door [to prop it open] because they are expecting someone and they don't want to have to come down and let them in. That infuriates me.

Do you ever take that out-- when you're leaving?

Yes, always.

Always?

Yeah. Um, yeah. The idea of somebody jeopardizing somebody else's stuff, somebody really, just-- I don't know. It's really very troubling to me. But, like, I know that I should probably lock both locks when I leave and just, "Oh God," then I have to remember which key goes with which.

(Laughs.)

I don't know. I don't have renters' insurance now. I used to when I lived in (Richmond). Just-- I don't know why. Somebody told me *(whispering)*, "You ought to get renters insurance with all your guitars and stuff." It made me scared.

I know that living like this is like not backing up your files on your computer. There's a certain leap of faith that things are going to be okay. And you maintain that faith by not thinking about it, as I suggested.

. . . It's hard to know where the happy medium is. I choose not to think about it, because you worry that to start thinking about it—security, that's what we're talking about, probably—is to kind of open up Pandora's box of worries. A kind of OC [obsessive compulsive] deal, sort of. Did I lock everything? Is there an oven on that I didn't turn off, and are the credit card offer pieces small enough, is--? And where does it end? . . . But I tend to err on the side of laziness in order to not be obsessive.

People in this study offer a variety of reasons for failing to embrace and/or act on privacy fears. Some, like Jim, consciously choose to worry only selectively about some things because they don't want to worry about other things. Other people worry only selectively because they believe there is nothing they *can* do about some things.

This next woman, for instance, not only engages in selective concealment and disclosure, but also in selective worry about her exposure. She finds that worrying about the things she can control actually distracts her from worrying about the things she can't.

So, I mean, I worry about things with my name on it being out in public and losing those things, and yet I know that my name is on the Internet. I've seen it on the Internet. And actually, there's been times where I've seen it on the Internet and I just want it off. Like, something you just, maybe, signed up for once or something when you weren't thinking. And, like, that feeling of, like-- I feel desperate. You're, like, I wish my name were not on the Internet here, you know? But the thing is, like-- I feel in control of this *(indicates purse)*. I feel in control of the things in my wallet. I can't control the other. So I can just pretend that my name's not on there [the Internet], and then I can, like, worry about not losing a [credit] card [instead]. That makes me feel better.

So you spend a lot of time worrying about what you can control because you know that there's so much that you can't.

Right. Yeah. And I think, like, by worrying about the things that I can control, it almost lets me forget temporarily.

. . . And even my to-do list. I was worried about something the other day. I think it fell out of my pocket or something, and I always write at the top of my to-do list whatever I have to do. It's like errand titles. And it's just like, oh, God, what if someone gets to see my to-do list? I was like-- You know? Just call me weird, but, like, I feel in control of the, like, the physical, little things around me, you know?

Some people refuse to worry about their privacy because they think that an obsession with privacy can result in stupid, dysfunctional systems— institutionally as well as personally. One such individual, for instance, de- scribed an extraordinarily cumbersome system invented by a health clinic to keep people from knowing the names of who else was there that day, only to result in many patients never knowing when it was their turn to see the doctor. Which was the worse alternative, he asked?

Other participants refuse to worry about their privacy and choose in- stead to simply, gleefully wreck the plans of intruders, from telemarketers and online retailers who sell their addresses to others onward. They engage in personal campaigns to poison (give false information for) databases, for instance, or otherwise circumvent data-collecting systems. One partici- pant separated her groceries as she shopped. When she reached the regis- ter, she swiped her customer loyalty card to buy the first batch and receive the deep discounts offered on certain items. She bought everything else as a separate order—with cash—so that these items could not be traced to her household. Stores legitimately need to keep track of their inventory, she says, but not what an individual buys.

Some participants refuse to worry about privacy, arguing that "feeding the fear" doesn't do anything to prevent what you fear from happening. It either will or it won't. And a number of individuals shared this next partic- ipant's perspective, a variation on that theme. She argues that most people misplace their fear, anyway.

Do you worry about your privacy or the privacy of the people you care about?

I can't say *worry*. But, I mean, if it's going to happen, it's going to come out. Because you never know who you're talking to—in the sense that your family, which is closest to you, can become your enemies. Because while family is the greatest thing that God made, the people that know you best are the people that can hurt you the most. And a person that don't know you or a person that you feel like is your enemy, you're not going to let them get that close to you. . . . The people that's closest to you are the ones that can hurt you the most because they know all the intimate details of your life. Your financial life, your relationship with who you're with or who you want to be with-- because you shared all that with family. So it's sad to say, but those are the people that can hurt you the most.

In other words, it's the people you're closest to who can really invade your privacy. There's nothing you can do about that, so why worry about it? And all those other people can't hurt you nearly as much as family can, so why worry about them, either? The woman whose cousin stole her identity and nearly wrecked her life might well agree.

Accordingly, I find two especially interesting moments in the development of participants' privacy fears and responses to them. First, there is the moment in which someone becomes genuinely worried about some aspect of their privacy. Knowing that something might happen does not instantly make us worry about it, though. Some people do, and some people don't.

Second, then, having developed a distinct concern about something, there is the moment in which a person might decide to simply shrug, perhaps, and learn to live with it. They may hope their worry is either unfounded or that they'll luck out and nothing too bad will happen to them— at least, nothing as bad as whatever they'd have to do in order to prevent it from happening. Others, however, may decide to actually act on their concern at this time, adopting a mindset and distinct behaviors designed to prevent what they fear from happening.

At this point, those who actually act on their privacy fears seem to fall into one or both of two categories. The first consists of individuals who have already witnessed the practical consequences of a particular privacy violation up close. As a result, this type of actor believes that the practical consequences of *not* trying to prevent this from happening are much more onerous than the practical consequences of adopting some well-defined preventive behaviors. They do so, accordingly.

There is a second category of people who actually act on their privacy fears, though, who seem much less concerned with the practical consequences of a violation and much more concerned with the symbolic consequences of it. Their symbolic meaning is what makes it well worth the practical trouble of trying to prevent violations. The most privacy-vigilant participants in this study fall into this category: a handful of single males in their mid-twenties to mid-forties, all employed in occupations that depended on their privacy expertise.

For these men, people both in and outside the workplace seemed to cast constant privacy gauntlets at their feet, winning swift, intensely felt responses in return. There was definitely a "may the best man win" attitude behind the personal privacy practices they described. It was just this symbolic meaning of a successful encroachment on their privacy—that is, that another person *was* better, at least that time—that seemed to mean such intrusions needed to be avoided whenever possible. Violations were to be contained and learned from—if not avenged—the rest of the time. If ever one needed to hire someone to protect one's privacy, these were precisely the people one would want on one's team. In many ways, they possessed mindsets and collections of skills that probably outstripped the vast majority of people's privacy toolkits.

In a couple minutes' conversation, for instance, look at all the things the following system administrator does to better control others' access to his time, his space, his agenda, his thoughts, and other private matters in his workplace. One gets the sense that he is not only highly motivated to do this, but that this is based on hard-won experience in the ways people are likely to challenge his privacy—and what the consequences of that are likely to be.

Can you arrange and use your workspace pretty much as you like?

I can arrange *my* workspace however. I think my desk is cluttered just so people won't touch my desk. It's impossible—

—to put anything down?

Yeah. No, seriously. I think that's half the reason. I also have it set up for a left-handed mouse on the Microsoft system so people don't use my Microsoft because I'm ambidextrous. People, like, go, "Oh, jeez."

They pick somebody else's.

Usually they do that.

So what kind of stuff do you clutter your desk with to keep people from using it?

Like glasses of stuff, you know. Usually beverages and paperwork just littered everywhere. No one goes near it because of it.

So here's sort of an odd question. So, she [Chris] says, pick one of your workplaces, any one, and think of three objects that you think are more private and three objects that you think are more public.

My voice-activated headset for my computer at my home workspace is more private. It's voice activated.

So, why?

It sits on your ear, and it's keyed to my voice.

So it's not necessarily that you wouldn't want someone touching; it's that it's not going to work for anybody else?

That's why I bought that one.

I don't understand quite what it is, actually.

I put it on my ear and I can do text, speech to text, voice recognition, and it can also operate the phone. I can say, "Dial Joe Smith at home." It would say, "Did you say dial Joe Smith at home?" Yeah.

Cool.

Dialing.

So there's some kind of security on it so it only responds to your voice?

No, it just doesn't get it right with other people. You have to train it.

If you really wanted privacy while you were working, what would you do? Is there a way you convey the message to others that you want to be left alone?

Headphones. By putting on headphones and turn the music up, I can't hear anything. People throw something at me to get my attention. There'll be, like, an endless supply of little toys like stress balls and stuff like that. And light, cushy devices that I get beaned with. And I do the same thing. People put headphones on. If you want to be left alone, you put headphones on.

Be left alone so you can concentrate more because it's just such an open space?

Yeah.

Do you ever put them on and not put music on?

Yeah. I did that all last week. You know, Mack walked up to me and he's like, "(Dude)." And I looked at him and I'm like, what? I just looked at him. He's, like, waiting for me to take the headphones off and I go, "They're not on." He goes, "Oh," and then he starts talking. He's like, "Why do you have them in?" I'm like, "So people leave me alone. I'm working."

If you don't have them on, people will just start, like, gossiping or chatting?

Chatting, usually. Like, hey! Look at this news article. You know, the DMCA, copyright protection, da, da, da, da, Internet something, you know.

Do you have much control over your schedule, including what you have to do and when you have to do it during the day?

Not a ton, but yeah. You can lie.

What do you mean?

If someone comes up to you and says, "Can you do this right now?" Like today, this guy's like, "Can you do this for me now?" I'm like, "No. I'm really busy right now." And then I had to make sure that for the rest of the day, I at least appeared busy. You know, because I knew that if he came around looking again, then I'd have to do it for him. Whatever.

Was the issue, like, control, that you didn't want to have to drop things and help him, or—?

Yeah.

Like you'd be happy to help him at another time if it were at your convenience? Or you never would help this guy?

Well, no. It's more that we just don't-- It's just bad to encourage people to come straight to you and then ask you directly when there's a help desk. And they should be calling the help desk or email the help desk. And they start coming to you and you're their solver, they'll keep continuing. It's like putting a saucer of milk out for a cat, you know? They'll keep showing up at your doorstep.

So even if you're the help desk, they shouldn't walk in? They should call or email?

We'd prefer that, yeah.

Why is that?

Documentation and control. Otherwise, you get into these reactionary modes. I've seen it so many times where all you're doing is reacting to problems and you can't actually get anything done. You know, there's so much more that we do besides solving the, putting out fires, that if you get into a fire-putting-out mode all the time, it screws you up. It screws everybody. You get into this mindset that's just terrible.

How do you kind of dissuade people from just walking in and asking for stuff? Do you think that most of the people in the company sort of know not to do that?

Well, like, this one guy came up to me this last week-- or was it this week? I don't remember. "Did you get that disc made for me?" I'm like,

"Did you put in a help desk ticket?" He's like, "Why do I got to put in a ticket? Can't I just ask you?" I'm like, "No, you've got to put in a help desk ticket." He's like, "This is bullshit." I said—we're all about customer service—I went, "No, it's not bullshit. It's how we do business." You know? And I stood by it. And he bitched about me. . . . And then my boss-- . . . I know that Mack has my back, too. . . . Because he knows how it is. It's the worst thing that can happen to an IT staff is that you become reactionary. It's like, "There is no crisis. There is no problem. You just wanted us to do it when you wanted it done." He came looking for some kind of-- I don't know, something. And that's not the only thing we do.

If he gave in, he has learned, then reacting to others' priorities might very well be the only thing he does. Everyone would soon treat him and the rest of the staff as if their time, their space, their agendas did not matter. Everything about the workday would become far more accessible and reactionary than they can afford it to be. Of course, the tactics mentioned here don't begin to address the detailed plans and practices he has for securing data files at work, much less everything he does to protect his privacy at home.

Whatever the combination of practical and symbolic consequences that motivates them, though, participants' most common responses to privacy worries are compromises between more thorough prevention strategies and those that are perhaps only adequate, but more livable. Here is Mike, for instance, a forty-year-old medical researcher, describing his approach.

Um, I work in a field where there is, there are protesters who could actually, you know-- I have colleagues whose homes have been attacked and things like that.

Right.

So it's important that we try to maintain a barrier between what, you know, what I do and where I live, for example.

Uh huh.

So, I've tried to do things like keep phone numbers in my wife's name and, you know, my name shouldn't appear in the white pages or—

Right.

—online with an address associated with it. Uh-- So I haven't given up total control of that, or hope to. But, but at the same time, it's not likely that I have been able to control it and if I don't, I'm just going to try to minimize it.

Okay.

But then other things I don't expect-- like my name is all over the lab, and people are going to find it.

. . . Uh huh. Has it ever happened to you, or just to colleagues?

I mean, not directly. The person I worked for has sort of been targeted by animal activist and terrorist groups. And other people down the hall have been.

So has their research been sabotaged or they as individuals?

Individuals targeted. I mean one person, they showed up in front of his home. And he has a wife and kids in the house. And they started throwing things in his home, and they sent him envelopes with white powder and razor blades. They sent him letters saying "We know where your children go to school." So that's a very scary kind of thing. So that's something you want to avoid.

It's not only parents and spouses who have privacy fears on behalf of others. Professionals do, too, then, on behalf of the people they serve and with whom they work. Their fears and preventive behaviors are designed to forestall future violations of others' privacy. Here, a nurse reflects on this aspect of her work in response to comments from the Canadian interviewer. (Canada enjoys socialized medicine and no citizen needs to worry about being denied medical care because they actually need to use it.)

[In the States], I'm very hesitant about telling even doctors and nurses just because I'm worried that, you know, it's going to somehow affect the kind of medical coverage that I get. So it must put you in a-- quite a bit of a position. 'Cause you're in a position where you have to ask for that information so you can help people.

And I respect that. And not everyone does in healthcare. And you're right, you have to be careful. Because-- Physicians and nurses are sometimes indiscriminate and sharing inappropriate information about patients. For example, you and I are working together and I'm the treatment coordinator. People tell me a lot of things. Let's say there's some personal crisis in their life. It's really not appropriate for me to indiscriminately talk about that to people. Now perhaps I would like to share it with the social worker 'cause I might think she should intervene and offer some assistance. But it's not something that I should just share indiscriminately with the whole group. And a lot of people are not there [in their understanding of that]. That's why I think that I'm a bit more, um, compulsive in that way about my sharing.

Uh huh.

'Cause you know healthcare has changed a lot. And we've had to learn to be very careful with what information is provided to whom. And as a patient you *should* be able to tell your healthcare provider anything and not be concerned about it.

Yet, as this next participant knows, that doesn't mean you *can*. Look at what she's done over the years to protect her privacy, as a result.

You have to be very careful about what you tell [doctors] and in what confidence and, um, how you tell them what information that they need to know.

We've gotten very good at saying, "All right, this is the information, and you cannot lay it down." I will not tell it to you until you promise not to write it down.

. . . And usually doctors are incredibly sympathetic. They are extremely cooperative and very sympathetic, and they won't write something down on your medical record if you tell them that you don't want it.

. . . I was denied insurance for years for a history of depression. And I'm still on medication after ten years, and there's not one paper trail that says that I am. I even go to [a different pharmacy] . . . to fill my prescriptions for [that] and medication that my insurance company does not know about. I started going to a separate pharmacy.

Anyone can learn to be secretive when the reward structure and nature of the relationship demands it. It can take a fair amount of effort to do so, though, whether as a professional or private citizen. One not only has to learn about what might go wrong with one's privacy, but one also must learn to anticipate and design solutions around that.

It can take a high level of motivation and insight—with the alternative perceived as completely unacceptable—for some people to give in to and act on their privacy concerns. Living a life focused on heading off potentially lost or invaded privacy is not necessarily the kind of "paranoid" road everyone wants to travel. Ignorance, carefully chosen, may well be bliss compared to the burden that comes from knowing and planning for everything that might go wrong.

Karen Cerulo (2006) offers another reason why people in the U.S. may avoid thinking about and acting on the possibility of bad things happening. She argues that we are both neurologically and socially predisposed to avoid thinking about worst-case scenarios. Our brains develop categories based on ideal types, she argues, which are the best case or clearest manifestation of a thing. Anything else—including a worst case—has increasing levels of categorical fuzziness about it, making it less good to think with. Accordingly, the way our brains are wired actually predisposes us to avoid thinking about these less clear, less clarifying, worst case scenarios.

On top of that, Cerulo explains, our social institutions—such as the organizations we work for, the education systems that teach us how to think and what to pay attention to, the politicians who lead and plan for us, and a whole slew of cultural manifestations as basic as our ideas of love and marriage (see Vaughan 1990 and Swidler 2003 on this, too)—encourage us to focus entirely on best-case scenarios. We are so rewarded for doing this that we simply don't consider less-than-optimal outcomes. Cerulo claims that when things go seriously awry, this is why we claim with complete honesty that we "never saw it coming"—even though in retrospect, the disastrous event was eminently possible and even probable.

Cerulo further argues that professional and organizational cultures can be developed to offset the broader biological and sociological tendency of Americans to be blinded by the most optimistic outcomes. Indeed, she says, it is imperative that in at least certain settings we embrace a culture actively dedicated to this, training ourselves to focus on worst-case scenarios so that we can actively plan for and cope with them. In her view, world health, economic, security, and environmental issues, for instance, demand that we think through the situations we fear most and put plans and resources in place to directly address those scenarios if they should occur.

Participants in this study cover quite a range of employment situations, including medicine, information technology, law, education, religion, real estate, social work, design, and architecture. Every one of these employees mentioned some capacity in which they acquired very real privacy fears on behalf of those for whom they worked. They also pointed out the specific practices they had adopted and wanted to adopt to prevent unwanted scenarios (i.e., privacy violations) from occurring. In this way, they exemplify Cerulo's thesis and show the direct value in having at least some people directly acknowledge specific privacy fears and plan around them.

After hearing enough stories about participants' privacy worries, I became interested in the shared elements of their narratives. Figure 5.2, A Privacy Fears Map,[6] is the result of an attempt to understand the dimensions of participants' privacy fears and the ways in which specific fears—and the actions taken to prevent them—might be related to each other. I

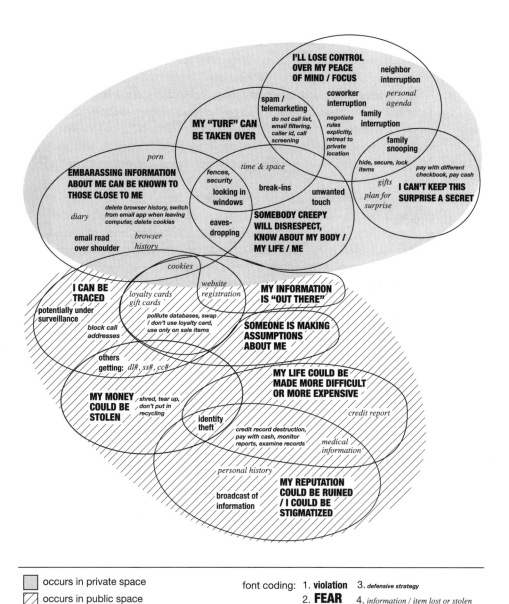

occurs in private space
occurs in public space

font coding: 1. **violation**   3. *defensive strategy*
            2. **FEAR**   4. *information / item lost or stolen*

FIGURE 5.2 A privacy fears map

focused on the formal, structural elements of the stories and allowed the unique details of each to follow.

The exercise confirmed that there are at least five dimensions along which any privacy fear and its associated behaviors may be categorized. First, of course, is the fear itself—the specific privacy-related worry at the heart of the story. Second is the actual violation of one's privacy that generates or taps into this fear. Third is the private information, item, or other matter that one is afraid of losing control over. Fourth, there is the behavior one adopts to prevent the violation from occurring in the future. Finally, among the many other potential dimensions along which this could be analyzed, one stands out in participants' accounts for its influence on the expected nature of the violator and the violation, and where, spatially, one's energy should be focused in trying to prevent it: whether the violation is expected to take place in more personal or more public space.

One further observation about this diagram bears discussion. At the time that this study was conducted, many participants focused a good portion of their privacy fears on electronic privacy matters. These were the newest (and often least understood) threats to their privacy,[7] so the concern is quite logical. I chose to reflect that heightened concern in the kinds of behaviors I selected for analysis during this exercise.[8]

Not only are these technologies fairly new in people's lives, but many of their implications for privacy are still not well understood.[9] Even the privacy implications of personal computers, which have been present on many of our desktops for two decades now, are not fully appreciated by many individuals. The following participant, a database consultant, offers striking insights on this subject, for instance. He provides further grounds for appreciating why it is that so many privacy fears are focused on matters of electronic privacy.

One of the things that I've noticed is that we grant privacy to people that we trust. First and foremost, that seems to be the rule. And we take it away the instant we do not trust somebody. That's when we start watching them a lot more closely, whether it's our kids or a co-worker or, I think, the FBI.

Anybody. I mean, I never check the box on the Web site that says, "Always trust certificates signed by Microsoft."

Yeah, right. Right.

Yeah, but you notice how they word that. They're not the only company that does that. If you want to download Macromedia's flash animation program to get a zippee doo sound or music on some people's Web sites, first box that comes up is "Do you want to install the flash reader?" with a check box. "Always trust certificates signed by Macromedia." No, I never check those boxes.

. . . It's sort of coming down to the basic rules that we've always had: Don't trust any stranger. Don't trust anyone that you haven't known

for *x* number of years and don't trust them outside of the scope of what you've known them through.

That's exactly right.

Is it that simple?

The definition of stranger has changed because—

How has the definition of stranger changed?

—because a stranger is now someone you invite onto your desk. You have invited IBM or Microsoft or CNN or Time or AOL into your house to sit on your desk and watch what you do. And you can't trust them either. They've been there for five years, and you've seen them every-day for five years. So the stranger is now not someone you haven't met. The stranger is someone that you have invited in and hosted and done business with for an extended period of time, and you can't trust them either.

Only you never realized you were doing that, because it's not a person.

That's right.

You know, if it was a person sitting on your desk for twenty-four hours a day everyday, you'd notice and you'd know.

But this is a machine.

I'm sure you must get as many ads as I do for, "Find out anything you want to know about anybody you want to know." Thousands of them and five million email addresses for ten bucks.

This is not a friend. This machine is not a friend. This machine is an intrusion device.

. . . It's a stranger, and it's a potentially hostile stranger. And it's a-- Even if it's a friend, it's a friend who suffers from bipolar. Sometimes it's friendly, helpful, fuzzy, enjoyable. Other times, it's an evil person watch-ing you and reporting on what you're doing. And you control it to some degree, but a degree to which you don't-- A degree which you cannot measure and don't know what it's doing, what it does.

. . . But it's a necessary fact of life, isn't it?

Sure.

And it can bring an awful lot of pleasure to an awful lot of people.

Absolutely. And an awful lot of communication to people who are otherwise isolated. It's a wonderful invention. So is nuclear power, you know?

Whenever participants' fears lead to specific, preventive behaviors—about electronic or other privacy issues—these behaviors may simultaneously serve two pragmatic functions. The first applies to everyone engaged in preventive behavior. It is to prevent the individual (or those for whom they are responsible) from being caught out of frame in the future. The second function, though, applies to individuals more selectively. It is to help get people back into frame—to recover their privacy—after it already has been violated.[10]

Preventive behaviors that stem from privacy fears thus show one way in which Cerulo's arguments hold true. If one actively reflects on a fear, if one mentally pursues and engages the worst case as well as the best, it may result in better practices and plans to prevent and address it. It may also lead to critical insights that lessen the fear. At the very least, our privacy fears and preventive efforts tell us a great deal about what is closest to our sense of who we are, given what we want most to protect.

Hochschild (1983) argues that to be social means to learn what emotions are appropriate when and how to manipulate them to achieve a desired outcome. As Katz puts it, "emotions are not just done to but done by" people (2000, 1). Like any other emotion, we learn to embrace, evoke, distance ourselves from, and otherwise control fear (Germain 2005). Privacy fears are as cultivated as any other and show individuals in this study responding to clear and constant demands that they seek out, nurture, and act on these fears. We get the message over and over again that, in a very fundamental way, privacy is not only about how others think of us, but also about how we will allow them to think of us. We need to act immediately and decisively, accordingly.

The demand for people in the U.S. to pay attention to privacy and become fearful of matters related to it comes from all kinds of institutions and their representatives: families, schools, churches, the government, political interest groups, healthcare providers and insurers, lawyers, system administrators, police and intelligence agencies, our professional colleagues and our employers, the media (e.g., Glassner 1999 and Altheide 2002), and other individuals we encounter on a regular basis. Fear and privacy are big business with lots of different kinds of stakeholders trying to either enhance or attenuate their presence in our minds via the attention we give to both. There are a lot of resourceful people with a vested interest in getting us to be (1) fearful and (2) obsessed with privacy, in other words—preferably at the same time.

They bring our attention not only to the sheer amount of worries we should have, but also what their specific nature should be. Which fears we are encouraged to embrace and which ones we ultimately reject is as much a function of history as it is of personal biography. Both constantly influence our relationships and our worried concern.

Although I've got to say, right after 9/11-- Mark is Arab. Mark is Lebanese, with a goatee. (*Laugh.*) You know. And we just started the day before-- Days before 9/11, we signed Kristin up at Jewish nursery school, and so Mark-- After 9/11, he's like, "I can't drop her off. They're not going to let an Arab guy walk up to the door with a goatee, walk up to the door to drop off a little girl."

Although he could look like a professor, an artist, or a rock star.

He could be anything. Right, exactly. But, um, you know-- So right after that, all of a sudden, we both had this sort of awareness that people are going to be looking at him differently. And I remember being on the phone and saying in, like, one phrase, saying, like, "Arab terrorism." All of a sudden, as I'm saying, I thought, you know, "If this phone call is surveyed for any of the buzz words that they're supposed to be looking for, I've just rattled off my tongue." So there are-- It's very weird that all of a sudden now I have this awareness of, you know, could somebody misconstrue something said and even something in an email because of Mark's name or identity?

We get mail now-- This is another topic that I thought might be interesting. We got on some mailing list for the Muslim American Association. We're not Muslim. Mark is Catholic. He's Christian. And we're getting this [unsolicited] mail now [from Arab charities], in his name. And I think to myself, "Is anybody looking at this?"

Yeah.

You know, "Is Mark going to be profiled or something?" I do wonder about those things. The mail now-- and very strange sort of surveillance-type things-- in light of the, sort of the climate now.

Yet there may be a more general-level phenomenon that also contributes to the increase in our privacy worries. Privacy fears are undoubtedly a function of a very interesting "what if" scenario-running kind of process, in which individuals assess the various risks associated with various choices they might make and then choose among them. We saw good evidence of this as people considered the privateness of their wallet and purse contents, for example. This scenario-running, risk-assessing mindset and the skills that go with it may be the defining sociocognitive dimension of late modernity.

Giddens (1991) asserts, for instance, that the perception of risk, of the potential risks associated with the different choices that one might make, and the attempt to manage risk, is the central feature of everyday life in such societies.

> Living in the "risk society" means living with a calculative attitude to the open possibilities of action, positive and negative, with which, as individuals and globally, we are confronted in a continuous way in our contemporary social existence. . . . In a post-traditional social universe, an indefinite range of potential courses of action (with their attendant risks) is at any given moment open to individuals and collectivities. Choosing among such alternatives is always an "as if" matter, a question of selection between "possible worlds." (1991, 28–29)

Both the development of fears over how one's privacy might be violated and the adoption of practices (or not) to prevent potential feared events from happening could be one manifestation of this overarching worldview.

The result can be a hard line to walk. We may simply try to use good common sense and prevent whatever predictable, pragmatic and symbolic consequences of privacy violations we can. However, we may also find ourselves obsessing over obscure, improbable, but deeply threatening, frightening scenarios. From Marge, a disabled seventy-six-year-old retiree:

I don't want anybody stealing my identity. I just, a few years ago, got a shredder. And I use it when I get around to it, and otherwise I just let the stuff-- Just an awful lot of stuff, I guess, I should shred because it's got my social security number on it or bank account numbers—

Yeah.

And I'm wondering. There's a thirteen-year-old in the building who has done some work for me. But do I ask her to shred these things? How do I know about her, essentially?

Right.

I don't want her-- I don't think she would try to steal my identity or charge things to me, but you never know.

If the tradeoffs for Marge are clear, the correct side to weigh in on is not. On the one hand, there are the completely predictable practical and symbolic consequences of potentially being a victim who should have known better. On the other hand, there is the possibility of accepting the messy—if not lonely and isolated—life of a fearful person who sees even children as potential identity thieves. If the preventive behaviors we engage in to protect our privacy reveal much about our sense of self, perhaps even more is revealed by the preventive behaviors we choose *not* to engage in.

Unlike Marge, some individuals, like Frank, a thirty-two-year-old investment analyst, adopt very clear, universal policies for themselves to make the decision-making process easier. There are no doubts taking up Frank's time. Here he refuses to discuss certain matters on tape, rejecting any reassurances about the safety of his privacy if he did.

Are there times when you've sort of been having a conversation and remembered some experience that you thought was relevant and then stopped yourself and said, wait, you know, I can't talk about that?

Uh huh.

Would you mind telling me what they were?

Sure. This situation. There are lots of things that-- This isn't a question about "Has anything been made public that you didn't really want to?" There are lots of things on that list, and a lot of them are things that I don't want to make public again. It was bad enough that they came out the first time. The last thing I want to do is have an actual tape of me discussing it, lest that tape fall into the wrong hands.

It won't.

Everybody says that. Trust me.

Frank did not hesitate. The interviewer's reassurances were countered by a very clear statement of whose predictions *really* could be trusted here—and it wasn't the interviewer's.

There is also an acute awareness among participants of the tradeoffs between their privacy fears and other fears they may have, a tension that means living with some privacy worries in order to achieve other goals or gain other reassurances. At the time of her interview, this Chicagoan had recently moved to New York City, to the Financial District. The tradeoffs between personal privacy and public security while living under high-surveillance conditions were on her mind.[11]

I just wanted to mention, since moving into this new neighborhood on the very tip of Manhattan, I had a little bit of concern about my personal safety walking around the neighborhood because, at night-- It's mostly commercial. And at night and on weekends, the place pretty much clears out. Then I quickly realized that there's so much security and surveillance in my neighborhood because of the World Trade Center being blocks away that I couldn't be in a safer place because there's so much surveillance. But then, of course, I started wondering, you know, my personal liberties are being probably—

When you say "surveillance," what kind of surveillance?

There's street-level surveillance. You see police cars patrolling, people walking. If you really look, you see them. And then, I would imagine, and I'm sure, there is all kinds of surveillance that we can't see, from buildings, from the sky, of who's coming and going.

Do you think it's people or is it cameras or—?

Probably cameras. Cameras and people.

But are they monitored cameras, do you think? Or are they cameras that are just-- you know, like, this is the store security camera and nobody watches it until after there's been an incident.

No, if they have them there, I think they're monitoring them. Because I know the weeks after and months after September 11th-- and the times when they've had heightened security alerts-- they have been monitoring certain areas in Manhattan for suspicious-looking activities, people, you know. And the areas right around all these financial-- The stock exchange is a hot spot. They've pretty much blocked off all the streets around it-- and other streets.

So does that bother you?

Well, it's a tradeoff. Because on the one hand, I feel safe that, you know, crime-wise or personal safety–wise, that I can walk around and I'm free to walk around. But on the other hand, you know, they know when-- Potentially, someone could know when I'm coming and going from my apartment. You know, I have to be very careful to close the blinds. And who knows what else? It just has started to dawn on me what, potentially, how my privacy could be invaded right now. I don't know. I'll have to let you know what I notice and how that evolves.

Yeah. I mean it's a really interesting issue because, generally speaking, Americans don't seem to really care about that very much.

Privacy. Giving up their privacy.

Yeah.

In general?

In terms of public surveillance. Whether it's surveillance through security cameras that are in the ATMs or 7-Elevens or in the parks, in parking lots of places, or anything. There's an interesting range of reactions, but they all seem to focus-- except for the real civil libertarian types-- they all focus on the sort of reaction of, "Well, I'm not doing anything wrong, so why do I care if anybody's watching me?"

Right. I think I pretty much feel like that. But then, there are some times where-- I don't know. When I'm at home, I certainly don't want to be watched.

And your comings and goings. I mean, that's an interesting thing, looking for patterns of apartment usage or anything. You know, who has access to the information?

Yeah. And I think a lot of people have shifted a little bit how they felt about surveillance ever since September 11th because they are willing to do whatever it takes, give away whatever information needed, to make sure things are safe.

Safety and security are not the only concerns that compete with the desire for privacy, though, as Etzioni (1999) reminds us, they are perhaps the most important ones. Among the other common worries people have that compete with their privacy concerns are: fear of not having enough time to do everything one needs or wants to do; fear of overpaying for products or services; fear of being unable to get out of undesirable situations like being lost or locked out of one's car; fear of being out of the social loop and/or fear of not getting as much attention as one would like. These all lead people to engage in behaviors that they *know* decrease their privacy—such as shopping online, using customer loyalty cards, buying services like OnStar or GPS-enabled cell phones, and setting up Facebook accounts. The disclosure tradeoff seems worth it.

As one participant put it, however, in those areas where we wish to maintain our privacy, the amount of vigilance that an individual has to take on now "is becoming burdensome—becoming very burdensome." Without doubt, one's individual burden of privacy rests heavily on the extent of one's privacy fears—including those we choose to act on as well as those we do not. Worries about privacy have gotten so bad for people like Susan, a thirty-year-old homemaker, that she now not only genuinely worries about and works to her protect her privacy in some very specific ways, but she also worries that she doesn't worry enough.

Do you worry about your privacy or the privacy of people that you care about?

I do worry about my privacy a little bit. I worry about it mainly in terms of identity theft, which you hear so much about these days. And I struggle with whether or not I should be more worried about it, just from a privacy standpoint-- in terms of companies wanting my information for marketing purposes, etc. Because I know a lot of people are really, really unhappy about that sort of thing. And I don't worry about that very much. But I'm always wondering if I should be-- if there's some reason that I just don't know about why it would be really, really bad for people to know that I buy a lot of clothes from Lands' End for my kids.

Ironically, this worry—that is, that her privacy burden is too light and should be greater, that she doesn't see her (and her children's) affairs as the "private" matters that they are and therefore doesn't protect them enough—is now added onto the rest of the weight that she carries. Her burden now consists of both the things she knows how to worry about and also those she doesn't. Both categories have a distinct impact on how successful she can be in her attempts to achieve privacy and ward off violations to it, to define and defend her island.

THE BEACH, REVISITED

Beaches and I have a mixed past. Raised in upstate New York, the movie *Jaws* is my clearest association with life on the ocean's edge. I am rather put off by salty water, in fact; it still startles me every time I taste it. I'm far too Calvinist for my own good, too. I can't just lie somewhere, sweating and squinting and getting sand into everything and pretending this is fun. As a poor student or academic for pretty much all of my existence, it is another sad fact that too many of the beaches in my life have been the pebbly, smelly, buggy, icky kinds—or the ones with a million other radios, Frisbees, and sand-kickers, along with the occasional Red Tide. Moreover, I have never come close to the six-foot-tall, bikini-ready body type that might have made me into more of a showoff at the beach. I burn, I don't tan, and now to make the whole sunbathing thing truly pointless, my dermatologist wants me to wear number 60 sunscreen from April to October. With a hat.

None of this has made it any easier for me to embrace the beach.

I still love it, though. I love the beach because it is a nexus. It is a place where things come together, juxtaposed against each other in the most enchanting of ways. Creatures that walk, creatures that fly, and creatures that swim intermingle here, scaring, fascinating, feeding, and amusing each other. Air is unpredictably sprinkled with water and sand and the gusts and breezes that move it in surprising ways. The fresh and the rotten, the salty and the sweet, the pungent and the subtle keep my nose and tongue and brain awake. The stillness is punctuated with sounds and motions that range from rhythmic poundings and furtive shiftings to the erratic splashes and insistent shrieks that pierce the constant. I love the beach especially at dawn and at twilight, when the diffused beginnings and endings of the day and night merge with the beginnings and the endings of the land and the water and the sky. The beach is a place where the temporally and spatially bounded nature of the classification of things is most beautifully manifested.

I love the beach, in other words, because I am drawn to the phenomenon of boundaries. The beach has been a most useful image to explore and express my interests in the boundaries and the concepts that are at the heart of this book, at least. It has helped me wend my way from "boundaries," "boundary work," and "boundary play" to "privacy," "publicity," and what it means to real people living real lives when they think and try to act as if something is "private" or "public"—or wish it was. It has been especially helpful in understanding what's going on when I see people engaged in so many of their daily activities.

The privacy behaviors described in this book focus on just a few locations along this particular shoreline. There are, no doubt, many more. Each constitutes an opportunity for another trip to the beach and another chance to see boundary success and failure, conflict and concurrence, negotiation and accommodation in action.

In part, this is because the work—and play—of privacy is never a static phenomenon. As high tide, low tide, and conditions during and after a hurricane suggest, the definition/territory of what is "private" and what is "public" may be highly dynamic. Some things, places, and times, for instance, may seem relatively stable for a given culture in terms of their more or less private/public natures; others most definitely are not.

As a result, professional cultural-categorical equivalents to those who work around geophysical beaches abound. Lawyers, nurses, system administrators, cultural commentators, policy makers, employers, public relations experts, the paparazzi, and marketing researchers, for instance, run parallel to people like civil engineers, lighthouse keepers, the Coast Guard, nature preservationists, and private land developers. Each may devote good portions of their lives to signaling, defending, and challenging the edges of the ocean, the island, and the beach—and anyone they bump into there.

At the personal level, our definitions of what is or should be "private" or "public" are clearly susceptible to negotiation and transformation. Here, especially, we see that the private/public nature of things is ultimately, remarkably, and profoundly artificial. As a culture and as individuals, too, we *decide* what we would like to be private and public—intentionally or by default—and constantly work to shape our beaches in particular ways. Often, we go further and try to impose our preferences on others, too.

This reflects the fact that no one is born thinking of privacy in any particular way, much less with the knowledge and skills needed to enact it. We must each learn what privacy is and reach an understanding of our own privacy expectations. We must learn to anticipate the ways in which those expectations might be challenged. And we must learn to manage our time, space, possessions, bodies, activities, information, and thoughts in accordance with both of these previous factors.

In the process, people in the United States also learn that privacy is both meaningful and important. Humans take their cues from others regarding what we should pay attention to and consider a priority. If adults (and, say, older siblings) make a big deal out of this thing they call "privacy" and repeatedly demonstrate what it is and how important it is to young children, then—at least initially—kids will learn to think in similar ways. To speak in terms of "violations," to worry so visibly about them, to spend so much time and effort each day trying to ward them off—all of this sends clear, constant messages about the importance of privacy for self-identity and for social status as well as for the smooth routines of our daily lives.

In addition to the importance of privacy, we also have to learn that it is, in fact, possible to classify things as more "private" and more "public." This is a key cognitive building block for thinking about and enacting privacy. As seen in each of the preceding chapters, we then also have to learn what these terms mean and what kinds of things others put in those categories. The possibility for variations on these categorical contents must be learned, too, along with the variations each individual prefers—especially if one's personal expectations for privacy are to be realistic and others' are to be respected.

Finally, given one's preferred variation on the private-public boundary, we must also learn to engage in specific kinds of work in order to achieve that vision. As we've seen, this is never done in a vacuum but relative to others' situated expectations of the same. Like the work of gender (West and Zimmerman 1987), the work of privacy is both dynamic and done in response to a specific interactional context. This is true whether the interactions are hypothetical and the "other" with whom one is interacting is internalized and resting inside one's head, or whether the other is one's mother, for instance, who has regular and unrestricted access to one's bedroom.

Metaphorically, in other words, socialization into specific, cultured understandings and practices of privacy means we need to learn (1) that there are these things we might call islands of privacy, (2) that these are distinguished from the ocean of publicness surrounding them, and (3) that we can and must negotiate not only the nature of the beach but also how far others are allowed to come up onto it.

Any culture is defined by its classificatory boundary-beaches, which act to separate all kinds of things into *this* and *that*, highlighting their commonalties as well as their differences. Thinking, acting, and being a member of a social group requires distinct categories to guide us in our sense-making efforts. This is precisely why it matters so much to us how these categories and their boundaries are drawn and redrawn over time.

But if beaches can keep *this* and *that*, ocean and island separated, they also facilitate the easy transformation of one into the other. Categorical beaches show us, therefore, how utterly artificial even the most basic assumptions are concerning their adjoining categories. Their extent, locations, contents, symbiotic nature, and immutability can therefore constitute highly contested terrain. What a tremendous amount of work we have to do, constantly, to keep these beaches, their contours, and the edges of the categories they join, right where we want them.

Perhaps it is now obvious that, above all, these metaphorical, categorical beaches—just like the geological ones in my life—seem to demand that I appreciate them. In their wonderful complexity, they make me think, they make me feel. They give me a place to experience the seemingly timeless, predictable, and comforting, as well as the new, the unexpected, the troubling, and the freeing. In Yi-Fu Tuan's (1997) terms, they are both a well-known "place" and adventurous "space." For me, and for all these reasons, the beach continues to beckon.

Appendix A: Study Questionnaire

Thank you very much for taking the time to meet with me today. As you know, your interview is part of a study in which I am exploring how people think about privacy. Please remember that I am interested in hearing as many stories as you wish to share with me. You needn't share any actual names or locations that might betray a confidence or make you uncomfortable, but personal stories that illustrate your insights are very useful to me.

1. Okay, I'd like to start with some pretty straightforward information about the key people and places in your life. First, could you tell me where you live? I don't need an address, just the town or area of the city in which you live.

    And where else have you lived during your life?
    Who lives at home with you?
    How old are they?
    How old are you?
    Do they work or go to school?
    Where?
    What kind of work do they do?

Name	*Age*	*Occupation*

    Do you have any pets?

2. What is your job title?
    And your employer?

Have you always worked in this kind of a job?
For this employer?
This industry?

Okay, now I'm going to just jump right in and hit you with the three hardest questions that I have for you today. Don't worry, I'm not even sure I could answer these; there's definitely no wrong answer.

3. First, what does "privacy" mean to you?

4. Next, what does it mean to you if something is "private"?

5. Finally, how would you define something that was "public"?

6. Have you ever been in public when something rather private happened to you and you felt uncomfortable? What happened? What did you do?

7. Can you think of a time when you saw someone else doing something in public that you thought was private and, therefore, inappropriate? Can you tell me what happened?

    Are there any other things that you see people doing in public these days that you generally find puzzling, insensitive, rude, or otherwise inappropriate because you think they're too private or impinging on the privacy of others?

8. Would you say that privacy is problematic for you right now? Why/why not?

9. Has there ever been a time in your life when someone you know or when you yourself felt that you were almost desperate for privacy? When was/is that?

10. Can you identify a single individual—or maybe a few individuals—who have seriously challenged your right to privacy, either intentionally or unintentionally, now or in the past?

11. Has there ever been a time when you felt you had too *much* privacy? Why/why not?

12. Do you know someone else who you think might have too much privacy? If so: What makes you think this person has too much privacy?

13. Do you think there is such a thing as a need for privacy among just normal, everyday people?

    (If yes: Why do you think we need privacy? What do you think happens when people don't get enough privacy?)
    (If no: Why *don't* you think we need privacy? What do you think might happen if we had too much privacy?)

14. Do you think there is such a thing as a right to privacy? (If appropriate: If not, do you think there should be a right to privacy?)

15. Can you think of any particular topics of conversation or kinds of information that you consider to be private?

    (Probe for: sex; fantasy; age; medical conditions/history/records; reproduction; DNA profiles; grades; religion; politics; finances; salaries; conflicts within the family; conflicts with workmates; intimate, tender feelings; grief; ethics/moral codes.)

16. Can you think of any specific behaviors or acts or experiences that you think are private? What about certain experiences—do you think any specific experiences should remain private?

17. What about objects—just fast, off the top of your head and without worrying about offending or puzzling me—can you think of any objects that you would define as private, whether or not you actually possess them or have ever actually seen them?

18. [See chart.] Are there any things, any objects, that you normally bring with you or wear when you leave your house to go to work each day? [List first, then ask: Where do you keep these objects while you're at your workplace?]

19. [See chart.] I'd like to take a closer look at something that most people think is pretty private and tends to go most places with them: your purse or wallet. If you're willing to have a little adventure, here's what I'd like you to do. I'd like you to take a look in your purse/wallet/pocket—or try to recall from memory what you've normally got there. I'd like you to separate all the stuff you've got in there into two piles or two lists. In one pile I'd like you to place all the things that you think are more private. In the other pile I'd like you to place all the things that you think are more public. And then I'd like to talk about why you placed each item in its particular pile.

    (If recalling from memory, provide chart with two columns for list.)

20. I'd like to take a quick look at your keys. Could you show or describe them to me and tell me what each key is for? Do you have any other keys that you don't normally carry with you to work each day?

21. Some people have a single calendar that they use to keep track of their commitments. Others use a system of calendars, across the spaces of home and work and throughout the day and the week. Can you either show or describe to me what kind of calendars you use to keep track of your scheduled activities with family and work associates?

Thank you. The next few questions I have for you focus more directly on your work and the places and times in which you do your work.

22. Could you tell me a little more about your job and the kind of work that you do?

23. Do you think your job is affected by or demands that you give your attention to issues of privacy? In what ways?

24. [See chart.] Where do you do your work? Is there one central location or is your work activity scattered over a number of places?

(If appropriate: How do you divide your work tasks and decide what to do in one place and what to do in another?)

25. (If appropriate: Do you prefer any of your workplaces over the others? Which one do you like least? Why is that?)

Next I have a few questions I'd like to ask you for each place in which you do your work. What I'd like to do is run through these ten questions for each of your workplaces, focusing on one workplace at a time.

[Repeat the next ten questions up to five times.]

26. Do you like being in this place?

WkSp#1	WkSp#2	WkSp#3	WkSp#4	WkSp#5
Y ~ N	Y ~ N	Y ~ N	Y ~ N	Y ~ N

What do you like about this workspace?

What do you dislike about it?

27. Can you arrange and use your workspace pretty much as you like?

WkSp#1	WkSp#2	WkSp#3	WkSp#4	WkSp#5
Y ~ N	Y ~ N	Y ~ N	Y ~ N	Y ~ N

28. Can people hear what you're doing in your workspace?

WkSp#1	WkSp#2	WkSp#3	WkSp#4	WkSp#5
Y ~ N	Y ~ N	Y ~ N	Y ~ N	Y ~ N

29. Can people see what you're doing in your workspace?

WkSp#1	WkSp#2	WkSp#3	WkSp#4	WkSp#5
Y ~ N	Y ~ N	Y ~ N	Y ~ N	Y ~ N

30. Are the articles in this workspace secure?

WkSp#1   WkSp#2   WkSp#3   WkSp#4   WkSp#5

Y ~ N   Y ~ N   Y ~ N   Y ~ N   Y ~ N

31. Are you happy with your ability to control aural, visual, and physical access to this workspace?

WkSp#1   WkSp#2   WkSp#3   WkSp#4   WkSp#5

Y ~ N   Y ~ N   Y ~ N   Y ~ N   Y ~ N

32. Who has access to this workspace—either in terms of hearing or seeing what's going on there?

33. Do you get to decide who can and cannot enter this workspace?

WkSp#1   WkSp#2   WkSp#3   WkSp#4   WkSp#5

Y ~ N   Y ~ N   Y ~ N   Y ~ N   Y ~ N

34. What about your access to other people's activities while you're engaged in work at this place: Can you hear what other people are doing from this space?

WkSp#1   WkSp#2   WkSp#3   WkSp#4   WkSp#5

Y ~ N   Y ~ N   Y ~ N   Y ~ N   Y ~ N

35. Can you see what they're doing?

WkSp#1   WkSp#2   WkSp#3   WkSp#4   WkSp#5

Y ~ N   Y ~ N   Y ~ N   Y ~ N   Y ~ N

36. Can you enter other people's spaces at will when you work here?

WkSp#1   WkSp#2   WkSp#3   WkSp#4   WkSp#5

Y ~ N   Y ~ N   Y ~ N   Y ~ N   Y ~ N

37. Do you like the fact that you have this level of access to others' space and activities when you're in this place?

WkSp#1   WkSp#2   WkSp#3   WkSp#4   WkSp#5

Y ~ N   Y ~ N   Y ~ N   Y ~ N   Y ~ N

38. Who typically has physical access to you while you're at this workplace?

WkSp#1   WkSp#2   WkSp#3   WkSp#4   WkSp#5

39. Who typically has electronic or telephone access to you while you're at this workplace?

    WkSp#1   WkSp#2   WkSp#3   WkSp#4   WkSp#5

40. Is there anyone that you actively try to *keep* from accessing you while you're engaged in your work here—either physically or via telephone or any other form of contact? Who is that?

    WkSp#1   WkSp#2   WkSp#3   WkSp#4   WkSp#5

41. [See chart and list respondent's workspaces.] I'm going to quickly write down the workspaces you've described to me on this list. I'd like you to classify each space for me according to how much privacy you feel it offers you while you're working there, at different times of the day. If you do not normally occupy that space at a certain time, just indicate that it's not applicable.

42. [See chart.] Now I'd like you to pick one of your workplaces—any one—and think of three objects that you think are more private and three objects that you think are more public. After you tell me which objects you're thinking of, I'd like you to tell me why you think each of them is more private or more public.

    (Probe: Is it visual/tactile access? Is it symbolic meaning regardless of physical access? Is there a particular workspace that seems associated with more private objects and a different one that is associated with more public ones?)

43. If you really wanted privacy while you're working, what would you do?

    Is there a way that you convey the message to others that you want to be left alone? Is there a special place that you go?

    Why might you be likely to want privacy at work—what kinds of things warrant a more private location or time?

44. If you felt like you needed or wanted highly public space at work, where would you go?

    What might you want to do that would require a highly public space?

45. Do you have much control over your schedule, including what you have to do and when you have to do it during the day?

46. What kinds of things do you do to try and control your time during the day?

47. What about longer-term control over your work time: How much do you get to decide what kind of work you do and when you do it over the

course of a week? A month? A year? Is there a pretty steady pace to your work or is it a real roller coaster? (If the latter: Is that roller coaster pace at all predictable?)

48. Do you have enough uninterrupted time to think about your activities during the working day? What about regardless of what the topic is and where you are—do you have enough to think, generally, these days?

49. Throughout the day, and often regardless of where they are, many people are now accessible to others through an assortment of electronic devices. I'd like to go through a list of these devices with you to see if you use any of them and, if so, how you use them.

49 A. Telephones—[see chart]

If I think of your day as a network of telephone numbers, how many telephones might I have to try to reach you during the day, both at home and at work? [List them in chart if pursuing optional qs.]

{Optional:} Now I'd like to ask you some questions about each of these phones to see how you use them. We'll take it one phone at a time, if that's okay.

1) Where is it located (for cell, where is it stored across the day)?
2) When are you likely to be near it?
3) Who answers it, usually?
4) If another person answers it on your behalf, what are the general rules for what happens next?
5) Does it have an automatic answering feature of some kind?
6) Do you use that automatic answering option and when are you likely to do so?
7) If this automatic answering device is activated, can other people usually hear the caller leaving her or his message as it is being left?
8) When do you usually answer this phone?
9) When do you usually not answer it, even if you are nearby when it rings?
10) When do you listen to or read messages from calls that came in over this phone?
11) Do you have any general guidelines for how you respond to or handle the messages from calls that came in over this phone?
12) Does anyone regularly monitor your calls on this phone?
13) (For cell) Do you receive or exchange any text messages using your cell phone? What are they about?

49 B. Beeper—Do you carry a beeper? Would you like to? Why/why not?

{Optional, if yes:}

1) Why do you carry this?
2) Where do you carry this?
3) When is it on?
4) When is it supposed to be on?
5) Have you ever turned it off or ignored it when you were supposed to respond to it?
6) What happens when you do (did) this?
7) Why do (did) you do this?
8) How do you feel about wearing a beeper?
9) Is your beeper activity monitored by anyone?

49 C. PDA—Do you carry any personal digital assistants, such as a Palm Pilot?

{Optional, if yes:}

1) Do you like it? Why/why not?
2) Why do you carry this?
3) What do you use it for?
4) Where do you carry this?
5) Do you have a pattern of when you use it?
6) Is there a pattern to when you are *not* likely to carry it? . . . When you're *not* likely to *use* it?

49 D. Computers—

Just as with the telephone, if I think of your day as the network of computers that you use, how many computers are you likely to use during the day, both at home and at work? [List them in a chart if pursuing optional qs.]

{Optional:} I have some questions I'd like to ask you about each of these computers, too, just like your telephones. Let's start with [first computer . . .].

1) Who owns it?
2) What do you use it for?
3) Does anyone else have physical access to it?
4) Is it networked into any other computers?
5) Does anyone else that you know of have access to the documents or databases that you create on it?
6) How many email accounts do you access from this computer?
7) What do you use each account for?
8) Does anyone else that you know of have access to this email account?

9) How do you know that someone does or does not have access to this account?

10) Does anyone else that you know of have access to your Web site activity history on this computer?

11) Has anyone else that you know of ever actually monitored your Web site activity on this computer?

12) (If so: Were you contacted before or after this happened? What happened after you knew this other person was monitoring your activity?)

13) Do you know if this computer's hard drive contains cookies that allow Web site administrators to track your Web site visitations?

14) Has this computer's hard drive ever been searched at a customs inspection?

15) Has this computer's hard drive ever been impounded or searched for evidence in a court case?

50. Do you ever feel as if your accessibility through telephones, computers, and other electronic devices is a problem for you? That is, do you ever feel overwhelmed by having to handle all the various ways that people can make demands on you with all this technology?

51. Has someone you know or have you yourself ever felt like your privacy was being invaded at work? What were the circumstances? Who was involved?

52. Were there any other times during which you thought your privacy was being invaded at work? Maybe not so seriously, but enough so that it made an impression on you?

53. I'd like to talk about monitoring other people's use of computers, telephones, or electronic devices in relation to work activity. Have you ever monitored anybody else's communications of this nature? This includes all kinds of monitoring, including, for instance, the formal monitoring of a subordinate's computer activity. It includes the friendly, instant-messaging kind of monitoring we do when we're looking to see if someone is online or reading email. And I'm also interested in a more illicit kind of monitoring in which the subjects are unaware that they are being monitored and you really shouldn't be doing it.

(If so: Can you describe the monitoring that you do?
Why do you do it?
Are you comfortable doing this? Why/why not?
Do others know that you are monitoring them? How do they know this?
Have you ever had difficulties over this activity?
What kind of guidelines do you follow in what you monitor and what you ignore and how you do it?)

54. Have you ever revealed deeply personal information or thoughts to some-
    one else simply because you had the assurance of complete anonymity
    with no possibility of someone finding out who you were?

55. Have you ever participated in an anonymous chat room? If appropriate:
    How long did you continue your participation? Did/do you like it? Why/
    why not?

56. Have you ever assumed an alternate identity online? If so: What did you
    find interesting and rewarding about that? Was there anything that you
    didn't like about it?

57. Do you know someone who is a good flirt? (If yes: Tell me about her
    or him.)
    What do you think makes someone a good flirt?

58. Have you or has someone you've known ever made a mistake and told
    or showed someone something that in retrospect seemed too private to
    have shared with that person? Can you tell me what happened? Did you
    or your acquaintance learn anything special from that experience or
    draw any particular conclusions from it?

59. Imagine that someone at work tries to engage in conversations or activi-
    ties with you that are more personal, more friendly than you would like.
    What would you do in a situation like this?

60. Do you know someone who has engaged in some kind of behavior in
    her or his workspace that others defined as too personal or private and,
    therefore, inappropriate?
    What happened?
    Why do you think this person did this?
    Do you agree that what happened was inappropriate for workspace?

61. Occasionally, someone we know might tell us about something that
    they seriously want to keep private from others but that we don't think
    would be so awful if others found out. Have you ever had that experience,
    maybe with a friend or loved one? Can you tell me about it?

    (If yes: Why do you think the other person wanted to keep this informa-
    tion secret? Have you kept this person's secret even though you don't
    think it would harm that person if others found out about it? Why or
    why/not?)

62. Has someone you know or have you yourself felt like you had to keep a re-
    lationship, event, or set of behaviors private because if it became publicly
    known there might be some negative consequences? What happened?

    Was/is it difficult to do this? Why/why not?

63. Has there been a time recently when someone did not want you to know something but (their) face or body gave (them) away, and as a result you found out what they didn't want you to know?

64. Has there been a time recently when you yourself felt as if your face or body betrayed what you were thinking when you would have preferred to keep that to yourself? What happened as a result?

65. What kinds of people do you think are most concerned with protecting their privacy? Do you think they should be concerned? Why/why not? Is there anyone else who you think should be concerned with their privacy these days?

66. Do you personally know anyone who seems unusually driven by a concern with or a quest for privacy? What can you tell me about this person?

67. Do you think there are people who should be less entitled to privacy than other people? Who?

    (Probe: What about children? Politicians? Criminals? Ex-criminals? People on welfare? Victims of crimes? People with bank accounts? Job applicants? Web site visitors? People who buy things on the Web? People who receive medical care? Gay and lesbian people? Gays and lesbians who want to adopt children or join the clergy?)

68. Do you personally know anyone who seems unusually driven by a concern with or a quest for publicity, for public attention and acclaim?

69. Do you regularly give speeches such as public or professional presentations?
    Do you like doing this?

70. a) As an adult, have you ever voluntarily participated in a public performance or exhibition of work in the fine arts of some kind?

    Did/do you enjoy this?

    b) What about as a child—did you ever perform or show art work outside the usual sorts of mandatory school activity?

    Did/do you enjoy this?

71. Have you ever been the focus of a newspaper or magazine article?

72. Have you ever been on the radio?

73. Have you ever been on TV or in a movie?

74. (If appropriate: Did you like your presence in the media? Why/why not?)

75. Would you like to be the focus of this kind of media attention in the future? Why/why not?

76. Do you think there is such a thing as a need for public recognition and a public presence among normal, everyday people?

77. Would you describe yourself as well known or famous?

    Have you ever fantasized or daydreamed about being famous?

    Why do you think being famous, being publicly recognized and rewarded, is so appealing to so many people?

78. Has there ever been a time when you personally felt a strong, almost desperate need for publicity and public recognition? When was—or is—that?

79. Do you feel like you are comfortable right now with the amount of public attention you receive?

80. Sometimes people feel like they need more public attention. When that happens, they might do things like join a volunteer organization, author a book, hire a publicist, go on radio or TV talk shows, give a speech, go to town meetings, publish a Web site, participate in a chat room, coach a sports team, demand the center of attention at a pub or party or public space, or dress specifically to attract attention. What do you do when you feel like you need more public attention, if ever?

81. What do you think happens when people don't get enough public attention, enough recognition of who they are and possibly what they've done?

82. What do you think might happen when someone gets too much public attention, too much recognition of their self and their acts?

83. Can you think of anyone who you think receives or has received too much publicity, too much attention in the public sphere?

    (Why do you think this person receives too much publicity?)

84. Can you recall a book or article that you read, a radio show that you heard, or a film or television show that you saw that said or showed something about privacy that you thought was important? What was the source and what was the message you got from it?

85. Have you recently received a privacy statement from a financial institution? (If so: Did you read it? Can you recall what it said?)

86. Have you ever visited a Web site? (If so: Have you ever read an online privacy statement? Can you recall what it said?)

87. Do you worry about your privacy or the privacy of the people you care about? Why/why not?

88. The term "electronic privacy" is a relatively new one, and not everyone is familiar with it yet. If you are familiar with it, can you give me a rough idea of what it means and why some people have become concerned with it? If you haven't yet heard of it, that's fine.

89. Have you ever taken any measures or adopted any practices or rules to specifically, intentionally protect your electronic privacy? For instance, you might have imposed some guidelines on yourself about using email in certain ways, or turned off some of the features on your computer to protect your privacy. Have you done anything like this?

    Do you intend to look into or adopt any other ways of protecting your electronic privacy in the future?

90. Do you think that the computer, e-commerce, and e-business industries are taking strong enough measures to protect your electronic privacy? Why/why not?

91. Do you think Congress and the president are taking strong enough measures to protect your electronic privacy?

92. Do you think Congress and the president are taking strong enough measures to protect your privacy, in general, these days?

Thank you very much. I'd like to talk about your home for a bit now.

93. What's your neighborhood like? Is it quiet, busy? Do people keep pretty much to themselves or are they out, about, and interacting a lot?

94. How would you describe your relationships to your neighbors?
    Do you know a lot of them?
    Are they acquaintances, good friends, relative strangers?
    Are they nosey? Respectful?

95. What do you and your neighbors do to respect each others' privacy?

96. What do you do if you want privacy from your neighbors? (Probe: inside vs. outside behavior.)

97. Have you ever lived somewhere where people did not respect each others' privacy as much as you would have liked? What was/is that like? What did/do you do about it?

98. What do your neighbors do—if anything—to interact, recognize, and create a healthy public life with each other?

99. Have you ever lived somewhere where people did not seem to work at making a certain level or kind of public interaction and recognition that you would have liked? What was/is that like? What did/do you do about it?

100. Okay, now let's turn to your home. What's it feel like at your home?

101. (Probe: Is it a busy, bustling place? Quiet, reserved? Mostly occupied by family at predictable times or Grand Central Station with lots of people coming through randomly? Is it snug and cozy? Large and spacious?)

    Do you like the way it feels there?

102. [See chart.] How many rooms are there in your residence? Could you list them, please?
    Is there a yard? What's that like?
    Where are the activity centers, inside the house and outside?
    Does anybody seem to have a certain turf, a certain room or space that everyone seems to know is associated with that person?

103. Could you describe a typical Saturday for your family? What about a typical Sunday?

    (Probe for work, parenting, and leisure activities; private time and space vs. public.)

104. Do you think that the responsibilities that you associate with home demand that you give your attention to issues of privacy? In what ways?

    (Probe for concerns with children/parenting; concerns with spouse; concerns with neighbors; business solicitations and information gathering; crossover with topics such as medical, financial histories, television content; Internet content; etc.)

105. What sorts of chores and activities are you responsible for at home?

    (If appropriate: Would you define yourself as the primary parent of your children, the person who is most responsible for their physical and emotional care on a daily basis?)

106. What about the other members of the house—what kinds of responsibilities do they have?

    (If appropriate: Would you say that you spend more time caring for your spouse or that your spouse spends more time caring for you, or are you pretty much equal in this regard?)

107. What do you do at home if you want privacy from your family? Is there anything special that you do to keep people from interacting with you?

108. Is it easy for you to obtain privacy at home?

Why is it so easy/hard for you to find some private time and space?
Is it easier or harder for you to acquire privacy than anybody else at home?

109. What do you do at home if you want to be accessible to everyone and interact with them?

Do you have to work at it to get other people to interact with you at home?

110. Think of someone else in the family. How do you know whether or not this person wants privacy or wants to interact?

What typically happens if you guess wrong and she or he wanted to be left alone or wanted company but you guessed the reverse?

111. What do you usually do if you're feeling a bit low or depressed at home—or anywhere else?

Have you noticed a pattern to what you do, where you go, whether you seek out others' company or keep to yourself when you're feeling a little blue?

112. Do you ever have conflicts at home over someone wanting privacy and not getting it?

If yes: What typically happens to start these conflicts and how do they end? What do you think is going on here?

113. Some people think that their homes are the last bastion of privacy that they have. Other people think that even this is dwindling away and our homes are no longer nearly as private as they once were. What do you think?

Is *your* home a private place?
Is this a good thing or a bad thing? Why?

114. What do you do at home if the doorbell rings?

115. People do all kinds of things to try to obtain and protect their privacy at home. Let me give you a list of the kinds of things I mean. For instance, they use curtains and doors and frequently lock their doors. They install security systems. They lobby for and acquire heightened neighborhood police patrols. They buy phones with multiple channels so their telephone conversations cannot be overheard so easily. They engage quietly in sexual activity, sometimes restricting sexual activity until after others are asleep. Some people remove the labels from pill bottles before putting them in their recycling bins. Some throw out credit card offers in their regular trash rather than recycling the paper the offers are printed

on. Others put the boxes leftover from purchases in front of someone else's house so no one will know that they just purchased a computer, stereo, or the like. Some people instruct delivery people to not leave packages with neighbors so no one will know what mail they're getting. Some people refuse to do paid work from their homes. Some people remove themselves to a private room if they need to cry. Individuals purchase potentially sensitive items online from home instead of in person at a local store. Other people discuss something over the phone at home instead of using email or a written postal letter to keep matters private. Many people hide objects in their houses so others will not discover them, such as a diary, love letter, personal hygiene item, a gift, or a treasured object. What kinds of interesting or everyday, normal things have you noticed other people doing—or have you done yourself—to acquire or protect your privacy at home?

116. What do you think is the funniest invasion of someone's privacy that ever happened to someone you know or to you, yourself, while this person was at home?

117. What's the worst, most serious invasion of someone's privacy that someone you know or you yourself did—either unintentionally or intentionally—to invade someone else's privacy in your home?

118. [See chart.] I'd like you to take a look at the following list of household objects and spaces and, believe it or not, questions about kissing at home! Could you indicate for me how private or public you think these are at the various times of day indicated?

119. Do you have a favorite time of day?

   (If so: What is it? Why is this your favorite?
   (If not: Why don't you think you have a favorite?)

120. Do you have a favorite day of the week?

   (If so: What is it? Why is this your favorite?)
   (If not: Why don't you think you have a favorite?)

121. I'd like you to tell me about three of your favorite places to be.

122. Do you have much leisure or spare time during a normal workday?

   If you do find yourself with some spare time, what kinds of activities do you like to do?
   Do your leisure choices differ during the week versus the weekend?

123. Do you normally take a vacation each year?
   If so: What do you do on your vacation? (Probe: visit family, certain work tasks, public vs. private orientation.)

Do other people know how to reach you while you're on vacation?
(If yes: Who knows how to reach you? Do they actually contact you?)

Do you like taking this kind of vacation?
Do the people with whom you share your vacation like this mixture of activities?

If you could do anything you wanted, with whomever you wanted on your vacation, what would it be?

Thank you. Now I have just four quick questions about your childhood.

124a. Would you say your childhood home is similar to or different from your current home life? In what ways?

124b. Are you still pretty much the same kind of person that you were as a child, or have your interests and behaviors changed? (Probe!)

125. Do you think you have more, less, or about the same amount of privacy now as you did when you were growing up?

126. A lot of what we think about privacy stems from lessons learned as a child. Can you recall any specific instances when someone you knew taught you something about privacy and what's private when you were a child?

127. And what about now—what would you say is the most recent or most important thing you've learned recently about privacy or what's private?

Is this something that somebody else taught you or that you picked up on your own?

And now, before I have to classify you into bland, demographic categories, I'd like to hear what kind of a person *you* think you are.

128. How would you describe yourself? What kind of a person would you say you are? What sorts of adjectives or characteristics come to mind?

Finally, these last four questions are purely demographic.

129. What is the highest level of formal education that you have achieved?

130. [See card.] Which of the following categories includes your household income level? [Show card.]

131. What race or ethnicity do you associate yourself with, if any?

132. What religion do you associate yourself with, if any?

Thank you so very much for your time and insights! I expect the initial results of this research to be published in about a year. Would you like me to drop you a note with the references for any articles or books that result from this study? (Where should the note be sent?) Thank you again.

Appendix B: Techniques of Secrets Work

Mark your stuff clearly
Compartmentalization of computer systems
Firewalls
Passwords
Use codes, ciphers to hide message content
Encrypt your data
Use a scrambled phone channel
Pass notes in class
Speak in a language unknown to those around you
Use jargon others do not understand
Use euphemisms (e.g., Friends of Bill)
Tilt window blinds
Tile computer screens
Use rigorous screensaver/logout protocols
Only let CEO and accountant see salary info, kept on a stand-alone computer
    in a very secure room
Tag locations as containing things specific people can know/access
Foster a public dialogue to keep the secret things secret (voting)
Don't park there (parents would know your movements)
Make personal calls from home, not work
Tag people as those who can know and not know
Only let IT group use the computer

Put up walls
Close curtains, blinds
Plant trees outside house to block windows
Keep secrets to interior rooms with no windows
Go into the bathroom
Fight inside the house
Email coworker to meet me in the bathroom, talk there
Go on the roof (to smoke)
Don't kiss boyfriend in public (gay man)
Don't be affectionate in public, esp. workplace (with coworker)
Nurse (breastfeed) in private, not in public places like a classroom
Lock your doors
Close the door
Don't wear a wrap-around skirt
Install an ATM (so undercover cops can't go outside and tell colleague to go
    bust prostitutes)
Use separate bathrooms and showers from students (teacher)

Be vigilant and don't create opportunities for violations (student stealing
    from teachers' file cabinet)
Don't let someone go in your purse or wallet
Never carry personal items in your wallet
Don't show or count your money in public
Protect your wallet
Closely attend laundromat machines to keep others from seeing and touching
    your laundry
Ask people not to hover over my shoulder while on computer
Intimidate others so they don't ask questions
Get a reputation so others stay away from you
Threaten the nosy tattletale ("Tell him stay away or I'll cut him.")
Catch a snoop at it, yell at them, don't leave them alone to do it again (dad in
    son's files)
If I see someone at my desk, I go in there and say this is *mine* and challenge
    their presence there
Put the guest chair too close to the desk and its occupant (discourages visitors
    and long conversations)
Use a left-handed mouse

Talk to neighbors on the sidewalk; don't let them in the house
Move to an unfriendly neighborhood
Don't talk to neighbors
Have a big yard and house so neighbors can't get too close
Have minimal contact with anyone whom you don't want to find out your secret

Don't hang out with bad (new) secret keepers

Don't date or get too close to anyone who might find out

Don't work for a snoop; quit the job (when he heard priest listening in on phone)

Don't take a high-profile job, especially a political appointment in a big city

Don't have kids

Don't have a cat (cat brought used condom out in front of church group in living room)

Don't get divorced

Don't do something that will send you to the hospital (e.g., drug overdose/convulsions; masturbation/lost testicle) (i.e., bring your behavior to another's attention)

Don't go into the army

Don't live in a dorm

Own your own home; don't rent

Don't be poor and forced to live in public housing

Have money—money lets you buy privacy and do things in private that others can't

Don't do things that advertise a status or identity that you don't want other people to think/know about (e.g., don't drive a "cop" car; don't buy a new car; don't buy a big, expensive house)

Leave your purchase box behind and put in a nondescript bag to transport

Wrap presents

Dress in the corridor, not in front of the window

Sit in the dark (so others at the party can't see your wet pants)

Don't include certain info on email

Pay cash

Use a prepaid phone card, bought with cash

Have your social security number removed from your driver's license

If I don't want the info online, I don't put the info online

Withhold info

Don't listen to or respond to others' questions or advice

Forget it—literally

Agree with what another is saying and let it go without correction or encouragement

Change the subject

Don't tell *any*one things you don't want anyone to know, esp. a priest

Tell, but do not allow anyone to write it down

Don't document it

Don't say it in a place or over a technological device where it could be recorded

Seal the documents and/or the case (legally)

Seal the envelope

Close files and log out before the next patient
Take labels off bottles, magazines
Put in regular trash, not recycling
Shred it
Rip trash in three pieces, put each in a different garbage can at different
     establishments
Burn trash
Destroy the evidence (burned parents' love letters)
Mandate burning of files after death
Sort the trash for the homeless, putting what they want on top (so they don't
     dig through and litter the rest)

Don't tell until you can't not tell, especially if you think someone is mentally
     ill and couldn't help it (wait until the police specifically ask)
Give yourself permission to not tell others and then don't do it
Adopt a professional demeanor where you don't acknowledge, don't talk
     about what you shouldn't have seen (realtor and interior decorator)
Follow professional codes of conduct that demand protecting others' secrets
Put yourself in another's shoes and imagine them seeing/hearing the secret
Imagine the likely emotional and relationship consequences of telling when
     you know they would be awful for you *and* the person you're thinking
     about telling it to
Convince and scare yourself of the dire consequences if you tell (job loss)
Live by the rule "Don't look there or you'll be fired"
Don't feel sympathy for the subjects of the secrets that you know and that
     you'd be tempted to tell them (people going to be fired)
Swear an oath not to tell
Swear an oath not to tell, prick fingers, and sign a contract in blood

Ask people explicitly not to share info with anyone else
Share it with a small circle of powerful, trusted, and trustworthy individuals
     who will then get others to stop asking and trying to find out
Tell him to leave me alone and stop asking what's wrong
Plead the Fifth (Amendment)
Physically defend your right to not let anyone know your secrets by trying to
     force them out of you
Force others to keep *their* secrets, so you can keep yours (don't ask, don't tell
     policies in military, educational, and religious institutions)

Lie
Broadcast an expected sign/sound but actually be/do something else
Keep good jewelry in the closet, leave the rest in the jewelry box
Have a fake journal in the desk and a real journal hidden elsewhere

Pay with a different checkbook

Use different pharmacies for different medications—the ones on the books and the ones off

Hide the secret in plain view (know what's normal, emulate it, and then you can keep what you're doing secret)

Use a fake eye; false teeth; prosthetic leg; wig; breast implants; nose job

Shave the goatee that makes him look Middle Eastern

Wear a "uniform" so your choice of dress gives away nothing about you (khakis and polo shirt)

Put your clothes on really quick (caught having sex when doorbell rings)

Have all the props (including money) you need to look like what you're pretending to be/know/have/do

"Put on a mask" (so no one knows how you feel)

Be willing to do the "hard, exhausting," and socially isolating work necessary to keep your secret (that you are gay)

Let yourself be known as sick and as a certain kind of troubled person rather than confront the real secrets you're keeping (e.g., bulimia, depression, alcoholism)

Be a good actor

Buy a phone service that lies for you

Poison others' databases (lie about personal info)

Spoofing (keeps the secret that you did it)

Run Web site anonymously

Send notes anonymously

Participate anonymously in chat room

Only use first names (AA)

Never discuss how you know this person (AA)

Don't introduce yourself

Try not to be noticed—become invisible (child in projects)

Get packages in the lobby, not at apt.

Put garden space and bench out of neighbors' lines of sight (so they don't know if you're there)

Disable cookies

Have an unlisted phone number

Use an 800 number to stay off LexisNexis

Screen calls

Use privacy manager

Have no phone in vacation home (no one knows if you're there or not unless they walk over)

Do something when no one (who cares) is around to see you do it (dump Christmas tree next door)

Keep moving the evidence (e.g., a present; one's body to hide swollen, red eyes from crying)

Turned to next (blank) page in diary whenever dad came to say good night

Hide laptop in couch cushions

Before a party, put my *Oprah* magazine at the bottom of the stack and *Bon Appetite* on top

Put things away the day the cleaning lady is coming

Roll up dirty underwear and put in bottom of laundry basket

Keep pornography in closet, in a box

Hide presents where receivers are unlikely to find them

Keep treasurers in sock drawer in dresser

Put things in the garage

Hide it under the mattress

Locate the evidence in a certain space; tell others and get them to agree to keep out/not look via threats, promise of fun, respect . . .

Don't invite or talk about the baby's father (only sister and her interracial baby ever present at family events)

Develop trust so others won't pry

Put the evidence of the secrets out in the open and let people know what it's about when you know they won't want to know (mother's journals that daughters won't touch)

Reveal just enough so people know they don't want to know any more and they stop and go away

TECHNIQUES FOR REVEALING SECRETS

Use a code, known only to those you want to communicate with (close curtains at dinner time to tell neighborhood kids but nobody else)

Parents talking in code in front of kids (e.g., use big words, or spell or use second language)

Translate to a known language (diplomatic communiqués)

Use words others can understand (e.g., not "pothead," not big words for nonnative speakers and children, not medical terms, not another language)

Put a chair in the shoveled-out parking space (another code, in Chicago)

Wear a wedding ring (e.g., crucifix, yarmulke, headscarf, burka, Star of David)

Put arm around boyfriend, hold hands in public (gay man)

Wear headphones at work (don't bother me)

Close the office door, maybe in front of someone (secretary knowing something's up at time of merger)

Display personally abnormal behavior (diabetic on street curb; diabetic friend disoriented on phone)

Isolate oneself, start taking drugs or drinking, change your appearance, change whom you hang out with

Scowl, look sad, gloomy (teenager at concert: "I don't want to be here")

Whisper it

Lower your voice

Say it in a certain way, i.e., *how* you say it reveals the secret (embarrassed, ashamed, humorous, tear filled, apathetic—tone and body language)

Lie badly, intentionally

Convince yourself that the truth is best, no matter what

Tell the absolute truth

Follow a professional mandate to tell (art teacher/therapist)

Instead of completely disclosing everything you know about someone, speak as if you're not quite sure/not presuming or intruding on their privacy

Put yourself in another's shoes and imagine if they'd want to know this and what a better/worse way would be to find it out

Tell them first, before arrest is published in the paper

Get someone else to tell for you

Wait for someone else to do it first (sister outed his alcoholism and drug abuse)

Let yourself feel compelled to tell on someone else's behalf (because what they know is wrong/you love them, etc.)

Feel compelled to tell in order to protect someone

Be willing to pay a price for telling via a corrupted or lost relationship

Be able to tolerate (even enjoy in the case of gifts or vengeance) others' reactions

Tell at the therapist's (with or without a third person present)

Talk to someone (don't use email)

Write it (don't say it)

Journal one's thoughts and let another read it but no discussion

Tell over time, selectively (teacher getting divorced)

Tag people or locations as being safe for revelation

Make sure Web site is credible before you put in credit card info

Cultivate a reputation so you discourage queries and reveal only to those you wish

Be very careful whom you tell—only those who need to know; only those you trust

Tell a stranger you'll never see again

Tell the barest possible facts—withhold any details or emotion

Just say it

Hold a meeting and discuss it

Gossip (tell people what you heard/saw/know)

Have a party (serve alcohol) (to encourage gossip and secret sharing)
Play truth or dare
Make a pass at someone
Get closer to someone
Go to counseling

Display one's artwork to others
Display personal objects, photos in workplace
Write it on a calendar, on your desk (wife's medical info)
Allow others in your desk, even inadvertently (assistant cleaning up found
    AA's Big Book)
Keep stuff where others can find it accidentally—or "accidentally"
Use a speaker phone
Hide it in plain sight (as an invitation to find it, e.g., *Where's Waldo?*, museum
    exhibit features)
Use a collective printer and/or collective computer files
Leave files lying around
Leave a paper trail
Leave an I.O.U. note in kid's sock drawer
Put social security number on driver's license, student ID
Show checks and bills (response to court subpoena)
Share/pass the evidence around so others can see for themselves (parents'
    letters)
Move from a place where people did not know your secret to one where they
    know it from the start (i.e., where it is no longer a secret)
Live a life that completely gives up the secret and the practices associated
    with it (AA member)
Do not allow doors to be closed (locked, or even present—cubicles)
Open curtains, blinds (don't have either)
Encourage/do not prevent drop-in visitors (neighbor's climbable gate for kids)

Use a phone that changes the number of rings and sequence and duration of
    remaining options to indicate recipient's phone activities
Talk in public
Play your music really loud
Let your presence be known on a buddy list
Yell it (person's name in MD's waiting room)
Announce the secret in class (gay/lesbian students in the room)
Write a letter and distribute by hand to neighbors (child molester in
    neighborhood)
Notify by mail or note from schools (Megan's Law molester notification)
Say it on radio, to the newspapers
Tell it on a talk show

Publish in a newspaper, on the front page

Talk to a reporter you trust

Sign a contract that gives you complete control over anything published about you

Make a sign (could be a note that is publicly visible)

Post info on the Web (e.g., my boyfriend's a cheat)

Email everyone in the office each time you communicate with your problematic boss

Do something when others are around to see it (walked in at 4 AM with a guy, never suspecting roommate was up)

Cry, emote strongly, try to pretend nothing's wrong in front of witness (child overhearing half of phone conversation)

Fight in public

Limp (lost leg); don't wear dark glasses (blind); give public speeches (stutterer); read out loud (dyslexic)

Get an erection

Trip/fall down, wearing a skirt

Go through an airport screening

Show passport, including stamps for entry and exit

Biometric info: thumbprints, retina prints, DNA samples

Carry something revealing in purse

Carry membership cards in wallet, etc. (blood donor/type, Costco, student ID)

Carry a badge, ID card, identity documentation

TECHNIQUES USED FOR FINDING OUT SECRETS

Wait until they tell you (until Christmas, birthday, merger announced)

Laugh and cajole in a highly interested but nonthreatening way

Give an art assignment

Get close—spend time and begin to trust and share stories with each other

Sleep with someone

Hang around a gossip/nosy person/insider seeking validation

Gossip

Ask someone who is likely to know or know someone who does (sometimes repeatedly—interrogation)

Snoop

Find other excuses to see/hear what you're really interested in

Drop in, unannounced

Listen (includes eavesdropping)

Read the paper/watch the news/listen to the radio

Watch/look

Gaydar

Look in windows

Milky door glass (secretary can see them, but not vice versa)

Cubicles, Plexiglas furniture, monitors facing the door

Look for physical evidence (lice check)

Look carefully at the package (mail), know what is and isn't normal for mail
packages

Touch it

Airport screening (search the person and their baggage)

Sniff/smell

Taste it

Open the refrigerator/medicine cabinet/drawer

Check places where it could be (pockets, toilet, drain, under mattress, behind
the door)

Look in the garbage

Clean (son's bedroom, found drugs)

Move the pillow (tidy up) (found paint dog spilled on rug, daughter covered up)

Walk in on someone doing something (accidental) (parents, college roommate having sex)

Go in someone's file cabinet when they're not there

Pick locks

Burgle a place

Go in someone's purse

Go in someone's purse for candy (diabetic?)

Look in his mouth for dentures (should be removed when unconscious)

Medical blood work

Read someone's diary

Read a dead person's love letters

Use a collective printer/computer

Monitor key strokes

Nanny cam

House security system

Telescope in office

Seek independent verification and confront (ask teacher about son's
homework)

Set up an opportunity/access and watch/check whenever the suspect was
likely to do/have done it (student stealing from teachers?)

Set a trap (housekeeper stealing from employer)

Have a party; serve alcohol

Play truth or dare

Conduct a police investigation

Don't let yourself experience sympathy—just find out

Take the mindset of an actor in a role and don't worry about the outcome

Look normal (no Crown Vic/Ford Taurus cars)

Be patient—do other things to stay focused and avoid acting too soon or too visibly

Work in groups and trade off to reduce visibility

Keep the contact as short as possible

Protect your identity (so you can do it again)

Use trickery and deceit

Pretend to be someone else

Use undercover—camouflaged—investigators

Use spies/informants

Hire a private detective

Purchase the information

Google, advanced people search, LexisNexis, phone book, sexual predator database, alumni directories

Use your imagination: put yourself in another's shoes and imagine where they went, who they talked to, what they did/might have done

Possess knowledge of what is normal daily vs. normal criminal daily life

Possess knowledge of associates and any criminals among them

Sort/label people quickly and correctly so you can focus on the right ones at the right time and find out what you want to know

Be able to tell when someone's lying

Polygraph, drug (urine) tests, blood tests

Photo lineup, live lineup, sketching perpetrator

Dust for fingerprints, DNA samples, breathalyzer tests

Know the laws that give you entry points and have the authority to find out what you want to know

Interview witnesses and suspects

Recognize when someone gives inadequate (abnormal) answers (indicates presence of secrets)

Search warrant

Collect and put lots of disparate bits of info together

Use and cultivate cross-agency cooperation; pool knowledge, skills, and authority

Use/have good protocol, equipment, and trained professionals to document and analyze the situations and behaviors of interest

Follow the paper trail

Check cell phone records

I-pass info

Lo-jacks

GPS

RFID

"tethers," "ankle bracelets"

Customer loyalty cards

Look at financial records (includes credit checks)

Depose the person, subpoena their records

Go to court—a trial

Go on shared files on computer

Read someone's documents on the computer

Possess a root account

Use an automatically generated list of users and their use patterns to show/
demonstrate their behavior to others

Use a Web-surfing robot

Use a sniffer

Hack in

Put a fraud alert on credit report

Privacy manager, caller ID, different ring tones

Listen for telltale sign of a caller's ID (computer-dialed solicitation calls)

Track spam senders by using specific email addresses

Trace intrusion by distinctive spelling of name (mortgage company spelled
name wrong; all junk mail that followed with that spelling was from there)

Notes

1. My use of this metaphor was inspired by the appearance of this three-word phrase in Barry Schwartz's classic essay "The Social Psychology of Privacy" (1968, 750).

2. A single response was coded into multiple categories if it focused on more than one aspect of privacy. For a fuller, more detailed analysis of these responses, see Nippert-Eng 2007.

3. Josh Gamson's (1994, 1998) and Jackall and Hirota's (2000) work are excellent on the problem of selective disclosure in the public relations industry and the trash talk-show circuit. Woody Allen's underappreciated film *Celebrity* is also just brilliant on this subject.

4. This is the central theme of Rod Lurie's film *The Contender*, but it receives a subtler and more compelling treatment in Mike Nichols's film *Primary Colors*.

5. See Lofland (1998, 35–36) for a general overview of behaviors regarding the staking out and defense of territory in public spaces.

6. Of course, other boundaries were being worked here, too. Orientation toward the water, toward the sun, or toward the beach house led people to self-organize into different sections of the beach. At the beach house, for instance, there was a live band playing in addition to the exciting buzz of people getting food, using the bathrooms, renting roller blades or bikes, or blasting through on the bike path that passes by here. At this particular beach, this is also the place to work out—or watch people working out—on the exercise equipment just outside of the beach house. Accordingly, some people are much more interested in what is going on here, and will face this way, opposite the water. Those who are interested in their tans and relaxation tend to occupy the middle areas of the beach, shifting their positions along with that of the sun. Still others go to the beach

to focus on the water (notably those with children and/or young adults), which is the case for those who set up closest to it. Not only is the direction in which one looks different here, but the purpose of one's bathing suit also tends to be different for those on the water's edge compared to those farther away from it.

7. Rabin (1993) and Jillson (1984) provide interesting reads on a variety of flirting behaviors.

8. Some people played with the boundary between being under the ground and on the top of it as they "buried" each other in the sand. It was, of course, mostly parents lying still, being buried, and mostly children who were doing the burying—a perfect game, suited to both their desired levels of activity. But most individuals here were focused on the land-water, not the land-air divide.

9. This was an excellent demonstration of Margulis's (2003, 248) observation that "Privacy is social in two senses: the social-psychological and the social-political. This duality is a bridge between social-psychological privacy as social behavior and socio-political privacy as a social issue." In their reflections, participants showed repeatedly how, for them, each aspect influences and reflects the other.

CHAPTER 1

1. As Simmel (in Levine 1971, 11) puts it, "All relations among men are determined by the varying degrees of this incompleteness."

2. A brief word about the transcription of these interviews. Transcribers were asked to capture pauses, vocalized place-keepers that signify thought, such as "um" and "uh," laughter, trailed-off sentences—all the things that are normally left out of interview excerpts. I think these are critical clues about a speaker's mental processing and intent. For that reason, I include such normally excised bits of information in the excerpts that appear throughout this book.

In addition, any time excerpt information appears in parentheses, it indicates a substituted word or phrase—usually a proper noun, like the name of a person, city, or company. This is designed to protect the speaker's confidentiality. Information that appears in brackets has been added for clarification. Two dashes attached to the end of a word indicate a thought or sentence that the speaker started and did not finish. This is distinct from the em dash—used in place of parentheses when participants made parenthetical phrases—so as not to be confused with the identity-protecting substitutions placed in parentheses.

Any time three periods appear in a row, it indicates that I have edited out some of the speaker's words at that point in the conversation. I did this as little as possible and only when a story was becoming disjointed. For the most part, study participants were stunningly articulate. I simply did not have to reset the storytelling dial or move the telling along very often. When I did, I did so for the same reason that I resisted it, for the most part: out of respect for the totality of the story, the nuanced thinking that was ever present in these speakers' words, and my belief that if one is going to treat people's words as data, then one needs to share as many of them as possible.

3. Chayko (2008, 160) puts it succinctly: "We are both identity *creators* and *consumers*," as we not only conceive and present our self to others, but watch them do the same.

4. An extreme case in point is provided by the socially isolated, poor, elderly population that bears such an undeniable cost during socioenvironmental crises. These people

need do nothing to obtain privacy; in fact, much work needs to be done to ensure the reverse and increase the amount of attention and social connectedness in their lives. See Klinenberg (2002) and Thomas's Green House Project, for example: http://www .ncbcapitalimpact.org/default.aspx?id=156.

5. Warren and Laslett (1977) use a comparison of families and homosexuals to argue that the difference between privacy and secrecy is a moral one. "Privacy and secrecy both involve boundaries and the denial of access to others; however, they differ in the moral content of the behavior which is concealed. Privacy is consensual where secrecy is not; that is, there is a 'right to privacy' but no equivalent 'right to secrecy'" (43). I completely disagree with this as grounds for distinguishing between the two as well as with the claim that individuals have no right to secrecy. However, I find the authors' secondary argument about the need to use secrecy and the degree of power possessed by social groups far more compelling and consistent with my own findings. "Those stigmatized or disadvantaged social groups who have little or no access to privacy utilize secrecy to conceal their behavior" (43). That is, privacy (for Warren and Laslett, morally neutral or approved behavior) persists where individuals have power. Secrecy (immoral behavior, for these authors) persists where they do not. If we drop the unnecessary and incorrect attempt to classify these conditions on moral grounds, these authors also support the idea that there are times in which people are constrained in ways such that they have to resort to more active behaviors, that is, those of secrecy, in order to achieve privacy. Even here, though, it's important to realize that sometimes people resort to secrecy just for the fun of it and for the specialness of the relationship to oneself or to another individual that can lie at the heart of the secrecy. Secrecy does not necessarily describe behavior that is either immoral or engaged in only by the powerless.

6. This is a critical point for Shils (1996, 26) in his work on governments and secrecy. It is an important reason why he also acknowledges a distinction between secrecy and privacy. For Shils, secrecy is "the compulsory withholding of knowledge, reinforced by the prospect of sanctions for disclosure." Privacy, however, is "the voluntary withholding of information reinforced by a willing indifference." I find the distinction interesting even where secrets are used as play. Here, the sanction for giving up a "play" secret may be the loss of the cloak-and-dagger machinations and/or the delightful relationship drama that may be at the heart of the play.

7. Bok (1982, 11, 14) puts it this way: "Privacy and secrecy overlap whenever the efforts at such control rely on hiding."

8. Sedgewick (1990) suggests otherwise about at least one stigmatizing secret. She argues that even when a gay/lesbian person is out of the closet, they're never totally out of the closet; every future contact, every interaction with another individual is a disclosure decision waiting to be made. From her perspective, being gay is a secret that never ends, never reverts to the land of merely unshared information. Several comments in this chapter support this possibility, as does Brekhus's (2003) study of suburban gay men, in which even those who define their sexuality as utterly irrelevant to most of their daily lives make conscious decisions not to tell others about it, if only because they see it as irrelevant.

9. Secrets are also the stuff of endless "boundary play" (Nippert-Eng 2005a). They still highlight the social relationships of those who do and don't share them, but the secret sharers do so by referencing and manipulating those boundaries simply for fun. The playful exchange of secrets that is the hallmark of childhood sleepovers simultaneously

achieves some rather amazing and amusing social boundary work. Of course there is nothing to prevent secrets from being used to achieve both fun and serious social boundaries. On this matter, see the conclusion of this chapter.

10. Simmel (1950b, 317–29) catalogs different kinds of relationships, the amount of secrecy associated with each, and the grounds for secrecy and disclosure that apply to them along with the consequences of each. Building on this work, Richardson (1988) looks specifically at the case of single women having affairs with married men. She argues that these couples' shared secrets—including the secret of the relationship itself—contribute greatly to the women's sense of how special these relationships are and their unwillingness to give them up. In a favorite essay, Dan Ryan (2006) offers further reflection on the social norms of notification and the socially exclusionary/inclusionary function of sharing and not sharing information, in general.

11. Vaughan's (1990, 11) observations on the decoupling of married persons could not be more on target. "Uncoupling begins with a secret," she writes. "Whatever their contribution to the maintenance of our unions, secrets also contribute to their collapse."

12. See also Nippert-Eng (2009b, 2009c) on the privacy lessons of childhood as well as the parental balancing act of gifting and withholding privacy to one's children.

13. In terms of unwanted connections to others via secrets, I think of Gene Hackman's private investigator character, Harry, in Francis Ford Coppola's *The Conversation* as a poignant example of this. Our parting shot of Harry takes place after he has discovered that he has been spied on by people as good at field craft as is he—perhaps better. In his anxiety to right the tables and regain his sense of superiority and control, he completely trashes his apartment only to realize he cannot find the mechanism used to bug him. Furniture slashed and upended, bare bulbs and wires exposed, everything stripped and destroyed, he is left sitting on the floor, a pathetic, devastated loner with nothing but his saxophone left intact. After a lifetime of trying to deny his connectedness to others and control it on his own terms, I see in his face the realization that it was all for naught. Their knowledge of his secrets, their invasion of his inner sanctum forces him to acknowledge that he is in fact connected to others who will not go away unless they choose to, and who may reassert themselves whenever they wish. It is a fundamental lesson about privacy. Here, it is also utterly debilitating to a middle-aged man who has never before been on the receiving end of such a lesson.

I first showed this film in a class on privacy on September 13, 2001, as previously scheduled. Afterwards, I could not help but point out to my students what else I saw in this final scene: a warning, and a stark potential parallel between Harry's fate and that of the United States. Would our leaders similarly make a shambles of our most treasured possessions and sense of identity as they realized—in a new and most terrible way—our connectedness to the rest of the world via the secrets we keep and the ones we try to find out? Even more importantly, would we wreck our own home through the ways they would choose to try to keep and find out those secrets? Would we eventually find ourselves, like Harry, sitting alone in the mess we made of and for ourselves, less secure than ever and more aware than ever of how much we and our privacy exist at the mercy of those around us? The weeks, years, legislation, and administration programs since that time have not provided the answer I would have hoped for.

14. See Fine (1987) on the importance of newcomers learning—or being denied—the shared stories of incumbent members of a Little League team for claiming full membership in the group.

15. In their work on mushroom collectors, Fine and Holyfield (1996) note that new members of a club dedicated to this activity often have to be taught not to share their knowledge of a particularly good place to find mushrooms. The authors argue that the desire to share this is rooted in novices' desires to prove competency, yet I suspect it may also be driven by a desire to affirm full membership in the group and assuage the feelings of relative isolation that are associated with being a newcomer. The connection between secret-swapping and intimacy seems to be learned early in the socialization process. In fact, Fine and Holyfield paint a convincing picture in which the denial of such unabated secret-swapping is critical to maintaining a group in which an individual member can be both competitive/highly differentiated and experience a collective measure of solidarity and companionship. Shared information assures membership. Withheld information assures individuation, a building block for a competitive organizational structure. Mushroom club members walk a fine line with what they let each other know, accordingly.

16. See Abbott (1988) on the historical ways in which this function has been transferred across all three professions.

17. The relief expressed among those who participate in an ongoing art installation, Frank Warren's "PostSecret," bears further witness to how important even anonymous disclosure of secrets can be in countering the troubles associated with solely known versions: http://postsecret.blogspot.com/. In this remarkable experiment in community art, people mail in a secret written on a (frequently beautiful, clever, and/or handmade) postcard. Among those who share their reactions to this act—whether the sender or a viewer who shares the same or a similar secret—the outcome tends to be highly emotional, liberating, and empowering. It is not a coincidence that this blog, dedicated to the ongoing project, includes a link to a suicide-prevention hotline for which the artist is a volunteer.

18. It is also interesting to think about whether there has been growth of the percentage of people in the U.S. who seek a paid professional as confessor due to the loss of others who might do the job. The leading sentence for a July 2, 2006, *New York Times* article was "Americans are not only lacking in bowling partners, now they're lacking in people to tell their deepest, darkest secrets." The article reported on research by Smith-Lovin et al. and these sociologists' findings that most adults in the U.S. have only two people with whom they discuss their most troubling issues. The question is, did we ever have more than that, and is the emergence of grassroots anonymous confessing outlets and the vastly larger use of therapy in any way related to an alleged loss of meaningful, non-professional, secret-sharing relationships for adults?

19. See Richardson (1988), for example, on the bonds formed between adulterous partners whose relationship is secret, as well as Fine (1987) on the importance of group-shared jokes and experiences in defining membership among Little League players. Both show secrets working in this way.

20. Simmel argues that the ever-present, implicit potential for betrayal is a key reason why people are fascinated with secrets.

21. I qualify this argument because in at least one type of case, shared secrets do not necessarily provide positive social benefits. Zerubavel (2006), for instance, writes hauntingly on situations in which individuals collectively share "open secrets" with a small group of others. Open secrets are information known to a number of people but kept from outsiders, thus helping to define the secret sharers' membership in a social unit. The fact that someone is a terrible teacher may be well known among other teachers and

the school administration, for instance, a focus of endless meetings and private conversations. Yet the entire school staff may remain pointedly mum about what they know when asked to discuss the matter with a parent. These kinds of open secrets clearly offer social rewards of the type under discussion here and are a key signifier of membership, in this case, on the employees' side of the classroom. In the open secrets Zerubavel writes about, however, the secret sharers do not openly discuss or otherwise acknowledge the secret among themselves, either. There appear to be social costs, but little or no benefits to a secret shared with others when the same others refuse to even acknowledge it—except via their pointed refusal to do so. In many ways, the forced silence around such secrets makes them more functionally akin to solely known secrets. Social isolation is just as likely to result from these kinds of secrets, therefore, as from those that are, in fact, solely known. It is quite possible that the psychological and social damage from them may be even worse, for, as Zerubavel writes, such secrets challenge even one's sense of what is real and how much one can trust one's self in the interpretation of the world. The secret sharers may be in it together in one sense, but they are also together alone. Socially, then, *this* kind of open secret is an exceptional case in that it cuts off the sociability—the bond—that one normally accrues from the sharing of a secret, negating the social rewards that usually follow. For an especially vivid and remarkable exploration of this, I highly recommend Vinterberg's film *The Celebration*, and I am grateful to Zerubavel for bringing it to my attention.

22. I am haunted by this knowledge when I think of the work of soldiers from such socially distant cultures as the U.S. operating in Iraq or Afghanistan. The finding out of secrets—life-threatening ones—is certainly one of these soldiers' foremost tasks. Physical evidence provides only so many clues. The ability to read another person, to second-guess what he or she might be hiding and how he or she might do it, is such a culturally infused talent. It seems a nearly impossible task for a foreigner from such a different culture, particularly one who does not speak any of the language, much less comprehend its nuances and the accompanying nonverbal, bodily forms of communication in that society. It is no wonder that terrorizing encounters and brute torture even with innocent civilians are so frequently used during such a war in an attempt to obtain information. It is questionable as to whether or not such tactics produce any useful information, however. Far more fruitful—as well as humane—is the kind of observation and questioning that might be used by those who have common cultural ground, even a personal relationship with the secret keeper. Participants in this study show a keen awareness of the fact that the people in the best position to discover your secrets are the people who know you well. Military and intelligence experts are increasingly vocal in claiming that extreme physical abuse is not nearly as effective for finding out valuable information as is the ability to read people well and develop trust and reciprocity with a secret keeper. This fact appears to be a basis of undercover work in all the intelligence professions. (See Marx [1977] on this in the domestic police force, for instance.) At best, as suggested in a recent *New York Times* article on the extraordinary success of one interrogator who eschews any physical means of extracting information, we do not know if the use of torture—alone or in combination with relationship-building techniques—is useful or not. There is no available data on the matter; it's been declared a State secret. See Scott Shane, "Inside a 9/11 Mastermind's Interrogation," *New York Times*, June 22, 2008: http://www.nytimes.com/2008/06/22/washington/22ksm.html?ex=1214798400&en=9fa0a687755764c3&ei=5070&emc=eta1, retrieved 6/22/08.

23. I love Goffman's (1986, 95–96) attention to the consequences of timing in *Stigma*, when he considers a situation in which someone finally discloses highly significant information that should have been confessed long ago. He writes, "In the case of post-stigma relationships that have gone past the point where the [stigmatized] individual should have told, he can stage a confessional scene with as much emotional fuss as the unfairness of his past silence requires, and then throw himself on the other's mercy as someone doubly exposed, exposed first in his differentness and secondly in his dishonesty and untrustworthiness."

24. Again, while I am concerned primarily with interpersonal interactions in this text, I cannot help but occasionally note the importance of the same principles and insights at higher, more macrolevel interactions. Countries adhere to the Geneva Conventions and refuse to engage in torture or prolonged and secret detention without due legal process because the way we treat others who may have even incredibly important secrets may be even more important for a nation-state's identity than the possession of the information itself.

25. Gladwell's *Blink* (2005) is a captivating discussion of just this kind of instantaneous decision-making process, what he calls "thin slicing."

26. A qualifier: in cases in which secrets are forced upon relatively powerless individuals, the moral claim of the dominant party's ownership may be offset or even superseded by the subordinate's eventual right to determine what happens with the secret, for reasons I'll discuss shortly.

27. Others may eventually second that sentiment, including the State. There are plenty of secrets whose ownership is claimed and whose nature is sealed by higher authorities than those who merely know about it. The courts produce such secrets everyday.

28. This is the same logic behind child abuse laws that legally require teachers and healthcare officials to file a formal report of suspected abuse. Such laws make it clear that by virtue of their occupation, these individuals, acting as agents of the State, must assume ownership over such information and must embark on a specific course of action as a result.

29. Zerubavel (2006, 29–32) discusses the fine line between the silence associated with social tact and the silence associated with denial and the refusal to act on knowledge one would prefer not to know. Unlike the latter, the former is what is embodied in etiquette rules and is often at the heart of the gift of privacy.

30. The public continues to debate whether or not Mike Rogers has the right to do what he does, too. Mr. Rogers uses his blog, blogactive.com, to out secretly gay Washington politicians and staffers who, in his view, are not only hypocritical but actively engaged in efforts that are harmful to the gay community.

31. In Vinterburg's film *The Celebration*, family members are invited to celebrate the sixtieth birthday of another father who sexually abused his children. The film is riveting and tells the story of what happens when the abused, estranged son announces in front of all the guests what this man did to him.

32. Bok (1982, 86) gets at the heart of at least part of the moral problem here with her observation that "Denying people the right to decide whether or not to reveal their own personal secrets would interfere in the most fundamental way with their freedom. . . . The burden of proof is on those who would override such personal control." In this case, both the mother and the daughter are making claims of ownership on the secret, with

antithetical plans of how to manage it. Each sees the other as fundamentally trying to interfere with her right to privacy, her right to control the secret.

33. Zerubavel (2006, 78) suggests this case displays a common pattern indeed. "Many groups, in fact, view silence breakers as threats to their very existence. . . . Indeed, many families seem to feel much more threatened by efforts to call attention to instances of incest within them than by the offense itself . . . In fact, we often view conspiracies of silence as far less threatening than the efforts to end them."

34. In George Orwell's 1984, we see a stunning sensitivity to the ways our bodies can betray our secrets in his concept of "face crime." We also see how the burden of all the work needed to keep his secret eventually leads Winston, the protagonist of this novel, to begin writing down his thoughts. He behaves in an increasingly reckless fashion as the story progresses—disclosing more and more in multiple ways, almost begging to be caught so that the charade will be over.

35. No one makes this point better than Keegan (2003), who further argues that it is failure at the point of communication that accounts for most intelligence failures.

36. Keegan also notices this and, in fact, says early on (2003, 2) that by the end of spy novels and the like we are often completely ignorant about how the spy's activity actually affected the state of affairs. We are so caught up in how they do things that we rarely seem interested in the bigger picture.

37. Again, Orwell's work in 1984 taps beautifully into the possibility of self-betraying actions that reveal a need to tell a secret. Why in the world would Winston, a man obsessed with the need and skills to never betray what he really thought, begin writing down his thoughts in a journal if he did not ultimately wish to be found out and to be relieved of the enormous burden of constantly living one life in his head and another outside it?

38. In this regard, readers might be interested in an extensive analysis of trash management in chapter 4.

39. http://www.youtube.com/watch?v=PmDTtkZlMwM;http://www.youtube.com/watch?v=H8oQBYw6xxc;

http://www.youtube.com/watch?v=zCozOLqYnRg.

40. See, for example, Michael R. Gordon, "A Platoon's Mission: Seeking and Destroying Explosives in Disguise," *New York Times*, July 12, 2006: http://query.nytimes.com/gst/fullpage.html?res=9C0CEFD91130F931A25754C0A9609 C8B63&sec=&spon=&emc=eta1. See also Benedict Carey, "In Battle, Hunches Prove to Be Valuable," *New York Times*, July 28, 2009, for a reflection that highlights the importance of perception in this kind of secrets work: http://www.nytimes.com/2009/07/28/health/research/28brain.html?emc=eta1.

41. Wikipedia offers as good a definition of this game as any other: "One player starts the game by asking another player, 'Truth or dare?' If the queried player answers, 'truth,' then the questioning player asks a *question*, usually *embarrassing*, of the queried player; otherwise, if the queried player answers, 'dare,' then the questioning player asks the queried to do something, also usually embarrassing." http://en.wikipedia.org/wiki/Truth_or_Dare, retrieved on June 8, 2007.

42. Bateson (2000, 181) argues that play and threat "form together a larger total complex of phenomena"; "such adult phenomena as gambling and playing with risk have their roots in the combination of threat and play." I argue instead that play itself can and frequently does incorporate threat and risk—just not too much of it, however

that is defined by the players. For more on the relationship between risk and play, see Nippert-Eng 2005a.

CHAPTER 2

1. Duneier (1999, 157–87) argues that a lack of access to decent, safe facilities leads homeless individuals to engage in behaviors that most people identify as "private"—such as sleeping and going to the bathroom—while out in public. The "housed" engage in private-public boundary work around these activities, in other words, partly because they can. People on the street, however, may be unable, rather than unwilling, to do so. This is but one example of how the lack of private space and time can indeed lead to rocky interactions, in this case between the "unhoused" and others in the public realm.

2. I would argue that this is one of the still unrecognized reasons why mandatory use of drivers' licenses and passports with implanted RFID devices is viewed by some as such an extreme invasion of people's privacy. When the adoption of such identifiers is voluntary, we see the selective access equivalent of giving a specific person specific permission to go into one's purse and get something out so that one doesn't have to go through the motions of doing it one's self. In cases where the use of RFID-implanted devices is mandatory, however—say, through the only form of a passport or driver's license one can get—people lose the selectivity of disclosure long associated with wallets and purses. These islands are supposed to be hands off to any and all others, their contents revealed and concealed only as we wish. Among adults, only those up to no good disregard this, from pickpockets and purse snatchers to those who surreptitiously extract only select contents. RFID technology now lets others take something (information) out of our wallets and purses without our even being aware of it, much less with our permission. Thus, for the government to force us to let them do this—and allow others to easily hack the information as we walk around in public—crosses a line for many people.

3. Incidentally, Lofland (1998, 36–38) argues that the general reluctance of urbanites to intervene in public even in emergency situations is at least partly rooted in their commitment to grant others their privacy. Privacy is a special challenge and an especially precious commodity in high-density areas. This is one of the reasons I chose to study urbanites. Lofland argues that in their desire to be polite by not drawing attention to things they wouldn't see in less crowded situations, city dwellers occasionally make mistakes. They sometimes also ignore people who would welcome their attention—and intervention.

4. In some cases, participants may see and acknowledge the possibility of characterizing an item differently but decide not to change its classification anyway. This happens for several reasons. First, they may think it highly unlikely that the scenarios they uncovered would ever actually happen, and it is therefore unnecessary to treat the object differently. Second, participants may find that defining an item in a particular way would require such a drastic change in their worldviews and their daily practices—and in such an undesirable way—that they consciously reject the alternate classification. Third, and in spite of what they know would be the self-imposed illogic of their original classification, participants may want to reinforce the correctness of their initial definition and/or their decisive nature by refusing to change their minds.

5. There is a fairly common exception to this. Whenever a participant feels that the information from these objects is already public, or believes it cannot be used in and of

itself to do them any harm, then these objects are not singled out for attention and protection any more than the other items they carry with them.

6. Expiration does not automatically change the nature of an item to the "intended only for myself" and/or "for myself and selected individuals" categories. Expired/outdated items still may be used in a practical but illicit way. Take, for example, the following participant: "My (college) ID. That feels a little more private, maybe because it's expired and I still use it to get discounts on books. I just will, like, not pull it out all the way." Only expired items that are not used for any practical, transactional reason may take on memento status.

7. Margulis's (1977, 10) definition of privacy is most obvious here: "Privacy, as a whole or in part, represents control over transactions between person(s) and other(s), the ultimate aim of which is to enhance autonomy and/or minimize vulnerability."

8. I am acquainted with individuals who carry an assortment of defensive weapons in their purses, from whistles and panic buttons to pepper spray and knives. Even these items are used to "establish" a relationship of a sort—one that makes it clear to a potential attacker that the carrier does not intend to be his or her victim. Of course, as self-defense experts remind us, a variety of common purse contents like keys, hairspray, and cell phones—even a heavily laden purse itself—can be used as weapons, too. In some ways they are more appealing because of their more multipurpose possibilities in both supporting one's own and one's friends' agendas and needs while thwarting those of the bad guys.

9. Writing about privacy and objects, Schwartz (1968, 750) argues, "There are two types of objects: those which may be observed by the public (and which may be termed personal objects) and those which are not available to public view (private property). Private property, as we are using the term, may be further delineated in terms of those intimate others who may have access to it in terms of visibility or use. Some private objectifications of self may be observed by family members, but some may be observed by *no one except the self.* There is no doubt that these latter objects have a very special meaning for identity; some of these are sacred and must not be contaminated by exposing them to observation by others; some are profane, and exposure will produce shame, but both are special and represent an essential aspect of self and, from the possessor's point of view, must not be tampered with." It is precisely the latter kinds of objects that are most likely to be classified into cell 1—and least likely to be carried in wallets and purses.

10. Notable exceptions are that we might form some personal attachment to an individual bill if it were especially rare, marked with a personal message, or reminded us of an especially significant transaction.

11. This reaction to coins is not just because these participants are largely well off; I would be very surprised if being born and raised in the U.S. isn't also important. Many of life's daily transactions in Europe are conducted using only coins, which have a much more substantial economic value than do U.S. coins. People utilizing the Euro or the British pound may have a very different gut-level reaction to coins for this reason alone.

12. In a previous study of wallet and purse contents (Nippert-Eng 1992, 1996) an interesting counterpoint to this phenomenon occurred. The study population included solidly working-class, highly skilled machinists. For these men, it sometimes happened that revealing the amount of cash that they carried was also a sensitive matter. In these cases, however, the sensitivity was due to worries about the how the interviewer—or anyone else—might interpret the presence of a fairly *small* amount of cash.

13. In November 2008, a friend in the information technology security business told me that identity theft for the purposes of using a victim's healthcare benefits is the latest crime of this type with a large expected growth curve. This seems reasonable since, according to the U.S. Census Bureau in 2007, there were nearly 46 million people or 15.3 percent of the U.S. population without healthcare coverage. http://www.census .gov/Press-Release/www/releases/archives/income_wealth/012528.html. See also the January 8, 2007, *Business Week* article on the subject: "Diagnosis: Identity Theft." http://www .businessweek.com/magazine/content/07_02/b4016041.htm.

14. See Snow and Anderson (1987), Vinitzky-Seroussi (1998), and Brekhus (2003) for consistent, yet slightly different uses of this term. Most notably, we focus here on the uses of objects in identity construction and place a greater emphasis on the self as audience in addition to others.

15. "Undercover" individuals (Marx 1988) also provide excellent food for thought regarding these processes. Similarly, Snow and Anderson (1987), Brekhus (2003), and Vinitzky-Seroussi (1998) offer provocative studies centering on the acts of selective concealment and disclosure among the homeless, gay suburbanites, and high school reunion attendees, respectively. For more sensational material, endless movies offer more harrowing treatments of this process; none is better than *Arlington Road*.

16. Identity disclosure and concealment is the key theme in Glaser and Strauss's work, incidentally. An awareness context describes "the total combination of what each interactant in a situation knows about the identity of the other and his own identity in the eyes of the other," which "surrounds and affects the interaction" between individuals (Glaser and Strauss 1964, 670). Given the kinds of situations in which wallets and purses come into play, the context established usually is one in which selective or only limited awareness of interactants' identities is expected.

17. We follow the groundbreaking work of Simmel (1990) and Zelizer (1995) in this respect. Zelizer's perspective is the one we specifically embrace here, however, while taking it into new territory. We give our attention to the actual objects that we call "money," the ways we use these objects during transactions, and the different kinds of social relationships, institutional systems, and everyday concerns that are revealed in the process.

18. As Newman (1988) shows, those who grew up during the Great Depression when the financial system proved itself to be utterly unreliable are much less likely to trust it now. They've seen and felt what can happen when this system fails. At the time of this writing, a new generation of people has recently learned that same lesson again, with the systemic failure of a whole new wave of financial institutions. Of course, there is a far better social safety net now. Nonetheless, a new population has now refreshed a decades-old level of distrust in financial institutions—and the individuals who were supposed to oversee their proper conduct.

19. Such an encounter may qualify as a "semi-focused" interaction, somewhere between Goffman's (1966, 24) bimodal option of "unfocused" and "focused" interactions in public. Naturally, exceptions to this mode of operation abound for urban dwellers, such as the interactions among "regulars" in "third places" (Oldenberg 1989, 2001). Morrill, Snow, and White (2005) also demonstrate wide variation in the extent to which urbanites expect to be—and are—"known" to each other through multiple studies of relationships that are sustained in public spaces.

20. Goffman (1959) is of course the main person to read on the dimensions and outcomes of impression management. Yet the popular movie *Catch Me If You Can*, starring

Leonardo DiCaprio, probably makes a more effective case for why means must exist independent of appearances to verify the trustworthiness of transactors. Masters of impression management—as well as those who fail miserably at it—remind us of the risk of conducting transactions based on the impression one makes on either side of the counter.

21. One exception to this may be inferred from occasionally resentful comments regarding grocery store loyalty rewards cards, which one participant describes as "punishment card[s]; if you don't have it, they punish you for not having it." While those cards do provide merchants with information identifying the customer, they are perceived by participants as primarily functioning to provide discounts.

22. Items imprinted with their names are amongst the most protected of our participants' wallet contents. Identification cards are considered private because "they refer to me," and even restaurant loyalty cards may be closely guarded "because my name is on them. . . . And why should anyone know my, where my name and address are, arbitrarily?"

Lofland's (1985, 161–75) engaging analysis of "identity games" and other encounters in the city rests on urbanites' love of anonymity, as does the seminal work of urban celebrant Jane Jacobs (1992). Of course, people like Sennett (1992) find less to celebrate about with the historical emergence of urban anonymity, largely due to the antisocial behavior that is associated with it in the U.S. Goffman (1966, 124) may have fingered at least one of the root causes of the quest for anonymity, though—the desire to be left alone: "in the case of unacquainted persons a willingness to refrain from unsolicited encounters saves the other from being exploited by inopportune overtures and requests." Yet Jasper (2000) offers another possibility, perhaps a more positive one, when he defines the quintessence of American culture as the belief in starting over. The less people know about who you are, the less they know about who you've been, the easier it is to become a new, better, different person. Family members may be most resistant to a black sheep's claims of turning over a new leaf and becoming a "new" person, for instance. Certainly, anonymity provides a great way to hide who you really are, no matter what the reason (Luna 2000; Charrett 1997).

23. This may well be more information than the *recipients* believe they must have, as in the case where an individual offers "too much" information, for whatever reason (e.g., the social obtuseness of Lofland's [1985] "hicks in the city," etc.). Not only sociologists, but countless sardonic comedians offer excellent observations on this point.

24. A staggering number of popular books take this observation as their starting point—perhaps contributing to it in the process. See, for example, Brin 1998; Whittaker 1999; Sykes 1999; Garfinkel 2000; Cate 1997; Lyon 1994, 2001; Staples 1997; and Levine, Everett-Church, and Stebben 2002. For a more entertaining, if darkly humorous review of the possibilities for accomplishing this kind of work, see Marx's (2002) fictitious essay on an electronic stalker, "Thomas I. Voire." Rule (1973) offers one of the earliest sociological and comprehensive looks at the foundations of digital surveillance and the use of this information against citizens.

25. Palen and Dourish (2003) identify a number of situations in which the original intent and expectations of an information technology user have been violated through the unexpected capabilities of the technology to reveal and repackage the information gathered with it. Smith (2000) is an excellent source on the historical emergence of the concept of misappropriated information (associated with the misuse of census data, ac-

tually) and the increasing, widespread concern with it in the U.S. during the twentieth century.

26. Flirtatious interactions are good examples of boundary play focused specifically on the private/public boundary. When someone playfully grabs another's wallet to examine its contents, they are challenging that object's normative status as private, often as a means of flirting with the wallet's owner. Neither author has ever seen someone try to make such a playful move by grabbing and going through someone's purse, though.

27. No one has written more provocatively on this subject than Tim O'Brien in his 1998 work of fiction *The Things They Carried*.

28. See Nippert-Eng (1996, 55–57) on occasions on which women choose not to carry purses as well.

29. On the sheer magnitude of kinds of purses as well as a bit of history about the purse, see Johnson (2002) and Holiner (1987). We have been unable to find any corresponding attention to wallets.

30. Special-occasion clutch purses are a notable exception to this general rule, coming closest to the wallet in terms of their exclusively self-oriented contents. Even these may contain items like tissues, mints, and tampons, however, which are reported as the kinds of items most likely to be shared with "anyone."

31. In fact, despite its private nature, the purse is also commonly used by women as an active tool in toddler management. It can provide a quiet and delightful archeological distraction whenever necessary.

32. Like the participant who earlier commented on how the meaning of $5 differs depending on one's geographic location, this is another example in which we extend Zelizer's (1995) thesis on the social meaning of money. Zelizer, for instance, discusses money that is earmarked for certain purposes, reflecting the social relationships that drive the separating of money into chunks. Here, we look at the object separation process itself—the ways in which tender is physically handled and separated—as well as the ways in which different social situations actually change the meaning of a given amount—or chunk—of money.

33. In this way, this fellow's money is not unlike the jewelry worn by Ahde's (2009) study participants. Publicly visible, jewelry may nonetheless have rich personal meanings and stories behind it, which the wearer may or may not disclose to others.

34. Scott and Lyman (1968) offer the seminal treatment of "accounts." Yet we embrace here the same kind of process indicated in a vast range of contemporary sociological work in the moderate social constructivist tradition, where "reality" constrains and is shaped by and perceived through the story about it. See, for instance, Berger and Luckmann (1968), Lyng and Franks (2002), Fleck (1982), Latour and Woolgar (1986), Gamson (1994), Spillman (1998), Schwartz (1987), Vinitzky-Seroussi (1998), Fine (2001), Smilde (2003), and Van Maanen (1980) for work in this tradition that runs the gamut from metatheory about accounts to individual biographies.

35. It is not a coincidence that the two individuals in figure 2.5 with such extensive wallet and purse contents were also in therapy, by the way. This is clearly an activity focused on exploring and defining the self. The minimalistic individuals represented in figure 2.4, however, had never sought counseling.

36. Pink's assertions are also supported by other studies on temporary and reduced-time employees, like those by Henson (1996) and Meiskins and Whalley (2002); they are all aware of the simultaneous frustrations of such work, of course.

CHAPTER 3

1. http://www.consumeraffairs.com/news04/2005/cell_sex.html.

2. See Morrill (1995) for a fine treatment of the ways in which the distribution of power is replicated in the recognition and resolution of conflict, particularly in organizations.

3. The distribution of power is situational, of course, and it is important to remember that the amount of it that one possesses relative to another person is entirely likely to change across sociophysical settings.

4. The only way this is not true is if the interrupter's agenda has already been assumed by the interrupted as her or his own. By definition, in such a situation the interruption is not perceived as an interruption at all (e.g., "No, no. You're not interrupting me. That's what I'm here for.").

5. See Lukes (1988) for a discussion of this definition of power and its complications. Here, I use a straightforward, situational definition: one person exerts power over another when someone has planned to do certain things at certain times in particular ways, and another forces her (or him) to abandon these plans, temporarily or permanently.

6. This also means a subordinate should not give attention when it is not wanted. That would constitute an interruption.

7. Interruptions are all about these attention-getting and attention-giving behaviors. They may take the form of a well-contained, temporary act, like a relatively short interruption in one's agenda for the day. They may be of quite lengthier durations as well, however, such as a single, multiyear interruption to one's career. As Perlow (1997) points out, workplace interruptions may also take the form of a long accumulation of daily interruptions, each of them relatively short, but the cumulative effects of which may be devastating to one's career. The same principle might apply to the experience of home and the relationships embedded therein, of course.

8. See, for instance, McLellan 1977.

9. Katz (2001) offers good support for this interpretation particularly in his striking analysis of road rage. See the conclusion of this book for more on the symbolic meaning of privacy violations.

10. The extraordinary adoption and use of personalized listening devices while in public space seems to me a direct attempt to prevent others' agendas—at least the auditory evidence of them—from displacing that of the wearer. I also see what Richard Sennett and others have identified as the flight of people in the U.S. away from public spaces and into private backyards and houses, parties, and clubs as an attempt to limit their exposure to others. Others' different agendas and behaviors may be quite effective in diverting if not totally arresting the agendas and attention-giving plans of seclusionists. It is not just the forced change to one's intended experience that causes some people to avoid public space; it is, even more importantly, the reminder they get that they are not as powerful—not as in control—as they would like to think. True urbanites, of course, revel in that reminder and may pay a great deal more money in daily living expenses than their suburban and rural counterparts to live their everyday lives with this possibility.

11. A typical instance of "flashing" is one in which an anonymous man walking in a crowd and on the move exposes his genitalia to random women who happen to look in his direction. It happens in a variety of public spaces, including while riding on public transportation. It is an act typically classified in criminal courts as "indecent exposure."

12. According to Ling (2000), for instance, this is precisely why so many Norwegian teenagers have cell phones, particularly males sixteen years of age and older who work for a wage.

13. Ryan's (2006) insightful essay on the social organization of notification further sets the groundwork for seeing how this not only complicates the sheer number of messages that we are supposed to respond to but also may challenge more traditional norms of whom we notify about what, and in what order.

14. See Zerubavel (2006) for a provocative treatment of the sociology of inattention.

15. In the business world, this is precisely what happens when organizations are more or less responsive to the electronic communications of their customers. Erika Morphy, "Study: Online Customer Service Is Dismal," June 8, 2005; http://newsfactor.com/story .xhtml?story_id=36133&full_skip=1.

16. See Nippert-Eng (1993) on immediate interruptions, but also Perlow (1997) and Bateson (1989) on the longer-term consequences of interruptions for individuals.

17. See Christina Duff's January 19, 1998, *Wall Street Journal* article, "Let Freedom Ring . . . and Ring and Ring and Ring."

18. http://www.guardian.co.uk/print/0,3858,5209945-111163,00.html.

19. This may well be because so many people now ask people "who matter" to call them on their cell phones.

20. See Duff (1998) and Crabb (1999) for work on screening behavior when it was still novel.

21. Gross (2004) presents a discussion of the many reasons why individuals have multiple e-mail addresses, including this one and others that appear in our participants' comments.

22. See Katz and Aakhus (2002) for an especially insightful collection of essays on the multiple implications of this point regarding cell phone use for people around the world.

23. The unwanted integration of different social worlds because of these technologies can create some interesting new problems. Palen and Dourish (2003), for instance, are interested in privacy and maintaining a given level of accessibility with regard to ICT-facilitated interactions. Their focus, however, is on the accessibility of information that individuals may wish to share with some individuals but not with others and applications that may facilitate this. Olson, Grudin, and Horvitz (2004) are similarly concerned with this subject in general, although they have also applied their attention to the problem of selectively sharing daily schedule items among colleagues.

24. See Nippert-Eng (1996, 105–51) on the nature of mental transitions between varyingly distinct social worlds, identities, and the mindsets associated with them.

25. Pink (2002) writes on the explicit attraction of such traditional boundary blurring for "free agents": entrepreneurs, consultants, temporary workers, and otherwise self-employed individuals.

26. One example of this is explored in the December 23, 2004, *New York Times* article by Joyce Cohen, "Email Doesn't Take a Holiday," on the dilemma of what to do with the huge numbers of email messages that pile up during vacation. http://www.nytimes .com/2004/12/23/technology/circuits/23vaca.html?scp=1&sq=email%20doesn't%20take% 20a%20holiday&st=cse.

27. It is no wonder so many people, especially teenagers, are getting into so much trouble over texting at the dinner table, as reported by Sara Rimer in a May 26, 2009,

New York Times article, "Play with Your Food, Just Don't Text": http://www.nytimes.com/
2009/05/27/dining/27text.html?scp=1&sq=texting%20etiquette&st=cse. Etiquette traditionally guides us to pay most attention to the people in physical proximity to us. But
when a cell phone is even closer, physically, than the people sitting next to you; when
talking to the person trying to reach you over that cell phone is of greater immediate
importance than talking to the other people at the table; and when you hardly even notice whether the mental connection and relationship you have with someone is accessed
via a cell phone screen and buttons or by simply looking up and saying something, the
problem of whom or what to pay attention to is not so simple.

28. Note that popular social networking sites like Facebook did not exist at the time of
these interviews. Now they are quite commonly used by people like these study participants. By the time of this book's printing, there is a good chance that a number of them
will have at least one additional access point of this nature, as well.

29. The "compulsion of proximity" is a phrase used by Boden and Molotch (1994) in
their analysis of the political economic rationale for companies to locate near each other.
It's a wonderful, visual phrase that also perfectly captures the effect that communication
technology devices have on so many people—that is, if they're in proximity, one feels utterly compelled to interact with these objects.

30. In some parts of the world, mobiles are not nearly so personal. A single phone may
be shared among a group of friends or even an entire village. In other parts of the world,
though—notably Southeast Asia—cell phones are personalized, accessorized, and glori-
fied to an extent that makes U.S. phones, at least, look bland by comparison. Genevieve
Bell's work (e.g., 2005) is excellent on this.

31. The problem with spam filters was captured nicely in Katie Hafner's August 5,
2004, *New York Times* article, "Delete: Bathwater. Undelete: Baby," for instance, about
how an important e-mail was targeted as spam and therefore never read, resulting in
some hard feelings as well as lost funding opportunities between colleagues.

32. Wirth (1938) argues that high density, high heterogeneity, and large size are the
definitive characteristics of cities.

33. Simmel (1950a) is certainly one of the more widely read (and, one must add, in
some ways the most antiurban) of these. Like Milgram, but in a less disciplined and more
sweeping fashion, he also focuses on the individual's response to the "intensification of
nervous stimulation" associated with city life. Lyn Lofland (1998, xvi–xvii) provides a
solid review of this perspective in an excellent volume with a decidedly more prourban
twist to it.

34. Many strategies used by participants to deal with overload are mentioned in this
chapter. In addition, individuals report generally slowing down their response rates
whenever possible and increasing their use of screening devices across channels. Some
also drop entire channels from their systems to ease their monitoring burdens.

35. See also Fischer (1981, 308) on this point.

36. Although the definition of technology is extremely varied, in this chapter I share
Fischer's (1992, 7) focus on its tangible, physical forms rather than the knowledge or way
of life embedded within them—that is, I focus on "devices, applications, and their systems of use."

37. See McLuhan's (1965) work for what may be the most famous instantiation of this
perspective. Gagnon's (1971) "Physical Strength, Once of Significance" is a succinct statement of this position, too. Couch's (1996) social history of information technologies,

Fischer's (1992) social history of the telephone in the U.S., Gergen's (1991) *The Saturated Self*, and Chayko's (2002) *Connecting* are quite different, favorite uses of it.

38. Meyrowitz's (1985) *No Sense of Place* on the embracement of television is perhaps the single best demonstration of this point. See also Katz and Aakhus's (2002) edited volume on the consequences of cell phone use patterns around the world.

CHAPTER 4

1. In "Back to the Shed: Gendered Visions of Technology and Domesticity," Bell and Dourish (2007) provide a fine example of another place along the perimeter ripe with privacy insights: the Australian shed. Prototypically masculine territory, its closest equivalent in the U.S. is the garage or basement workshop. Very few individuals in this study possess such a space, however.

2. This is one of the key points made by a MoMA installation entitled "The Un-Private House" (2002). The installation included a number of built and theoretical architectural reflections on accessibility and the blurring of the boundary between the interior and exterior of private homes.

3. In "A Knock on the Door: Managing Death in the Israeli Defense Forces," Vinitzky-Seroussi and Ben Ari (2000) explore a situation in which the job of military officials announcing the death, serious injury, disappearance, or captivity of soldiers bears remarkable resemblance to that of a door. First, the team sets up and secures a buffer zone to keep others away from the family and keep interaction located within the home. After that, they selectively open or "dismantle" the buffer zone, permitting access between the family and, for instance, neighbors and various institutions, allowing those inside and outside of the home to interface more freely with each other.

4. In *Doormen*, Bearman (2005) claims that this kind of personalized service is the hallmark of a good doorman. Their primary function, it might be argued, is to screen attempts by the public to access building residents, letting through the desirable contacts and keeping out the rest, according to the specific desires of each individual resident.

5. In the U.S., Halloween involves children dressing up in costumes and, once night falls, going door to door in the neighborhood asking for candy. The children ring each doorbell in turn, and as each resident opens the door, the kids yell, "Trick or Treat!" The resident is then supposed to drop pieces of candy into the containers children carry just for this purpose. The play-threat uttered by the children means that should a resident fail to give them treats, they may be subjected to a "trick" of some kind instead. Neighborhoods have varying levels of participation in the annual ritual, yet it is unusual for a community with children present not to adhere to it in some way.

6. Among the most generous and excitement-generating techniques used by adults for distributing Halloween treats that I have noticed are: allowing children to reach into a bowl or sack of candy and grab a handful; commenting on the wonderfulness of a costume or some other attribute of each individual while giving out the candy; sitting outside on the steps to hand out candy when others use interior apartment building doors as an excuse not to participate; wearing a costume or even a single prop to increase the fun and sense of camaraderie; scaring the children before giving them the candy—but not too badly; lavishly decorating the house in a spooky or fun Halloween theme; or combining a number of these, as the families on Harper Street do in my neighborhood. (See Balliet 2004 for a description.) Not only do most residents on this neighborhood block

decorate profusely beforehand, but they create interactive dramas for the evening, too. One family, for instance, had someone lie in a coffin then suddenly sit up when the kids reached in to get a piece of candy. Another woman dressed as a witch the same year and cackled while stirring a vapor-spewing cauldron on the balcony; an assistant gave out candy below. One house dressed up a rooftop mermaid statue as a witch each year, stuck a garden hose in her hands, and randomly sprayed it at trick-or-treaters. At another house, spooky sounds were piped onto the street, and an unseen person spoke in ghoulish tones through a microphone, commenting on the children and what was happening on the sidewalk. Another family flies cabled, swooping spooks over kids' heads each year while they wait in quite remarkable lines to walk up the porch steps. In this way, over two thousand trick-or-treaters, on one neighborhood block and in the span of just a few hours, are granted a remarkable degree of accessibility to its residents.

7. This makes it all the more remarkable to me that so many urban households hold to the traditions of opening doors to unknown people on Halloween.

8. "Jehovah's Witnesses Official Web Site" states the following: "Like the prophet Ezekiel of old, Jehovah's Witnesses today try to find those who 'are sighing and groaning over all the detestable things that are being done.'—Ezekiel 9:4. The best-known way they use to find those who are distressed by present conditions is by going from house to house. Thus they make a positive effort to reach the public, just as Jesus did when 'he went journeying from city to city and from village to village, preaching and declaring the good news of the kingdom of God.' His early disciples did likewise. (Luke 8:1; 9:1–6; 10:1–9) Today, where it is possible, Jehovah's Witnesses endeavor to call at each home several times a year, seeking to converse with the householder for a few minutes on some local or world topic of interest or concern. A scripture or two may be offered for consideration, and if the householder shows interest, the Witness may arrange to call back at a convenient time for further discussion. Bibles and literature explaining the Bible are made available, and if the householder desires, a home Bible study is conducted free of charge. Millions of these helpful Bible studies are conducted regularly with individuals and families throughout the world." http://www.watchtower.org/e/jt/index .htm?article=article_03.htm, retrieved June 26, 2007.

9. Favorite readings to date for thinking of a building, room, or feature as part of a system—and therefore defined, in part, by the rest of it—are those by Alexander, Ishikawa, and Silverstein (1977) and Jacobs (1992).

10. For this reason, windows are also the quintessential architectural tool for blurring the inside-outside dichotomy of the home—or any other building. See Bachelard (1994, 211–31) for some of my favorite musings on the inside-outside dialectic. No film better uses windows to highlight the inside-outside/private-public dichotomy than Sam Mendes's *American Beauty*, incidentally.

11. Florian Henckel von Donnersmarck's film *The Lives of Others* is an exceptional exploration of this principle.

12. Recent concern about Google's street-level photos should be seen precisely in this light. (See, for example, Miguel Helft, "Google Zooms in Too Close for Some," *New York Times*, June 1, 2007: http://www.nytimes.com/2007/06/01/technology/01private.html?_r= 1&ex=1183608000&en=1228839ff23cb204&ei=5070). For primates, stopping and staring at what others are doing may be interpreted as extremely rude, if not threatening and predacious. Google "Street View" photos can feel like a stare, directly into one's house. Worse, there can be many, many starers whom one can't even see—anyone with access

to the Internet is a potential starer. While some people are willing to live with the trade-offs of having light, a sense of connection with the outside, and the ability to see what's going on outside at the risk of local, embodied passersby looking in, the idea of anyone with Internet access doing so is quite a different story. Normally one has recourse for in-person encounters, too. A direct counter to such an intrusion would be to confront the offending individual and try to make him or her move along, call the police to do the same, or simply close the curtains or blinds on them. None of the normal options exist for defending oneself against cyberstaring into one's windows, though.

13. While this last individual may describe a level of inhibition that is slightly lower than the others, all three participants demonstrate what may be a fundamental part of human nature—the ability to get used to just about anything. This certainly helps sociologists and anthropologists do useful fieldwork among study populations. Once we've been around for a while, people start taking us—like windows—for granted. When subjects' awareness of the researcher drops sufficiently, their behavior typically reverts to something that is far closer to whatever is normal for them, allowing the researcher to have better access to it.

14. A friend who worked in a military think tank never could figure out how to sort and dispose of his trash according to the very specific guidelines he was given. As a consequence, he simply threw it all—including his lunch leftovers—into the burn bag and then dumped it down the incinerator chute.

15. In U.S. cities, homeless and poor but housed individuals regularly try to make money by combing trash receptacles for items they might resell or consume themselves. See Duneier's (1999) book on street vendors who sell the magazines and books they collect the night before recycling pickup in New York, for instance. People such as "freegans," who dumpster-dive for food and nonperishables as part of an anticonsumerist political agenda, also exhibit these behaviors. (See Steven Kurutz, "Not Buying It," *New York Times,* June 21, 2007.)

16. The legal definition of the private-public nature of one's trash varies enormously, according to local, state, and federal statutes. In some cases, law enforcement may have to get a subpoena to comb through one's trash. In other cases, particularly if a criminal has passed by an outside trash receptacle in the course of committing a crime or trying to evade police, trash cans are fair game. The location of a trash can outside one's home also seems to affect the public/private definition of the contents. The closer the can is to the house, the more its contents are thought of as private. The closer it is to the curb—in fact, if it is on or easily accessed from public property—the more public they are.

17. I make it a personal point never to underestimate the impact of payment structures on human behavior, especially in the United States. One need go no further than here to study what social scientists mean by agency and innovation.

18. I recall reading a bit of advice in a women's magazine once. To help very young children cope when it's time to throw out a Christmas tree, one should take a photo of the tree before taking off the ornaments and putting it outside, placing the photo near the child's bed. This advice recognizes not only the brutal speed at which Christmas trees are transformed into garbage, but also the key, magical role they might have in a child's fantasies.

19. Hans Christian Andersen's utterly maudlin "The Fir Tree" proves that this may not be the worst ending to a story one might imagine about a Christmas tree's classificatory transitions.

20. I am generally fascinated by the moment in which an object is suddenly, instantaneously (re)defined as trash, no longer of use or interest, its very presence no longer tolerated, no matter how useful, interesting, or tolerated it was up to a split second earlier.

21. See McKeown and Stern (1999) and Luna (2000) on what can be learned from reading someone's mail or going through their trash.

22. Smith (2000) argues that the invention of the envelope was key in the history of privacy in the United States for just this reason—as well as the fact that it can betray evidence of individuals trying to see what it contains.

23. See, for instance, the *Chicago Sun-Times* article "Local Mail Delivery Worst It's Ever Been," http://www.suntimes.com/news/metro/291829,CST-NWS-mail11.article; or the NPR story "Chicago Cited for Failure to Deliver Mail," http://www.npr.org/templates/story/story.php?storyId=9615598.

24. Jesse Walker's February 17, 2006, article in *Reason* magazine, "This Asphalt Is Mine! Homesteaders in the Snow," not only summarizes these arguments perfectly, it includes highly accurate descriptions of this behavior and a report on the controversial remarks of the Chicago mayor endorsing and warning people of the acceptability of it. http://www.reason.com/news/show/34172.html. See also Mark Brown's *Chicago Sun-Times*, January 11, 2001, article, "Time to Jettison Chicago's Space Junk," where he also addresses these issues, but reports on the fact that the "private" objects that were claiming these spaces at that time were about to become public trash, per the mayor's decree. http://www.highbeam.com/doc/1P2-4585953.html.

25. In fact, many urban areas also have ordinances that are a function of people agreeing to make public sidewalks private, in a sense, also according to the weather. In Chicago, for instance, private building owners are responsible for the wintertime upkeep of the public sidewalks adjacent to their properties. A home/building owner is legally liable and may be sued if a pedestrian harms her- or himself due to an icy or snow-covered sidewalk and a private property owner's neglect.

26. In Chicago, "Section 8 housing" refers to apartments—usually entire buildings of apartments—that are occupied by low-income individuals and families who receive a federal subsidy to help pay their rent. The amount allocated is adjusted according to government standards for the "fair market value" of a rental unit that fulfills the family's needs and the expectation that the family will pay 30 percent of their monthly income toward that rent. In this case, the participant is referring to the destruction of entire buildings ("projects") that had been set aside by local authorities to house individuals who qualify for Section 8 housing. The government Web site on Section 8 housing (now called the Housing Choice Voucher program) may be found here: http://www.hud.gov/offices/pih/programs/hcv/. The following Web site provides somewhat clearer, more accessible information about Section 8 housing and how it works: http://www.affordable-housingonline.com/section8housing.asp.

27. For more on design and its impact on privacy, see Nippert-Eng 2007.

28. There are literally dozens of sparkling, classic ethnographies in sociology that document and discuss urban neighborhoods. There are dozens more in urban planning and other disciplines that do the same. Some of these are burned into my mind because of early coursework (e.g., Whyte's 1993 *Street Corner Society*, Gans's 1982 *Urban Villagers*, Hunter's 1982 *Symbolic Communities*) and later curiosity (e.g., Anderson's 1992 *Streetwise*, Duneier's 1994 *Slim's Table* and 1999 *Sidewalk*, Klinenberg's 2002 *Heat Wave*, Patillo-McCoy's 1999 *Black Picket Fences*, Venkatesh's 2002 *American Project*). These have

undoubtedly helped shape how I think here. However, in this chapter I refrain from pointing out the rather endless ways in which my participants' observations implicitly and explicitly complement the observations on the nature of community and neighborhood that are put forth in these other books. Instead—in part because it would be cumbersome to do otherwise—I stay focused here on the original data of this study and the precise topic at hand, that is, the ways in which mostly well-educated, upper-middle-class individuals negotiate privacy within the community and between neighbors. It is a topic that has received far less attention than it might have. I highlight Hunter's and Lofland's works because they provide a uniquely rich theoretical entry point to this matter.

29. Lofland (1998) argues that the connection between these social realms/moral orders and physical space is not so obvious: "Realms are not geographically or physically rooted pieces of space. They are social, not physical territories" (11). Unfortunately, she then immediately goes on to argue, "Whether any actual physical space contains a realm at all and, if it does, whether that realm is private, is parochial, or is public is not the consequence of some immutable culturally or legally given designation. . . . It is, rather, the consequence of the proportions and densities of relationship types present and these proportions and densities are themselves fluid" (11).

The problem with this argument lies in the leap between the first proposition—that interaction in the neighborhood is guided by social, moral orders that are not linked to physical space—and the second proposition—that the number and density of the dominant social relationships then defines the overall nature of the physical space. This line of thought requires two important corrections if we are to understand my study participants' interactions in their urban neighborhoods. First, the concept of social realms must be completely decoupled from physical space, resisting any temptation to fuse and confuse them. Second, we need to focus on relationships, only, to analyze and understand the nature of interactions in urban space. It is a distraction to try to type the space itself into categories that may or may not be relevant to any interaction taking place there. Urban space is not, for instance, private space over here, morphing into parochial space over there, and eventually to public space farther on. Indeed, it is not even conflict between "what kind of space this is," or "where the boundaries between different kinds of spaces are located," nor even "uncertainty of knowing exactly where one is," in Lofland's terms (14), that underlies the problematic nature of urban communities. The problem is that urban neighborhood space supports all three moral orders at once, and novices can easily make mistakes about how to treat different people, given the moral order that applies to each person—and the importance of getting it right.

30. Wellman's work on rethinking neighborhoods in the age of sophisticated communication technologies is consistent here (see Wellman 2001, for instance). Rather than thinking of the people in physical proximity to each other as a community, each individual should be seen as a member of multiple social networks or communities that may or may not be associated with a physical location like a neighborhood. In other words, the individual becomes the entry point to community, not the geophysical location where she or he lives. As Chayko (2002) notes, all relationships have a mental connection; some also have a physical manifestation. Likewise, all communities have a social foundation. In the era of ubiquitous and mobile computing, they may or may not have a physical one as well.

31. In Zerubavel's (1993) terms, such space is "flexible" rather than "rigid."

32. There are many exciting works on the factors influencing one's experience of space that support an argument such as mine. Schama's *Landscape and Memory* (1996) may be the seminal piece of work on this theme. I also like, in a different way, Bell's *Childerley* (1995), which is a more embodied and contemporary work on this point. But I also like the accessible, short, yet sweeping work of Rybczynski on architecture (1993, for instance), Gallagher's (1994) and Hiss's (1991) broader popular treatments on the experience of place, Urry's (1998) writing on "the tourist gaze," a collection on "Spatial Hauntings" edited by Degan and Hetherington (2001), and my favorite works on the meanings of space and place, belonging to Tuan (1997 and 1982 in particular, here).

33. For instance, this understanding gives us the underlying framework for enacting Lofland's (1998, 28) "five principles that appear to guide . . . the intricacies of public face-to-face interaction: 1) cooperative motility, 2) civil inattention, 3) audience role prominence, 4) restrained helpfulness, and 5) civility toward diversity." These are clearly important dimensions of our interactions with neighbors as well as others in our neighborhoods, and our stance along each of these dimensions is at least partly determined by the categories in which we place each person whom we encounter. In fact, Lofland argues that "persons draw upon—employ—their knowledge of these principles, as well as their presumptively shared understandings about the meanings of body language, appearances, and space-specific appropriate behaviors and identities to produce . . . privacy, disattention, and avoidance," among other urban behaviors (34).

34. Goffman is the consummate expert on how we manage ourselves during such encounters, and four of his books are especially essential reading for anyone who wishes to know more about how we "present our selves" (1959) "in public places" (1966) using "face-to-face behavior" (1982), whether we are trying to hide some particular stigma (1986) or not.

35. The Robert Taylor Homes is a notorious public housing complex in Chicago. Life in these projects is documented most thoroughly and thoughtfully by Sudhir Venkatesh (2002).

36. See Gilliom (2001) for more on the full range of surveillance and privacy-intrusive measures imposed on those who receive public assistance, but in a rural setting. Even better, see his work for a discussion of the ways that these individuals adapt to these measures and try to achieve privacy—and sustainable income, anyway.

CONCLUSION

1. One reason the lower right-hand part of this chart interests me is that it underscores the fact that there is no expected guarantee of publicity that equates with the generally held belief in one's right to privacy in the U.S. A number of authors' works suggest this may be changing, given a culture that teaches us to covet attention and 24/7 connectivity (e.g., Braudy 1997, Derber 1979, Gamson 1994, Gergen 1991, Grindstaff 2002, Lasch 1979, Wilson 2000). But conversations with people in this study did not reveal anything like this. Participants relayed stories in which they did not receive due credit for their achievements, or were disappointed in their expectations for attention at an event or within their families. In such cases, they had been led to believe—with their happy complicity—that they or some matter/object/entity that was important to them existed (or would shortly exist) at a higher level of notoriety than turned out to be the case. Yet no one spoke of these kinds of situations in the language of "violations" or a denial of their

civil rights. For a sense of violation to occur, there must be a feeling of fundamental entitlement to something as well as the belief that one does/did, indeed, possess this thing to which one is entitled. There also must be a corresponding emotional shock when one realizes that what one thought was the case simply is not—and that the implications of this are not good. In the stories I heard of missing publicity, there simply was not the kind of outrage, depression, fear, or activation of institutional protections that regularly accompanied participants' accounts of violations to their privacy.

2. I do not mean to suggest that a difference between one's perception of how much privacy exists and others' demonstrated reality of this must always be a bad thing. Because I am focused here on explaining privacy violations, I have been discussing so far only situations in which the experiential consequences of a mismatch are negative. Yet framing mismatches along this dimension may be emotionally positive or negative. In fact, there is a corresponding but emotionally opposite heuristic that mirrors figure 5.1 and its focus on negative outcomes. It may be best thought of as a mapping of privacy/publicity *reprieves*. Here, an individual's personal understanding of the degree of privacy/publicity she or he possesses also is out of synch with the "real" definition of the situation. The "objective" definition trumps that of the individual in these scenarios, too. Yet, unlike the outcomes depicted in figure 5.1, in these cases the mismatch proves desirable; individuals experience relief upon discovering that they were wrong about how private or public something was.

3. Since I did not ask individuals to actually rate the severity of the violations they reported, it is not possible to say this with certainty. It is a hypothesis worthy of further exploration, though.

4. Katz is superb throughout his volume on the importance of shame in bringing forth extremely strong emotional responses from us.

5. See Kassanoff (2001) and Cavoukian and Hamilton (2002) for more provocative observations on the tension and proper resolution between the corporate promise of personalization and choice in exchange for individuals' permitting their privacy to be violated.

6. I am grateful to Eric Swanson and Jay Melican for helping to analyze and flesh out these relationships and bring them to diagrammatic life, and for Gitte Jonsdatter's final grayscale-friendly version of their work.

7. See Hunter 2002 for an interesting collection and discussion of the kinds of threatening and even criminal behaviors now associated with pervasive computer systems' use.

8. See Nippert-Eng et al. 2005 on the link between the introduction and adoption of computer technologies and the soaring attention to privacy in the newspapers between 1985 and 2003, for instance. In many ways, the story of privacy over the last twenty years is strongly driven by the story of new technologies, especially the Internet.

9. Agre and Rotenberg's (2001) work is notable, for example, because the authors not only saw new technologies as transforming the privacy landscape, but also because they tried to lay out the policy implications of this.

10. There are individuals with such excellent imaginations and abilities to empathize that although their privacy has not been actually violated, they can hear about a violation and deeply feel what it would be like if it were to happen to them. For these people, the effect on their ensuing preventive behaviors may be almost a pseudorecovery from the violation they imagined could have been their own. Moreover, when a violation happens to their friends or loved ones, the same kinds of people hint at what seems to be an

attempt to help the actual victim recover faster by adopting the preventive behaviors themselves. It is as if the friend is saying to the victim, "See? This could happen to anyone; let's both change our behavior so it doesn't happen to either of us again and we'll just put it behind us."

11. Etzioni's (1999) *The Limits of Privacy* is the best book I've read on this tradeoff.

References

Abbott, Andrew. 1988. *The System of Professions: An Essay on the Division of Expert Labor.* Chicago: University of Chicago Press.

Adler, Peter, and Patricia Adler. 1991. *Backboards and Blackboards.* New York: Columbia University Press.

Agre, Phillip E., and Marc Rotenberg. 2001. *Technology and Privacy: The New Landscape.* Cambridge, MA: MIT Press.

Ahde, Petra. 2009. "Multigenerational Possessing: Pieces of Jewelry Mediating Generations." Paper presented at 40 IADE 40 conference, October 2. Lisbon, Portugal.

Alderman, Ellen, and Caroline Kennedy. 1997. *The Right to Privacy.* New York: Vintage Books.

Alexander, Christopher, Sara Ishikawa, and Murray Silverstein. 1977. *A Pattern Language: Towns, Buildings, Construction.* Oxford: Oxford University Press.

Allen, Anita. 1988. *Uneasy Access.* Lanham, MD: Rowman & Littlefield.

Altheide, David L. 2002. *Creating Fear: News and the Construction of Crisis.* New York: Aldine de Gruyter.

Altman, Irwin. 1975. *The Environment and Social Behavior: Privacy, Personal Space, Territory, Crowding.* Belmont, CA: Wadsworth.

Anderson, Elijah. 1992. *Streetwise: Race, Class, and Change in an Urban Community.* Chicago: University of Chicago Press.

Bachelard, Gaston. 1994 [1964]. *The Poetics of Space: The Classic Look at How We Experience Intimate Places.* Boston: Beacon Press.

Balliett, Blue. 2004. *Chasing Vermeer.* New York: Scholastic Press.

Bateson, Gregory. 2000 [1955]. *Steps to an Ecology of Mind.* New York: Ballantine.

Bateson, Mary Catherine. 1989. *Composing a Life.* New York: Atlantic Monthly Press.

Bearman, Peter. 2005. *Doormen*. Chicago: University of Chicago Press.

Beck, Ulrich. 1992. *Risk Society: Towards a New Modernity*. London: Sage Publications.

Bell, G., and P. Dourish. 2007. "Back to the Shed: Gendered Visions of Technology and Domesticity." *Personal and Ubiquitous Computing* 11(5): 373–81.

Bell, Genevieve. 2005. "The Age of the Thumb: A Cultural Reading of Mobile Technologies from Asia." In *Thumb Culture: Social Trends and Mobile Phone Use*, ed. Peter Glotz, Stefan Bertschi, and Chris Locke, 67–88. Bielefeld, Germany: Verlag.

Bell, Michael. 1995 [1994]. *Childerley: Nature and Morality in a Country Village*. Chicago: University of Chicago Press.

Berger, Peter L., and Thomas Luckmann. 1968. *The Social Construction of Reality*. Garden City, NY: Anchor Press.

Bethke Elshtain, Jean. 1981. *Public Man, Private Woman: Women in Social and Political Thought*. Princeton: Princeton University Press.

Boden, D., and H. Molotch. 1994. "The Compulsion of Proximity." In *NowHere: Space, Time and Modernity*, ed. R. Friedland and D. Boden, 257–86. Berkeley: University of California Press.

Bok, Sissela. 1982. *Secrets: On the Ethics of Concealment and Revelation*. New York: Pantheon.

Bowker, Geoffrey C., and Susan Leigh Star. 2000. *Sorting Things Out: Classification and Its Consequences*. Cambridge, MA: MIT Press.

Braudy, Leo. 1997. *The Frenzy of Renown: Fame and Its History*. New York: Vintage Books.

Brekhus, Wayne. 1996. "Social Marking and the Mental Coloring of Identity: Sexual Identity Construction and Maintenance in the United States." *Sociological Forum* 11 (3): 497–522.

———. 2003. *Peacocks, Chameleons, Centaurs: Gay Suburbia and the Grammar of Social Identity*. Chicago: University of Chicago Press.

Brin, David. 1998. *The Transparent Society: Will Technology Force Us to Choose between Privacy and Freedom?* Reading, MA: Perseus Books.

Brittin, Alexander J., and Dennis Melamed, eds. 2001. *The HIPPA Handbook: What Your Organization Should Know about the Federal Privacy Standards*. Washington, DC: URAC/ American Accreditation HealthCare Commission.

Cate, Fred H. 1997. *Privacy in the Information Age*. Washington, DC: Brookings Institution Press.

Cavoukian, Ann, and Tyler J. Hamilton. 2002. *The Privacy Payoff: How Successful Businesses Build Customer Trust*. Whitby, Canada: McGraw Hill-Ryerson.

Cerulo, Karen. 2006. *Never Saw It Coming: Cultural Challenges to Envisioning the Worst*. Chicago: University of Chicago Press.

Charrett, Sheldon. 1997. *The Modern Identity Changer: How to Create a New Identity for Privacy and Personal Freedom*. Boulder: Paladin Press.

Chartier, Roger, ed. 1989. *A History of Private Life: Passions of the Renaissance*. Cambridge, MA: Belknap Press of Harvard University Press.

Chayko, Mary. 2002. *Connecting: How We Form Social Bonds and Communities in the Internet Age*. New York: State University of New York Press.

———. 2008. *Portable Communities: The Social Dynamics of Online and Mobile Connectedness*. Albany: SUNY Press.

Chesbro, Michael E. 1999. *Privacy for Sale: How Big Brother and Others Are Selling Your Private Secrets for Profit*. Boulder: Paladin Press.

Coser, Rose. 1991. *In Defense of Modernity: Complexity of Social Roles and Individual Autonomy.* Stanford: Stanford University Press.

Couch, Carl J. 1996. *Information Technologies and Social Orders.* New York: Aldine de Gruyter.

Crabb, Peter B. 1999. "The Use of Answering Machines and Caller ID to Regulate Home Privacy." *Environment and Behavior* 31 (5) (September): 657–70.

Csikszentmihalyi, Mihaly, and Eugene Rochberg-Halton. 1981. *The Meaning of Things: Domestic Symbols and the Self.* Cambridge: Cambridge University Press.

Degan, Monica, and Kevin Hetherington, eds. 2001. "Spatial Hauntings." In *Space and Culture,* 11–12. London: Sage Publications.

Derber, Charles. 1979. *The Pursuit of Attention: Power and Individualism in Everyday Life.* Boston: G. K. Hall and Company.

Duby, Georges, ed. 1988. *A History of Private Life: Revelations of the Medieval World.* Cambridge, MA: Belknap Press of Harvard University Press.

Duff, Christina. 1998. "Pick Up on This: Just Don't Answer, Let Freedom Ring." *Wall Street Journal,* January 14.

Duneier, Mitchell. 1994. *Slim's Table: Race, Respectability, and Masculinity.* Chicago: University of Chicago Press.

———. 1999. *Sidewalk.* New York: Farrar, Straus and Giroux.

Etzioni, Amitai. 1999. *The Limits of Privacy.* New York: Basic Books.

Fine, Gary Alan. 1987. *With the Boys: Little League Baseball and Preadolescent Culture.* Chicago: University of Chicago Press.

———. 2001. *Difficult Reputations: Collective Memories of the Evil, Inept, and Controversial.* Chicago: University of Chicago Press.

Fine, Gary Alan, and Lori Holyfield. 1996. "Secrecy, Trust, and Dangerous Leisure: Generating Group Cohesion in Voluntary Organizations." *Social Psychology Quarterly* 59:22–38.

Fischer, Claude S. 1981. "The Public and Private Worlds of City Life." *American Sociological Review* 46 (3) (June): 306–16.

———. 1992. *America Calling: A Social History of the Telephone to 1940.* Berkeley: University of California Press.

Fleck, Ludwig. 1982 [1935]. *Genesis and Development of a Scientific Fact.* Chicago: University of Chicago Press.

Foucault, Michel. 1990 [1976]. *The History of Sexuality: An Introduction.* Vintage Books: New York.

———. 1995 [1975]. *Discipline and Punish.* 2nd ed. Vintage Books: New York.

Gagnon, John H. 1971. "Physical Strength, Once of Significance." *Impact of Science on Society* 21:31–42.

Gallagher, Winifred. 1994 [1993]. *The Power of Place: How Our Surroundings Shape Our Thoughts, Emotions, and Actions.* New York: HarperPerennial.

Gamson, Joshua. 1994. *Claims to Fame: Celebrity in Contemporary America.* Berkeley: University of California Press.

———. 1998. *Freaks Talk Back: Tabloid Talk Shows and Sexual Nonconformity.* Chicago: University of Chicago Press.

Gans, Herbert J. 1982. *Urban Villagers: Group and Class in the Life of Italian-Americans.* New York: Free Press.

Garfinkel, Simson. 2000. *Database Nation: The Death of Privacy in the 21st Century.* Sebastopol, CA: O'Reilly & Associates, Inc.

Gergen, Kenneth J. 1991. *The Saturated Self*. New York: Basic Books.

———. 2002. "The Challenge of Absent Presence." In *Perpetual Contact: Mobile Communication, Private Talk, Public Performance*, ed. J. Katz and M. Aakhus, 227–41. New York: Cambridge University Press.

Germain, Brian. 2005. *Transcending Fear: Relax, Focus and Flow*. Ashland, OH: Atlas Books.

Giddens, Anthony. 1984. *The Constitution of Society*. Berkeley: University of California Press.

———. 1990. *The Consequences of Modernity*. Stanford: Stanford University Press.

———. 1991. *Modernity and Self-Identity*. Stanford: Stanford University Press.

Gilliom, John. 2001. *Overseers of the Poor: Surveillance, Resistance, and the Limits of Privacy*. Chicago: The University of Chicago Press.

Gladwell, Malcolm. 2005. *Blink: The Power of Thinking without Thinking*. New York: Little, Brown and Co.

Glaser, Barney G., and Anselm L. Strauss. 1964. "Awareness Contexts and Social Interaction." *American Sociological Review* 29 (5) (October): 669–79.

Glassner, Barry. *The Culture of Fear*. 1999. New York: Basic Books.

Goffman, Erving. 1959. *The Presentation of Self in Everyday Life*. Garden City, NY: Doubleday Anchor Books.

———. 1966 [1963]. *Behavior in Public Places: Notes on the Social Organization of Gatherings*. New York: Free Press.

———. 1974. *Frame Analysis: An Essay on the Organization of Experience*. Cambridge, MA: Harvard University Press.

———. 1982 [1967]. *Interaction Ritual: Essays on Face-to-Face Behavior*. New York: Pantheon Books.

———. 1986 [1963]. *Stigma: Notes on the Management of Spoiled Identity*. New York: Touchstone.

Grindstaff, Laura. 2002. *The Money Shot: Trash, Class, and the Making of TV Talk Shows*. Chicago: University of Chicago Press.

Gross, Benjamin M. 2004. "Multiple Email Addresses: A Socio-Technical Investigation." Ph.D. diss. proposal, University of Illinois at Urbana-Champaign, Department of Information Sciences.

Hall, Edward T. 1966. *The Hidden Dimension*. New York: Anchor Books.

Henson, Kevin. 1996. *Just a Temp*. Philadelphia: Temple University Press.

Hermanowicz, Joseph. 2008. "The Punishment of the Adept." Paper presented at the annual meeting of the American Sociological Association, Boston.

Hiss, Tony. 1991 [1990]. *The Experience of Place*. New York: Vintage Books.

Hochschild, Arlie Russell. 1983. *The Managed Heart*. Berkeley: University of California Press.

Holiner, Richard. 1987. *Antique Purses: A History, Identification, and Value Guide*. Paducah, KY: Collector Books.

Holm, Bill. 2001. *Eccentric Islands: Travels Real and Imaginary*. Minneapolis, MN: Milkweed Editions.

Honigmann, John Joseph. 1973 [c. 1970]. "Sampling in Ethnographic Fieldwork." In *A Handbook of Method in Cultural Anthropology*, ed. Raoul Naroll and Ronald Cohen. New York: Columbia University Press.

Hunter, Albert. 1982. *Symbolic Communities: The Persistence and Change of Chicago's Local Communities*. Chicago: University of Chicago Press.

Hunter, Richard. 2002. *World without Secrets: Business, Crime, and Privacy in the Age of Ubiquitous Computing*. New York: John Wiley & Sons, Inc.

Jackall, Robert, and Janice Hirota. 2000. *Image Makers: Advertising, Public Relations, and the Ethos of Advocacy*. Chicago: University of Chicago Press.

Jacobs, Jane. 1992 [1961]. *The Death and Life of Great American Cities*. New York: Vintage Books.

Jasper, James M. 2000. *Restless Nation: Starting Over in America*. Chicago: University of Chicago Press.

Jillson, Joyce. 1984. *The Fine Art of Flirting*. New York: Simon & Shuster.

Johnson, Anna. 2002. *Handbags: The Power of the Purse*. New York: Workman Publishing.

Kassanoff, Bruce. 2001. *Making It Personal: How to Profit from Personalization without Invading Privacy*. Cambridge, MA: Perseus Publishing.

Katz, Jack. 2001. *How Emotions Work*. Chicago: University of Chicago Press.

Katz, James E., and Mark Aakhus, eds. 2002. *Perpetual Contact: Mobile Communication, Private Talk, Public Performance*. Cambridge: Cambridge University Press.

Keegan, John. 2003. *Intelligence in War: Knowledge of the Enemy from Napoleon to Al-Qaeda*. London: Hutchinson.

Kimmel, Michael. 2005. *Manhood in America: A Cultural History*. 2nd ed. New York: Oxford University Press.

Klinenberg, Eric. 2002. *Heat Wave: A Social Autopsy of Disaster in Chicago*. Chicago: University of Chicago Press.

Lally, Elaine. 2002. *At Home with Computers*. Oxford: Berg Publishers.

Lane, Belden C. 1998. *The Solace of Fierce Landscapes: Exploring the Desert and Mountain Spirituality*. New York: Oxford University Press.

Lane, Frederick S. 2003. *The Naked Employee: How Technology Is Compromising Workplace Privacy*. New York: AMACOM.

Lasch, Christopher. 1979. *Culture of Narcissism: American Life in an Age of Diminishing Expectations*. New York: W. W. Norton & Company.

Latour, Bruno, and Steve Woolgar. 1986. *Laboratory Life: The Construction of Scientific Facts*. Princeton: Princeton University Press.

Levine, Donald. N., ed. 1971. *Georg Simmel on Individuality and Social Forms*. Chicago: University of Chicago Press.

Levine, John R., Ray Everett-Church, and Gregg Stebben. 2002. *Internet Privacy for Dummies*. Indianapolis: Wiley Publishing.

Ling, Richard. 2000. "We Will Be Reached: The Use of Mobile Telephony among Norwegian Youth." *Information Technology and People* 13 (2): 102–20.

Lofland, Lyn H. 1985 [1973]. *A World of Strangers: Order and Action in Urban Public Space*. Long Grove, IL: Waveland Press.

———. 1998. *The Public Realm: Exploring the City's Quintessential Social Territory*. New York: Aldine De Gruyter.

Lukes, Steven. 1988 [1974]. *Power: A Radical View*. London: MacMillan Education Ltd.

Luna, J. J. 2000. *How to Be Invisible: A Step-by-Step Guide to Protecting Your Assets, Your Identity, and Your Life*. New York: St. Martin's Press.

Lyng, Steven, and David Franks. 2002. *Sociology and the Real World*. New York: Rowman & Littlefield.

Lyon, David. 1994. *The Electronic Eye: The Rise in Surveillance Society*. Minneapolis: University of Minnesota Press.

———. 2001. *Surveillance Society: Monitoring Everyday Life*. Philadelphia: Open University Press.

Margulis, Stephen T. 1977. "Conceptions of Privacy: Current Status and Next Steps." *Journal of Social Issues* 33 (3): 5–21.

———. 2003. "Privacy as a Social Issue and Behavioral Concept." In *Contemporary Perspectives on Privacy: Social, Psychological, Political*, ed. Steven T. Margulis. *Journal of Social Issues* 59 (2): 243–61.

Marx, Gary T. 1988. *Under Cover: Police Surveillance in America*. Berkeley: University of California Press.

———. 2002. "Technology and Gender: Thomas I. Voire and the Case of the Peeping Tom." *Sociological Quarterly* 43 (3): 407–33.

McKeown, Kevin and David Stern. 1999. *Your Secrets Are My Business: A Security Expert Reveals How Your Trash, License Plate, Credit Cards, Computer, and Even Your Mail Make You an Easy Target for Today's Information Thieves*. New York: Plume.

McLellan, David, ed. 1977. *Karl Marx: Selected Writings*. London: Oxford University Press.

McLuhan, Marshall. 1965. *Understanding Media: The Extensions of Man*. New York: McGraw-Hill.

Meiksins, Peter, and Peter Whalley. 2002. *Putting Work in Its Place: A Quiet Revolution*. Ithaca: ILR Press.

Meyrowitz, Joshua. 1985. *No Sense of Place: The Impact of Electronic Media on Social Behavior*. New York: Oxford University Press.

Milgram, Stanley. 1970. "The Experience of Living in Cities." *Science* 167 (3924): 1461–68.

Monmonier, Mark. 2002. *Spying with Maps: Surveillance Technologies and the Future of Privacy*. Chicago: University of Chicago Press.

Morrill, Calvin. 1995. *The Executive Way: Conflict Management in Corporations*. Chicago: University of Chicago Press.

Morrill, Calvin, David A. Snow, and Cindy White, eds. 2005. *Together Alone: Personal Relationships in Public Places*. Berkeley: University of California Press.

Nathan, Rebekah. 2005. *My Freshman Year*. Ithaca: Cornell University Press.

Nelson, Deborah. 2002. *Pursuing Privacy in Cold War America*. New York: Columbia University Press.

Newman, John Q. 1999. *Identity Theft: The Cybercrime of the Millennium*. Port Townsend, WA: Loompanics Unlimited.

Newman, Katherine. 1988. *Falling from Grace: Downward Mobility in the Age of Affluence*. New York: Basic Books.

Nippert-Eng, Christena. 1992. "Identity Kits: A View of Your Self from Your Wallet or Purse." Paper presented at the annual meeting of the Society for the Study of Symbolic Interaction, Pittsburgh.

———. 1993. "'Mommy, Mommy' or 'Excuse Me, Ma'am': Gender and Interruptions at Home and Work." Paper presented at the annual meeting of the American Sociological Association, Pittsburgh.

———. 1996. *Home and Work: Negotiating Boundaries through Everyday Life*. Chicago: University of Chicago Press.

———. 2004. "Disclosure and Concealment: Wallets, Purses, and Modern Identity Work." With Jay Melican. Paper presented at the annual meeting of the American Sociological Association, San Francisco.

———. 2005a. "Boundary Play." *Space and Culture* 8 (3): 302–24.

———. 2005b. "Usable Privacy." Paper presented at the Usable Privacy conference, Intel Corporation.

———. 2007. "Privacy in the United States: Some Implications for Design." *International Journal of Design* 1(2): 1–10. http://www.ijdesign.org/ojs/index.php/IJDesign/article/view/67/30.

———. 2009a. "Gender and Privacy: A Hidden Effect of 'Good' Mothering on Social Status." Unpublished paper.

———. 2009b. "Parenting and Privacy: The Balancing Act." Unpublished paper.

———. 2009c. "Privacy: The Lessons of Childhood." Unpublished paper.

Nippert-Eng, Christena, Meghan Carlock, Nicholas Nimchuk, Jay Melican, Nalini Kotamraju, and James C. Witte. 2005. "Privacy and Technology: Newspaper Coverage from 1985 to 2003." Paper presented at the annual meeting of the American Sociological Association, Philadelphia.

Nippert-Eng, Christena, Jay Melican, Rachel Hinman, and Ryan Pikkel. 2005. "Social Accessibility and ICTs: New challenges to an Old Problem." Paper presented at the annual meeting of the American Sociological Association, Philadelphia.

Nock, Steven L. 1993. *The Costs of Privacy: Surveillance and Reputation in America.* Hawthorne, NY: Aldine de Gruyter.

O'Brien, Tim. 1998. *The Things They Carried.* New York: Broadway Books.

Oldenburg, Ray. 1989. *The Great Good Place: Cafes, Coffee Shops, Bookstores, Bars, Hair Salons and Other Hangouts at the Heart of the Community.* New York: Marlowe & Company.

———. 2001. *Celebrating the Third Place: Inspiring Stories about the "Great Good Places" at the Heart of Our Communities.* New York: Marlow & Company.

Olson, Judith S., Jonathan Grudin and Eric Horvitz. 2004. "A Study of Preferences for Sharing and Privacy." Proceedings of the 2005 Conference on Human Factors in Computing Systems, 1985–88. New York: Association for Computing Machinery.

Orwell, George. 1977. *1984.* New York: Harcourt Brace.

Palen, Leysia, and Paul Dourish. 2003. "Privacy and Trust: Unpacking 'Privacy' for a Networked World." Proceedings of the Conference on Human Factors in Computing Systems. New York: Association for Computing Machinery.

Patillo-McCoy, Mary. 1999. *Black Picket Fences: Privilege and Peril among Black Middle Class.* Chicago: University of Chicago Press.

Perlow, Leslie. 1997. *Finding Time.* Ithaca: Cornell University Press.

Perroy, Michelle, ed. 1990. *A History of Private Life: From the Fires of Revolution to the Great War.* Cambridge, MA: Belknap Press of Harvard University Press.

Pink, Daniel H. 2002. *Free Agent Nation.* New York: Warner Books.

Prosy, Antoine, and Gerard Vincent, eds. 1991. *A History of Private Life: Riddles of Identity in Modern Times.* Cambridge, MA: Belknap Press of Harvard University Press.

Rabin, Susan. 1993. *How to Attract Anyone, Anytime, Anyplace: The Smart Guide to Flirting.* New York: Plume.

Richardson, Laurel. 1988. "Secrecy and Status: The Social Construction of Forbidden Relationships." *American Sociological Review* 53 (2): 209–20.

Riley, Terence. 2002. *The Un-Private House.* New York: Museum of Modern Art.

Rosen, Jeffrey. 2000. *The Unwanted Gaze: The Destruction of Privacy in America.* New York: Vintage Books.

Rule, James. 1973. *Private Lives and Public Surveillance.* London: Allen Lane.

Ryan, Dan. 2006. "Getting the Word Out: Notes on the Social Organization of Notification." *Sociological Theory* 24 (3).

Rybczynski, Witold. 1993 [1992]. *Looking Around: A Journey through Architecture.* New York: Penguin Books.

Schama, Simon. 1996 [1995]. *Landscape and Memory.* New York: Knopf.

Schrage, Michael. 1997. "The Relationship Revolution." *Merrill Lynch Forum.* http://web .archive.org/web/20030602025739/http://www.ml.com/woml/forum/relation.htm.

Schutz, Alfred. 1973. "On Multiple Realities." In *Collected Papers*, 1:207–59. 4th ed. The Hague: Martinus Nijhoff.

Schutz, Alfred, and Thomas Luckmann 1973. *The Structures of the Life World.* Evanston: Northwestern University Press.

Schwartz, Barry. 1968. "The Social Psychology of Privacy." *American Journal of Sociology* 73 (6): 741–52.

———. 1975. *Queuing and Waiting.* Chicago: University of Chicago Press.

———. 1987. *George Washington: The Making of an American Symbol.* New York: Free Press.

Scott, Marvin B., and Stanford Lyman. 1968. "Accounts." *American Sociological Review* 33 (1): 46–62.

Sedgewick, Eve Kosofsky. 1990. *Epistemology of the Closet.* Berkeley: University of California Press.

Sennett, Richard. 1992 [1974]. *The Fall of Public Man.* New York: W. W. Norton & Company.

———. 1998. *The Corrosion of Character: The Personal Consequences of Work in the New Capitalism.* New York: W. W. Norton & Company.

Shapiro, Susan P. 1987. "The Social Control of Impersonal Trust." *American Journal of Sociology* 93 (3) (November): 623–58.

Shields, Rob. 2003. *The Virtual.* London: Routledge.

Shils, Edward A. 1996 [1956]. *The Torment of Secrecy.* Chicago: Ivan R. Dee, Inc.

Simmel, Georg. 1950a [1902]. "The Metropolis and Mental Life." Trans. Kurt Wolff. In *The Sociology of Georg Simmel*, 409–24. New York: Free Press.

———. 1950b [1902]. "Secrecy." Trans. Kurt Wolff. In *The Sociology of Georg Simmel*, 330–44. New York: Free Press, 1950.

———. 1955. "The Web of Group-Affiliations." Trans. Reinhard Bendix. In *Conflict and the Web of Group-Affiliations.* New York: Free Press.

———. 1990. *The Philosophy of Money.* Ed. David Frisby. Trans. Tom Bottomore and David Frisby. 3rd ed. New York: Routledge.

———. 1997 [1909]. "Bridge and Door." In *Simmel on Culture: Selected Writings*, ed. David Frisby and Mike Featherstone, 170–73.

Smith, Robert Ellis. 2000. *Ben Franklin's Website: Privacy and Curiosity from Plymouth Rock to the Internet.* Providence: Privacy Journal.

Snow, David A., and Leon Anderson. 1987. "Identity Work among the Homeless: The Verbal Construction and Avowal of Personal Identities." *American Journal of Sociology* 92 (6): 1336–71.

Spillman, Lynette. 1998. "When Do Collective Memories Last? Founding Moments in the United States and Australia." *Social Science History* 22:445–77.

Staples, William G. 1997. *The Culture of Surveillance: Discipline and Social Control in the United States.* New York: St. Martin's Press.

Swidler, Ann 2003. *Talk of Love: How Culture Matters.* Chicago: University of Chicago Press.

Sykes, Charles J. 1999. *The End of Privacy: Personal Rights in the Surveillance Society.* New York: St. Martin's Press.

Tuan, Yi-Fu. 1982 [1966]. *Segmented Worlds and Self*. Minneapolis: University of Minnesota Press.

———. 1997 [1977]. *Space and Place: The Perspective of Experience*. Minneapolis: University of Minnesota Press.

Urry, John. 1998 [1990]. *The Tourist Gaze: Leisure and Travel in Contemporary Societies*. London: Sage Publications.

Van Maanen, John. 1980. "Beyond Account: The Personal Impact of Police Shootings." *Annals of the American Academy of Political and Social Science* 451 (3): 145–56.

Vaughan, Diane. 1990 [1986]. *Uncoupling: Turning Points in Intimate Relationships*. New York: Vintage Books.

———. 1996. *The Challenger Launch Decision: Risky Technology, Culture, and Deviance at NASA*. Chicago: The University of Chicago Press.

Veblen, Thorsten. 1994 [1899]. *The Theory of the Leisure Class*. New York: Penguin.

Venkatesh, Sudhir. 2002. *American Project: The Rise and Fall of a Modern Ghetto*. Cambridge, MA: Harvard University Press.

Veyne, Paul, ed. 1987. *A History of Private Life: From Pagan Rome to Byzantium*. Cambridge, MA: Belknap Press of Harvard University Press.

Vinitzky-Seroussi, Vered. 1998. *After Pomp and Circumstance: High School Reunion as an Autobiographical Occasion*. Chicago: University of Chicago Press.

Vinitzky-Seroussi, Vered, and Eyal Ben Ari. 2000. "A Knock on the Door: Managing Death in the Israeli Defense Forces." *Sociological Quarterly* 41 (3): 391–411.

Warren, C., and B. Laslett. 1977. "Privacy and Secrecy: A Conceptual Comparison." *Journal of Social Issues* 33 (3): 43–51.

Warren, Samuel D., and Louis D. Brandeis. 1890. "The Right to Privacy." *Harvard Law Review* 4 (5).

Weintraub, Jeff, and Krishan Kumer. 1997. *Public and Private in Thought and Practice*. Chicago: University of Chicago Press.

Wellman, Barry. 2001. "The Persistence and Transformation of Community: From Neighbourhood Groups to Social Networks." *Report to the Law Commission of Canada* (October 30). http://www.chass.utoronto.ca/~wellman/publications/index.html.

West, C., and D. Zimmerman. 1987. "Doing Gender." *Gender and Society* 1:125–51.

Westin, Alan F. 1967. *Privacy and Freedom*. New York: Atheneum.

Whitaker, Reg. 1999. *The End of Privacy: How Total Surveillance Is Becoming Reality*. New York: New Press.

Whyte, William Foote. 1993 [1943]. *Street Corner Society: The Social Structure of an Italian Slum*. Chicago: University of Chicago Press.

Wilson, Cintra. 2000. *A Massive Swelling: Celebrity Reexamined as a Grotesque, Crippling Disease and Other Cultural Revelations*. New York: Viking.

Wirth, Louis. 1938. "Urbanism as a Way of Life." *American Journal of Sociology* 44 (1) (July): 1–24.

Woolf, Virginia. 1929. *A Room of One's Own*. New York: Harcourt, Brace and Jovanovich.

Zelizer, Viviana. 1995 [1994]. *The Social Meaning of Money*. New York: Basic Books.

Zerubavel, Eviatar. 1979a. *Patterns of Time in Hospital Life*. Chicago: University of Chicago Press.

———. 1979b. "Private Time and Public Time: The Temporal Structure of Social Accessibility and Professional Commitments." *Social Forces* 58 (1) (September): 38–58.

———. 1982. "Personal Information and Social Life." *Symbolic Interaction* 5 (1982): 97–109.

———. 1985 [1981]. *Hidden Rhythms: Schedules and Calendars in Social Life*. Berkeley: University of California Press.

———. 1987. "The Language of Time: Toward a Semiotics of Temporality." *Sociological Quarterly* 28 (1987): 343–56.

———. 1993. *The Fine Line: Making Distinctions in Everyday Life*. Chicago: University of Chicago Press.

———. 1996. "Lumping and Splitting: Notes on Social Classification." *Sociological Forum* 11 (3) (September): 421–33.

———. 2006. *The Elephant in the Room: The Social Organization of Silence and Denial*. London: Oxford University Press.

Zussman, Robert. 1996. "Autobiographical Occasions." *Contemporary Sociology* 25 (2) (March): 143–48.

Index

Page references followed by f or t refer to figures and tables, respectively.

Braudy, Leo, 378n1

Brekhus, Wayne, 359n8, 367nn14–15

Brin, David, 368n24

Brokeback Mountain, 41–42

business card(s), 104–5, 108, 110–11, 127, 133, 154–55, 183, 242; private-public hybrid nature of, 130–31, 139–41; symbolic meaning of, 140–41. *See also* objects; objects, classification of

caller ID. *See* telephone(s); telephone(s), cell(ullar)

Cate, Fred H., 368n24

Catch Me If You Can, 367n20

cats, 284–85, 308, 347 (appendix B)

Cavoukian, Ann, 298

Celebration, The, 361–62n21, 363n31

Celebrity, 357n3

cell phones. *See* telephone(s); telephone(s), cell(ullar)

Cerulo, Karen, 312, 316

Charrett, Sheldon, 368n22

Chayko, Mary, xi, 146, 169, 177, 358n3, 372–73n37, 377n30

Chesbro, Michael E., 298

children: abuse of, 23, 32–33, 72–74, 115t, 273, 352, 363n28, 363n31; affect on private-public boundary, 223, 259; awareness of boundaries, 13, 32–33, 44–45, 218, 257, 259–61, 349, 351; at the beach, 13, 357–58n6, 358n8; boundary concerns on behalf of, 6, 13–14, 23, 44–45, 72–74, 83, 140, 227, 249, 244; as boundary management assistants, 174, 184, 202; bullying of, 170; neighborhood, 73, 215, 223, 249, 254–55, 257–58, 265–66, 352, 373nn5–6; phone answering and, 171, 184, 202; photos of, 125, 149, 154t, 350; purses and, 97, 369; secrets and, 22, 27, 30, 32–33, 36–37, 38–39t, 44–45, 48, 65, 83, 85, 97, 227, 350, 359n9, 363n28; sidewalk life and, 258. *See also* privacy; privacy, fears; privacy, places associated with; privacy, types of; privacy, violations

class (social), 2, 16, 18, 366n12, 376–77n28, 378n36

classification, 108–9, 116–18, 128, 131, 251, 253, 270, 323, 365n4. *See also* beaches; boundary(ies)(categorical/classificatory);

business card(s); credit cards; government; information; "islands of privacy" metaphor; mail; money; neighborhoods; neighbors; objects; objects, classification of: hybrid (public/private); parking (street); private; privacy; privacy, fears; privacy, places associated with; privacy, types of; privacy, violations; public; publicity; scenarios; trash; wallets and purses; wallets and purses, contents; yards

Contender, The, 357n4

Conversation, The, 360n13

corporations, 3, 6, 145–56, 298–301, 316, 321–22, 374n12, 379n5

Coser, Rose, 155

Couch, Carl J., 168, 372n37

Crabb, Peter B., 371n20

credit cards: fears concerning, 119, 124, 137–38; financial reputations and, 121–24, 136–38, 367n18; identity theft and, 121–24, 137; private-public hybrid nature of, 100, 102–3t, 108, 110, 113t, 117, 119, 124, 130, 136–38, 242; symbolic meanings of, 131, 138, 145

Csikszentmihalyi, Mihaly, 147, 149

culture: anonymity and, 368n22; boundary-beaches of, 325; material, 142, 152, 157; organizational, 312; privacy and, 4, 6, 17, 301, 323–25; publicity and, 147, 378n1; of secrecy, 67, 362n22

customer loyalty cards and, 148, 304, 321, 356 (appendix B), 368nn21–22

databases, 190, 300, 314, 349, 355; poisoning, 304

Degan, Monica, 378n32

Derber, Charles, 164, 169, 378n1

dogs: consequences of walking, 253–55, 263, 270; door-answering with, 217–18; as "familiar strangers," 254, 257; neighborhood interactions and, 210, 253–55, 270–71; and other pets, 256–57, 283; pretending to have, 257; as privacy managers, 213, 257; security and, 219, 257; visibility of, 73, 251, 253–57, 270–71

door-answering behaviors, 209, 213–23, 270; changes in, 219–20; cultural expectations regarding, 214, 218–23; dogs door-answering behaviors (*cont.*)

and, 217–19, 257; fears associated with, 219, 257; front vs. backdoors, 214, 222–23, 280; goals of, 214; on Halloween, 217–19, 258, 373–74nn5–7; Jehovah's Witnesses and, 23, 62, 220–22, 374n8; screening and, 214–16, 373n4; similar to answering the phone, 214, 221, 223; systems surrounding, 215–17, 223, 373n5, 374n9

Dourish, Paul, xi, 368n25, 371n23, 373n1

driver's licenses, 5, 100, 101t, 111, 115–16, 119, 124, 127, 144–45, 149, 153t, 154t, 347, 352, 365n2

Duff, Christina, 371n17, 371n20

Duneier, Mitchell, xi, 365n1, 375n15, 376n28

email: filtering of, 180, 184, 188, 192, 195–96, 198–99, 371n26, 372; identity and, 146, 317; management through multiple addresses, 173–74, 177, 184, 188, 195–96, 356, 371n21; monitoring others', 75; as part of a sociotechnical system, 177, 178t, 181–84, 187–89, 195–96, 209, 306, 308, 367; as a preferred channel, 182–84, 199–200; resistance to, 189–90, 192, 197, 351, 371n26; rules for checking, 179–81, 184; spam, 172–73, 180, 184, 192, 195–96, 198, 207, 315, 372n31; specific uses of, 200, 308, 346, 353, 356

Etzioni, Amitai, 7, 321, 380n11

Everett-Church, Ray, 368n24

Facebook, 170, 321, 372n28

filtering/screening behaviors: at the door, 214–16, 222–23, 373n4; logic of, 169, 180–81, 184, 185f, 192, 198, 204–5, 214, 370n20; email and, 180, 184, 188, 192, 195–96, 198–99, 371n26, 372n31; policies about, 180–81, 192–93, 196, 200, 203, 214, 216–17, 245; priorities guiding, 196, 202–3, 214, 373n4; resistance to, 193, 202–3; telephones and, 172, 182–85, 187, 192–94, 196, 198, 200, 202–3, 214, 223, 370n20; worries about, 193–94, 214. *See also* email; technology(ies); technology(ies), information and communication (ICTs); technology(ies), information and communication (ICTs), channels/

channeling among; telephone(s); telephone(s), cell(ullar)

Fine, Gary Alan, xi, 143, 360–61nn14–15, 361n19, 369n34

Fischer, Claude S., 168, 372–73nn35–37

flashing, 166, 204, 295, 370n11

Fleck, Ludwig, 369n34

Foucault, Michel, 165

framing/frame analysis: "breaking frame," 290; "in frame," 290, 295, 297, 316; mismatch, 289–90, 379n2; of objects, 117, 128, 131; out of frame, 297–98, 316; play and, 88–89; privacy violations and, 289, 290f, 291–93, 295, 379n2. *See also* privacy; privacy, fears; privacy, places associated with; privacy, types of; privacy, violations; publicity

Franks, David, 11, 369n34

Gagnon, John H., 372n37

Gallagher, Winifred, 378n32

Gamson, Joshua, 143, 357n3, 369n34, 378n1

Gans, Herbert J., 376n28

Garfinkel, Simson, 7, 298, 368n24

gender: discrimination, 96; doing, 148, 373n1; identity, 148; trans-, 89–96; work, 148, 324. *See also* interruptions; wallets and purses; wallets and purses, contents

Gergen, Kenneth J., 168, 175–77, 209, 372–73n37, 378n1

Germain, Brian, 316

Giddens, Anthony, 116, 142–43, 155, 318

Gilliom, John, 378n36

Gina and Sarah, 3, 5–7, 9–11

Gladwell, Malcolm, 363n25

Glaser, Barney G., 142, 367n16

Glassner, Barry, 316

Goffman, Erving, 24, 128–29, 141, 160, 162, 204, 289–90, 363n23, 367–68nn19–20, 368n22, 378n34

Google Street View, 374n12

government: Bush (George W.)–Cheney Administration, 17, 70, 298, 301, 316, 360; housing (Section 8), 260, 273, 279, 376n26, 378n35; as intrusive, 3, 212, 291, 298, 301, 316, 360n13, 365n2; public nature of, 115t, 131; and secrecy, 17, 26, 37, 82, 291, 298, 301, 359n6, 362n22, 363n27. *See also* privacy; privacy, fears;

privacy, places associated with; privacy, types of; privacy, violations

GPS/Onstar, 321, 355

Green House Project, 358–59n4

Grindstaff, Laura, 378n1

Gross, Benjamin M., xi, 371n21

Grudin, Jonathan, 371n23

Halloween, 73, 217–19, 258, 373–74nn5–7

Hamilton, Tyler J., 298, 379n5

Henson, Kevin, 369n36

Hermanowicz, Joseph, 33

Hetherington, Kevin, 378n32

Hirota, Janice, 357n3

Hiss, Tony, 378n32

Hochschild, Arlie Russell, 87, 316

Holiner, Richard, 369n29

Holyfield, Lori, 361n15

home. *See* privacy, places associated with

Honigmann, John Joseph, 19

Horvitz, Eric, 371n23

Hunter, Albert, 268–70, 376–77n28

Hunter, Richard, 379n7

identity: accessibility of, 22–23, 175; anonymity, 34, 141, 144–45, 152, 156, 232, 268, 280–81, 368n22; autobiographical objects and occasions and, 127, 147, 149–51, 280, 366n14; centrality of secrets for, 27, 41, 60, 66, 94, 360n13, 363n24; concept of, 23, 152–53, 358n3; continuum, 141; kit(s) (wallets and purses as), 99, 141–42, 150, 152, 154t; modern, 144, 152, 154t, 168; postmodern, 153t, 154–55t, 168, 209; privacy as control over, 22–23, 324, 366n9, 378n33; selective disclosure and concealment of, 22–24, 141, 145–46, 148, 151, 157, 367n16; theft, 23, 25, 112, 120–25, 137, 152, 157, 236, 240–42, 295, 305, 318–19, 322, 367n13; types of items carried to support, 124, 127, 138, 141, 148–52, 153t, 154–55t, 366n9; uses of wallet and purse contents to achieve/support, 120, 124, 127, 136, 145, 147, 151; work, 142, 148, 152–53, 156, 371n24. *See also* credit cards; email; gender; modern/modernity; privacy; privacy, fears; privacy, places associated with; privacy, types of; privacy, violations; private; relationships; secrets

and secrecy; secrets and secrecy, work; self; strangers; trash; wallets and purses; wallets and purses, contents

information: as increasing focus of privacy, 6–7, 117, 236; private nature of, 110–15, 117, 120–26, 131, 134–37, 140, 143, 145–46, 209, 283–85, 299–311, 315–31, 320–22, 359n6, 360n10, 361n15, 362n22, 363n23, 363n28, 365n2, 368n25, 371n23; "too much," 79, 368n23. *See also* money; neighbors; power; privacy; privacy, fears; privacy, places associated with; privacy, types of; privacy, violations; secrets and secrecy; secrets and secrecy, work; sociotechnical system(s); technology(ies); technology(ies), information and communication (ICTs); technology(ies), information and communication (ICTs), channels/channeling among

instant messaging (IM), 177, 182, 187–88, 191

Intel Research Council, xi, 16

interruptions: agendas and, 163, 170, 370n4; attention management and, 163–64, 175–76, 370n7; as demands for attention, 7, 161–63, 175–76, 370nn6–7; gender and, 370n7, 371n16; power and, 163–64, 170, 370n6; status and, 163–64, 370n7, 371n16; waiting and, 163. *See also* attention; power

interviews (for Islands of Privacy study): confidentiality and, 19; description of, ix, x, 2–3, 16–19, 99–100, 162, 372n28; Intel Research Council funding for, xi, 16; nonrepresentative nature of, 18–19, 84; objects and, 99–100, 134, 149, 366n12; participants, 17–19, 18t, 366n12; questionnaire, 19, appendix A; transcription conventions, 358n2

Ishikawa, Sara, 374n9

"islands of privacy" metaphor, 3–6, 10–13, 26, 98, 156, 160, 294, 322–23, 325, 333, 365n2

Jackall, Robert, 357n3

Jacobs, Jane, 258, 368n22, 374n9

Jasper, James M., 368n22

Jehovah's Witnesses, 23, 62, 220–22, 374n8

Jillson, Joyce, 358n7

Johnson, Anna, 369n29

Center), 17, 60, 297–98, 317, 320–21, 360n13, 362n22

Nippert-Eng, Christena, 4, 10, 99, 112–13, 131, 141, 147, 150, 161, 163, 357n2, 359n9, 360n12, 364–65n42, 366n12, 369n28, 371n16, 371n24, 376n27, 379n8

Nock, Steven L., 142–44

objects: private, 98, 108–9, 112, 117, 119, 124, 127–30, 129f, 149, 291, 306–7, 366n9, 369n26, 376n24; public, 110, 117, 127–30, 129f, 137, 147–48, 366n9, 376n24; related to self, 108–9, 112, 116–17, 120, 124–30, 129f, 137, 147–49, 151, 213, 366nn9–10, 367n14; as representations of relationships, 128, 138, 140, 148, 150, 243, 367n17, 369n32; secret, 78, 213, 285. See also framing/frame analysis; identity; interviews (for Islands of Privacy study); self

objects, classification of, 109, 112, 116–18, 128–30, 129f, 365–66nn4–5; hybrid (private-public), 100, 109, 111–12, 116–17, 128–29, 129f; business cards as, 101–4t, 108, 130–31, 139–40; contents of wallets and purses as, 131, 136; credit cards as, 101–2t, 108, 116–17, 130–31, 136–38; homes as, 212–13; mail as, 245, 250, 376n21; money as, 101–3t, 108, 124–25, 130–36, 369n33; streets as, 249, 251, 376n24; trash as, 238, 242–43, 245, 376nn20–21

O'Brien, Tim, 147n27

Oldenburg, Ray, 143n19

Olson, Judith S., 371n23

Orwell, George, 364n34, 364n37

Palen, Leysia, 368n25, 371n23

parking (street): Chicago, 85, 249–51, 376n24; private-public hybrid nature of, 85, 249–51, 376n24; social accessibility and, 251–52

Pattillo-McCoy, Mary, 376n28

Perlow, Leslie, 370n7, 371n16

Pink, Daniel H., 155, 369n36, 371n25

power: accessibility and, 162–65; agenda-setting as, 162–64, 166, 170, 174, 177, 179, 190, 370n4, 370n10; attention and, 163–64, 166–67, 170, 174, 181, 199, 202; boundary-setting and, 7, 10, 163; control

of information and, 51–52, 56; distribution of, 17, 41, 45, 51–52, 162–63, 167, 173, 199, 370nn2–3; group versus individual, 6, 9–10, 170; interruptions and, 163–64, 174, 370nn4–5; privacy and, 7, 9, 51–52, 163, 166–67, 290–91, 294–95, 359n5; relationships and, 51–52, 60, 202; secrets and, 33–34, 41, 45, 51–52, 56, 60, 359n5, 363n26; use of ICTs to regain, 179–81. See also attention; interruptions; secrets and secrecy; secrets and secrecy, work

Primary Colors, 357n4

privacy: achieving, 2, 3, 5–8, 17–19, 22, 24–25, 88, 99, 156–57, 160, 169, 177, 208–9, 261, 270, 282, 284, 297, 322, 324, 359n5, 378n36; acquisition of, as work, 8, 22, 24, 324; active-passive continuum of techniques to achieve, 25; Bush (George W.)–Cheney Administration, 17, 70, 298, 301, 360; classic liberalism and, 6, 298; constraints on, 3, 7, 11, 260–61, 365, 378; control, as central to, 7–8; definition of, 5, 7–8, 22–23, 366; de-/resensitization towards amount of, 233–36; desire for, in balance with publicity, 5, 7, 22; dynamic nature of, 8, 22, 280, 323–24; as an endpoint on an accessibility continuum, 4–5, 141–284; etiquette and, 24–25; gifted nature of, 7–9, 24, 230, 289, 363; "good," 7–8, 281; history of, 6–7, 117, 169; identity and need for, 22–24; as inaccessibility, 6–8, 22, 125, 157, 160, 162, 166, 169, 219–20, 223, 284; individual burden of, 157, 179, 311, 321–22, 364n34; law, 3, 6–7, 11, 26, 56, 58, 60–64, 73, 82, 86, 96, 112, 114, 121–22, 128–29, 132, 142, 147, 211–12, 252, 291–92, 298, 312, 316, 323, 352, 355, 363n28, 375n16, 376n25, 377n29; managerial conception of, 3, 7–8, 11, 22–24, 87, 96, 99, 128, 141–42, 156–57, 160–61, 168–69, 173–74, 176–77, 179–81, 182, 184, 185f, 195–96, 199, 202, 204, 209, 213–14, 223, 238, 243, 257, 281–82, 324, 363–64n32, 367–68n20, 378n34; media and, 16–17, 291, 316; negotiated nature of, 2, 4, 7, 11, 44, 99, 118, 156, 160, 177, 251, 257, 261, 271–72, 281, 323, 325; race and, 268; "right to," 6, 13–14, 22–23, 41–42, 45–47, 49–51, privacy (*cont.*)

67, 73–74, 174, 274, 294, 348, 359n5, 363n26, 363n32, 378n1; security and, 17, 142, 200, 224–26, 257, 269, 303, 307, 319–21, 380n11; signaling desire for, 6, 9–10, 13, 28, 85, 167, 205–6, 218, 223–24, 262, 307, 323, 350; status and, 33, 129, 131, 147, 150, 163–65, 185, 268, 291, 294, 324, 347; surveillance and, 21–31, 80–82, 143–44, 368n24, 378n36; trade-offs, 6, 234, 319–21, 355, 379n5, 380n11. *See also* accessibility; accessibility, social; culture; dogs; framing/frame analysis; identity; information; "islands of privacy" metaphor; neighborhoods; neighbors; power; publicity; relationships; risk; secrets and secrecy; secrets and secrecy, work; selective concealment and disclosure; strangers; technology(ies); technology(ies), information and communication (ICTs); technology(ies), information and communication (ICTs), channels/channeling among; wallets and purses; wallets and purses, contents; windows

privacy, fears, 3, 90, 116, 125, 134, 137, 220, 284–85, 297, 303–5, 310, 312, 313, 316, 317–22; on behalf of children, 72–74, 124–25, 309–10, 322; consumers and, 299–301, 321–22, 379n5; corporations and, 3, 6, 145–46, 298–301, 316, 322, 371n15; decision to act on, 302–3, 305, 309, 311–12, 316, 318–22, 380; definition of, 297–98, 301, 358–59; dimensions of, 298, 313–14; electronic, 299, 301–2, 313–16, 379nn7–9, 368n24; emotion and, 298, 316; fears map, 313–14, 313f, 379n6; frame analysis and, 297–98, 316; "general," 298–301; government and, 298, 301, 316; importance of, 3, 312; learning about, 297, 316–17, 324–25, 360; media and, 16–17, 291, 316; practical consequences of, 298, 305, 318–19; preventive behaviors, 301–3, 305, 316; professionals' vigilance based on, 305–10, 312; resistance to, 304–5, 311–12, 316; scenarios and, 317–18; sources of, 316–18; "specific," 298, 301–22; strangers and, 271, 304–5, 314–15; symbolic con-

sequences of, 298, 305–6, 318–19; types of, 298; value of worst case scenarios about, 312. *See also* accessibility; accessibility, social; culture; dogs; framing/frame analysis; identity; information; "islands of privacy" metaphor; neighborhoods; neighbors; power; publicity; relationships; risk; secrets and secrecy; secrets and secrecy, work; selective concealment and disclosure; strangers; technology(ies); technology(ies), information and communication (ICTs); technology(ies), information and communication (ICTs), channels/channeling among; wallets and purses; wallets and purses, contents; windows

privacy, places associated with: bathrooms, 1, 29, 40, 43, 52–53, 108, 113t, 167, 244, 275, 357n6, 365n1; bedrooms, 1–2, 5, 10, 31–32, 52, 57, 79, 244, 284–85, 324, 354, 375; cars, 115, 119, 121, 132, 165, 186, 207, 213, 225, 227, 234, 246, 250–53, 261, 282, 300, 320–21, 355; cities, 166, 204–5, 219, 228, 232–33, 236, 244, 247, 249, 251, 253, 281, 319–20, 365n3, 368nn22–23, 372nn32–33, 374n8, 375n15; the home, 1–3, 9, 111, 113t, 173–74, 191, 211–17, 221–23, 226–27, 230, 233, 241, 243, 247, 254, 258–61, 270–73, 279, 282–83, 309–10, 360n13, 373nn2–3, 375n16; the home, in public housing, 18, 235, 260, 273, 279, 376n26, 378n35; in public, 2–4, 11, 13, 31 52, 98, 113–14, 115t, 126, 132, 134, 160–61, 165–66, 212, 235, 239, 242–43, 249–51, 268–69, 279, 286, 295, 303, 357n5, 365nn1–3, 370n10, 376n25, 378n34; the shower, 1, 9, 113t, 197, 233, 288–89; the street, 98, 166, 226, 236, 249–51, 268–69, 365n1, 374n12; the United States, 2, 6, 16–18, 60, 76, 82, 148, 185, 212, 218, 221–23, 310, 324, 360n13, 375n37, 376n22; workspace, xi, 175–76, 189, 225–26, 230, 287, 306 (*see also* neighborhoods). *See also* accessibility; accessibility, social; culture; dogs; framing/frame analysis; identity; information; "islands of privacy" metaphor; neighborhoods; neighbors; power; publicity; relationships; risk; secrets and secrecy;

secrets and secrecy, work; selective concealment and disclosure; strangers; technology(ies); technology(ies), information and communication (ICTs); technology(ies), information and communication (ICTs), channels/channeling among; wallets and purses; wallets and purses, contents; windows

privacy, types of: auditory, 13–14, 85, 112, 207, 272–76, 296, 307n10; electronic, 170, 198, 209, 212, 299, 301–2, 313–16, 368n24, 379nn7–9; financial, 23, 104, 108, 113t, 129, 135–38, 144, 238, 242, 246, 301–2, 305; informational, 110–15, 117, 120–26, 131, 134–37, 140, 143, 145–46, 209, 236, 283–85, 299–311, 331–15, 320–22, 359n6, 360n10, 361n15, 362n22, 363n23, 363n28, 365n2, 368n25, 371n23; medical, 44–46, 58, 89–96, 113t, 124, 140, 285–86, 291–92, 295–96, 304, 310–11; olfactory, 13–14, 165, 212, 226; visual, 13–14, 48, 166, 207, 211–13, 222–34, 266, 373n2, 374–75n12. *See also* accessibility; accessibility, social; culture; dogs; framing/frame analysis; identity; information; "islands of privacy" metaphor; neighborhoods; neighbors; power; publicity; relationships; risk; secrets and secrecy; secrets and secrecy, work; selective concealment and disclosure; strangers; technology(ies); technology(ies), information and communication (ICTs); technology(ies), information and communication (ICTs), channels/channeling among; wallets and purses; wallets and purses, contents; windows

privacy, violations, 9, 14, 37, 42, 48, 165, 173, 221, 279, 283–97, 290f, 301, 305–6, 310, 312–14, 313f, 318, 324, 370n9, 378–79nn1–3, 379n10; definition of, 14, 42, 48, 284–85, 289; experiential impact of, 289, 291, 293–95, 297, 379n3, 379n10; frame analysis of, 289, 290f, 291–93, 379n2; Google Street View and, 374n12; along household perimeter, 221, 225–26, 236, 247, 279; information and communication technologies and, 173, 187, 313–15, 368n25; Linda Tripp and, 290–91; list of exam-

ples of, 285–89; as a mismatch in perception versus reality, 289; nature of, 37, 84, 173, 283–84, 289–95, 305–6, 313–14f, 378–79n1, 379n2; practical consequences of, 3; prevention of (*see* privacy, fears); prevention of, professionals' versus lay people's interpretations, 291–93; prevention of, realization of, 285, 289, 291–94, 322, 368n25; recovery from, 295–97, 316; secrets and, 42, 48, 72; self and, 294–95; symbolic consequences of, 165–66, 293–95, 305–6, 309, 318, 370n9, 379n10; tsunami-like, 291; wallets and purses and, 119, 126. *See also* accessibility; accessibility, social; culture; dogs; framing/frame analysis; identity; information; "islands of privacy" metaphor; neighborhoods; neighbors; power; publicity; relationships; risk; secrets and secrecy; secrets and secrecy, work; selective concealment and disclosure; strangers; technology(ies); technology(ies), information and communication (ICTs); technology(ies), information and communication (ICTs), channels/channeling among; wallets and purses; wallets and purses, contents; windows

private: conflict over what is, 4–5, 14–15, 46, 49–51, 162, 175, 188, 190, 213, 240, 251, 323, 370n2, 377n29; culturally specific nature of, 16–17; definition of, 4–5, 109–15, 323; as endpoint on access-based continuum, 4–5, 242; requiring personal protection, 9, 11, 24–25, 109–10, 112, 129–30, 138, 152, 176, 185, 209, 236, 366n9; as requiring social consensus, 9, 10; secret versus, 24, 25; space, 2–3, 7, 9–10, 13–14, 22, 24, 48, 54, 98, 117, 160–61, 167, 170, 173, 179, 186, 190, 209, 212, 221–23, 227, 243, 249–51, 254, 261, 263, 269, 279, 282, 306, 309, 313–14, 324, 357n5, 365n1, 373n1, 377n29; subjects commonly considered, 108–9; things, defined, 2, 4, 24–25, 108–9, 112, 113t, 114–15, 323; time, 2–3, 6–7, 9–11, 22, 27, 98, 160–61, 163–67, 170–73, 175–77, 179–80, 186, 198–200, 209, 214, 220–21, 262, 264, 284, 291, 309, 323–34,

private (*cont.*)
365n1, 370n5, 376n24. *See also* beaches;
boundary(ies) (categorical/classificatory);
business card(s); credit cards; dogs;
information; mail; money; neighborhoods; objects; objects, classification
of; parking (street); secrets and secrecy;
secrets and secrecy, work; trash; wallets
and purses; wallets and purses, contents;
yards

public, 14; conflict over what is, 4–5, 14–15,
46, 49–51, 162, 175, 188, 190, 213, 240, 251,
323, 370n2, 377n29; culturally specific
nature of, 16–17; definition of, 4–5, 109–
15, 323; as endpoint on access-based
continuum, 4, 5, 242; housing, 18, 235,
260, 273, 279, 376n26, 378n35; requiring
others' collective protection, 114–15;
things, list of, 114–15, 115t. *See also* accessibility; accessibility, social; beaches;
boundary(ies) (categorical/classificatory);
business card(s); credit cards; dogs; government; mail; money; neighborhoods;
objects; objects, classification of; parking (street); privacy; privacy, fears; privacy, places associated with; privacy,
types of; privacy, violations

publicity: as accessibility, 3–4, 157, 166;
definition of, 4–5; desire for, in balance
with privacy, 4–5, 7, 76, 138–39, 225, 261;
economy of strangers and need for, 144;
as an endpoint on an accessibility continuum, 4–5, 323; frame analysis of, 290,
378–79n1, 279n2; individual burden of,
83, 144, 157, 176, 218; mismatches in perception versus reality of, 290, 379n2; no
"right to," 378–79n1. *See also* accessibility; accessibility, social; culture; privacy; privacy, fears; privacy, places associated with; privacy, types of; privacy,
violations; wallets and purses; wallets
and purses, contents

Rabin, Susan, 358n7
RFID (radio frequency identification), 355,
365n2
relationships: demands for attention and,
170, 202, 370n7; identity and, 22–23;
increase in number of, due to tech-

nology, 168–69, 174, 177; managing privacy to manage, 3, 6, 8, 22–24, 51, 167–68,
170, 202, 209–10, 230–31, 262, 282; nature
of, in urban neighborhoods, 265–66,
269–71, 367n19, 377n29–30; objects as
representations of, 128, 138, 140, 148, 150,
243, 367n17, 369n32; secrets as a measure
of intimacy in, 23, 27–33, 35, 46, 51, 360–
61; the "self" and, 6, 22, 34, 74, 96, 209;
social accessibility and 160, 167–70, 200,
202, 205, 209, 262, 265–66; violations
as reflections of, 293–94, 316–17. *See
also* accessibility; accessibility, social;
neighborhoods; neighbors; objects;
objects, classification of; power; secrets
and secrecy; secrets and secrecy, work;
self; technology(ies); technology(ies),
information and communication (ICTs);
technology(ies), information and communication (ICTs), channels/channeling
among; windows

Richardson, Laurel, 360n10, 361n19
risk: decision making and assessment of,
16, 74, 83, 124–25, 145, 231, 233, 240,
364n42; privacy fears and, 317–18; scenarios and, 317–18; "society," 116, 204. *See
also* trash

Rochberg-Halton, Eugene, 147, 149
Rosen, Jeffrey, 7, 23, 229
Rotenberg, Marc, 379n9
Rule, James, 368n24
Ryan, Dan, xi, 35, 360n10, 371n13
Rybczynski, Witold, 378n32

scenarios: classification and, 48, 116, 271,
312, 365n4; running, 40, 45, 87, 116–18,
312, 317–18; worst-case, 271, 312. *See also*
modern/modernity; privacy; privacy,
fears; privacy, places associated with;
privacy, types of; privacy, violations
Schama, Simon, 378n32
Schrage, Michael, 168
Schutz, Alfred, 289
Schwartz, Barry, 7, 98, 143, 147, 151n34, 163,
268, 357n1, 366n9
Scott, Marvin B., 369n34
secrets and secrecy: birth and death of,
25, 36, 37, 42; boundary play and, 359,
360; boundary work and, 27, 31, 360n10;

Bush (G. W.) Administration and, 17, 60, 298, 360n13; codes, 82, 85, 104, 112, 114, 235, 263, 265, 345, 348, 350; collective, 26, 34, 36, 44, 77–84, 88–89, 361n15, 361n21; confession and, 34, 35, 361n18, 363n23; disclosure/exposure of, 36–38, 78, 363n23; dynamic nature of, 26–27, 78; formal versus informal, 25; form versus content of, 25–28, 33, 35; importance to self-identity, 27–30, 363n24; intentionality and, 25, 27, 37–40, 45, 77, 83; intimacy and, 23, 25, 27–28, 45, 76, 361n15, 366n9; isolating effect of, 34, 205–8, 349, 361n15, 362n21; learning about, 22–23, 30, 33, 52–53, 64, 76, 83–84, 87–88; life of, 36–40, 42; managing, 3, 22, 24, 34–36, 53, 60, 72, 77, 80, 87–89, 96; mapping the, 38–40t; morality of, 42–43, 46–47, 86, 89, 359n5, 363n26, 363n32; open, 361n21; organizational, 33, 55–56, 67, 74–76; outed, 27, 36, 48–50, 66, 275, 351; PostSecret community art project and, 361, 361n17; power and, 7, 17, 33, 41, 45, 51–52, 56, 60, 66, 77, 359n5, 361n17, 363n26; "private" things and privacy versus, 24–25, 359nn5–7; relationships and, 22, 24, 27–37, 41–53, 60, 71–72, 74, 89, 96, 360n10, 361n18, 363n23; socially binding effect of, 27–28, 30–34, 230, 361n19, 361n21; solely owned, 26, 33–34, 42–43, 361n17, 362n21; state, 26, 82, 362n22, 363n27; structural logic of, 35–38; as a subset of unshared information, 25, 37, 30–34, 230, 361n19, 361n21; temporal nature of, 26, 35, 40, 44–45, 363n23; torture and, 362n22, 363n24

secrets and secrecy, work: anticipated consequences of, 70–76; competency in, 35–37, 41, 52–53, 55–56, 58–60, 64, 67, 70, 77, 82, 88, 89; decision making, 8, 22, 25, 28, 30, 35–37, 41–43, 45–48, 52–53, 55–56, 58, 66, 67, 70–76, 78, 86–89, 96, 359n8, 363n25; definition of, 22, 34–36; fieldcraft, 76–77, 89, 360n13; importance of how it is done, 27, 34–36, 363n23; individual versus collective, 36, 52, 67, 77–80, 82, 88; knowledge of, 35–37, 41, 53, 70, 76, 83, 87, 88, 324; knowledge of, nonhumans and, 87; "ownership" and, 363,

364; skills and techniques, 35–37, 52–54, 61–64, 67–70, 76–88, 96, 324, 345–56, 362n22, 364n37; "successful" (definition of), 34–35; tangibles versus intangibles, 36, 77–78, 89; transgendered case of, 89–96; trash and, 87–88, 238, 364n40; willingness to do, 66–67, 71. See also children; identity; power; privacy; privacy, fears; privacy, places associated with; privacy, types of; privacy, violations; relationships

security, 17, 142, 200, 224–26, 257, 269, 303, 307, 319–21, 380n11

Sedgwick, Eve Kosofsky, 359n8

selective concealment and disclosure: daily need for balance in, 5, 7, 10, 24, 99, 145; decisions about, 17, 22, 24, 27, 36–37, 49–51, 70, 146, 303, 359n8, 361n17, 364n34, 367nn15–16, 369n33; difficulty of former versus latter, 8–9, 36–37, 56–60, 359n6, 363n23, 364n34; as a goal, 7–8, 262, 357n3, 364n34; "good" privacy and, 8; as method to achieve privacy, 2–3, 5–7, 10, 22, 50–51, 70, 99, 141, 148, 238, 303, 359n6, 364n34; relative difficulty of, 8–9, 27, 50–51, 55–66, 77, 359n8, 360n10, 361n17, 363n23. See also identity; wallets and purses; wallets and purses, contents

self: affect of ICTs on the, 167–70, 175–77, 371n23; -centeredness of wallet/purse contents, 151–52, 156; free agency and the, 153, 156; "narratives of the," 147, 149, 151–52, 312–13; objects related to, 99, 112, 126–30, 129f, 213; "reflexive project of the," 146–47, 152, 155–56; relationships and the, 6, 22, 34, 74, 96, 209; therapy and attention to the, 33–34, 50, 89–96, 361n18, 369n35; wallet and purse contents as props for the, 156–57. See also modern/modernity; objects; objects, classification of; privacy; privacy, fears; privacy, places associated with; privacy, types of; privacy, violations; relationships; secrets and secrecy; secrets and secrecy, work; technology(ies); technology(ies), information and communication (ICTs); technology(ies), information and communication (ICTs), channels/channeling among;

prereceipt, 182–85, 185f; participants' total access points via, 177–78, 178t; preferences for, 182–85, 196, 205; response rates of different, 184–85, 185f; use of, in a sociotechnical system, 179–85. *See also* beepers; email; filtering/screening behaviors; Instant Messaging (IM); RFID (radio frequency identification); telephone(s); telephone(s), cell(ullar); telemarketers

telemarketers, 23, 169, 186–87, 191–93, 196, 295, 304; changes in phone answering behavior due to, 170–74; gaming, 173–74; Jehovah's Witnesses similar to, 23

telephone(s): answering behaviors, 161–62, 170–71, 173–74, 180, 186–87, 189, 191, 193–94, 196–98, 201–3; answering machines, 184, 195, 201, 202, 221; caller ID, 171, 180–81, 184, 192–94, 200, 203; channeling and, 182–84, 185f, 191, 195; filtering/screening and, 182–85, 187, 192–94, 196, 198, 200, 214; home, 171–72, 183, 191, 197; integration of social worlds/selves, 160–62, 175, 371; as part of a sociotechnical system, 179–82, 195, 202; social accessibility and, 168, 185–89; voicemail, 171–72, 181, 186, 196, 202; work(place), 161, 180, 196–97. *See also* children; door-answering behaviors; privacy; privacy, fears; privacy, places associated with; privacy, types of; privacy, violations; telemarketers

telephone(s), cell(ullar), 185–87, 191, 371; annoyance with, 13, 165, 175–77, 187, 191, 203, 296, 372n27; at the beach, 15; giving out numbers for, 23, 111, 139, 175–76, 180–87, 223, 371n19; "interruptus," 161, 175, 370n1; versus other phones, 181–85, 187, 190–91, 195, 223, 272n30, 273n22, 321, 355, 366n8, 371n22, 373n38; personal nature of, 186, 195, 223, 371n12; for work, 63, 105, 107, 111, 139, 175–76, 179, 181–87. *See also* children; door-answering behaviors; privacy; privacy, fears; privacy, places associated with; privacy, types of; privacy, violations; telemarketers

trash: Christmas trees, 243, 375; classification of, 235–36, 238–40, 242, 271, 375n14,

376n20, 376n24; definition of, 375n16, 376n20, 376n24; effort versus risk of violation via, 235–36, 239–42; identity theft and, 240–42, 376n21; mail, similar to, 244–45, 248–49, 376n21; paying attention to, 234–36, 241, 281; private nature of, 235, 242, 376; private-public hybrid nature of, 110, 210, 213, 235–38, 242–44, 249, 375n16, 375–76nn18–20, 376n24; public nature of, 236, 238, 244, 252, 375n15, 376n21; secret, 87–88, 238, 240, 244, 285, 318, 348; shredding, 234, 236–42, 318, 348 (appendix B); sorting, 235–42, 348, 375n14; at work, 235, 239. *See also* mail; objects; objects, classification of; secrets and secrecy; secrets and secrecy, work

Tuan, Yi-Fu, 325, 378n32

Urry, John, 378n32

Van Maanen, John, 369n34
Vaughan, Diane, 32–33, 312, 360n11
Veblen, Thorsten, 185
Venkatesh, Sudhir, 376n28, 378n35
Vinitzky-Seroussi, Vered, xi, 147, 367nn14–15, 369n34, 373n3

wallets and purses: as autobiographical occasions/props, 127, 146–57, 369n34; choreographies around, 148; extensive vs. minimal, 151–56; flirting and, 15, 147, 369n26; gendered nature of, 148; as identity kits, 99, 141, 145; identity theft and, 120–25; as islands of privacy, 97–99, 156, 185; modern versus late-modern, 152–56; oriented toward self versus others, 148; protection of/control over, 118–20, 124–26; reflexive project of self and, 146, 152; role in achieving privacy, 3, 98–99; self-identity and, 146–57, 213; socialization regarding, 97–99, 126, 148–49; trust, reputation and, 142–44; twin burdens of privacy and publicity and, 144–45, 156–57. *See also* beaches; identity; objects; objects, classification of; privacy; privacy, fears; privacy, places associated with; privacy, types of; privacy, violations wallets and purses, contents: private-public classification of, 96, 99–115 (stem and leaf diagram, 100–107); selective concealment and disclosure of, 96, 126–30, 129f, 141–46, 149, 365n2, 367n16; sorting model, 129f, 130–40, 366n9. *See also* beaches; identity; objects; objects, classification of; privacy; privacy, fears; privacy, places associated with; privacy, types of; privacy, violations

Warren, C., 359n5

Warren, Samuel D., 7

Weintraub, Jeff, 114

Wellman, Barry, 377n30

West, C., 148, 324

Westin, Alan F., 6, 170, 208

Whalley, Peter, 369n36

White, Cindy, 369n19

Whyte, William Foote, 376n28

Wilson, Cintra, 378n1

windows: adapting behaviors due to, 227, 231, 233, 375n13; car, 234; curtains, blinds, and other treatments for, 207–8, 211, 223–24, 227–29, 231–32; Google Street View and, 374–75n12; lack of, 55, 226; managing relationships via, 230–31; as part of a system, 213–15, 223; privacy violations and, 48, 233, 279; security problems with, 225–26; signs in, 223–25; two-way nature of, 225–27, 229, 231, 234, 374n10; visual accessibility of others through, 48, 213, 220, 223–24, 229–31, 233–34, 279

Wirth, Louis, 204, 372n32

Woolgar, Steve, 369n34

yards: accessibility and, 212–13, 223, 253, 255, 259–62; designed boundary features, 222, 257, 259–61; front versus back, 222–23, 261, 270; interaction in/across, 223, 253–54, 259, 261–63; private-public nature of, 212, 222–23, 252, 261, 266

Zelizer, Viviana, 133, 367n17, 369n32

Zerubavel, Eviatar, xi, 4, 33, 51, 159–60, 165–66, 361–62n21, 363n29, 364n33, 371n14, 377n31

Zimmerman, D., 148, 324

Zussman, Robert, 147